WANTED ONE
SURROGATE MOTHER

Other Books By Las Chance

Short Time Wife ISBN: 978-1-4634-3255-3
ISBN: 978-1-4634-3254-6
ISBN: 978-1-4634-3253-9

RON ISBN: 978-1-4670-6074-5
ISBN: 978-1-4670-5439-3
ISBN: 978-1-4670-6073-8

WANTED ONE SURROGATE MOTHER

Las Chance

authorHOUSE®

AuthorHouse™
1663 Liberty Drive
Bloomington, IN 47403
www.authorhouse.com
Phone: 1-800-839-8640

Published by AuthorHouse   12/05/2012

ISBN: 978-1-4772-6281-8 (sc)
ISBN: 978-1-4772-6280-1 (hc)
ISBN: 978-1-4772-6279-5 (e)

Library of Congress Control Number: 2012915144

CHAPTER ONE

"Austin you seem determined to go through with this thing. Would not it be simpler if you would just get one of your lady friends pregnant and then you support your heir?"

Peter King was Austin's attorney as well as his friend. He had known Austin for many years and he never thought of Austin as being the family man type, but things have a way of changing sometimes. Peter along with everyone else, because of the type of business their friend owned, just assumed that Austin would be a player all his life.

"No, Pete. I don't want my heir living with anyone but me. I don't want any problem with any one of the women I know. They would want marriage and money. The money part I don't mind, but the marriage part is not for me. All I want is a surrogate to have a baby for me. I will gladly pay her the money we decide upon to get the job done and then she will be out of my life and my heir's life forever." At this time Austin believed every word he was saying to his attorney was the truth.

"Well Austin, I hope it goes just that easy, but for some reason I doubt it will." Pete knew things rarely go as planned.

"Pete, as my attorney, it will be up to you to see that it does go well." Austin knew his friend would do everything in his power to make things go his way.

"I will do my very best, but you need to let someone other than yourself do the interviewing of these women. You don't need to get into the middle of it all until it is totally necessary. However if I were you I would not ever meet the lady in person. I would not want her to be able to pick me out of a crowd of people as I walked down the street one day and then she decides to cause me a lot of trouble."

"Maybe so, but no, I will be doing all of the interviewing myself. I want to be the one who decides who will be carrying my child. Not someone else. I know what I want and what I don't want better than anyone. It's my baby the woman will be carrying. So Pete, I will be doing all of the interviews myself, I will just have to take a chance that the woman I pick will not be that kind of person."

"Austin, you know this may take some time. Are you willing to put that much time into this project?" He knew how busy his friend's business kept him most of the time.

"Yes, I know, but I will make time for this. Would you let someone else pick the woman that would carry your child?" Austin asked his friend.

"No, but I believe in the old fashion way. You know with that good old stuff called sex." Pete had married his childhood sweetheart and he knew how good all that stuff could be when it was being done with the woman you love.

"Yes and the old fashion way can get in the way of business." Austin knew what Pete was saying, but he also knew things didn't always turn out as well as it had for his friend Pete.

"Austin, there is just nothing that can out do the old fashion way. You should try it someday." Pete had a big smile on his face from just thinking about his life with his wife.

"I have tried it that way. Maybe way more times than I should have. That's one of the reasons I decided to go this way." Austin knew his friend was really still speaking about marriage and not a one night stand or some brief affair, but that was even less appealing to him. Marriage may be for some men, but right now Austin did not think it was for him at all.

Austin Blackburn was a very wealthy business man who had no siblings. For that reason alone he was very anxious to have at least one heir. However, he did not want a wife just to get an heir. He said he didn't have the time to invest in a woman. That they require a lot of a man's time and he had all he could do without having to be responsible for a wife too. Austin did not like small talk and he did not want to be tied to just one woman. That was an inconvenience he did not want nor needed.

Karen Belmont was a young girl just out of high school when she came to New York City three years ago. She lived alone and worked as a secretary to Reverend Thomas St. Johns. She came in search of a better life than the one she had lived so far. Karen thought that working at a church as a secretary to a minister would be a safe and respectable job, but she soon found out even a preacher can be sinful.

"Karen, could you please come into my office?" It was only eight o'clock in the morning and the Reverend had just gotten into his office, but he was already after her.

Karen hated it more and more each time when the Reverend called her to come into his office. He would always tell her to close the door behind her whenever she came into his office. "Yes sir, I will be right in," she answered as she picked up her writing pad and a pen and started into her boss' office. She wished she had a whip she could take with her every time she had to go into his office, but of course she didn't have one.

"Karen, please close the door. I need you to take a few letters, so have a seat right up here close to me. That way I won't need to be talking so loud." She already knew what the good Reverend had on his mind, but he could forget all of it. She was not going to play his game now or ever: any more than she had played them in all the time she had worked for him at the church, and that was not at all.

"That's alright Reverend St. Johns. I can hear you just fine from over here," she answered as she took a seat in the chair that was the furthest from him. Karen wanted to feel safe and that meant staying as far away from the Reverend as she could get and as near to the door as she could get. "I'll just sit here," she answered.

Every day it was a battle she had to fight all over again. The Reverend St. Johns was no Saint behind closed doors, but let some church member show up and he was so good, you would have believed he could walk on water.

Karen wanted another job, but she needed this job too. During lunch time she read the ad that was placed in the news paper by Austin, asking for a woman who would be willing to become a surrogate mother for forty thousand dollars plus room and board and medical expenses. Karen read and reread the advertisement. She didn't believe that was something she could ever do herself. She didn't believe she could ever just give up her own baby after it was born and that was exactly what any woman who answered that ad would be asked to do.

Even after going back to work after lunch, she could not get the ad out of her mind. Forty thousand dollars was a lot of money and she could sure use it. She was young and healthy and could have her own babies later, after she finds a man to love. The ad said for any woman interested to send a short profile to the post office box stated in the ad. "A short profile, I can do that. Most likely it won't get any farther than that," she thought to herself. Karen sat down at her little desk and began to write

Chapter Two

"My name is Karen Belmont I'm over eighteen years old. I live alone. I work for a church." She didn't know anything else to say about herself that would be of any interest to this person. She placed her short note into a stamped envelope and mailed it without adding any more information.

Austin's secretary went everyday to the post office box to get Austin's mail. He would read them at night when he was at home and alone. He must have read five or six hundred letters when he picked up Karen's short to the point note. That intrigued Austin so much that he decided to write her back and ask her to come in for an interview.

"Dear Miss Belmont, I would be very much interested in interviewing you for the advertised position. If you are still interested please call me at this number 555-1171." Austin did not sign his name to his note nor did he give any indication to Karen as to whom he may be.

Two days later Karen received Austin's note. She decided to give this person a call. After all at this point she still was not committed to anything and she didn't have anything to lose by just making the call and going on the interview. She would call the number the first chance she got. It must have been her lucky day because as soon as she had gotten back to her desk after lunch the phone rang and it was a very upset church member. The good Reverend had no choice, but to leave his office and meet with his church member in their home that very afternoon. Karen waited until she was sure that the good Reverend was gone before she placed her call. She let it ring several times and she was just before hanging up when Austin answered.

"Hello," Austin answered in his very business like voice. He knew who it had to be. No one else so far had been given that number.

"Hello Sir, I'm Karen Belmont. I was asked to call this number for an interview. Are you the person I'm supposed to be talking with?" She was getting very nervous while she waited for the party to answer her back. Again she almost hung up the phone.

"Yes Miss Belmont I am that person. I have been waiting for your call. Will it be convenient for you to meet with me this afternoon around three o'clock?" Austin wanted to get this thing rolling as soon as possible.

"No sir I will still be at work at that time. I can meet you later or even during the weekend if that would be better for both of us." Karen hands were even shaking now and her voice had broken a little. She just hoped the man on the other end of her call would not be able tell all of this.

"Alright then could you come to my house tonight if three o'clock this afternoon is inconvenient for you?" Austin waited for her answer. He could tell by her hesitation that she didn't like what he had just suggested either.

"No sir, I would rather meet you in a public place, or maybe I'm not what you need. I'm sorry for wasting your time." Karen was ready to end this call.

"No, don't hang up. I will meet you in a public place. I should have thought of that myself. Austin was even more interested in this person after hearing her voice on the phone.

"Okay, I will meet you, where would you want to meet?" Karen asked and then she let out a long breath. She was so relieved that this man had agreed to meet with her in a public place. She felt she would be a lot safer if there were other people around.

"Miss Belmont why don't you decide the time and a place where you will feel the safest and then I will meet you there." Austin was beginning to like this woman more and more.

"I will meet you at the coffee shop across the street from the church where I work at five fifteen this afternoon if that is alright with you?" Karen then told Austin exactly where the church and the coffee shop were located.

"Alright, I will be there at five fifteen today." Austin knew he would be there before the appointed time. He wanted to be there early to check things out before Karen got there.

At five o'clock that afternoon, Karen put on her jacket and got her pocketbook out of her desk. The good Reverend had come back to his office only a few minutes earlier. "I'm leaving now Reverend St. Johns." She called out from the door. "It's already five o'clock."

"Well then Karen, I guess I will see you tomorrow," he said while he had his hand over the mouth piece of the phone. The Reverend was on the phone and Karen knew she would be able to get away if he was busy with another one of the church members.

Austin had found the little coffee shop without any trouble. He parked in front of the shop and went inside as quickly as he could. He took a seat in a booth that had a window with a good view of the church across the street. He wanted to be able to see Karen even before she came into the little coffee shop. He had just gotten seated, when he saw a woman coming from the church. The closer she got the easier it was for him to see that this was a beautiful woman, more beautiful than he would have ever expected a surrogate to be, but she was a little on the short side he could already tell. He was used to being surrounded by tall beautiful models. However this woman sure was beautiful to him. That made Austin wonder why such a beautiful woman would want to be a surrogate at all, that is if this was the woman he was there to meet. It had to be for no other reason other than for the money, but forty thousand dollars was not that much money, at least not to a person like him. Austin was still watching the woman from the window and she was still coming his way. This had to be the person he was there to meet he kept thinking. The caller had told him that she would be coming from the church where she worked. Austin smiled to himself as he sat in the booth. "This may not be such a bad job after all." He thought to himself.

"Hello Karen." The waitress said as the young girl walked into the coffee shop. The waitress had been behind the counter since Austin came into the coffee shop. She had not gone over to his booth at all to get his order. She had a feeling he did not come there to be alone. Anyway she was too busy looking at him and his car until Karen came in the door.

"Hello Beth." Karen was looking around to see if there was anyone there. Beth was the only employee in the coffee shop. At this time of day business was always slow.

"What brings you here this time of day?" Beth asked. "I would think your boss would be on his way home and not wanting something else this late in the day." Beth did not like the good Reverend at all. He did not impress her in the least. She was always glad she was not one of his church members.

Karen smiled over at the waitress. "Oh he is still there, but I'm not here for him today. I came here to meet someone."

"Oh well I guess then, that is why that tall good looking guy is here too. He's in that third booth. I knew I had never seen him in here before." Beth wondered how Karen knew him. She had never seen Karen with any man before. She knew that Karen deserved to meet a nice man if anyone did. Working at that church for the good Reverend was no picnic.

"Thank you Beth." Karen said as she hurried down to the third booth. She didn't want to be late for her interview. Austin had his back to her so she was unable to get a look at him. "Hello, I'm Karen, are you the person I'm here to meet?" She was so nervous she could feel her knees shaking.

"Yes, I guess I am." Austin answered. He didn't get up from his seat he just motioned for her to take the seat across from him in the booth. Karen slid into the booth as he had indicated for her to do. She was sitting across from him now and she could look right into his eyes. That is if she had raised her head up high enough. They were the only people in the coffee shop other than Beth the waitress.

"Would you like to have a cup of coffee?" Austin asked her. He was trying to help her to relax, but he was not doing a very good job of it he could tell.

"No sir, I don't drink coffee." She answered.

Austin looked over at Karen in more of a stare than just a look. "Then why in the world did you suggest we meet here at a coffee shop?" He asked.

"Why not, it was close and I knew where this place was." Karen answered.

"Well I guess that's a good enough reason." Austin answered. At first all he could do was gaze at Karen. Then he started with his questions. He hoped this would take his mind off of how beautiful this woman was sitting across the table from him. "Let me ask you something Miss Belmont and I hope you have some good answers for all of my questions. Why would you even consider becoming a surrogate mother?" He could not imagine why a woman who looked as she did would ever do such a thing. He knew none of the woman he knew would ever carry a baby for someone else and mess up their perfect body, and this woman had as perfect of a body as he had ever seen.

8

Karen took a deep breath. She didn't really have a good answer for that question, but she didn't want to wait too long before she gave him an answer. "I don't know," was all that came out of her mouth. She was sure that was not the answer he wanted to hear and it didn't take but a second or two for her to know that for sure.

"If you don't know why you are doing it, then why are you wasting my valuable time?" He asked and he didn't look any too pleased with her at the time. But if the truth be known Austin did not care why she answered his ad. The only thing he cared about was the fact that she did answer it.

Karen just sat there for the longest time. She didn't know if she needed to leave or stay, but she was sure that she did need to decide one way or the other and soon.

"Is that a question, you again don't have an answer for?" Austin asked.

"No sir, I have an answer to your last question. I didn't know I was wasting your valuable time. You are the one who asked me to meet with you and not the other way around. I'm just here trying to answer your questions the best way I can and you don't make it an easy thing to do."

Austin wanted to know why a beautiful girl like her would answer such an ad and what made her want to be a surrogate. "Tell me Miss Belmont, why did you answer my ad?" He was looking right at her, and by him doing that it did not help Karen at all. He was asking her the same question, but in another way.

"I answered your ad, because I need to make more money than I'm making working at the Church and I need to have time to look for a better job. I thought after your baby was born and before I would be able to go back to work at the church I would have time to look for a better paying job somewhere near to where I live." Karen was now even more nervous now than she was earlier.

"Why? What's wrong with your present job at the Church? I would think that would be an ideal place for a young woman like you to work." Austin asked.

"The preacher, that's what is wrong with my job, along with the pay. He won't leave me alone." Karen's face was turning a little red now.

She had not meant to tell this man so much about her relationship with her boss, the good Reverend St. Johns.

"Oh! So you are having a little thing going with the preacher?" All of a sudden Austin felt himself feeling a little jealous, but he could not understand why.

"No! I am not. I don't want a little thing with him. All I want is for him to leave me alone." Austin could tell how this thing with the preacher was making Karen very upset.

Oh! I see he thinks because he is a preacher he gets the pick of the crop." Austin was enjoying the whole interview except for the few seconds earlier when he felt somewhat jealous. After all he wasn't the one in the hot seat, but this beautiful woman was.

Karen didn't like the way Austin spoke about her situation. "Mister, there is no crop as far as I'm concerned. I'm not doing anything with him or any man I'm not married to. I've seen too many of my friends, back home taking the short cut and then all they got was a baby to take care of out of it. That's not the way I want to start motherhood. Not by myself. I want a family, but only when there is a husband to share it with me."

"Okay, I get it you don't mess around, but that does not answer my question." Austin still wanted an answer.

Karen had to raise her eyes back up from looking at the table so she could look direct at Austin. "Oh, now you have made me forget what your question was. I'm so sorry." Karen didn't feel as if her interview was going very well.

"Then I will ask it again. Why do you want to be a surrogate mother?" When asking his questions Austin had no expression on his face at all. That made it impossible for Karen to read his face as to how things were going for her.

"I did answer your question mister. I told you, so that I could afford to look for a better job, so that I could make myself a better living. I'm sorry if that isn't the answer you may have wanted, but it's my answer and like I said I have already given it to you."

"You are right. You did answer the question, but then you went off into telling me about you not letting your boy friend get his way with you." Austin knew very well she had not said any such thing.

"No, I did not. I never said one word about having a boy friend. You just made that up in your own head." Karen was beginning to think this man was not listening to one word she had to say. Was she wasting her time now she wondered?

"So you didn't. Does that mean that you don't like men?" This was an answer Austin wanted to hear and he sure hoped it was the answer he wanted.

Karen wondered just where in the world did he get such an idea? Not from her she knew. "No! It only means I just have never had a boyfriend. It also means I would never just let a man mess around with me for the fun of it."

Austin wanted to laugh. This little girl was not at all like any of the sophisticated women he was used to knowing. However there was something about her that interested him more than he liked. "So tell me Miss Belmont, what do you do over at the church across the street?" He waited for her answer again.

"I'm the Reverend's secretary. You would believe a good safe job, but it is not, as I have already told you." Karen was about to tell Mr. Blackburn that she didn't think they could come to any agreement and that she needed to leave. After all it was getting late and it would be getting dark soon and she still would need to walk home.

Austin noticed how Karen kept her head down most of the time during the time he was talking to her. "What do you mean by it is not?" Austin asked in a low voice, not wanting the waitress to over hear their conversation.

Karen raised her eyes once again just enough so she would be looking at Austin's face. "It doesn't really matter, because it doesn't have anything to do with what you are wanting."

Austin smiled over at Karen before he answered. "You are right, it doesn't." But he for some reason was still upset with her situation at the Church. "So Miss Belmont, tell me all about you." Austin wanted to know more about this beautiful girl.

"I have already done that in my letter to you." Karen answered. Again Austin just stared over at her for awhile. "Yes Miss Belmont you did do that in that one and half line letter. You told it all, but I'm nosey and I want to hear a little more about your most interesting life if you don't mind."

Karen didn't say anything for a few seconds. Then she asked. "Like what?" She had told him everything she thought he needed to know about in her letter. So what else was there to tell?

"Oh, I don't know Miss Belmont. Maybe you could dwell on your education perhaps?" Austin was interested in anything and everything this beautiful woman had to say.

"Okay, I went to school." She answered.

Now Austin was getting a little upset with her. Karen could tell by the way he had squinted up his eyes. She didn't know what else she could tell him. There had never been much happening in her life and what had happened she was sure was nothing that would interest him. "Could you elaborate a little more on your education?" He asked.

"Yes, I graduated from high school three years ago." She answered. "So, you are almost twenty one years old?" He asked.

"Yes and no, yes I am nearer than I was this time last year and no I have just turned nineteen last week. I will be out of school three years in June." Karen was not going to tell anymore than she needed to tell. If he wanted more he would have to ask for more.

"So you were sixteen years old when you graduated from high school?" Austin asked.

"Yes sir I was." Karen answered.

"Did your school only go to the tenth grade?" he asked.

"No we went all the way to the twelfth like all of the other schools." She gave him a smile this time with her answer. That made Austin a little nervous himself.

"So tell me Miss Belmont, how did you get out of school so young?" He was smiling at her now, but it was not a friendly smile more like one a person does when they think they have caught you in a lie.

"I studied a lot and I didn't date and waste my time doing things that would cause me any trouble." Karen still had her hands folded in her lap. "Where did you graduate?" Austin still had that smile on his face.

She wanted so badly to wipe it off of his face.

Karen answered right away. "We graduated out on our football field."

Austin wanted to laugh again. "I didn't mean the place the memorable occasion actually took place. I meant where in your class did you finish one or three hundred?"

"Oh, I understand now, one," she quickly answered.

"One, you were first in your class of how many, two?" he asked. "No, I was the one of one hundred thirty five." This time it was

Karen who was doing all of the smiling.

"So, I gather you did very well in school. Why didn't you go on to college?" Austin just didn't understand.

"I didn't have the money to go to college." Karen answered.

"I don't understand how you finished first in your class and you didn't get a scholarship to a good college?" Austin thought anyone who had graduated first in their class would have gotten a scholarship to any college of their choosing. He and Bo his best friend had done that everything.

"That's easy I didn't play sports," she answered.

"Oh I see you are not athletic and what else are you not, may I ask?" Austin was just enjoying himself at this point. She was beautiful and smart. She would make a perfect mother.

"I'm not a dope head, a drunk, nor am I stupid, do you wish me to go on with my list or is that sufficient enough for you?" Karen asked.

"No I think that is enough, so I take it then that you are still a virgin." Austin really wanted to know the answer to this question.

"Yes and again I think I have already told you that." Karen could feel her face heating up and turning red at the same time.

Austin just ignored what she had said and went on with his questions as if she had only answered "yes." "Tell me Miss Belmont, why would you be willing to have a baby for money and yet, you would not sleep with a man?"

"They have nothing to do with each other. That is why. At least I hope not. I hope you aren't expecting me to sleep with you. You do know it can all be done medically?" Karen was now wondering what she had gotten herself into by answering this man's ad. He could well be a man right out of the crazy house as far as she knew.

Austin smiled at Karen. He wanted her to worry a little while before he gave in and answered her question.

"Yes and that is the only way I will be doing it. I'm not looking for an affair and if I was, you would not be the type of woman or should I say in your case girl I would ever want." Austin was trying very hard to convince himself what he had just said was true, but he knew it was as far from the truth as it could get.

"Thank you that sure busted my ego. Are you this nice to all the women you meet?" Karen was watching Austin's face to see how he would react to her last remark.

"No just the ones I pay to do a job, and before you get any smart idea about what they are being paid to do for me, I can tell you right now I have never had to pay for sex. So you can get all of that right out of your head. And anyway what I do is none of your business Miss Belmont."

Karen had not even thought about him paying for sex. She could not imagine a man like this needing to pay for sex. She would think there were plenty of women waiting to give him what he needed. There maybe even a few women out there that would be willing to pay him for sex. After all, to Karen he was the most handsome man she had ever seen in her life.

"No sir I had not given that one thought. I was only going to say good, because I would hate to think I was giving my sweet baby to someone who was so rude to everyone they meet. I'm glad it's only me you feel the need to be so rude to Mr. Blackburn"

Austin had not given much thought to the woman giving up her own baby. "That Miss Belmont brings up another question. Will you be able to give up your baby once it is born? Will you be able to walk away from this child and never look back?" Austin wasn't sure he would want her to say she could.

"I don't know," Karen answered fast.

"Well, Miss Belmont you need to know, because that is exactly what you will need to do, if I should select you to be my surrogate. Maybe you are just far too young for this project." Austin wanted to seem as cold hearted as he possible could.

"No, but I don't look at it as just a project either." Karen was looking down at her hands which were still lying in her lap. She kept them there so he would not see how much they were shaking.

"Excuse me, but could I take your order?" the waitress asked.

"Yes, I will have a cup of coffee, Miss Belmont what would you like to have?" Austin wanted to touch just her hand, but Karen still kept them in her lap. He wondered if she did that all the time or was she just keeping them in her lap because she was with him and she was nervous.

"I don't need anything, thank you Beth," Karen answered. She didn't want him to see her hands shaking if she tried to hold a glass or anything else in them.

"Okay. One coffee, will you need cream with your coffee sir?" Beth asked as she turned back to Austin.

"No thank you I drink my coffee black," he answered.

Beth looked over at Karen, wondering what she and this man were doing together. She had never known Karen to be with anyone. She just worked over at the Church and she went back to her room every afternoon. Beth was sure the preacher didn't know about Karen's man. If he did he would be right over there at the coffee shop this very second checking him out.

"Now where were we?" Austin asked. "Oh, yes you were saying you don't consider this to be just a project. May I ask then what do you consider it to be Miss Belmont?" Austin was very interested in what Karen thought this little ordeal that they were discussing would be to her. This little girl was holding his interests more than any of the women he had ever known.

Karen took a deep breath and began to answer his question. "Right now it's just a means to an end. It's not something I will want to do every day or in this case every year. I am trying to look at it as though I will be doing something good for someone who is unable to do it for themselves. That still doesn't mean I won't regret it later. I don't mean doing it for someone who can't do it, but I mean I will always love my Baby and it will always hurt me to think I will never be a part of its life. That will be something I will need to learn to live with. I will always love my baby forever. I can't change that no matter what happens. I'm sure you have at least one thing in your life you have done that you have regretted, and you have had to learn to live with it, no matter how painful it is. At your age I bet there has been more than just one thing you have done that you still regret." Karen only referred to Austin's age because he had done the very same thing to her earlier in their interview.

"Young lady how old do you think I am?" Austin asked. He was very interested in knowing what she thought his age was.

Karen gave him a good long look before answering as if she was trying to decide his age. "Well I would say a lot older than me for sure. I would say forty or maybe forty five, or maybe even a little older." Karen knew he was way younger than that, but she was not going to let him know it. She was just saying all of that to make him mad.years old. That is not very much older than you, but apparently it "Well I hate to disappoint you, but I'm not. I'm only thirty four is to you." This time it was Austin's face that was turning red. No one had ever thought he was even the age he was.

"No it's not. Your age is none of my business. I was just doing you the way you have been doing me. How did it feel?" She asked.

"Not good at all," he answered.

The waitress brought Austin's coffee. "Are you sure you won't have a coke or a glass of milk or something?" He asked.

"No thank you. There you go again insulting my age. Did you insult, all of the other women you have interviewed, the way you have been insulting me?" she asked.

"No, but only because you are the first one I have asked to meet with me for an interview." Austin loved just looking at this girl. He did not know what had come over him. He had never had such feeling about a woman before.

"So you are having trouble finding someone to do your little deed?" Karen was so glad she was the only woman he had wanted to interview.

"No I'm not having any trouble getting responds to my ad and how did this turn into you interviewing me?" Austin was not used to anyone but himself being in control.

"I just asked you a question, that's how." Karen answered.

"Miss Belmont I wasn't really looking for an answer to that question. I was just making a statement."

"Well it sounded like a question, to me and you were looking right at me when you asked it. Karen was scared to death, but she was not going to let this man know. "Sir, do you mind if I ask you just one more question? I promise I won't take control of your interview."

Austin was just starring at Karen again. He could not get over how beautiful she was. Her skin did not have one flaw. "Did you say something," he asked?

"Yes Sir I did," Karen answered. Then she started to repeat her question.

"Go ahead I'm very sure I wouldn't be able to stop you even if I would want to.

"You could if you really wanted to stop me," Karen answered.

She was right, he could, but like she said only if he really wanted to stop her. All Austin wanted to do was watch Karen's mouth move when she talked. He had never seen a more beautiful mouth, and in his business he had seem a lot of mouths. "Well go ahead and ask your question before I change my mind."

"What is your name?" Karen asked. She was still looking at him and waiting for him to answer her.

Austin looked so surprised. "Didn't I tell you my name when you first got to the table?" He asked. He thought for sure he had done that the second she sat down at the table. This had never happened to him before in his life.

"No sir you did not, however I did introduce myself to you," she answered.

"Alright then Miss Belmont I apologize my name is Austin Blackburn." Austin still could not believe he had forgotten to introduce himself to her.

"Is that all you are going to say?" Karen still had not taken her hands out of her lap yet.

"Miss Belmont that is all you need to know right now. And I'm not at all sure you even really needed to know my name yet." Austin was not going to give Karen all the information she wanted at this one meeting. He wanted her to come back for more meetings even if he did not use her as his surrogate. This decision even surprised Austin. He was used to very sophisticated women not little young secretaries, but this girl fascinated him more than he liked.

"Well I guess our business is over. It was nice to meeting you, Mr. Austin Blackburn. Good luck to you in your hunt. I'm sure you will find just the right woman for your needs." Karen started to slide out of the booth.

"Where are you going? I'm still talking to you." Austin needed to talk fast if he wanted Karen to come back for a second meeting.

"No I think we have just finished our talk." Karen said as she put her hand up on the table to help push her way out of the booth.

Austin quickly placed his hand over the top of hers. "Karen, I wish you would reconsider and let me continue with my interview. After all isn't that why we are both here today?" He could not let her leave.

"Yes, I guess so, but I feel I need to know something about the person I could be giving my precious little baby to one day." That caught Austin's attention. He had not thought much about this baby in the way Karen kept bringing it up. She was putting life and value to this baby.

"Karen, ask me any question you want and need an answer to, I will do my very best to answer all of your questions." Austin had made his decision. Karen would be his surrogate. That is if he still needed one after their meeting. He did not need to interview anyone else. That one statement touched his heart. She may be very young, but she was very concerned with the welfare of her child.

"Do you really mean that? Will you really answer all my questions?" she asked.

"Yes I do Karen, ask me anything." Austin had a smile on his face at last, making him appear years younger than he did at the first of their meeting. This pleased Karen. She liked this man a lot. More than she had ever liked anyone and in such a short time. There was something about him that kept drawing her to him.

"Okay, then I will ask you why you want a baby and why you need to use a surrogate. Oh, are you gay? I never thought about that, you could be gay."

"No! I am not gay. I need an heir and a surrogate removes the emotional conflict that goes along with being involved with a woman. This way it will be all business. There won't be anything personal." Austin sat there sipping his coffee. He hoped his answers would please Karen.

"How can you say it won't be personal? Having a baby is a very personal thing. Do you know where a baby comes from? And do you know where a baby comes out?" Karen was very serious. She wanted an answer from Austin.

"Yes Miss Belmont, I do believe I am an adult. I know all about the birds and the bees." Austin had a small smile on his face.

"Well Mr. Blackburn, I do believe that is a very personal place at least it is on me," Karen answered.

Austin just sat and listened to Karen talk. He wanted to laugh again, but he was sure she would not like that at all.

"Mr. Blackburn, would you want to be in the room when your baby is born?"

That was another something he had not given any thought to at all, but now that Karen had brought it up he would just give her his answer. "Yes of course I would. I want to see my baby coming into the world."

"Well, then you need to cross my name off your list right now, because, you are not going to be looking at my cootchie. Until the baby is out of me completely and wrapped in a nice little warm blanket and has one of those little stocking caps on its sweet little head, it is still mine. I don't care if it is going to be your baby later. It is still my baby as long as my legs are spread apart and my cootchie is still showing."

Austin was fighting not to laugh. "Miss Belmont, I am not interested in your cootchie, at all. All I'm interested in is the baby coming out of your cootchie."

"Mr. Blackburn, if you are watching my baby come out of my body, you will be seeing my cootchie and I don't want to show you that part of me. Do you understand me?" Austin could not hold back his laugher any longer. He began to laugh and the more he thought about what Karen had just said the harder and louder he laughed. "What is so funny?" Karen asked.

"You, Miss Belmont," he answered.

"Me, what did I say that was so funny?" Karen didn't understand him at all. She was sitting there with such a serious look on her face.

"All of that you have said about your cootchie. I have never in my life heard anyone call it that before."

"Well Mr. Blackburn, that is what it is called back home and I don't want my cootchie put on display for anyone. Would you want me looking at your stuff? That is what they call it even in this big old city isn't it?" Karen was as red in the face as she had ever been in her life.

"Well, Miss Belmont I would not mind that at all. If you want to look I would be happy to let you." Austin answered with a smile on his face.

"Well then what are you waiting for a better offer?" Karen asked. "Karen, I don't think this is the place for all of that do you?" She had not noticed that he was using only her first name now.

"Well it's just as much the right place as it will be when I give birth to my baby. You will probably even want pictures of the whole thing." Karen was getting more than just a little upset, Austin could tell.

"Yes of course I will and I will want a movie of it all too. So I could play it over and over again for myself and all my friends. Plus I will show them the pictures of your cootchie I will have enlarged." Austin had another big smile on his face. He knew this was upsetting her even more.

"I hope Mr. Austin Blackburn you don't think that remark is helping your case any?" Karen was red and warm, she was border line hot and it was all noticed by Austin.

19

"Did I say in color and a lot of close ups?" Austin was just adding fuel to his fire. He was enjoying it all. For a few second he wished his best friend was there so he could share all of this with him.

"No, you did not. Mr. Blackburn, I'm not even sure I would give my husband permission to do all of those things. That is whenever I get one." Karen answered.

"Now Miss Belmont, don't tell me you will be this shy with your own husband?" He bet if he was her husband he could get her to change her mind.

"Yes, I would. So what? If God had wanted my cootchie to be seen he would have put it in a more convenient place."

"Miss Belmont, God did put it in a very convenient place as far as I'm concerned." Austin still had that smile on his face.

"Not for you to make pictures of it he sure did not." Karen was still a nice shade of red.

CHAPTER THREE

"**M**iss Belmont, would you feel safe enough with me to go out to dinner?" Austin asked.

"When Mr. Blackburn, would you want me to go out to dinner with you?" she asked. Thinking anything would be better than him talking so much about her cootchie and by tomorrow night he would have forgotten all about her cootchie.

"Well I was thinking about right now. It is getting near dinner time and I'm sure we both could use a good meal," Austin answered.

"You mean you want us to go right now, this very day?" She didn't expect he would say right then. But he was right, she was getting a little hungry.

"Yes Miss Belmont, I think so. Is this not a convenient time for you, do you have another date for tonight?" he asked.

"No I don't have another date and you very well know that already. So alright I will go to dinner with you, just as long as you don't think you will have the urge to make any pictures." She answered.

"Why would I want any pictures of you?" Austin knew he would love a picture of this beautiful girl, but he was not letting her know that for a second.

"Oh, I don't really know. Maybe to pass around to all your friends to show them what a stupid girl looks like, I guess." She answered.

"I think all of my friends already know what stupid girls look like and I don't think you are stupid. You may be a little frigid, but I would never say you were stupid."

"Mr. Blackburn, I'm not frigid, I'm just wholesome. Haven't you ever been around a virgin before?"

"Yes back in grade school." Karen would have liked to have been able to stay seated across from him all night. She wanted to look at this handsome man as long as she could. She had never met any man that was even near as handsome as this Mr. Austin Blackburn.

"Now, are you going to dinner with me or not?" He asked her again. Austin was watching her as hard as she was watching him.

"Are you paying?" she asked.

"Yes of course Miss Belmont, I'm paying. I am the one who asked you out to dinner aren't I?"

"Will you be deducting the price of the meal from my money you will be giving me should you pick me to have our baby, Mr. Blackburn?" Karen wanted to know if she would be paying for this meal in the long run.

Austin smiled. He almost said yes of course I am, but he changed his mind. "No Miss Belmont I will just throw in the meal for free." Austin was still watching her.

Karen was still full of questions that she needed answers too. "Will you bring me back here after we have had our dinner or will I need to walk back?"

"I will be glad to bring you back. You will not need to walk back. It may be too long of a walk for a short person like you." Austin wanted to see what Karen would have to say about that little comment. But she didn't have anything to say about it at all. She had always been kidded about her height.

"Where do you live from here?" Austin asked. He assumed she lived close.

Karen looked out the window and pointed to the right. "I live about five blocks that way."

"Do you live in an apartment?" Austin asked. He wanted to learn a little more about this beautiful woman.

"No I just have a small room at a big rooming house." Austin didn't even know there were rooming houses anymore. He had never known anyone who lived in a rooming house. All he knew about them were from old movies.

"Do you have a car?" He had not seen, but one car over at the church when he arrived at the Coffee Shop and he assumed that car belonged to the good Reverend.

"No, that's why I have to walk everywhere I go and that is why it is so important for me to know if the places I am going will be near enough for me to walk to or in our case near enough for me to walk back from. I have just one more question if you don't mind?"

"Alright ask away." Austin said as if he could stop her from doing anything.

"Will you bring me back here to this Coffee Shop or will you drive me all the way to my rooming house?"

"I will drive you all the way to your rooming house if you will trust me to do that for you," he answered.

I will trust you, because it will be dark by the time we have had our supper and I don't like walking in the dark."

"Now that we have all that out of the way, are you ready to go Miss Belmont?" Austin asked.

"I guess so Mr. Blackburn." Karen had on a pair of jeans and a nice little sweater. She looked real good in her old outfit. Austin could see why the preacher would want to make a pass at her. After all, preachers were men too.

"Do you dress like this every day?" Austin asked as he continued to look her over.

Karen gave Austin a funny look. "Is there something wrong with the way I'm dressed Mr. Blackburn?" she asked.

Austin smiled and rubbed the back of his head. "No, not at all, I like the way you are dressed and I'm very sure most men would. You have the body that would make any outfit you put on look great."

Karen didn't like what he had just said. "Are you saying I look cheap Mr. Blackburn?"

"No not at all. I was just admiring how good you really look in your jeans and top." He answered, but he was still looking at her body.

"Now you have me wondering if I look cheap." This did not make Karen feel good at all.

"Miss Belmont, you do not look one bit cheap. You look like a million bucks in your jeans." This little woman was having a great affect on Austin. He did not want this meeting to end. He did not want to leave her. He wanted to take her home with him tonight.

"Mr. Blackburn, if you don't mind can I ask what you do to make your living?" Karen was only curious.

"Yes you may ask. I'm an entertainment promoter. Do you know what that is?" he asked. He knew most people had no idea what he did even after he had told them.

"No, but it's alright, I'm sure it's something real interesting and important, because you are that type of man." She was back to not looking at him again.

"You are right, I am." Austin lead Karen out of the Coffee shop to his little sport car.

"Wow, is this your car? It's so cute. What is it?" She could not close her mouth. She had never known anyone who owned a regular spots car before let alone one that had to be an out of this world sports car.

"It's a Ferrari," he answered. "What's that?" she asked.

"It's an Italian made sport car." Austin was helping Karen into his pride and joy, his baby as he called it.

"How much does a car like this cost?" Karen asked. She had never seen anything like it before in her life.

"Oh, are you planning to buy one soon?" he asked her.

"No, but it doesn't stop me from wondering," she slowly answered as she started looking at inside of his car.

Austin was starting to like this little girl more and more. "No, I guess it doesn't. It cost around three hundred and fifty thousand dollars and at that price I got it at a steal."

"What! You paid that much for a car and you think you got it at a steal. Now you want my baby for only forty thousand dollars. I guess my baby doesn't have the get up and go that your little red sports car has." Karen did not look any to happy.

"Do you have a problem with me having this car?" he asked.

"No, not at all as long as you love my baby as much as you love your car." She answered.

Austin had not thought anything about loving this baby. He was only wanting, an heir. Now Karen had planted another seed something else for him to think about.

"Karen, I may not pick you to be my surrogate," he said.

"I know, but I hope no matter who you pick you will love their baby, because it takes a lot to leave your baby with someone forever especially if you don't know anything about this person." Karen felt a little sad for her and her baby and even a little sad for Mr. Blackburn.

Austin, had not even turned on his car, he was still listening to what Karen had to say. She was very thoughtful. Why couldn't he meet some woman like her? Then he would not be interviewing women to be a surrogate mother for his heir. Instead he would be married to her and they would be waiting for the birth of their child together.

"Mr. Blackburn, are we just going to sit here?" Karen asked.

"No, of course not," Austin then started up the engine to his baby. "Now tell me Miss Belmont, do you like Italian food?"

"Yes, I sure do, do you?" She asked.

"Yes I do. So let's go and get some of the best Italian food in all of NYC." Austin drove them to his favorite Italian restaurant.

They were greeted at as soon as they were in the door of the restaurant. "Hello, Mr. Blackburn, how many in your party tonight?" A young Italian man in his early thirties asked.

"There will be just the two of us tonight, Gino." Austin replied to the handsome Italian man at the front check-in podium. Even as handsome as Gino was, with his coal black hair and his deep set dark eyes he didn't hold a candle to Austin in the least.

"Oh, and what a dish she is." Gino said in a low voice just for Austin to hear. Austin was a frequent patron of this restaurant and over the years he had gotten to know the owner and his sons quite well.

"Now Gino, she is already taken by me. So put your eyes back into your head. I'm very sure before the evening is over you will have found at least one young lady that will be glad to spend her time with a nice young man like you."

"If you say so, Mr. Blackburn, but she is worth the look." Gino said as he got two menus and started to lead them through the main part of the restaurant to a very nice out of the way booth.

Everyone in the restaurant that knew Austin was giving Karen a good looking over. They all wondered how long Austin had been hiding her from all of them. She was nothing like the woman he was always associated with so they all knew this had to be something serious. She was different.

"Hello Austin, now who do you have here?" a man about Austin's age asked as he was walking by.

"She is taken Dan, so just walk on before you and I get upset with each other." Dan was an old friend of Austin's who over the years had stolen each other's girlfriends. Austin was not going to let Karen be Dan's latest conquest.

They were soon seated in their very private booth. The waitress came to take their drink orders.

"Would you and your lady like a glass of wine tonight, Mr. Blackburn?" the waitress asked.

"No not tonight. I want to be aware of everything that I plan to do," Austin answered.

The waitress just smiled at Austin and then at Karen as if she knew what they would be doing later that night and it was not just business.

As soon as the waitress was gone from their booth Karen lit into him. "What did you mean by that little remark, Mr. Blackburn?"

"Nothing at all as far as you are concern. I was just letting her believe you were my date that's all," he answered.

"Oh, well I guess I can live with that this one time." Karen was enjoying being with Austin, he was so handsome and if he wanted his friend to think she was his date that was all fine with her. She would like to do a little pretending herself.

"What do you mean you can live with it, this one time?" Austin asked. He was sitting very near to Karen. Maybe even a little too close considering it was business and maybe even to close for a first date.

"I just meant you are usually here with beautiful sophisticated women not people like me. If you could put up with me, I can put up with you for one night at least," she answered.

Austin was still not pleased with what Karen had to say. He was not used to anyone and especially a woman putting him down. "Well, Miss Belmont, I hope you won't need to put up with me for a full night."

"No I guess you don't. I know I'm not that all interesting to you. I'm just a no body and you are used to stars and people like that around you. So I will just shut up and leave you alone. That way you won't be so irritated with me." Karen was close enough to Austin she could feel his arm next to hers. Austin could feel her arm leaving his as she moved a little away from him. "Mr. Blackburn, I can slide over to the other side of this booth and give you more room if that would make you more comfortable?"

"No you will stay right where you were. So get back over here near me and don't move away again." Austin wanted her as near as he could get her, but he didn't understand why.

"Why?" Karen asked.

"So you will not be bothered by all these men in this room who have all their eyes on you at this very second." He answered, but he knew that was only partly true. He wanted her near him.

"Mr. Blackburn, no one in this room cares about me one way or another. Not even you, Mr. Blackburn and, I'm even here at this restaurant with you." Karen had never been in such a situation before.

"Well we will still make sure all those men know you are not available." Austin answered.

"How are you going to do that?" Karen asked in an almost whisper she didn't want anyone else to hear what was being said at their table.

"Like this." Austin turned to her and pulled her into his arms and began to give her a very long and passionate kiss. When the kiss was over Karen's eyes were as big as saucers. "Miss Belmont, don't look so shocked. People are watching us." Austin still had her in his arms.

"But I am shocked." She answered in a somewhat weak voice.

"I know, but you need to do something that would go along with what I just did." Austin told her.

"Like what? She asked "Do you want me to slap your face? That's the only thing I can think of right now that would go right along with what you just did."

"No! I do not want you to do that for sure." Austin never thought she would want to slap his face for him only kissing her.

Karen looked over at Austin. Then she put her hands one on each side of his face and turned his head so he was facing her completely. "Don't you ever do that to me again or I will slap your face so hard people will see your head rolling down on the floor." She said it in such a sweet voice and her face looked so loving the whole time she was talking, anyone watching them would think they were having another very private loving moment.

Austin could not move. He wanted to kiss her again so badly, but he knew she meant what she said. "Karen, are you going to kiss me or just hold my face between your hands all night?"

Karen thought for a split second only. "I will kiss you. I don't want your friends to think we are not a couple at least for the time we are here." She pulled him close to her. Then he put his arms around her and they began to kiss.

The second their kiss had ended Austin started. "Karen I can't have you as my surrogate."

"Why Mr. Blackburn, did I do something wrong already? I need to make some money so bad. I can't get a better life without money and I will never make enough working at the Church. Mr. Blackburn was it because I kissed you?" She was heartbroken.

"Yes, and I kissed you back." Karen could feel the pure life pouring out of her. Now what was she going to do?

"What's the matter?" Austin asked. He could see she was beginning to look pale.

"Nothing is the matter." She answered in a sad voice.

"Yes there is so out with it." He wanted to do anything he could to help her, but she was not going to be his surrogate.

"Mr. Blackburn, is it that you just don't want any baby I would have?" Karen felt so sad and disappointed. If it was up to her she would be happy to have his baby even if he didn't want her baby.

"No, that is not it at all. I don't want to get involved with the woman I choose to be my surrogate, and I can see we are headed for nothing, but that already."

"No, Mr. Blackburn, we don't have to get involved. I'm not your type of woman you have already said so. I'm not rich, I'm not pretty, and I'm too young for anybody to have much interest in me at all. You are just being nice, that is all. By tomorrow you won't remember anything about my kiss, but I sure will remember yours," Karen answered.

"Karen, if you still want to stay on my list, I will keep your name there, but I just can't see it happening. You are too easy to get involved with, at any minute in my life." Austin wanted her for more than just a surrogate and he already knew it.

"No I'm not. I've never been involved with any man in my life. You don't even know me." Karen was fighting back the tears that wanted to fill her eyes and then run down her cheeks.

"You are right, I don't know you." But Austin sure wanted to get to know her.

Karen didn't feel like eating anymore. She felt she had just blown it all. "Mr. Blackburn, you were never going to pick me ever, were you?" she asked.

"No. Karen I wasn't," Austin answered.

"Then why did you go to all this trouble?" She wanted to cry, but they were still in the restaurant and she did not want all of the people there seeing her cry.

"Karen, I don't really know." He did not have an answer to her question. At least one he wanted to give her.

"Okay, I understand. I'm ready to leave if you are?" Karen was just sitting there without saying another word.

"But, we have not eaten yet. We will eat and then we will go." Austin was not letting her walk out of his life so quickly.

Karen ate very little, in fact she only ate two bites of bread. She never even touched her plate. She could not understand why Austin had invited her to dinner if he knew she was not what he wanted in a surrogate. They left the restaurant as soon as Austin's meal was over.

"Mr. Blackburn, I'm sorry I wasted your time. I did not mean to waste any of your valuable time. That's all I know to say to you. I hope you find a surrogate for your baby. I'm just sorry it won't be me." She didn't say another word until Austin asked her for the directions to her rooming house. She gave him the directions, but said nothing else and neither did he.

Austin drove for several miles. "Is that your building there?" Austin asked as they approached the big house.

"Yes, thank you for the ride and the meal. Good luck in your search Mr. Blackburn. I do hope you find the right woman for your project as you call it." Karen started to get out of Austin's little car, but before she could he stopped her.

"I will help you. Stay right there." Austin got out and hurried around to Karen's side of the car. Once he had opened her door he started. "Karen, I do hope you get your new life."

"No, you don't." She snapped back at him in a way that was so unlike her, but she wasn't feeling at all like herself tonight.

"What?" He snapped back at her.

"No you don't. If you did you would not be writing me off so quickly. I would be a good surrogate and you know it. I'm healthy, I don't have any bad habits and I'm not involved with anyone. I'm still a virgin, what more do you want your baby's mother to be? If you doubt me, you could keep an eye on me to be sure I'm not seeing anyone. You could even have me checked by a doctor so you would know I have never been with a man." She was giving every reason for him to keep her she could think of at the time.

Austin didn't know what to say. He had only known Karen for a few hours and she was already under his skin. "Karen, if I put you back on my list, would you be willing to move?"

"What do you mean move? I can't afford to move. I need to be near enough to the church to walk to work and home each day." She was now feeling sick again.

"I mean into my house. You did say I could keep an eye on you." He reminded her.

"Yes I did, but I didn't mean I would live with you." She never expected him to say such a thing.

Austin was shooting in the dark now and hoping. He hoped she would not see it as living with a man, but as being critiqued for a very important position.

Karen thought for a few seconds. "I don't know. I guess you have your point." She didn't want to take too much time to think it over. "When would I need to move and how would I get to work each day?"

"I will drive you to work every morning," Austin answered.

"Oh, that should go over real well with the good Reverend. Okay, I will do it, but you didn't say when?"

"No I didn't, but what's wrong with now?" Austin asked.

"Do you want me to go in there now and pack up all of my things and go with you tonight?" Karen had never done anything like this in her life.

"Yes that is exactly what I want you to do. I will go in with you and we can get it all done in a little while." He was ready to take her home with him and he wasn't even sure why yet.

"Okay, but what will I do if you decide you hate me and you want me out of your house?" This worried Karen a lot.

Austin only smiled over at her. "Then we will move you out." He answered.

"But Mr. Blackburn, then where will I go? I won't have a place to go or any place to live." Karen was already worrying about later. That was one of her downfalls, worrying.

"Karen, I will get you a place to live." Austin didn't see that ever happening for awhile anyway. This was not something he did every day. In fact he had never had a woman living with him. That was something he and his best friend Bo had decided a long time ago that they would not do.

"Yes, I'm sure you would, but any place you would find for me would cost way more than I could afford." Karen didn't know what she should do now.

"Karen, I would pay for your rent." Karen looked up at Austin, who was still standing at the open car door.

"Why would you do that?" Karen was puzzled, she had never known anyone like Austin before.

"Let's just say because I'm a good guy and let it go at that for now." If truth be known he didn't know why he would do it either. He would do it if it ever came to that, but he hoped it never would.

"Mr. Blackburn, I would not let you do that, if you don't want me at your house you should not be paying my rent. People would think I'm a kept woman." Karen did not want this man to get the wrong idea about her, now or later.

"No we sure don't want anyone thinking that you are a kept woman do we?" Again Austin wanted to laugh, but he was sure that would be as dangerous as kissing her and he was not in the mood to have his head slapped off of his shoulder as she had said she would do.

"Mr. Blackburn, are you making fun of me?" Austin was not smiling, but Karen could see the devil in his eyes. "Are you making fun of me again?" she asked.

"Yes Karen, I am," he answered.

"Why would you want to do that to me?" she asked him.

"Because I can and if anyone has ever needed to be kept by someone it is you." Austin kept thinking he did not want her to change her mind.

"Mr. Blackburn, why do you think that I need to have someone to take care of me? Why would you say I need to be kept by someone?" She was very interested to know his answer. After all she had been out on her own for almost three years and she had made it so far by herself.

"Oh Miss Belmont, I don't know. Maybe from all the things you have said." Austin just wanted to be that person no matter what. What was wrong with him? He did not know. "Well are you ready to get out of my car and go to your room and pack up all of your things?"

"Yes, but you don't need to go with me. There isn't that much to pack and I will be out here in ten minutes." He helped her out of the car and watched as she walked into the old building. She was like music in motion. He could not take his eyes off of her. Then he remembered the good Reverend Thomas St. Johns. "I may need to pay the good Reverend a little visit one day if he doesn't stop his advances on my woman." What had he said? He had said it out loud, but there was no one there to hear it, except him, and he had heard it loud and clear. His woman, he wanted Karen, but not just for overnight.

Karen went straight to her room and unlocked the door and hurried in to pack. Like she said there wasn't much to pack. There was just a little underwear, two gowns, three pairs of jeans, five tops, two skirts, two dresses and three pair of shoes. Then she packed her tooth brush, tooth paste, hair spray, two towels and that was it. Ten minutes later she was walking out of the front door of the rooming house with her one bag in her hand.

"Is this all of your things?" Austin asked.

"Yes, this is it. I told you it would not take me long." Austin was taking Karen's old bag from her to put it in his car.

"Yes, but I thought you were speaking in woman time," Austin answered.

"What's woman time?" Karen had never heard that before.

"That's when a woman says short and she really means long and she says long you may never see or hear from her again," he answered.

"Oh wonderful, so you think all women lie." Karen didn't know if she was up to changing his mind or not, but she would try.

"Yep that's how it seems," Austin answered.

"Well Mr. Blackburn, I try to never lie if I can help it." Karen had always been as honest as the day is long, but there were a few things she had to lie about.

"Good, then we should get along fabulously. I will not tolerate a liar." Austin was sounding all business like once again.

CHAPTER FOUR

"**M**r. Blackburn, may I ask where do you live?" Karen had forgotten to ask this very important question.

"I have a brownstone in the city." He answered. He doubted if she knew what he was talking about.

"Won't that be out of your way to bring me here to work every morning?" She almost told him to turn around and take her back to the rooming house.

"Yes, maybe, but after the good Reverend learns that you are now living with me, he may fire you and you won't have your little job anymore." Karen knew she did not need to lose her job at the church even if she hated it until she had a new job.

"Well Mr. Blackburn, I just won't tell anyone I have moved and maybe then the Reverend won't know. I still need my job." Austin was speeding down the interstate

Austin was going to make sure that the good Reverend heard that Karen was living in sin and with a man she had just met.

"Well now you have just started to lie." Austin glanced over at Karen to see her reaction to his statement.

"No I have not. I just don't think it is any of the Reverend's business where I live or with whom I live." She wished that Austin would stop trying to upset her.

Austin got a little smile on his face. "I bet the Reverend won't see it that way."

"No I'm sure he won't." Karen didn't know what she would do if she lost her job. Austin had a lot more on his mind going back into the city than he had when he drove out of the city earlier.

"Mr. Blackburn if I should lose my job what will I do?" Karen was so afraid.

Austin gave a quick look over at this beautiful woman sitting in the passenger seat. He knew the possibility of her losing her job was really worrying her, and he did not want her to worry about anything. He was going to be the one taking care of her from this night on. "You would just stay at home and wait for me to come back home each night," he answered.

Now that he had answered that question she had already thought of another question for him to answer. "Mr. Blackburn, you said how I would get to work, but you didn't say how I would get back to your house after work each day?" This was another thing that was bothering her. The thought of having to ride the bus frightened Karen to death. She had never been on any of the buses or trains in the city.

Don't worry Karen, I will go and get you, as long as you still have your job." Austin would see to it that her job would not last much longer. He wanted Karen at his house waiting for him to get home from work every night.

It took over thirty minutes to get to Austin's house. The traffic was nothing compared to what it will be in the mornings when he would need to drive her back out of the city to work. "She won't need to work," he kept thinking to himself. "I will take care of her."

"Wow, you have a beautiful house, is it just as beautiful inside as it is outside?" Karen asked. She had never seen such a nice house before. "I think so, but what do I know?" Karen turned to look at Austin.

She wondered what had brought that on.

Austin had parked right in front of his brownstone. As soon as he had stopped his car he had the door open and he was out. He hurried to open Karen's door. Then he got her little bag out. "Are you ready to go in and see if the inside of my house lives up to the outside?" he asked.

Karen didn't bother to answer. She didn't really know if it was a real question or just again one of his statements. She just smiled up at him and let him lead the way.

After Austin unlocked the front door he stepped inside to a large entrance hall. She could see the stairs case that ran up to the next floors and there were several other large rooms that came off of the entrance hall. All of the rooms she could see had beautiful shining hardwood flooring. "Come on in, don't just stand there," he told her.

Karen stepped inside. Her heart skipped a beat. It was every bit as beautiful if not more so than the outside. "Wow, you do have a very nice home. How long have you lived here? It all looks brand new." She could not get her eyes to take it all in at first glance. All she could do was say wow and she did that three or four more times.

"Well no it is not new, it's over a hundred years old. I have lived here for eight years." Austin was very proud of his home and seeing how it had affected Karen made him even prouder.

"Do you live here all by yourself?" She sure hoped there was no girlfriend living there with him.

"Why are you asking that? Have you now become my mother?" Austin had never had a so called live in girlfriend.

"No I'm not your mother or anyone else's mother you know that, but I was wondering if you would be sharing your baby with someone or were you going to raise it with a nanny's help. I am sure you won't be doing it alone." Karen could not see this handsome man taking any of his time away from what he normally did at night after he had finished his job for the day to stay home and raise a baby.

"You are right you aren't anyone's mother, and you may not ever be anyone's surrogate mother." Austin was going to say more, but Karen cut him off.

"What did you say?" Karen asked. She did not like what he had said at all. If he felt that way she may as well go back to her room at the rooming house tonight before things had time to get any worst for her she thought.

"You heard me." Austin wanted Karen to learn to respond to his statements. He knew she was somewhat shy, but that was one of the things he loved about her.

"Why would you say such a thing to me Mr. Blackburn if you think I may never be a mother then what am I doing here with you?" She did not understand any of what Austin had said. Austin didn't bother to answer her he just turned and walked away. Karen was not going to let him do that to her. She followed after him. "Mr. Blackburn, what am I doing here if I'm not at least someone you may pick to be your surrogate?"

"Miss Belmont, did I not say I would keep you on my list, but you would most likely not ever be my surrogate," he reminded her.

"Yes sir." She answered in a low voice, but she was still not satisfied with his answer.

"So there is your answer." He smiled and started to walk away once again.

"Wait, are you going to keep all the women you keep on your list here at your house?" Karen wanted to know this before she moved into his house.

"No, why would I?" Austin still had that little smile on his handsome face. That smile, of his only make it harder for Karen to feel relaxed around him. She had never been around very many men and none as tall and handsome as Austin or as rich.

"For the same reason you want me here I would suspect," she answered.

Austin didn't bother to answer her again. He just started up the stairs that led to the second floor guest bedrooms. Karen was right on his heels the whole time.

"Which room do you want?" he asked as soon as they had gotten to the second floor landing. Karen looked at all of the closed doors, before asking.

"Which room is yours?" she asked.

"None of these, my room is up there on the next floor." Austin was pointing to the upper floor.

"Good then I will take that one." Karen pointed to the door that was the furthest from the third floor stairs at the other end of the hall. "To bad that's not a bedroom it's a closet. So you will need to pick again." Karen didn't know what door to pick now. She knew she would look even more foolish if she picked another door and again it's not a bedroom.

"Alright then, you pick for me," she answered quickly.

Of course he picked the door that was the nearest to the stair case. Then he smiled. "This way you can run either way upstairs or downstairs. Whichever you may feel the need to do." He gave her another big smile. He already wanted to kiss her again, but he knew he could not. Not yet any way.

The room which Austin chose for Karen was decorated in the Victorian era. As soon as Austin opened the door to the bedroom Karen's face lit up. "Mr. Blackburn, this is the most beautiful bedroom I have ever seen in my life. Are you sure you don't mind me staying in it? I could stay in another room unless of course all of your bedrooms are this nice and in that case I guess I could stay just anywhere. I don't want to mess up anything in your beautiful house."

Austin put her old bag down on the bed, before he asked. "Karen why on earth would I mind you staying in this bedroom or any of the other bedrooms here? Just how many bedrooms have you ever slept in other than your own?"

Karen didn't need any time to think on that question at all. She already knew the answer. "Two."

"So you aren't as pure as you have said," he replied.

"What does that mean Mr. Blackburn?" Karen was not happy at the way things were going at the time. He talked in riddles to her most of the time she thought.

"It means you have slept with someone." He answered with that little smirk of a smile on his face.

"No I have not. I have stayed overnight at my grandma's house and my aunt's house." This time Austin didn't have a comment. "Now Mr. Blackburn, you didn't really mean that I had slept with someone did you?"

Austin gave Karen another one of his little smiles. "No I meant you have had sex with someone."

"That is just what I thought you meant. The answer is no." Karen did not look any too happy with Mr. Blackburn at that moment.

Austin had gone up to the head of the bed and was turning the covers back. "You don't need to do that. I do know how to turn down the covers on a bed for myself." Karen didn't want him to think she was from the backwoods and she didn't know anything.

"Well I do hope so after all you are a grown woman. At least you pretend to be one. Now tell me what time do you need to be at work tomorrow morning?" Austin knew he would not be doing whatever he had to do tomorrow morning to get her to work for very long. He had some plans of his own.

"Mr. Blackburn, at eight, now are you sure, you still want me here. Especially with you needing to get up so much earlier, just to get me to my job before you go to yours." She was still standing in the middle of the bedroom holding on to her purse.

"Yes I am very sure. There is a bathroom with a tub and a shower, through that door. The other door is your closet." Austin began to tell her. He wanted Karen to be as comfortable as she could.

"Thank you Mr. Blackburn, but I think I will be able to learn which door goes where. If I should have trouble figuring it all out then I will give you a loud call and I'm sure you will come running."

"Now if you are through being such a smart mouth. After you have unpacked your things and have put them all away would you care to go down stairs and watch some television with me before bed time?" He wanted to sit and look at her some more before going to bed alone.

"Sure why not. I haven't done that in quite awhile," Karen answered.

Austin was still standing in the bedroom with Karen. He seemed to be looking for any excuse to stay with her. "Alright then if there is nothing else I can get for you, or do for you, I will go. Like I said before get your things put away and go back downstairs. I will be down in the den." Austin then turned and left the room.

Karen opened her old bag as soon as Austin had left out of the room and she began to put her few things away. She didn't need very much of the large closet at all, but she did wish that she had enough things to fill it all.

"Well that was quick," Austin said the second that Karen came into the den.

"Well you saw I didn't have much," she answered.

"Yes I did." Austin decided he needed to take Karen shopping over the weekend. She would need better clothes, although he did like the way she looked in her jeans. She still needed more clothes if she was going to be living with him and she most definitely was living with him and with any luck she would be fired from her job at the church before the end of the next week.

"Oh well come on in here and have a seat and enjoy the rest of the evening. Do you want something to eat? You didn't eat much of your dinner. It was a total waste of my money to have ordered you that meal. No more than you ate you could have eaten off my plate with me. The next time we go out that's exactly what we will do." Austin was sitting in his big chair.

"Mr. Blackburn, you don't need to take me with you when you go out to eat. I can just stay here." Karen felt so small sitting on the big sofa. Everything in the room was very nice and manly. She could tell it all cost plenty.

"And what will you eat while you are here alone?" Austin was watching Karen's every movement.

"I don't know. Maybe, I would make myself another peanut butter sandwich," she answered.

"You would want to eat a peanut butter sandwich while I'm out at some wonderful restaurant eating some delicious meal? Why would you want to do that, Karen?" Austin could not understand this young woman at all.

"I just didn't think you would want me around you when you are with your friends. After all I'm not here as your company." She reminded him.

"No you are not. You are here so I can keep an eye on you. So how am I to do that if you are here at home eating a peanut butter sandwich?" Austin was starting to want Karen more and more.

"I don't know. I guess the same way you will be doing it while you are at work and I am at work and we aren't together," she answered.

That gave Austin another idea for when he gets Karen fired from her job. He was ready to take on all of the responsibilities for this young beautiful woman. "No matter, you will not be here alone eating a peanut butter sandwich. You will be with me." He hoped that settled it all for her.

Karen was still sitting on the sofa. She didn't want to add anything to what Austin had said. It would only make him mad, she was sure.

By ten thirty, Karen was past ready for bed. She was trying very hard not to fall asleep while sitting on the big sofa waiting for Austin to announce that it was bed time. Even the television program had failed to keep her awake.

"Miss Belmont, are you ready for bed yet?" He made it sound as if she was the one keeping them both up past their usual bedtime.

"Yes sir, I am. And what do you mean yet?" she just had to ask. Austin's little remark seemed to have, woken Karen right up. She didn't feel one bit sleepy anymore.

"I only meant you have been sitting there on my sofa almost asleep for the last thirty minutes, and I was just wondering if you would rather be in bed, that's all." Austin had been watching Karen and he could have asked her about going to bed minutes ago, but he wanted to just watch her for a while longer.

"I'm so sorry I'm just not used to being in someone else's home," she answered.

"I can tell that for myself. Just how long, have you been here, Miss Belmont?" Austin could sit and watch her for hours without ever getting tired. She had that strong of an effect on him.

"Mr. Blackburn, you already know the answer to that question. I came here with you just a few hours ago." Karen could not understand why he would be asking her such a question. Did he have a really short memory she wondered.

Austin smiled to himself as he sat in his chair watching her every move without her even being aware of it. "I can see I will always need to paint a little picture for you every time I ask you a question that requires more than a one syllable answer. I was wondering how long you had been living away from your family Miss Belmont not how long you have been here in my home."

After Austin had explained what he meant Karen had no trouble answering. "Three years in June. Didn't I tell you all of this back at the coffee shop earlier?" Karen still had a very puzzled look on her flawless face. She was sure she had told him this back at the coffee shop.

"Are you telling me you left home at sixteen and have been out on your own since?" Austin had never heard of such a thing.

"Yes sir, I have," she answered.

"Why?" Austin could not believe it even though he was hearing it from her.

"Why not, I am an adult. At least that is what everyone said at my graduation. KAREN YOU ARE AN ADULT NOW. GO OUT AND GET YOURSELF A JOB. DON'T BE EXPECTING YOUR POOR MAMA TO ALWAYS TAKE CARE OF YOU."

Austin could not take his eyes off of Karen. "So you just packed up and left?" he asked.

"Yes, I packed and left on the bus that very afternoon, and I've never been back or spoken to anyone of them since," she answered.

They had walked up the stairs to the second floor and Karen was ready to turn to go to her room. "Karen I'll see you tomorrow morning. I will come down and wake you." Austin said as he started up the next set of stairs that led to the third floor.

"No, you don't need to do that, I have my alarm clock. I will just set it for five o'clock." She didn't want him to think she was nothing, but trouble. Someone who he would need to look after all the time she would be in his home.

"Okay, it's up to you. Good night Miss Belmont I will see you tomorrow morning." Austin went up to the next floor to his bedroom. That night all he could think about was Karen being in the bedroom one floor down from him. "Man you have just made things very hard on yourself." Austin said out loud. He was lying in the middle of his big king size bed thinking about how beautiful Karen was and how very young she was. She was way too young for him he thought. Austin had never had a live in girlfriend and he had never wanted one. That was up until today when he saw Karen crossing the street from the church to the coffee shop. He must have lain awake until way past two o'clock in the morning.

Karen on the other hand went into her room and took a nice warm bath and dressed for bed. She was so tired by the time she got into bed she fell right off to sleep. When she got up the next morning she put everything back in its place before she went down stairs. She did not want Mr. Blackburn to get upset with her for not taking good care of his things while she was there in his house. When she went to leave the bedroom that's when she discovered she had not even closed the bedroom door all the way. It was standing half way open. "Too late to worry about that now," she said to herself. "I need to go now and find his kitchen and borrow a knife."

CHAPTER FIVE

When his alarm went off at six o'clock Austin was not in any hurry to get out of his bed. However he had no choice but to get up, Karen needed to get to her job. That's when he decided to make her late getting there. That should upset the good Reverend, Austin thought, besides, the good Reverend may even see her with him and that may upset him even more. He also decided he would send roses to her job today and again on Monday, that is if she still had her job on Monday. Austin was on a mission to get Karen fired from her Church secretary job.

After he showered and had dressed he went down to the second floor. He could not hear a sound coming from Karen's room. He knocked several times, but there was no answer. Then he called out her name and still there was no answer, so without any hesitation he went right into her room.

The bed was already made and the whole room looked as if no one had ever used it. Austin checked the closet to be sure she had not left during the night, but how could she. He had set the alarm before going upstairs to bed. She had to be there somewhere. Downstairs was the only other place she could be.

"Karen, are you down here?" Austin called out, as he began to walk through the main floor of his house.

"Mr. Blackburn, I'm in your kitchen. I hope you don't mind. I made me a sandwich for lunch. I had my bread and peanut butter, but I didn't have a knife. I must have left my knife at the rooming house. So I came down to use one of yours. Was that alright?" She looked so sweet to him standing there in his big nice hardly used kitchen.

"Yes of course Karen, that's alright, but why are you taking a sandwich?" Austin had never taken his lunch to work before in his life.

"Why not Mr. Blackburn? It doesn't cost as much to take something to eat as it does to buy something every day. I have always taken my lunch. I know that the coffee shop is only across the street, but I have never been there except to get something for the Reverend and yesterday when I went there to meet you.

"But you take a peanut butter sandwich?" He asked.

"Sure, like I already said, why not? I didn't have a refrigerator in my room at the rooming house so I always got peanut butter because it didn't need to be refrigerated." Karen began to wonder if he had ever had a peanut butter sandwich before or if he even knew what it was.

"Do you take that every day for your lunch?" Austin had never heard of such in his life. He knew he would not want a peanut butter sandwich for his lunch one time let alone every day.

"No, sometimes I just don't eat. I used to use that time to read, but most of the time now I use that time studying the Bible. Reverend St Johns said I needed to know the Bible better and if I didn't start doing my studying on my own time, he would take some of his valuable time and teach me about the Bible. I sure didn't want that to ever happen so I started memorizing the Bible. That way if he started to ask me a question, hoping I would not know the answer, I could just quote all the verses which he was questioning, me about. That always made him mad and he would tell me to go back to my desk and close the door behind me. That would always be the best part of my day."

Austin did not like the good Reverend at all and the more Karen told him about her interactions with the good Reverend the less he cared for him. "He is not a very good man, is he?"

"I don't know. I only see him at the office. I don't care to see him anywhere else." Karen had her sandwich made and in a little plastic bag.

"Do you need a napkin or anything else?" Austin asked.

"No, I will use a paper towel from the ladies' room," she answered.

"What do you drink with your tasty lunch each day?" Austin had only eaten a few peanut butter sandwiches in his life. He could not imagine having to eat one every day. He didn't believe he would be able to eat them that often. If he remembered right even as a boy he did not care much for them.

"Water," Karen answered. "That's free at the church and they don't mind if I drink it even if I'm a sinner."

"Have you always worked at the church since getting to New York?" Austin asked.

"Yes, I got my job there right away. I told them I was eighteen years old and they believed me. So they think I'm twenty one now." Karen had not realized until it was too late that she had just told Austin one of her secrets.

"You mean to tell me you lied to the good Reverend St. Johns?" Austin had a little more material to use against Karen in getting her fired if his first plan should fail.

"Yes I guess you could say I lied, but I needed a job and it's not like it is something I do all the time. I try very hard to avoid doing that if all possible. Karen was not happy about Mr. Blackburn knowing that she had lied and to a Church at that.

"Are you ready? We need to be leaving." Austin already had his car keys in his hand. He knew it was going to be a very long drive this morning back to the Church. Austin left out of the kitchen and was standing by the front door when Karen got there.

"Yes sir, I'm ready. Just let me get my jacket and purse." Karen hurried up to the second floor and got back down as Austin was unlocking the front door.

"Oh, were you going to leave without me?" she asked.

"No Karen I would have remembered you before I drove away." Austin said as he opened the door. Before long they were in Austin's little red sport car going down the highway.

"Mr. Blackburn, I don't think this is going to work. You are too set in your ways. I may be too much trouble for you. You have no idea how much trouble I can be." Karen said as she sat there trying not to look Austin's way. She wanted to give Austin another chance to change his mind.

Austin again gave her one of his looks. She didn't know what trouble really was, but she's about to find out he thought to himself. "Miss Belmont, I am not set in my ways and you can be trained."

"Mr. Blackburn, do you think I'm a dog or some other type of animal that you can train?" Karen did not like his statement at all. In fact she had not cared for several of his statements.

"No, I said you could be trained. Not the same at all." Austin was going to have himself a very good time living with this woman he could already tell. "Would you like to have some breakfast before going into work?"

"No sir, I'm alright. It will be lunch time in four and half hours." Karen stopped talking and began to look for her peanut butter sandwich.

"What's wrong now?" Austin asked as he watched her looking for something.

"I don't have my sandwich. I must have left it in your kitchen. Oh well I can eat it tonight for supper." She was disappointed that she would not have anything to eat until after work and until after she got back to Mr. Blackburn's house and who knows how late tonight that may be.

Austin looked over at Karen for only a second. The traffic was very heavy and he was keeping his eyes on the road. He sure did not want anything to happen to his baby. "What are you going to eat at lunch time now that you have left your delicious sandwich at home?"

"I won't, I will just do my Bible studying today instead of eating. I can eat that sandwich for supper and it won't go to waste that way." She answered.

"No, you will not eat that old sandwich for dinner tonight. We are going out." He had not even taken his eyes off the road a second to answer her.

"Mr. Blackburn, you don't need to feel as if you have to feed me. I will do alright. I have for three years almost and I'm still alive. Haven't you noticed?" Karen was sitting in her seat worrying so much about her job and everything else that crossed her mind. She was not even looking out of the car window at the sites. Now she was worried about the good Reverend and what he was going to do. All of that was on her mind too much for her to care about anything she could have seen out of the window.

Austin smiled. "Yes Miss Belmont, I have noticed that you are very much alive. What time do you go to lunch?" Austin was driving as slow as he possibility could. He wanted to be sure he made her very late for work.

"Why do you need to know about my lunch time Mr. Blackburn?" Karen was now looking over at Austin. She could not help herself. She wanted to know what he was up to.

"Well I need to know in case I want to give you a call for some reason and I want to be sure you are there and not out to lunch. I'm sure you don't want the good Reverend taking your personal calls while you are out studying your Bible lessons." Austin had another one of those smiles on his face.

"No, I sure don't, especially a call from you," she quickly answered.

"Now Miss Belmont, should I be flattered or insulted?" he asked. "I'm not sure myself as to which one Mr. Blackburn, but as soon as I decide I will sure let you know. I'm young and a lot of things thrill a girl my age. You know we young girls are just boy crazy and to get a call from a Big Old Adult like you may just thrill me way too much and I may just do something real crazy, who knows?" she was trying to irritate him some.

"Miss Belmont, if you decide to do something crazy, I would prefer you to do it with me rather than with the good Reverend," Austin answered. The traffic was getting a lot heavier now.

"Oh me too Mr. Blackburn I would never want that man to get that near me. Just the thought of him being that near me makes my skin crawl." Karen was even making a face.

"Well at least we are on the same page." Austin answered. He was already in trouble and he knew it. This young girl without even being aware of it was changing his life forever.

"Mr. Blackburn, could you drive any slower?" Karen was getting very anxious.

Yes I could if that's what you want me to do." He answered as he let up on the gas paddle as his car began to slow down even more.

"No! I don't really want you to drive any slower I was just being rude. We seem to be crawling along the road, not at all the way you drove last night." She wondered if he was afraid of driving in such heavy traffic.

"Oh, I haven't noticed. I thought I was just being very careful with my passenger. After all you are going to be the mother of my baby," he answered.

"Yes I may, but you said last night that I most likely would not be your surrogate." Karen still did not understand why she was living at his house, but right now she did not want to go into all of that with him. All she wanted now was to get to her job at the Church and on time. "Mr. Blackburn, if you don't speed up just a little I will be late for work and Rev. St. Johns does not want me to ever be late. He said it was a bad reflection on him and the church."

"So he believes you being late for your job would be a bad reflection on his church, but his making passes at you is perfectly alright?" The more Austin heard about the good Reverend the less he cared for him.

"Yes, I guess so," Karen was getting very anxious again.

"I do believe he has a lot to learn." Austin said and he felt he was just the man to teach it to the good Reverend.

"Mr. Blackburn, what are you doing now?" Karen asked as she watched him leaving the road. Austin had decided to stop at a fast food drive-in. He knew that would take up quite a bit of time.

"I need a cup of coffee, do you want something?" he asked.

"No! I don't want anything. All I want is to get to work and on time, but I don't think I will make it. So just go ahead and get all the coffee you want. After all it's not your job on the line, it's only mine." Karen had knots in her stomach from thinking about the good Reverend's reaction to her being late.

"Miss Belmont, I was under the impression, you were employed by me at the present time," Austin answered. "So what if you lose the job at the church you still have your job with me.

"Employed by you, at doing what?" she asked.

"Yes Miss Belmont, at having my baby," he answered.

"No, I'm not yet and you said I most likely would not be your surrogate at all. Now you are telling me I am employed by you and I'm having your baby. When did I get pregnant? Was it while we were crawling down the highway this morning?

"No, you did not get pregnant while we were going down the highway this morning, but if you want to give it a try we can." Austin had that smile on his face again that only meant trouble, but Karen had not learned that yet.

"No, you know I don't want to do that. We aren't married. What's wrong with you?" she asked.

"Nothing is wrong with me, but you are employed by me like it or not young lady and as for being married we will see." Austin smiled he knew at that moment he was wining.

"Employed at what Mr. Blackburn that's all I want to know," Karen asked again. She had forgotten all of what he had said about being married. She was all puzzled once again.

"At having my baby Miss Belmont, what else do you think?" Austin had said it again. It was out of his mouth before he knew it. He had already told her he would most likely not pick her to be his surrogate, but now he had said it twice that she would be having his baby. What in the world did he have on his mind? At that time he even wondered.

"Mr. Blackburn, if you should pick me, I will have your baby, but if you pick some other woman, then she will be the one having your baby not me. The thought of that ever happening makes me sad." Austin wanted to tell Karen no one else would ever have his babies, but of course he said nothing.

"Are you sure you don't want something to eat? I could order you something. They seem to have quite a large menu." Austin was still looking at the menu at the drive-in fast food restaurant. He was wasting as much time as he possibly could. After all he was in no hurry at all.

"No sir I'm nervous enough. I don't need any caffeine in me." Karen was not able to keep her hands still. She kept moving her fingers up and down in her hands.

"It's just as well you don't drink coffee, it's not good for you or my baby." There he had said it once again. "There will be a lot of things you will need to change." Karen did not ask him, what those changes would be. Right now she really didn't care what they were.

"Mr. Blackburn, could you just order your coffee and stop talking so much. We really do need to get going. I'm very sure the Reverend is already at the church and he is wondering where I am."

"Yes Miss Belmont, I will, now let me see if there is anything else I may want. I would sure hate to be half way down the road and remember something I wanted and then need to come back here to get it."

Karen could not take it any longer. "No, there is nothing else you want, and stop calling me Miss Belmont. You sound just like Reverend St. Johns. He is always calling me Miss Belmont."

Austin gave her a long stare. "You are nervous aren't you?" he asked as if he didn't know that already.

"Yes I am. I told you Reverend St Johns does not want me to be late." Karen even had tears in her eyes now.

"Karen, what will happen if you are late?" Austin was very concern about this woman now. He had so much feeling for her that it almost scared him.

"All hell will break loose," she answered.

"Karen exactly what does that mean, all hell will break loose?" Austin wanted to know exactly what would happen to her if she is late.

"It only means he will find every reason in the world to have me sit right under him in his little office all day." Karen could no longer hold back her tears now. "Then he will tell me for the hundredth time the proper way to run an office."

"Oh, no he won't. I will be telling him a few things, if he does one more thing to you." Austin face was turning a light shade of red. Karen wondered what had made him want to do that for her, but she was not going to asked him right now. "Alright we will go."

"You aren't going to order your coffee?" Karen asked.

"No, the coffee can wait. We are going to get you to work." Austin pulled back out into the heavy traffic, but he was not crawling this time he was racing instead.

"Well you don't have to get us killed. Reverend St. Johns could do that if I was ready to die." Karen told him.

"Woman is there any pleasing you?" Austin asked as he continued to race down the highway.

"Yes, you know there has to be," she answered.

Austin gave Karen a quick look. "How would I know? I sure haven't done any of it yet."

Karen smiled. "Just keep trying and maybe you will someday," she answered.

"Whoever said I wanted to try?" Austin answered back at her, but he knew he want to please her more than anything in the world.

Karen didn't need to see Austin's face to know his eyes were all squinted up. "Not you that is for sure," Karen answered.

"Miss Belmont, didn't your mother ever tell you not to be such a smart mouth?"

"Yes sir, Mr. Blackburn, lots of time. Especially, just before she would hit me." Karen did not like being reminded of those old days.

"What! Just before she would hit you," Austin was now even angry at Karen's mother.

"You see Mr. Blackburn my mother was and still is a drunk. I spent my time dodging her and her no good for nothing boyfriends."

"Where was your father during all this time?" Austin asked.

"I have also wondered that many times myself. I don't have any idea who my father is. He could be you for all I know or even the good Reverend, but I doubt it is either of you. You two would have been running away from my mother as fast as you could. She only wanted bikers. Do you know what bikers are Mr. Blackburn?"

"Yes as a matter of fact I do." Austin had spent lots of weekends and vacations riding his big bike, around the country with his best friend, but he never got involved with any biker women. Besides he was only fifteen years older than Karen. At fifteen he was in prep school under the watchful eyes of all his teachers and house mother.

"Miss Belmont, there is no way in this world I could be your father, but I cannot speak for the good reverend. Let's just hope he is not your father. I have a feeling having no father is better than having the good Reverend as your father. We sure would hate for your family tree to be a tumble weed."

"Didn't I make it clear to you he is only my employer," she answered.

"Yes, you did and I do apologize." Austin could not get enough of this young woman. She had clearly captured his heart already.

"Well we are here and in one piece, but I'm afraid you are still a little late." Austin said as he glanced over at the clock on the dashboard as he pulled his car into the church's parking lot. As soon as he had parked his car he got out and went around to the other side and opened Karen's door.

"Why did you need to do this? Karen asked as soon as he opened her car door. "I could have gotten out without your help. Now if the Reverend sees you with me, he will assume that we are sleeping together, Mr. Blackburn." Karen was so afraid she was being watched by the good Reverend and he would have a lot to say to her about it all as soon as she was in her office.

"Oh well then in that case it won't hurt if I." Austin then pulled Karen out of the car and into his arms and kissed her.

"Mr. Blackburn, you most likely just got me fired." Karen said as soon as he had released her.

"Then maybe Karen, I need to go in with you just in case I did get you fired and then you would have a ride home." Austin was in no hurry to leave her there. He did not want the good Reverend to upset her.

"No Mr. Blackburn, I will run the chance, that maybe he was busy doing something and he missed the whole thing." That's what Karen hoped, but she had her doubts. Knowing the Reverend he was watching for out of his office window.

"Maybe he did, Karen." Austin said as he pulled her close one more time and leaned way down to kiss her again.

"Will you, please stop with all of the kissing." She said as she pulled away from him. "You are acting like we are lovers. Not at all like someone who can't stand me."

"Who said I could not stand you?" Austin sure knew it was not him.

"You may not have said it in words, but you have made it quite clear by the way you look at me." Karen was still standing with Austin's arms around her.

"I most definitely, do not look at you as if I cannot stand you. I can assure you of that one thing." Austin did not want to let her go.

"Mr. Blackburn, it doesn't really matter right now. I just need to get in there and take my medicine. Mr. Blackburn, thank you for the ride. I'm sorry I have been so unkind to you this morning." Karen found she liked his kisses and being held in his arms. She only wished that they were real kisses and hugs just for her and not just for the good Reverend to see.

"Karen, could you call me Austin? That is my name." Austin got back into his red sport car and drove away, while Karen watched.

CHAPTER SIX

"Miss Belmont, I see that you are late. What did I tell you about being late when I hired you?" The good Reverend was sitting at his desk and Karen could tell he was not happy at all.

"Reverend St. Johns, I'm very sorry I was late this morning, but this was the first time I've ever been late in the three years I have worked here at your church." She hoped he would consider all of that before he decided on her punishment.

"Never the less, you are still late. You will need to make up the time, this afternoon. You will work an extra hour to make up for your tardiness." The Reverend had one of his tight little smiles on his lips.

"Rev. St. Johns, I was only three minutes late." Karen said as she stood in the Reverend's office as near to the door as she could get.

"I know how late you were. I saw you and your boyfriend kissing and right here on the church property too. Who is he, some rich man that you met at some bar? He must be very rich to be able to drive that kind of car. Is that what you've been holding out for? I bet you didn't make him wait." The good Reverend said all of that in such a hateful voice. That it scared Karen. She turned and walked out of the Reverend's office. Once back at her desk she called the number Austin had given her to call about the ad. She only hoped he would answer.

"Hello, Karen what's wrong, honey." Austin had been waiting for her call.

"Everything, I can't stay here. He saw us and he said I had to stay an hour after work to make up for the three minutes I was late." Karen was already starting to cry.

Austin wasted no time he just made a big U turn and sped back to the church while still talking to Karen on his cell phone. He didn't ask her if she needed him to come and get her. He just decided that's why she had called.

"Mr. Blackburn, what should I do?" She was so afraid. Now she had no job and that meant she had no income. When she thought things could not get any worst they did.

"Karen honey, I'm on my way. Just get ready to leave. I will be back there in a couple of minutes." Karen hung up her phone. She was going to stay as far away from the Reverend as she could while she waited for Austin to get there.

"Miss Belmont, come in here and bring your writing pad. You need to learn some respect for the position you hold in my church. I will give you a few things you can do this weekend to help you learn that respect. That is if you aren't too busy with your boyfriend. Just how long has all of that been going on and right here under my very nose?" Karen didn't bother to answer. She had tears running down her face. She could hear the good reverend as he went on and on about her morals. She could picture how hateful his face must be looking in her mind.

Austin pulled his red sport car back into the church parking lot and hurried into the building marked office. He could see another sign that led him down the hall to where Karen's desk sat. She was still sitting there listening to the good Reverend go on and on about her morals.

"You didn't answer me. How long has your affair with that man been going on? How many times have you slept with him, while you still pretended to be a virgin?" The Reverend kept talking and talking. Karen wished one of his church members would come in now and see what a good man he really was.

"Karen." Austin whispered softly as he leaned over her desk at her. He didn't want the Reverend to know that he was there until Karen had time to get out of the building completely.

"Mr. Blackburn." She was surprised to see him there so soon. "Karen, go out to the car and wait, I will be out in a short while."

She got up out of her chair and started walking out of the building with her jacket and purse in her hand. She was never so glad to see someone before in her life as she was to see Austin.

Austin took a few steps and was in the Reverend's office before the good Reverend knew that he had company. "Sir," Austin said as he stood at the door of the office.

Reverend St. Johns stopped talking and looked up from studying his Bible. He had not expected to be hearing a male voice. "Yes, could

I help you? My secretary must be away from her desk." The Reverend did not recognized Austin as being the man out in the parking lot this morning with Karen.

Austin smiled. "No sir, you are right she is not there and she is not your secretary anymore. She is my woman and she lives with me. I hope you get a good mental picture of us together. We live together do you understand what all that means? I sure hope so. Now multiply that by a million, that's how often I get her. She is completely mine. Karen Belmont is my woman and she will never be yours." Without, saying another word Austin turned and walked back out the door. While leaving the good reverend still sitting at his desk with his mouth wide open.

Austin hurried out of the building, and as he came out of the door he could see Karen standing at his car. "Karen, what did he do honey?" Austin asked as soon as he was near enough to her.

She was crying. "He saw us and he wanted to know, how long I had been sleeping with you, Mr. Blackburn? He was saying such ugly things to me. Things I would have never expected a mister to say. Austin had Karen in his arms. He was holding her very close. She stood there letting him hold her. Austin didn't want to ever let her go. Her head came just to the middle of his chest even with her heels.

"Karen, let's get into the car and we will go to my office and check in and then I will take you back home later." But before he let her go he kissed her again. Then he looked right into her big beautiful tear filled eyes. "Karen, you need to be calling me Austin. Can you remember Austin? I'm Austin to you."

"Yes, I will remember." She said in a soft voice. She was still crying a little, but having Austin there helped matters so much.

On their drive back to the city, Austin could not help, but to be happy that Karen's job at the Church with the good Reverend was all over and done with. It would save him a lot of trouble, but he had been ready to do whatever it took to get her out of the good Reverend's reach. Karen was not the reverend's woman, she was his woman. "Karen, please stop crying it's alright you do not need that job." If Karen wasn't so upset Austin may have subjected that they celebrate in some way.

"Yes I do and now I won't even be able to get another job, because I'm very sure the Reverend will not give me a good recommendation and I will have lost all those years I put up with his mouth and advances.

I feel sick." Austin kept driving. He was listening to her every word, but he did not take it literally. "Austin, I really mean I feel like I'm going to throw up. You need to stop and let me out of your car and I do mean in a hurry." She already had her hand over her mouth.

"Okay Karen, hold on honey until I find a safe place to pull over." Austin took the next exit off the interstate then he pulled over to the side of the road. "Alright get out, I will wait here." He did not want to make her wait for him to get around to her side of the car to open her door. He was afraid it would be too late and she would have done it all in his baby. After a few seconds he decided he could not just sit in the car and wait any longer while Karen was leaned over outside throwing up. He got out and took her several tissues. "Karen honey, are you feeling any better?"

"Yes Austin, I'm sorry, but this has upset me a great deal. I don't know what I'm going to do now. I don't have any place to go and now I don't even have a job anymore. I'm right back to where I was three years ago when I got here and needed a job."

"Karen you do have a place to go. The same place you stayed at last night and you don't need that job. In fact you don't need any job." Austin was going to be the one to take care of her now. She was ready to start crying all over again.

She looked up at him with the saddest eyes he had ever seen. "But for how long will I have a home Austin? If you pick another woman to have your baby you won't need me. So where do I go that day?" She asked.

"Karen, don't worry about something that hasn't taken place yet." That was all Austin could tell her. It would have to do for now. He just hoped that would be enough for her at this time.

By the time they had gotten back to the city, Karen was back to normal. Her stomach had settled down, but she was very quiet. "Karen, you can talk, you don't have to just sit there and not say a word. We are something to each other you know."

She cut her eyes over at him without moving her head. "What are we to each other Austin? Yesterday at this time you didn't even know me. Now I'm living with you. No wonder the Reverend got so upset with me. I am a bad woman. Good women don't live with men they aren't married to at least I didn't think I would."

"Yes they do Karen. Every day there's good women living with men that they aren't married to and they are even sharing their bed. Unlike us, we don't even share the same floor, but we still manage to have just as many arguments as any married couples."

"No we do not. If we did you would be divorcing me, but that is only if we were married." She answered.

"Maybe then we should just get married and then I could divorce you, every time you upset me." Austin said in a very serious voice.

"Austin, we are not getting married you and I both know that. You were just making a point. I know, but I will never get a divorce. If I love someone enough to marry him I will love him enough to work at being married to him. After all I want lots of children and I may need my husband for that little job."

"And will he get to see his babies being born?" Austin asked. "Maybe he will," Karen answered. Austin just smiled. Karen saw him smiling, but she just let it go again.

CHAPTER SEVEN

It wasn't too long before Austin was pulling into a big underground garage. "Austin, where do you want me to wait?" Karen asked when they got out of his car and was walking towards the elevator.

"What do you mean, wait for me?" He asked.

"I mean while you go upstairs at your job. Where do you want me to wait while you are up there? Here in the garage or someplace else?" She asked.

"I will take you with me to my office," he answered. He led her into the elevator. While in the elevator several people spoke to him. He didn't even need to say what floor he wanted. The people seemed to know a lot about him. Karen noticed.

As soon as the door opened on the forty seventh floor he led Karen out of the elevator where Premier Entertainment agency covered the whole floor.

"Do you work here?" She asked.

"Yes I work here," that was all the answer he gave her.

"Hello Mr. Blackburn." One lady said as she passed them. She was going out of the front door as they were going into the business. Austin just nodded his head as they passed.

"Mary Helen, do I have any messages?" Austin asked as soon as they were in the door.

"Yes sir, about three dozen of them. I will bring them down to your office right away." Mary Helen was the receptionist at the front desk. She handled almost all of the incoming calls to the business each day with the help of the switchboard operator.

"Okay, do that and get me a cup of coffee if you don't mind. I have had a very hard time this morning getting a cup of coffee." Austin gave the woman a little smile and then he looked down at Karen.

The woman looked over at Karen as to say, "I bet you were the reason my boss didn't get his coffee this morning." But it was a cute smile she gave Karen not a mean jealous look.

"Come on Karen, we will do a little here and then we will go." Austin took hold of Karen's hand and then he led her down a long hallway.

"Good morning Mr. Blackburn," someone else said as they passed them in the hall.

"Good morning." Austin repeated that several more times before getting to his office. He was well liked by his employees.

"Lisa, hold all of my calls. I have something I need to do this morning that just can't wait."

This woman gave Karen a look that asked, "Is he doing you?" But this time it was a mean jealous look. Not a sweet cute smile like the one the nice woman from up at the front desk had given her. Karen wanted to scream, back at Austin's secretary, "NO! He is not doing me."

"Come on in Karen, and close the door behind you." For some reason she didn't mind at all being in Austin's office with the door closed. "Karen there is a bathroom through that door and there is a new toothbrush and toothpaste plus mouthwash under the sink. It's all waiting for you to use." Austin was already taking his seat behind his desk.

"Thank you Mr. Blackburn." Austin didn't say anything to her for calling him Mr. Blackburn. He decided to let it go for this once. Karen went right into his private bathroom but once she was in there she took a few minutes to just look all around it. It was so big and beautiful. It was not at all like a bathroom she would have expected a person to have at their job. After she had recovered from her tour of his bathroom she brushed her teeth and rinsed her mouth with his mouthwash. She felt a lot better with a clean mouth again. She even used the potty while she was there.

As she opened the bathroom door she could see that Austin was waiting for her. "Come back in here and have a seat." Karen picked a chair way over on the other side of the big room. "Karen, if I had wanted you to sit so far away, I would have left you outside with my secretary. Now move over here like you should."

She got up out of that chair and moved to the chair that was right in front of his big desk. "Karen, do I need to re-raise you to be what I need?" He asked.

"No sir, you don't need to do that, because we both know I will never be what you need or want no matter how much you try to change me. I will still be the same old me," she answered.

"Why would you say that?" Austin liked everything he saw and more.

"Look." Karen stood up with her arms open wide. "Just look at me then look at all the beautiful women you have here at your job. You have it all and all those pretty woman trying to catch your attention." Karen did not think she measured up to Austin's standards in any way.

"And here you have all of my attention Karen and you can't tell me you don't want it." Austin was still sitting behind his desk listening to her talk. He was very powerful and intimidating to her.

"Austin, I never said I didn't want it. I just know what I can have and what I will never have. You are one of those things I will never have." If she could only read his mind she would have known how he felt about her.

"Karen, why would you say you could never have it? From where I sit you could have it all," he answered.

"Austin look at me, I'm small town nothing. You are up town everything. You are surrounded by beautiful women all the time. What in the world would you want with a plain Jane like me?" Karen looked so sweet and innocent to him. It was taking all he had to stay behind his desk and not go over and take her into his arms.

"Oh, I don't really know Karen, maybe just a good time." He replied. That sure didn't sit well with her.

"Well you won't ever be just having your good time with me. I'm not a good time woman and I don't know anything about having a good time and I don't care to learn. So you need to just find yourself another plaything because it will never be me."

Austin waited a few more seconds before adding, "What if I'm not looking for just a plaything? What if I wanted you permanently?"

"What does that mean? What if? I played what if in Jr. High School. You know the game; what if I was tall, what if I was rich, what if what, Austin?" Karen was feeling scared again.

Karen, I mean what if I wanted to marry you." Karen could tell that Austin was very serious.

"No, Austin, you don't want to do that, you don't know me and I'm not your kind of woman. You said that yourself. Nobody in his right mind would want to marry me," she sadly answered.

"Well I have never before in my life heard a woman give so many reasons why a man should not want to marry her. Do you ever take what someone says to you at its face value?" He asked.

Karen's eyes were like two big circles. She could not believe what she was hearing. She was sure it was all just a dream, and any time now she would be waking up. "Austin, I don't know. I don't think I understand what you are saying."

"Well does that mean that I will need to spend the next sixty years or so explaining everything to you?" Austin had a playful smile on his face. He wanted Karen to marry him. He had never been this serious about anything other than his parents, his business and of course; his best and dearest friend Bo.

"I guess, because you always say so much I forget half of what you say before you have finished saying it and I don't always understand the other half." She was still just as puzzled.

"Karen, I want an heir." Austin said in a low clear voice. He wanted to say everything that he needed to say without upsetting her or him.

"Yes, Austin I know that, and that is why you ran the ad in the paper. That's why I'm here." Karen was now sitting on the edge of her chair.

"No, Karen, it is not. You are here because I want you here." He hoped what he had to say now would not scare her off, but instead bring them very close together.

"Yes, so I can be a surrogate mother for your heir," she answered. She was not getting one word of what Austin was trying very hard to tell her.

"No Karen, so you can be the mother of my heir." He was speaking so softly when telling her all of this.

"Isn't that what I just got out of my mouth?" Karen asked.

"No honey, you said you were here to be my surrogate. I said you are here to be my heir's mother." He answered.

"Aren't they both the same thing?" Karen asked.

"No, the surrogate would be impregnated medically, but I don't want it done that way with you. That is why you will not be my surrogate anymore." Karen was almost in tears. She still was not getting what Austin was telling her. For some reason she was not getting it at all. Maybe because of all that had upset her earlier she was not thinking right.

"So you have already made up your mind, and you don't need me anymore." She began to cry.

"No, Karen I did not say that at all. I just don't need a surrogate anymore. I need you to have my heir by the old fashion way." Austin did not know any other way to say it to her, but he would soon learn he would need to say it another way.

"And what way is that?" By Karen's reaction Austin could tell she did not understand what he had said at all. All she had heard was that she was not going to be his surrogate.

"I want to make love to you and get you pregnant. Do you understand that much?" Austin asked.

"Yes and no, yes I understand that, but no I can't." Karen had never been asked to do such a thing before in her life.

"Tell me why not, Karen?" Austin could not understand why she would not want to do as he had asked.

"Because, for one thing Mr. Blackburn, I want to be married when I do that with a man." Karen thought that would put an end to his big idea.

"Yes, I know and I'm willing to marry you so I can make love with you." Austin had said it all so matter of fact. As if this was something he did every day without thinking. He was not ready to show his hand yet.

"Mr. Blackburn, are you telling me you would go as far as to marry me, just so I would sleep with you until you get me pregnant. So I can have you a baby." Karen could not believe what she was hearing.

Karen had never even dreamed of ever being married. "Then what do you do with me then? Divorce me and send me on my merry way?" The thought of being sent away from him was bad enough, but to have to leave her baby too would be too much.

"No Karen, I told you it would take me sixty years to teach you what I needed to teach you. So I expect we will be married a very long time." Austin had a little tinkle in his eyes now.

"Mr. Blackburn, have you lost your mind?" She asked. That was the only reason she could think of that would make him want to marry her.

"No Karen I don't think so. How about you Karen, have you lost your mind?" He asked her.

Karen just sat there staring at him without saying anything. She again did not know if he had asked her a question or if he had just made another one of his statements. "I will give you a few weeks of courting so you can get to know me better, but I do expect us to marry in a couple of months and I expect you to want me." Austin still had no expression on his face that would give Karen any clue as to what his real feelings were concerning her other than that few seconds she saw a small twinkle in his eyes earlier.

"How do you expect me to want you?" Karen asked while she was still sitting on the edge of her chair.

"Boy this is going to be some kind of marriage. I mean I want you to want me sexually. You do know what that means, you do know about sex, don't you?" This was getting to be almost funny to Austin. If it was happening to two other people he would be laughing right now, but he was very sure laughing right now would not help his cause at all.

"Yes, I do know about sex. I did take Marriage and Family in school like everyone else in my school," she answered. He could not tell if she was joking or not.

"But Karen did you learn anything?" He asked.

"I passed the course if that's what you mean with an "A" how about you?" She answered.

"But sweetheart, do you know anything about sex?" He asked. "No, are you happy now?" She answered. Austin had a very big smile on his face now and that did not help Karen one bit.

"Yes, in fact I am. This means, I will be your only teacher," he answered.

"You already knew that, so why did you need to ask me that awful question?" She asked.

"Karen, sex is not awful. It's a very wonderful thing if shared by two people who love each other." Austin could already see them having a very good marriage.

"And who are married to each other," she answered.

"Yes Karen, and two people who are married to each other, you are right." Austin was somewhat pleased at how things were going at the time between the two of them.

Karen was still staring over at Austin and she was wondering where all of this was going.

Then from out of the blue, she asked. "Just how many women have you slept with or should I say had sex with up until now?"

That question caught Austin off guard. "That's none of your business." He didn't want to answer that question. Especially if it is being asked by the woman he wanted to marry and who happens to be a woman he had not slept or had sex with at all.

Karen was the one who had the little smile on her face now. "Oh, now it's none of my business, when it comes to me asking you about your sex life, but it's alright for you to question me on my sex life."

Austin had never been asked such a question before. "Yes, I'm glad you see it that way and you understand," he answered.

"No you aren't, because you know full well I didn't understand one bit of what you said. Austin, why don't you want me to know about the women you have slept with and done more with than you have done with me? After all I'm the one who would be giving up my freedom to have your baby."

"If you put it that way Karen, maybe you won't need to give up your freedom to have our baby. We could just live together and we both could keep our freedom," he answered.

"No I will never do that and you know it. Besides I'm not sure at all about even marrying you." She wasn't sure if Austin was serious or just testing her.

"Yes, you are. We both knew we were headed that way even at the coffee shop yesterday afternoon."

"No, I did not." Karen quickly answered.

"Liar," Austin answered. Karen stopped playing with her fingers and looked at Austin. She did not like being call a liar.

"Mr. Blackburn, I am not a liar." She had never been called a liar before, but now she wasn't too sure she wasn't a liar. "If I thought anything about wanting you as a husband I sure would have known it." Then her face started heating up and turning red.

"I see you have at least thought about it." Austin had another smile on his face.

"Yes, yes, yes, I have thought about it are you happy now? What woman would not give it a thought if they met you and saw how nice you are? After all they could already see how handsome you are." She answered with a red face.

Austin got out of his chair and walked around his desk. Karen was still sitting on the very edge of her chair. "Karen, slide back into the chair before you fall out onto the floor." Karen slid a little farther back into the chair, but still not all the way. "Karen, I have changed my mind we are going today and get married. We are doing it now because we need to do it today." Austin was kneeling down in front of Karen's chair.

"Mr. Blackburn, why do we need to get married today?" Again she didn't understand what he was saying.

"Because Karen, I think it is dangerous for us to sleep in the same house without being married. And as you have said you have no other place to go."

"Okay, I guess you are right." Then Austin pulled Karen into his arms and kissed her.

"Stay right here, I will be right back." He said as he left her still sitting in the chair.

Karen didn't move. All she could think about was the fact she was getting married to a man she didn't know and she was happy about it. Was she just as crazy as Austin? Maybe so, but she wanted that man.

"Lisa, I will be gone the rest of the day, but I will be back on Monday, just take my messages and tell them I will see them Monday." Then Austin went back into his office. "Karen, are you ready to go?" He asked as soon as he had closed his office door.

"Yes Austin, I'm ready," she answered.

"That's my girl. Now let's go. We will need to make a couple of stops, before we get married." Austin said as he hurried around to his desk to be sure everything was put away and even some things he wanted locked away.

Karen didn't ask any questions. She didn't need to ask anything, she knew Austin would take good care of her.

When they came walking out of his office, Austin had his arm around Karen. He wanted all of his employees to see that this was his woman. The next time he came in with her she would be his wife.

They were already in the elevator, before they said anything else to each other. "Are you nervous, Karen?" He asked.

Karen raised her head up high enough so she was able to see Austin's face. "No, I'm just scared to death."

"That's my girl," Austin said as he gave her arm a little squeeze. "There is nothing like a scared bride, on her wedding night."

"You think so?" Karen answered.

"Yes Karen, I do." He had been with lots of women over the years, but it had been a long time since he had been with a virgin.

"Oh, that is easy for you to say. You know what's going to be happening." Austin, still had his, arm around her, and her little comment brought a smile to his lips. Yes he did know what was going to happen and he was very much looking forward to their wedding bed. There were several people in the elevator with them now. Karen did not want to be discussing their wedding plans in front of strangers. She decided to wait to say any more until they were back in Austin's little red sports car.

But as soon as they were in his car she had things she needed to know. "Mr. Blackburn," Karen said once again.

Austin stopped her before she had a chance to go any farther. "Karen, what is my name?" He asked.

"Austin," she answered.

"So use it. You can't be going around calling me Mr. Blackburn, in our bed can you?" He had just put his key into the ignition and started the engine.

"No, I don't guess so." Karen forgot all about wanting to ask him a question about their wedding. The mere mention of their bed made her forget everything.

"Well Karen, what was it you were going to ask me?" He said as she smiled over at her.

"I forgot," she answered.

"Karen, do you have a problem with remembering things?" Austin asked.

"No, I do not. You just scare me. So I forget what I'm thinking about. Oh, now I remember, are my jeans alright for your bride to wear when she marries you?" She asked.

"Yes I think so. After all you do look great in them. I bet all the women at my job wished they looked as good in their jeans as you do in yours. I'm very sure they have already discussed you and your jeans by now."

"Austin, did you see how tall all of those women were? Like model tall. I'm very sure not one of them wished they looked like me in any way at all." Karen had never seen so many beautiful tall women in one place in her life.

"Karen, a lot of them were models when they were younger and some are still models, but you are more beautiful than any of them." Karen's face was turning a light shade of red. "Honey, you need to get used to people saying that you are beautiful, because I'm very sure you are going to be hearing it a lot."

"Austin, how, tall are you?" Karen asked, she wanted to know how much taller he was than her.

"Oh, six foot three or four, why?" He asked. He hoped she didn't have any hang ups about his height.

"I was just wondering why, a tall handsome man like you would settle for a short small town girl like me." Karen felt so insecure.

"Maybe Karen, I have feelings for you that I have never had for any other woman before, and you do look good." That was the only answer he was going to give her. She would need to learn the real reason for herself.

That last remark did not go over too well with Karen, but she knew he was just baiting her. "Austin, I will try very hard to be a good wife to you."

I know you will Karen. I have no doubt about that at all." Austin was driving them down the busy street. "Karen, do you know how to drive?" He asked.

"No, I was too young to take drivers education in school, so I never learned," she answered and after seeing all of the traffic in this city she was so glad she was not a driver.

"Well honey, you need to know how to drive." Austin was keeping a close eye on the cars around him.

"Why, I don't have anything to drive." Karen decided she would not push the subject any farther after all cars cost a lot of money.

"Karen, I will get you a car to drive." Austin answered.

"No Austin, I don't need one. I would be scared to death to try to drive in this place. I would rather walk."

"That's okay for now, but I want you to learn to drive. We may not always live in the city. We may buy a place out of town, when we start our family. Then you would need to know how to drive." Without even knowing it Austin had just given her something else to worry about.

"Well Mr. Blackburn, we will just see if you still feel this way later."

CHAPTER EIGHT

Austin was taking them to some certain place Karen could tell. "Austin, do you mind if I ask you where we are going?" Austin smiled over at her. "No not at all sweetheart. We are going inside that jewelry store right there." Austin pointed to a very nice store that was directly in front of his car. "And I'm getting us our wedding rings. A band for me and a nice set of wedding rings for you."

Karen was getting real upset. She didn't want Austin to be buying a set of rings for her. "Austin, please don't, I don't need a set of rings. A band will do for me as well."

Austin wanted Karen to have what she wanted, but he preferred she had a set of rings. "Alright, if that is what you really want. Later if you change your mind we will just come back and get you a nice set of wedding rings."

"Austin, I won't be changing my mind. The price of a band is enough for you to be spending on me. I know you have to be paying a lot on your car and your house each month. And now you have me to feed. So please Austin, don't spend much on a ring for me." She was very serious.

"Karen if you are worried about money; don't. I own my car and my house. I can afford to buy you a very nice set of wedding rings." He didn't want her to think he was a man in debt up to his ears living from pay check to pay check when that was so far from the truth.

"No, I don't want a set of rings that I can't wear later even if you can afford them," she answered.

"Why in heaven would you not be able to wear them?" Austin didn't understand what she was saying. They were still sitting in Austin's car. He was not about to go into the jewelry store until they had this problem settled.

Karen was close to tears. She was already dreading the day she would not get to wear his wedding rings anymore. "Austin, no matter what you say now, one day you will regret marrying me and then you will divorce me. And then you will take my baby and put me out and send me on my way. So please don't buy me anything, but a little plain band, it doesn't even have to be real gold. Don't spend a lot on me please."

It was up to him to show her that he loved her and he was never going to fail her. It may have seemed to others that he may have made the decision to marry her in somewhat of a hurry, but not to him. He has always acted fast on any deal that he knew to be a sure winner and marrying Karen was just that kind of deal to him. She was everything he would ever want in a woman. He already knew that yesterday.

"Karen honey, you have not heard one word I have said to you. We will not ever be getting a divorce, so you will be getting a set of rings do you understand? I'm marrying you for keeps. I'm not a young boy getting married on a whim. So let's get our rings so we can get to the court house before lunch time and get our license. We will get married this afternoon."

They got out and went into the jewelry store. In less than a half hour they were back in Austin's car with their rings and on their way to the court house.

"Austin, the rings are so beautiful. I love all three of them. But you didn't need to buy me an engagement ring. I've never been engaged."

He had not given it one thought that he had not asked Karen to marry him yet in the normal way. He had just told her they were getting married. "That's right you haven't." At the next traffic light, Austin took the engagement ring out of the small box and turned to face Karen. "Karen Belmont, will you marry me?" He asked.

Karen smiled real big. "Yes, Austin I will. I will be happy to marry you." Then she kissed Austin even before he, put the ring on her finger.

"Now Karen, we are engaged, our children will never believe all of this." Someone behind them blew their horn. The traffic light had turned green so Austin had to start driving again.

"Maybe not, but we will. Austin, there is only one thing missing from all of this. You don't love me. I guess that is too much for me to want or even to ask for." She knew that she had feelings for him, but she didn't think he had any feelings for her at all. It was all business to him she thought.

"No Karen, it's not. I do find myself in love with you and I suspect you love me too. You are very young and you may not have realized it yet, but I can assure you the feeling is there."

She smiled over at him. "Yes I do realize it yet or whatever way I should say it. Austin I do love you. I'm not sure why yet, but I do love you."

Alright things are beginning to look up for both of us. Now woman, let's get in that court house and get that marriage license, so we can get married. I feel the need for a honeymoon." He was a happy man. Karen had said that she did love him and he knew he loved her.

"Oh, Austin, you don't need to take me on a honeymoon. We can just go back to your beautiful house. There is no one else there and it will be a wonderful place to have our honeymoon."

"Okay if that is what my woman wants to do we will go straight back to our house and make love." He wondered if Karen had thought anything about them making love or had that part of their honeymoon slipped her mind.

Karen just sat there. She was hoping Austin had not noticed that she had not said anything about them making love even after he had brought it up. She needed to get his mind on something else she decided. "Austin, isn't there some kind of paper you want me to sign before we are married?"

"No Karen, that is only for people who get married while all the time they are planning to get unmarried. That is something we will never do. There is only one paper for you to sign and that is our marriage license." Austin was just the kind of man Karen would have wanted to marry if she had ever thought she could ever get a husband.

They got their license and went right on into the Judges' Chamber and were married in less than an hour.

"Mrs. Blackburn, where do you want to have lunch?" Austin asked his new bride.

"I would like to go back to the same place we almost ate at last night. You remember the place where we had our first date. While we were still dating long before you asked me to be you wife." That was the only restaurant, Karen had even been into if you don't count the coffee shop across the street from the church.

"Oh yes I do believe I vaguely remember that place. After all Karen as you said we did go there on our very first date and look how long ago that has been now. Are you going to eat your meal today, or will I be only wasting my money again?" Austin had a boyish grin on his face.

"I will eat. You have wasted enough money for today," Karen answered.

"Oh Mrs. Blackburn, I don't feel at all as if I have wasted one cent today. I plan to cash in on my investment real soon, even before it gets dark." Austin had that look on his face again, but now Karen was learning to love that little smile of his.

Austin drove right back to that same Italian restaurant. "Hello and welcome again Mr. Blackburn, I never expected to be seeing you back so soon, and I see you still have the same beautiful lady with you." Gino was eyeing Karen today as much as he had last night.

"Yes Gino, and this beautiful lady here is my wife. You will always be seeing her with me and later even a few little ones. Remember I told you last night she was taken."

"Yes Mr. Blackburn you sure did, I remember. Just follow me, would you like that same private booth in the back?" Gino wanted to put Mr. Blackburn and his wife where ever they wanted to sit. He was sure the back booth again would be that place. It was the most private place in the restaurant.

"Yes Gino, we would as a matter of fact. We could use a little privacy right now." Austin already knew what he wanted to do, but all he could do there would only be a warm up for later.

"I can tell Mr. Blackburn, you sure got yourself a dish."

"Thank you Gino," Austin thought, "I sure did, but I got the complete meal too".

They were back in their old booth now. Austin had his arm around his bride. "Karen, are you happy?" He asked.

"Yes Austin, I'm very happy. I never knew people could be this happy. Are you happy Austin? I sure hope so and I hope we will always be happy?"

"Yes Karen, I am very happy and we will always be happy because we will work at being happy together." Austin, could not resist it, he had to give Karen a kiss. "Now, let's order so we can get home. I have something else I want to do."

"Austin, you need to forget about all of that for right now or I will just faint." She was already shaking a little. She didn't know if it was from her nerves or from the restaurant being so cool.

Austin pulled Karen real close to him and whispered, "No my wife will not faint, because she is just as anxious as I am to have our wedding night."

"Maybe I am." Karen said as she smiled up at Austin.

"No, more maybe about it Karen, you and I will work it all out. There will never be any maybe between us. We will always be there for each other. That's what makes any marriage work." He knew this from witnessing his parents' marriage.

"Yes Austin, I am just as anxious as you to be your wife all the way even if I am real scared of the whole thing."

"That's my girl. Austin said as he took her hand and kissed it. "Now let's order so we can eat and go. I've already been as patient as I can be."

The waitress came to their table to get their drink order. "Would you like to have a little wine maybe? Karen looked up at Austin, and said, "Let's go I don't need anything to eat." This surprised Austin and made him happy at the same time. "Sorry my wife has decided on something else." Austin left a very large tip and they left the restaurant.

"Karen, you are going to be just the woman I thought you would be and that makes me very happy. Let's go home. Karen, its times like this, I wish I had a different kind of car."

"No you don't, you love your little car," she answered.

"Yes you are right. My wife knows me better than I thought." Karen knowing he loved his car and the fact she was good with knowing that made Austin very happy.

The ride home today seemed ten times as long as it had last night. At least that's how it felt to both of them, but at last they were home.

"Mrs. Blackburn, let's go inside and start our married life." Austin opened Karen's door and helped her out. Then he started kissing her right there on the sidewalk. When they got to the front door and after he had unlocked it Austin scooped her up into his arms and carried her into the house.

"Austin, that was so sweet. I saw someone do that in a movie one time and I hoped right then that someday my husband will want to do that with me."

"Oh, but sweetheart this is no movie. It's all real life and it's our life and it all starts today."

"I know Austin, and I'm glad it's our life and no one else's." Austin kissed Karen once again as he held her in his arms. They were both very happy.

"Shall we go upstairs Mrs. Blackburn?" He didn't wait for Karen to answer he just carried her up to the third floor to his bedroom. It was the first time Karen had ever been into Austin's bedroom. Considering how long they had known each other, it had not been altogether a very long wait at all.

"Austin, your bedroom is so big and it's so beautiful. It is nothing like my room downstairs." Karen was still being held by Austin as she looked, around the bedroom.

"Karen this is our room from now on. You no longer have a room on the second floor. Your bedroom is up here on the third floor with me."

"I know Austin. I'm not that young and naive. I did finish first in my class of one hundred and thirty five not two like you think. I know a lot of girls younger than me that are married, so I know I can do this. I have always done things that were meant for older people and nineteen is not that young as far as love goes. I am an adult, you know."

"Yes Karen, I do know that, but I hope you don't do this much talking every time we start to go to bed."

"Well you knew I had to give it a try," she said just before she began to laugh.

"So all of that was to delay us from getting down to business in bed?" He asked.

"Yes if I had not done it you would think I am easy and eager. What kind of blushing bride would I be if I didn't try to delay some things." She felt too shy to even say what those things were.

"Oh Karen, I don't think you are easy. Didn't I marry you to get you up to the third floor? But I do hope you are eager." Austin had that look in his eyes again as he put her down onto the floor.

"Yes you did, but is the third floor the only place I need to worry about?" She asked him.

"No you can worry about all three floors and the basement." Austin answered.

"You have a basement, and you never told me you had a basement." Karen had found something else she could ask him about and he was the one who had given her this latest bit of information.

Austin just took her hand in his and pulled her close up to him. "We will talk about all of that later. Now it's time to get down to business."

"I can't." Karen quickly answered as she stood there looking up at him while doing nothing.

"What?" Austin didn't know what to do now. After all this was his first time at being a groom.

I can't." Karen's face was turning red.

"Why?" He wondered if it was because she was afraid of him. "Austin, I need to go and brush my teeth and put on my gown like a lady." Karen didn't know a lot about wedding nights, but she did know most girls back home had pretty gowns that they bought especially to wear on their wedding night.

"Karen, do you have a gown?" Austin was so relieved. She only wanted to be like all other brides.

"No, but I have a big tee shirt," she answered.

"So do I; and you can go right into our bathroom and brush your teeth and put on one of my undershirts, I'm sure it will fit you like a gown." Austin went to his chest of drawers and got her one of his nice white undershirts.

Karen went into the bathroom and changed out of the jeans and into Austin's undershirt. She had on her plain white cotton underwear. After she had changed out of her jeans she walked slowly back into the bedroom. As Austin had said his undershirt fit her like a gown. "Austin, I don't have on pretty underwear."

"Who cares, I'm only going to take them off of you anyway," he answered.

"Oh but," she started to say something. "Oh, but what is it now Karen?" He asked.

"Austin, I'm sorry, but I'm scared." Karen looked so beautiful standing there.

Austin had expected her to have another excuse that would keep them out of the bed awhile longer. He held out his hand for her. "Karen, come here." She walked over to her husband. "Are you scared of me or are you scared of the act?" He asked.

"All of it," Karen answered in a low voice. Austin put his arms around her and held her close.

"That's alright honey, you should feel this way the very first time, but you will began to feel different the longer we are married. I will not hurt you. You are my wife and I want you to be happy with our love life as much as I want you to be happy with everything else we do and have together."

Karen was now in Austin's arms and she was holding on to him tight. "Karen, we are going to take this nice and slow. We have a life time together to get it right. So stop your worrying, we are married and there is nothing wrong with what we are going to do. In fact that's why God created marriage." Austin wanted to help her to feel comfortable in their marriage bed.

They soon got into bed. Karen laid in Austin's arms in his king size bed. She was still a little scared, but she trusted her husband completely and they did get it right that very first time.

"Was that too scary Karen?" Austin asked his wife.

"No, I guess not," she answered, but she was glad that their first time was over. She now knew what to expect.

"Karen, don't look so upset. You have done nothing wrong and if we are going to have that large family we will need to do this many, many more times. I hope you will learn to love doing it with me as much as I love doing it with you."

"Austin, I don't mind doing it with you, but I don't want to ever do this with anyone else and I'm very sure I will love doing it with you as soon as I stop turning so red."

"Good that's the way it should be. We are only, suppose to want to do it with each other. It will get easier and better Karen, I promise you." Austin had enough experience to know what he was talking about.

"Austin, I know it will get better, because I will get used to being naked with you one day. I know it being the first time ever for me it has upset me some, but I, know it is what is suppose to happen when a man and woman get married. I just don't want to disappoint you." She hoped that her new husband wasn't disappointed already.

"Honey you did not disappoint me at all. You were everything I could have ever wanted. I'm very proud of you. It could not have been any better." Austin was in love and he knew he had made the right decision when marrying Karen. His life already seemed a lot better.

Karen kissed her husband before saying, "I hope so."

"The next time will be much easier Karen. I Love you even though we only met yesterday. I want you to believe that because it is true.

"Austin, I know and I love you, even if I am young. I do know how I fee,." she answered.

"Karen I'm so glad you love me. It will make the next sixty years or so much nicer." He had gotten her over the first hurdle now he had one more for her to jump.

CHAPTER NINE

"N ow let's get a shower and get dressed. We need to get something to eat." Austin said while still holding Karen close.

"Austin, do you mean together?" Karen wasn't sure she was up to this next step of marriage so soon after just finishing her first step which she felt she may never completely recover from.

"Yes, why not, we will shower together today and any other time now that we are married I want us to do everything together that we can.

After they had showered they had to run down to the second floor to get Karen's clothes so she could re-dress. "Austin, I could keep my things down here and you would not need to move any of your things."

"Karen, there is another closet up there for you. It has been empty all these years waiting just for you." Somewhere in the back of Austin's mind he had always been waiting for his wife, even back when he and Bo worked those years at night to redo their homes.

They took all of Karen's things up to third floor. After hanging her few things in the large closet they both stood at the door and looked. "Well I never realized how few pieces of clothing I had until we hung them in here." Karen was so embarrassed over her few pieces of clothing.

"Tomorrow we will change all of that for you." Austin pulled his new wife into his arms and gave her a kiss.

"How, are you going to put a couple of new walls up to make it a smaller closet, so my things won't get lost?" She asked.

"No Karen honey that would be too much work. I thought we would just go shopping. I think that would be easier."

"No Austin we don't need to do that, I have enough clothes. How many things can I wear at once?" She asked him.

"Now I have heard it all. A woman who says she doesn't need any new clothes, but Karen, you do need a new gown to sleep in like a lady." He reminded her.

"Austin, I think me being a lady is all over. After what we have just done I don't think I could ever be a lady even if I had a million pretty gowns."

"No honey it is not, it has just started. You will always be my lady with or without any pretty gowns." He didn't care if she never wore a gown. She was beautiful and he enjoyed looking at her body.

They decided to go out to eat at a nearby big mom and pop's restaurant. "Austin, do you eat out every meal?" Karen had never known anyone that really did that before.

"Yes I do. I don't cook and if you don't cook we will be eating out." Austin was helping Karen with her Jacket. It was a little cool outside.

"I do cook Austin. My grandma taught me to cook. I just haven't done it since coming here, because I didn't have a kitchen. Really I can cook, but not fancy food like you eat. I cook like old people. You know vegetables, corn bread, chicken, roast, macaroni and cheese, that kind of food."

"So you cook comfort food. I got myself a little cook as well as a lover. I guess today really was my lucky day." Austin had that cute little smile on his face again.

"Now Austin, don't go and start thinking that, you don't know anything about food like I cook, I can tell. You like rich people food. I don't know how to cook your kind of food. I only cook regular food that regular people eat and we both know you are no regular person."

"Mrs. Blackburn, I may surprise you. I have eaten food like you cook while I was down in the South and I enjoyed it very much. Now I have not eaten a lot of it and I don't know the names of a lot of it, but I will learn to eat what my wife cooks. Tell me Mrs. Blackburn, what else can my new wife do?"

They were getting back into Austin's little sport car again. "Oh, I don't know just the usual things a person does to run a home."

Austin was so happy. "So I have managed to marry myself a real wife." He had never expected in his wildest dreams that he would marry a girl as young as Karen and at her age she would even know how to run a home. He was so full of joy. Austin had always wanted to have a normal family life. Now if she could just hurry and get pregnant, he thought everything would be perfect.

After they had eaten, they hurried back home. "Karen, we need to sit down here on this sofa and just talk. There are things we need to decide."

"Like what Austin?" Karen was sitting right next to Austin on his big long sofa. He had his arm wrapped around her.

"Like what you can expect from me as your husband," h e answered.

"Like what Austin? I have no idea what I should expect. My mother and I lived alone most of the time, but sometimes she would have a boyfriend over for awhile. All they ever did was to eat and sleep."

"Well Karen, in our house, things will be done a lot different. I go to work five days a week. Sometimes I have to go out of town or even out of the country, but anytime I go away I will take you with me. I see no need for you to stay home by yourself when you could be with me. So one of the first things we need to do is apply for a passport for you. I'm usually up by seven a.m. and I leave by nine. I always try to be home by seven o'clock in the evening."

"Wow, you have a long day. Your boss must be kin to the Reverend St. Johns."

"No Karen, but my boss is akin to you," Austin answered.

"You say that he is akin to me, Austin, who am I kin to?" Karen was puzzled.

"Yes Karen I said kin to you. I'm your husband that makes me your next of kin," he answered.

"Oh, so you are the boss," she answered.

"Yes I'm the big bad boss." Austin would tell her all about his business later.

"Austin I'm mad at you. Why didn't you tell me that this morning when I was so scared that I would get you fired because you had to go back to the church to save me, from the good Reverend St. Johns, wrath." Karen was so relieved.

"I kind of like seeing you worrying about me," he answered. Then he gave her a little squeeze.

"I bet you did. Especially when it made me so sick I almost threw up in your three hundred and fifty thousand dollar car."

"Now honey that part I could have lived without." Karen loved it when he called her honey or sweetheart. It made her feel so loved by him.

"Austin, what do you want me to do? I can get a job and help pay my way." Karen had always had to do something to pay her own way in life, even when she was very young and still in grade school. She would rake people's yards and later she did a lot of babysitting.

"No Karen, you do not need a job. I'm the husband. I've waited this long to have a wife to take care of so don't deprive me of that pleasure. Austin was a good man.

"Do you think taking care of me is a pleasure?" No one has ever said that to her before. Karen felt as if she was going to cry.

"Yes Karen it is my pleasure like I said. I love you and taking care of you is the only thing I want to do." Austin had a very pleased look on his face. "That means you stay home and take care of our home, me and our children. That is when we begin to have them. That will be your full time job. Because young lady I will require a lot of taking care of from you."

"Austin just how many babies do you want?" She asked. She hoped he would want a lot more than just one.

"One at least, but I would like more if you would be willing. However that would be up to you. After all it's you who will be doing that job all by yourself. No matter how much I may want to help. My part will be long over way before you give birth to our baby." Karen took a good look at Austin. "What's wrong Karen?"

"Nothing I was just thinking how wonderfully you put all of that. Austin I want a whole house full of babies. If you want them I want them too. We will have as many as you want." She was so happy with her new husband of a few hours just as a bride should be.

"Karen we will start with one and then we will go from there." Karen was already making him very happy.

"Okay I will try to get pregnant as fast as I can," she answered. "Little lady not without me to help with that job," Austin said as he pulled her up close to him.

"No never without you. After all I'm not the surrogate anymore," she happily answered.

"No Karen you were never going to be a surrogate. I changed my mind about needing a surrogate the second I saw you coming across the street from the church to the coffee shop. If someone had told me that was going to happen to me yesterday I would have laughed in their face. But it did happen and here we are."

"Austin, why did you change your mind, about us just living, here in the same house? What happened to your plan of courting me for the next two months?" She asked, but she knew the answer already.

Austin still had his arms around his new wife. He leaned over and gave her a little kiss before answering her. "Because I knew I could not go on just sleeping up there on the third floor while you slept on the floor below. I didn't want to wait two long months. I wanted you now. So I asked myself, why did we need to wait? I just didn't see a need in putting us both through that when we didn't have to do it. Would you have preferred to have waited?" He asked her.

"No Austin I would have married you yesterday if you had asked me." Karen answered.

"Well I guess the long wait was good for us both." Austin laughed. "Now let's get back upstairs and try to start our family again."

"Austin will you show me some of your house while we are down here?" Karen had only been in the den, the kitchen, the entrance hallway, the bedroom and bathroom and the second floor and now their bedroom and bathroom and the third floor. She had not been into any of the other rooms at all.

"Yes of course if that's what you want to do right now." Austin knew this was just some more of Karen's shyness coming out.

"Yes I do right now. Everything is so nice and big here." She was looking all around the room while sitting on the sofa next to him.

"Karen have you been in the city before now?" Austin wanted to learn as much as he could about his wife.

"You mean this city that we are in right now?" Karen asked. "Yes this big city," he answered.

"No it was too far away and I was afraid I would get lost. So I just stayed near the church and my rooming house." She was still afraid of getting lost, but she knew as long as she was with her husband she would have nothing to be afraid of again.

"For three years you never went any farther than that rooming house and the Church?" Austin could not have stayed in one place that long if his life depended on it.

"Nope, that's all I did. That was still a larger area than I had lived in back home," she answered.

Austin realized right then he didn't know anything about his wife, but he would learn everything about her in time. "Karen honey, where are you from?"

"Georgia, have you ever heard of it?" She asked.

"Yes I do believe I have. Isn't that a little state down South somewhere?" He was being funny.

"Yes, it is down South, but it is not a little state, Mr. New York City," she answered. What she said and how she had said it made Austin laugh at her.

"Just where in Georgia do you come from?" He asked as soon as he had stopped laughing.

"It's just a very small place with only a couple thousand people and no I do not know the names of all of them. But I did know the names of all those who went to my school. Most of them were two to three years older than me. I didn't have anything in common with any of them. I was never asked to any of the school dances, or to the movie or to anything else. I was smart in books, school and work, but I had no one, except my Grandma to love me until you and I hope you really do love me. Austin I'm so thankful that you ran that ad in the paper." Karen was so young with such a grownup mind.

"Honey I'm so glad you answered my ad with all that information about yourself and yes, Karen I do love you." Austin was telling her the truth.

"My teacher told me, one time to never give everything to a person the first time, because they will have no reason to come back for more if you give it to them all at once. So that's what I did. I gave you a reason to come back and it worked."

"You sure did and in a very big way. Now back to us as married people. I will write down all of my telephone numbers for you. That way you will be able to call me anytime you need me or just want to talk with me. I will always be available for you. We will just keep the phone I got for the ad, and when it rings I will know it's you because no one else has ever had that number."

"Austin, are you going to tell all of those pretty ladies at your work that you are married now so they can stop flirting with you? Or will I need to go down there and tell them myself?"

"Yes I will tell all of my employees Monday when we go in for my weekly meeting. Then we will come back home for awhile.

"Austin, are you really happy? You aren't just saying you are to keep from hurting my feelings." Karen would die if she ever found out that he did not really love her.

"Karen I would never go as far as marriage to keep from hurting a woman's feelings. I would chance her getting over her feelings a lot quicker than me getting over marriage. So believe me when I say I love you. There is no getting out of our marriage ever. Do you understand me?"

"Yes Austin, I do, and I will never want out of our marriage. I love you too." Karen was really in love with her husband.

"Karen if you are going to be cooking our meals we may need to do a little shopping. You may want to check your kitchen to see what we have already and what else we may need. I don't open doors to the cabinets enough to remember what's in them. I don't even know if we have any dishes or pots and pans. I do know we will be needing food. We don't have any food in the house except, your bread and peanut butter."

"Austin this is going to cost you a lot of money." Karen was already worrying again.

"Yes it will cost, but sooner or later we will need to do it. So I suggest we do it the first thing tomorrow morning. Karen, will you stop worrying about money. I'm not exactly a poor man. I can afford about anything I want." He kissed her again. He found that he liked doing that a lot. They still had not looked at anymore of the house. They just spent the time talking and kissing each other.

After another hour or so of talking, Austin was ready to make love again. "Now young lady are we going back up to the third floor? We need to do that if we are going to start planning our family." He took Karen's hand and led her up the stairs.

"Austin how many bedrooms are there in this house?" Karen asked as they passed the second floor.

"We have five, counting our bedroom, why do you ask?" Austin knew Karen had some reason for asking.

"I was just deciding how many times I wanted to come up these stairs." Karen gave Austin a big smile.

"So how many times did you decide?" He asked as he smiled back at her.

"Eight times at least," she answered as she kept walking up the stairs.

"Karen honey, are you saying you would be willing to have eight babies?" This pleased Austin a lot. He was always seeing people with large families when he was out on business; he envied the love that they all seemed to have for each other whether they were well off or living from pay day to pay day, but he never thought he would be lucky enough to be one of those people.

"Yes, that would be a house full," Karen was still smiling.

"Yes Karen, it would be a big house full, but you don't have to have that many if you don't want that many." Although he would love being the father to eight kids he did not want Karen to feel as if that was all she was there for.

"Austin we will try for one and if I feel I can do it again I will, but eight is our goal." Karen wanted to have a lot of people around her that she could love and that would love her back. That was something she had so little of during the years of growing up.

"If you say so honey, eight will be a nice round number." He had never thought he would marry and now he was married to a nineteen year old woman and she wanted eight children. Now he could only imagine what his and Karen's life was going be like with eight children.

CHAPTER TEN

Karen slept all night in her husband's arms. Things were going great. They both felt blessed to have found each other. Neither one had expected to find love so quickly or at all. The next morning they went shopping.

"Karen I hate to say it." Karen was almost afraid to hear what he was going to say. "I may need to get us another car. I can already see this car is not going to work now that I have a beautiful new wife and she needs things I never dreamed of needing."

"Well get used to it big shot. You are married now. Your playing days are all over. The only playing you will be doing from now on will be with me, get it? We are a family and families need family things and most of the time they are big things."

"Like what?" Austin asked.

"Oh heck Austin I don't know. Let's just pretend we do and we will learn it all one day just like I'm learning those other little things I didn't know anything about until yesterday."

"How did all of that come out of me saying we needed another type of car?" He asked.

"I don't know Austin, all I know is, I wanted to take your mind off of getting rid of your little car that you love so much, even more than me," she answered.

"Karen I would not say that now. Maybe last Saturday I would have said I loved this car more than anything or anyone, but this Saturday I have changed my mind. I could live without this car, but I could not live without you. So we are going right now and get another car."

"Austin, why don't you keep your little car and get another car for us to use when we go shopping and do things that we can't do with your car? You could get something that doesn't cost so much. You know a regular person type of car."

Austin listened to his young wife. She made a lot of sense. They did need two cars and he could keep his baby.

"Alright let's go and look at a regular type of car. What type of car do you want us to have Karen?" He asked, but he was not at all prepared for her answer.

"A truck, a four door Ford truck, what else? We can use it to haul things and use it when our babies start coming," she answered.

"What are we planning to haul?" Austin was so amazed at his young wife. He had never in his life thought for one second about driving a truck. It was just not his cup of tea.

"Baby beds, rockers, high chairs, things like that Austin. We may even want to take our children camping one weekend." Karen didn't know people from big cities knew so little about trucks. Everyone back in her home town drove trucks.

"Alright we are going to go and find us a big Ford truck, but Mrs. Blackburn you will be learning to drive and soon. However I'm not real sure about a camping weekend."

"Austin I don't want to learn to drive. I'm just too afraid to drive," she answered. She wished he would just forget about her needing to drive.

"Yes you do. You just don't know it yet. Just like yesterday you didn't know what you were missing until I showed you." Karen gave her husband an evil eye look. She did not want him to remind her of all the things they had done yesterday and this morning in bed.

"Now little lady you can just wipe that look off your face. You know you can't wait to get back home and get busy with me again." Karen could not help it; she just had to pop him.

"Now why did you do that?" He asked.

"I felt like it. All you need to do is hope I don't feel like doing it again today. The next time it may hurt," she told her husband.

"I think you need to be saving all of your energy for tonight and not wasting it popping me. This may well be your lucky night and you may get pregnant."

"Mr. Blackburn I know when I can get pregnant or not. Remember I took that class in school and all of this we are doing right now is just for practice. I can tell you that for sure. So if you think you are perfect at it already and you don't need any more practice to be sure you get it right when it comes that time; then you don't need to be getting on top of me until next week."

"So why didn't you tell me that last night. You could have saved me a lot of trouble. So you are saying all of that love making, I have been through has been for nothing? Woman now you tell me I could have spent that time watching television instead of making love with my new bride."

"Austin, are you mad at me?" She thought he was serious.

"No honey I was just teasing you. I will love all the practice we get to do until your fertile days are here. It's not your fault we got married so soon. I think we got married at the very right time."

"Me too Austin I will never regret it. I will always be glad I sent that letter to you." Karen was all smiles now.

"So will I sweetheart," Austin said as he turned the corner.

Austin found a Ford dealership. "Hello folks, how can I help you today? My name is Kevin Moody and you are?" The salesman asked.

"Austin Blackburn and this is my wife Karen. We are interested in buying a truck." Austin had no idea at all what he should be looking for in a truck. He would have to trust Karen with their truck buying.

"Mr. Blackburn you're not trading off your Ferrari, are you?" Kevin just could not see a need for any man to do a silly thing like that no matter what his wife wanted.

"Heavens, No!" Austin answered so fast that it scared Karen. "We just need a truck too," he answered.

After looking at several different types of trucks Austin decided with a lot of Karen's help on the one he disliked least of all. They got themselves a big heavy duty king cab four door truck. Austin had never driven anything near as large as his new truck.

"Now Karen, we have a truck, but how do we get it home?" Austin asked.

"Don't look at me, unless you want me to drive your baby home." She answered. She was pretty sure Austin did not want her to drive his baby.

"Mr. Blackburn we will deliver it to your home later today if that will be alright with you? Let's say in about three hours. Will you be home then?" Kevin asked.

"Yes we will. We will go straight home and wait for you to come with our truck. I'm sure my wife can find something for me to do while we wait." Karen took her foot and gave Austin a big kick under the table. She knew exactly what he was talking about and she was pretty sure Mr. Moody did too.

"I gather you two are newlyweds and you need something bigger because of a little one on the way?" Kevin asked.

"Yes we are. How did you ever guess?" Karen asked. Knowing it was from all the things Austin had said and done while they were there.

"Oh M'am, that was real easy to see. Your husband couldn't keep his eyes off of you." Kevin wanted to add and keep his hands off of you, but was sure that would have lost him a sale.

"Oh." Karen said as Austin smiled over at her.

"See sweetheart everyone knows we are expecting." Karen gave Austin the evil eye again.

"Mr. Blackburn you are a lucky man. Not every wife will let her husband keep a car like yours after they are married." Kevin had seen a lot of sports cars traded for a family car over the years. The first thing to go after the wedding was always the man's sport car.

"Then Mr. Moody I am a lucky man. My wife insisted on me keeping my car. She likes to ride in it and still make out in it. Maybe that is why we are expecting now." Austin just looked down at Karen and smiled. He knew she could do nothing more than just give him another big kick under the table right now. He waited for her kick, but she never did it nor did she say anything.

Mr. Moody walked them back out to Austin's car. He wanted to get a better look at Austin's baby. "I will see you two later." Kevin said before he walked away, but only after he had gotten Austin to let him sit in the driver's seat and play with all of the equipment that was in his little sport car.

Austin opened Karen's door and helped her into his car then he leaned down and gave her a big kiss. He knew she was waiting until they were along before she got him for all those things he had said and done while they were there.

"Austin Blackburn you made, those men in that place believe we have made love in this little car." Karen's face was already red.

"Yes I did and right now they all are in there imagining how we did it." Austin wished he knew a way himself that they could make love in his car. It would give him something good to remember every time he got into his little car.

"No they're not. They're all in that show room wishing they had your little red car." Karen said as she gave Austin another little kiss. She didn't seem at all upset with him now. It didn't take them long to get home. Austin knew the city well and he had no trouble getting from one place to another in record time.

"Mrs. Blackburn we have time to get in a little practice before our truck gets here. So what do you say Mrs. Blackburn? I do like the ring of your new name. Do you want to go up to the third floor with your husband?"

"I'm surprised you haven't already wanted us to try it in this little car," she answered.

"I will once it gets dark and we are parked some place other than out in the street in front of our house. So right now let's just use our bed for all of our practicing."

"Alright Mr. Blackburn, but I don't see where you need any practice at all. But what do I know. For all I know you may need as much practice as I do." Karen was teasing him. She had already forgotten all about what she had told him earlier about him being perfect already and not needing anymore practice until it is time to get her pregnant. "Yes Mrs. Blackburn you are so right. I sure do need all of the practice I can get. So get your butt up those stairs and into our room.

We are wasting time." Three hours later the door bell rang.

"Mr. Blackburn we have your truck. I parked it right behind your red car. That sure is some car. I bet a real woman getter." Mr. Moody could not stop talking about Austin's car.

"Hello Mr. Moody." Karen said as she stepped out from behind Austin. "Yes it was a woman getter, but now it's just a baby getter. My husband is very proud of that fact. He can't wait for me to have this one so we can get the next one started in the very same way." Karen then turned and walked out to the new truck.

"Wow is that your wife?" the other man with Mr. Moody asked. "Yes that is my wife and she is really everything you see." Austin had never had as much fun as he had in the last two days with Karen. She had changed his life forever and he didn't mind it at all.

Austin didn't know if his so call sophisticated women friends would like Karen, but he was real sure all of the men would be crazy about her. The women he was sure would just be jealous of her, but did he care? No, he loved Karen and he loved everything about her.

"Austin come on let's go for a ride in your new truck." Karen was like a school girl wanting her boyfriend to do something with her.

"Karen trucks must be a really big thing in the South?" Austin wasn't sure why he had even bought this truck. To please Karen was the only reason he knew.

Karen was standing outside of the front passenger's door trying to look in, however she was too short to see very much even standing on her tiptoes.

"Yes I guess they are. Everyone drives a truck even the banker, and the preachers, they all drive trucks. Austin you don't like your new truck, do you?" This made her a little sad. Had he done all of this just to please her she wondered?

"Karen we haven't even tried our new truck yet. I'm sure we will like it once we take it for a nice long ride." He didn't want his feelings to disappoint her.

"But Austin you won't ever like it, will you?" Karen felt as if she had made a big mistake and she wasn't sure how to make it right or even if she could. "Austin I'm so sorry I told you to get a truck. I should have known better. People like you are not truck people. I should have realized that you are and will always be just a sport car man. You are still a single man at heart. I think you should have just stuck with your plan and got yourself a surrogate and you would not be in this mess right now. Austin maybe you can get it all changed. Maybe there is some way you can return the truck and me. Then you can get yourself out of this whole mess. I'm sorry I now see how wrong I was. You are sport car and I'm unemployed and I don't even have a home anymore."

Karen turned and went back inside of Austin's house. He found her packing her things into her old bag getting ready to move her few things out of his house. She had already gotten her things out of the closet and was almost ready to leave. "Karen what happen? I thought we were happy. I thought you were happy with me." He had a very serious look on his handsome face.

"Austin I love you, but you are just a dream man to me. Someone I will never have. I see all of that now. It is all very clear to me now. You are someone I can only have in my dreams."

"Karen is all of this happening because of the truck? I will enjoy the truck when we need to use it. Yes I am a sport car man who now happens to own a truck also. Honey I love you and this is your home now with me. Put your clothes back into your closet right now before I start getting upset with you." Karen started to cry.

"Austin I'm not good enough for you. I will never fit into your world you need to let me leave. You need someone who you won't need to be always worrying about embarrassing you. In the back of your mind you will always have that tiny little spot of worry if you stay married to me."

"Karen I don't care if you never fit into my so call world. I only want you to fit me." Austin held Karen close in his arms. "Karen I will buy ten trucks if that is what it takes to make you happy. I love you so much don't you ever do this to us again. Honey we are married and we are staying married. You are employed by me as my wife. It's a full time position which no one, but you can fill. You are the only person in this world who will ever have that job. You need to stop thinking about what other people will say about us being a couple. I can tell you they will all be jealous. Your home will always be here or any other place that our home may be. I can see that our home needs my wife's touch. So let's you and I go do a little shopping and use that big Ford truck of ours to haul it all home."

Austin picked Karen up and carried her down the stairs and out the front door, all this time she had her arms around his neck. However, before they were able to get off their steps to go to their new truck their neighbor walked over.

CHAPTER ELEVEN

"Austin whoever is this pretty young lady you have in your arms?" The man was as nice looking as Austin and he was also well educated Karen could tell.

"Bo this pretty young lady just happens to be my wife. Karen, meet Dr. Bo Brooks. He's an OBGYN doctor." Karen was still in Austin's arms and he was holding onto her very tight.

"Hello Mr. Doctor nice to meet you." Karen said in her sweet southern voice.

"Nice to meet you Karen I'm sure we will become best of friends. I already know you will need my service very soon. When you play with fire someone always gets burned and I'm very sure you two are playing with fire. If I know my old friend here he will want a family real soon. Now tell me how did he sneak you in here without me knowing anything about you?" Bo was a very nice person Karen could already tell and she could also tell he and Austin were very close.

Karen just smiled and said nothing. She was going to let her husband tell his friend what he wanted him to know about their private life.

"Bo I just did what I had to do to get Karen to marry me and I didn't want to take any chance of her meeting you before I had her good and married to me." Austin wanted his friend to know that he was really in love with his wife. And he was not just playing a game.

"Mrs. Blackburn, your husband sure is a smart man." Bo had not taken his eyes off of Karen. She was very beautiful to him. He thought his friend was smart to marry her so fast. He sure would have done the same if he had been given the chance.

"Yes sir I know. He is very smart." Karen answered.

"Bo how do you like my new truck?" Austin still had Karen up in his arms.

"I was wondering who got that big black shiny truck. It sure is nice. Now back home you would be the envy of every man around and even some of the women folks." Bo sounded like the boys from around where Karen grew up.

"Mr. Dr. Bo where are you from?" She asked.

"Miss Karen honey I'm from the great state of Georgia," Bo said so proudly.

"Oh so am I!" Karen was so happy to meet someone from home. "I thought I heard a little Georgia in your voice. Bo gave Austin a little smile. "Well Austin I see you did real good. I bet she even knows how to cook and I don't mean like these city girls do. I mean really cook."

"Yes she does Bo. In fact we were just going shopping now to get some pots and dishes and some silverware. All those things a wife needs to use when she cooks her man a good meal." Austin was a happy and proud man.

"Now when you get ready to entertain don't you go and forget about me Miss Karen," Bo said.

"We sure won't Mr. Dr. Bo." Karen loved to cook and now she had two men she could cook for all the time.

"Austin you take your wife and go on and do that shopping so your new wife can start cooking for us." Bo was ready to go back to his house and catch up on some much needed reading in some medical journals he had been putting off for sometimes.

"Nice meeting you." Karen said one more time as they both watched Bo go back to his house next door.

"Honey, are you ready to go?" Austin still had Karen in his arms. "Yes I am. Austin I do love you so much and I will be the best wife in the world to you." She knew that was all she would ever want to be along with being the mother of his children.

"Karen I love you too and I hope I will be the husband you will want me to be."

After awhile Austin found he was really enjoying his new Ford truck. He could see over almost everything that was on the road and they had room for everything they had bought.

"Karen I love this truck." He now wished he had waited until after he had given his truck a try before he told Karen he didn't like his truck.

"Do you really Austin? You aren't just saying that now to keep me from hurting you?" She asked.

"No honey I really love driving it. I may even start driving it to work." Austin looked real pleased with his truck now. It made him feel different.

"See Austin it does something to a man when he drives a big Ford truck." "IT MAKES A MAN FEEL LIKE THE MAN HE THINKS HE IS AND IT LETS A WOMAN KNOW SHE IS A WOMAN WITH POWER RIGHT UNDER HER FOOT."

"I believe it." Austin had a big smile on his face now. He couldn't have been any happier with his new truck.

"Austin have you really changed your mind about your new truck?" She sure hoped so. She hoped he was not just saying that because of her.

"Yes Karen I have. Like I said I may start driving my truck to work now. It handles a lot different than I thought it would." Austin thought that his answer had sounded southern. He hoped Karen noticed.

"Oh Austin you are something. No wonder all those women at your job like you so much. Not only are you drop dead good looking, you are funny and smart. Oh and I almost forgot your rich too." She didn't want to leave out any of his good qualities

"Yep that's my wife. Any other woman would have started with he's rich, but not my wife she almost forgot that little fact. Another reason I love you so much. And where did you learn that phrase "Drop Dead Good Looking?""

"From watching television that's where we small town girls learn most everything about you big city boys," Karen answered.

"Well I may need to start censoring your television programs. You may be watching something you aren't old enough to see."

"No you won't I may learn something you may like." Karen said as she smiled up at Austin.

"From watching television you think you will learn something I will like?" Austin was quite puzzled. "What kind of programs do you watch?" He asked.

"Cooking shows what else?" She answered.

"Oh sweetheart you had me worried there for awhile. I just could not decide what was on the television that you could learn to do that I would like."

"No I didn't, I had you hoping." Karen was sitting as close to Austin as she could get with a console between them.

As they rode down the street Karen found she had another question for her husband. "Austin, do you ever wear jeans?" Karen asked.

"I have on occasions worn them. Why, do you want me to get some jeans and then we both can wear them?" He liked that idea.

"Yes I do. You look so handsome and I know you will look even better in jeans." She could tell he had just the kind of body all the girls back home want their men to have, but only a very few of their men would ever come close to looking like Austin.

"Alright I will get some jeans. Let's just go back now before we get any farther away from the mall. I will get a few pairs of jeans and I will get you something that's not just for the kitchen." They got Austin several pair of jeans and a couple of long sleeve white shirts to go with his new look.

"Austin you need some boots. Do you have any boots at home? I forgot to ask you that earlier."

"Yes, but I'm quite sure they aren't the kind you will want me to wear with my new outfit. So let's get boots too while we are here." After Austin had his new boots they went to the ladies department and got Karen a few things.

"Karen, get yourself a lot of those little fancy panties so I can take them off of you." He wanted to see his wife all dolled up before he undressed her.

"Austin, are you trying to embarrass me?" She had never worn panties like the ones he wanted her to have. All she had ever worn were white cotton ones.

"No honey I was only trying to get you ready for tonight." Austin had that little smile on his face. Like the cat that ate the canary.

"Then I will need a pretty little gown for you to take off of me along with my panties. No need in going half way," she answered.

"Yes you do need a pretty little gown because, that's a part of the chase. Like you said no need in going only half way." They didn't get home until eight thirty that night. They had spent a full day shopping.

"Austin I'm worn out." Karen said as she flopped into the first chair she came to in the den.

"I am too. Let's just call for a pizza tonight. Tomorrow we will go to the grocery store."

"That's okay with me Austin. I just want to get a shower and put on my new night clothes and a pair of those pretty tiny panties."

"Not without me. We can order that pizza later." Two hours later they called for the pizza.

"Married life may just starve me to death." Austin said as he took another piece of pizza.

"Austin you don't have to use up all of our sex life in just two days. We can save some to use tomorrow. I really don't think it will spoil."

"Honey are you real sure of that? Did they teach you that in your Marriage and Family class?" He wanted to tease her a little.

"No I just figured that out for myself." Karen and Austin were sitting at the little table in the kitchen eating all the pizza they could hold and have a nice cold coke with it.

"Honey I'm glad it won't spoil, but there is no reason for us not to do all we want is there?" He hoped there was no reason after all this was their honeymoon.

"Austin I think I miss figured my time. I may be at my time already." Karen hoped she had not messed up everything for him.

"Okay let's just check and see." Austin knew just the person to ask such a question.

"How will we do that?" Karen asked.

"I will call and ask Bo. Karen when was your last period?" Austin wanted to be ready to tell Bo all of the information he would need.

"The eighth of this month and today is the twenty second," Karen answered.

"Now let me call Bo and ask him about all of this baby business. If anyone knows he will." The phone rang twice before Bo answered.

"Hello Austin why are you on the phone with me instead of being in bed doing the deed with your beautiful wife?"

"Well that is sort of why I am calling. We have done the deed several times. Now we need some information?"

"Oh now you want to know if it has been safe to do it at this time." Bo was already laughing at his friend. "Don't you think it's just a little too late to worry about that now?"

"No we want to know if it's time for us to get pregnant. We want to get pregnant you see." Austin was very serious his friend could tell. So he stopped laughing.

"Okay, but this has got to be a first. Someone calling me and wanting to be sure they will be doing it at the time to get pregnant.

Alright tell me when did Karen have her last period?" Bo was being all doctor now.

"The eighth of this month and today is the twenty second. What do you think?" Austin was anxious to have a family Bo could tell. He hoped his friend didn't marry just to get a baby.

"By my calculation I would say that your bride may already be pregnant. So keep up the good work and I'm very sure you will be a daddy in nine months."

"Oh thanks Bo," Austin hung up the phone. "Well Mrs. Blackburn we may already be pregnant Bo said."

"Austin, are you upset or happy?" She didn't know how she should be feeling until she knew how Austin felt.

"Happy of course Karen, that's what I wanted." Austin answered as he sat back down at the table.

"Austin you know everyone is going to think we had to get married." Karen knew how people talked about every newlywed couple back in her home town. They were all waiting for the first baby to be born then they would all start counting backward to the couple's wedding date.

"Do you think for one minute I care what everyone else thinks? We know better and that's all that counts and even if we were that would still be only our business and no one else's business." Austin wondered if Karen thought every woman who got pregnant before marriage married the baby's father.

"What do we do now?" Karen was waiting for her husband to tell her what to do next.

"Bo said to keep up the good work, so I guess we do what the doctor says." Austin had a smile on his face and Karen knew exactly what that smile meant.

"Oh, maybe I should have called Bo instead of letting you. I wonder if he would have told me, to do the same thing," she said.

"I'm sure he would have. After all he would want only the best for his friend." Austin was thinking how far he and Karen had come in such a very short time.

"Oh you men are always sticking together aren't you?"

"Karen you still want a baby don't you?" Austin's voice told Karen he was worried that she may have changed her mind now that they were married.

"Yes, more than ever. I want a family so badly Austin that I can't stand it. And I want that family only with you. I'm very sure it's going to take a whole lot of love making to get eight babies here. Besides we don't need to just be making a baby to make love." She knew her answer wiped away all of Austin's fears and worries. He already had her in his arms and into his lap even before she had finished her little speech.

"Mr. Blackburn you sure have some fast moves." Then Karen began to laugh.

"Yes, don't I Mrs. Blackburn. Now let's get up there and be sure we get pregnant."

"Austin do you have a Mother and Father?" He had never said anything about them to her at all. Karen thought they both may be dead.

"Yep I sure do and they will blow in here one day and you will call me and say come home Austin right now. There are two weird people sitting in our living room claiming to be your parents. I hope our baby don't take after them." He was just laughing up a storm.

"No, I will not do such a thing," Karen answered. "I will just say I see where Austin gets it all from." Then it was her turn to do all of the laughing.

"No you won't. You will love them both just like I do. My parents are in Europe somewhere, but they will be home anytime now." Austin was beginning to miss his parents a great deal now. More even since he married Karen and had so much he want to share with them.

"Austin, do they know you are married?" Karen asked.

"No not yet. I wanted to wait and tell them in person. I want to see the look on their faces. They won't believe it, but they will be happy. I can assure you." Austin knew his parents well. He was their only child and they were all very close.

"But Austin will they be happy you married me?" Karen had not thought one time about having in-laws. Now she was worried that they would not like her at all.

"Karen, stop worrying so much. My Mother and Father will both love you. What is there not to love about you?" Austin was not worried at all.

"Austin what does your Father do?"

"You mean other than chase my Mother around the bed room? He owns the business with me. We are partners, but I'm the one who works and he is the one who plays now, but he put many years of hard work into our business before he had a chance to play. My parents deserve to be able to play now." It was easy for Karen see how much her husband loved his parents.

"Austin they sound like wonderful people. Do you have any brothers and sisters?" Karen was realizing how little she knew about the man she had married.

"No I'm their only child. My Mother could only have one baby although they tried to have more. She was a model before she married my father. They have been married thirty six years. They met right up on the forty seventh floor where I work today. My father was the sole owner then and my mother worked as a model through his agency."

"So I'm the only short person in this family." Karen was feeling a little out of place. She didn't feel as if her new in-laws would want their only son to be married to some unknown short woman who didn't know anything at all about being the kind of person they all were.

"Yes I guess you are. Just think about it this way, there will always be someone around that can reach everything in the cabinets for you." Austin didn't want his wife to feel that she was an outsider among a house full of tall people.

"Yes that's true." Austin started kissing Karen again.

"You know you do look nice in this lady looking gown and I do believe those pretty little panties will come off of you very soon."

"Austin Blackburn you can't see my new little panties. Do your parents know what a sex hungry man they raised? If they don't maybe I need to tell them."

"Oh I think they already know, but they are glad they never had to worry about me doing something crazy," he answered.

"Austin don't you think, they are going to think you marrying me after just one day isn't crazy? If that's not something they would consider as being crazy what is crazy to them?" Now, Karen was worrying again.

"No, if I had not married you after the one day, they would think that was the crazy part." He answered.

"So Mr. Blackburn you are telling me your whole family is crazy right along with me." Karen felt she was going to love being in this crazy family.

"Yes woman at last you have it. We are all crazy, you, me and my parents."

They sat in the kitchen a little longer talking before Karen decided to clean up everything before going back up stairs. The next morning they slept in. After all they had been awake most of the night making love.

"Karen we will go to the grocery store first, do you want to make us a list?" Austin asked.

"Yes, but Austin we don't need to get everything now. We can go back to the store next week after you have another pay day. Austin, that's how normal people do it." Karen tried to explain to him.

"So my wife thinks we aren't normal?" Austin could not help, but laugh.

"No I didn't say that at all. All I said was normal people don't always have the money to buy everything they want or need every time they go to the store, but that doesn't seem to be a problem for you. If that makes you not normal well all I can say then, if the shoe fits then wear it." Karen answered as Austin pulled her down into his lap. They spent the rest of the day grocery shopping and putting their new things away.

"Well Karen we have it all done." Austin said as they put the last thing away. He had never worked so hard at putting things away before in his life and especially kitchen things.

"Yes we do Austin, now it's time to cook," she answered.

"Do you mean we are going to drag it all out again? After we have just gotten it all put away." He could not believe it.

"Yes that's how you do it. We didn't just buy it all to fill up your nice big cabinets. We got it all to use and we are starting to use it today."

"Mrs. Blackburn, they are our cabinets." Austin corrected her. "Austin, thinking of this place as mine as well as it is yours may take some getting used to, but I know I'm going to enjoy using all your things. So let's get started."

Three hours later. "Karen that was a real good meal, I never expected you to cook that well." Austin was so proud of his little wife.

"Yes Karen, I felt like I was back home in Georgia eating at my Mother's table." Bo really enjoyed his meal. He had not been home in some time and eating Karen's cooking made him feel like a boy again.

"Thank you both, my Grandma would be pleased." Karen said as she got up from the table.

"Now you two get out of here so I can get it all cleaned up." She wanted to get it all done and put away so she would have some time with her husband.

"Don't you want us to help?" Austin asked.

"No Austin, I will love doing it. Now go and enjoy your little friend. I'm very sure you two have a lot to talk about. If not I will give you both something to talk about."

"Alright if you say so, but give me a holler if you need me."

"I will do just that Austin if I find this to be too much work for me." Karen gave Austin a big kiss and Bo a kiss on his cheek.

Once Bo and Austin were in the den and far enough away that Karen could not hear them talking Bo couldn't wait to start question his friend. "Okay, Austin, tell me how you met her and when did you two get married?" He wanted the whole story.

They went into the den and over to the big chairs which they always sat in when they watched television together.

"I met her Thursday after work." Austin didn't look over at Bo when he answered his friend's question. He wasn't so sure how Bo was going to take his news.

"What, you met her Thursday and its only Sunday and you have already married. You are really married aren't you?" Bo was so confused.

"Yes we got married Friday." Austin was not going to just tell Bo everything if he didn't ask him something specific he was not telling him.

"Now this is getting very interesting. Tell me more." Bo wanted to find out how in the world his best friend who was never getting married just a week ago was now a happily married man.

Before Austin knew it he was telling Bo everything. "Bo you know I wanted to have an heir and that I had ran an ad for a surrogate mother. Karen answered my ad, she, sent me a one and a half line note telling me all about herself. That just made me more interested in her. So I got a cell phone just for this project and I sent her a note back and asked her to call me at that number. She did and we arranged to meet, but Bo the second I saw her crossing that street to come to the coffee shop where I was waiting, I knew I wanted her for my wife and nothing less would do."

"But Austin she is not like the women you have always dated." That was one of the things Bo liked so much about Karen.

"No Bo she is not. She is a lot better." Bo could see how much his friend had changed already. He was ready to share everything he had in this world with a woman he had only known less than four full days. The old Austin would have never done this.

"Yes I can see that for myself already. After all she is in the kitchen cleaning it up while we are in here sitting. Your other lady friends would be in here waiting for you to take them out to some expensive restaurant to eat. I believe you lucked out old friend. I can see you two having that family and being married a very long time." Bo was really happy for his friend.

"Me too, Karen is so sweet and I love her so much. I never believed anyone could really fall in love so quickly, but you can." Austin was proof.

"Austin I think you did the right thing. Now does she have a sister for me?" Both men had a good laugh over that.

"No Bo she is the only child too." Austin had a big smile on his face.

"Now about her getting pregnant, if she is healthy and those were the right dates you are most likely going to be a daddy in nine short months my friend. Austin are you ready for all of that in your life?"

"Yes I sure am. That would make us both very happy." Austin answered with another big smile on his handsome face.

"Who would have ever guessed the play boy would get hitched so quickly. How old is she?" Bo asked.

"Nineteen." Austin answered. "She graduated at sixteen, and she was first in her class. She is so sweet and innocent too." Austin now had a love sick look on his face.

"I could see she looked a lot younger than the women you usually dated, but I never guessed nineteen. Man you are married to a teenager." Bo could not help himself he had to laugh.

"Bo you are right, I have never thought about it that way, but you are right. My wife is a teenager." Bo had stop laughing and now both men had a big smile on their faces.

"You know Austin I think we are two lucky men to have your wife." Bo could see how Austin having Karen was going to even make his life better.

"Now Bo my friend I believe I'm the only one having my wife." Austin joked with his friend.

"Oh so you just want to have her all to yourself." Bo asked.

"Yes I do and you knew that already. Get your own wife." Austin joked back.

"I would if I could find a wife like yours," Bo answered.

Bo already had his eye on a young girl that worked for him at his office. So far he had been too shy to even speak to her, but he did do a lot of looking at her during the day.

"Well maybe you need to run an ad." Austin said as he looked back into the kitchen to get a glance at Karen.

"No not me, buddy you just lucked out, that doesn't always happen. Now tell me about your new jeans? Is this some more of her doings along with the truck?" Bo had his chair all kicked back and his feet up. He was ready for a long night of listening.

"Yes." Austin answered as he began to smile. "Yes, she said I would like the truck, but I didn't think I would. Then yesterday afternoon they delivered it. I can say at first I truly hated it, but then it almost cost me my wife. She came back into the house and was packing up her things to leave when I found her. Only because she felt if I had bought a truck I hated, I may have married and now changed my mind about that too."

"You haven't changed your mind have you Austin?" Bo asked.

"No Bo I haven't so you are out of luck. Now let me finish telling you the rest of my story before you try to take my wife from me. I talked to Karen and proved to her in our special way that I loved her and we were always going to be married. Then we went off all day in that truck and now I find myself wanting to drive it to work instead of my car. Isn't that the funniest thing?"

"That little wife of yours sure has a spell on you. I hope she keeps you just this way and the jeans are a nice touch too, but you already had jeans. I do say the white long sleeve shirt is a good touch too. They all go right along with having a big black Ford Truck." Bo knew the look well from back home. Most all the men back in his home town that were lucky enough to own a nice truck like Austin's dressed the same way. His dad being one of them too and even Bo himself had dressed that same way when he was still living at home and driving his pickup.

Karen came into the den just as Bo had finished talking. She had taken off her apron and Bo got a real good look at her for the first time. His eyes almost popped out of his head. She had the best shape he had ever seen on a woman and being a doctor Bo had seen a lot of female bodies.

"Austin you may want to take her to work with you every day because you don't want to leave something that nice just laying around. Someone may come along and pick it up."

Austin didn't hear half of what Bo had said. His mind was on Karen and her little tight jeans.

"Bo, were you saying something?" Austin asked while still watching Karen. In fact Bo was doing the exact same thing. "Nothing," he answered. "Not one word."

Karen went right over to her husband's chair and he pulled her in his lap and then he leaned back his recliner.

"Well I see it's time for me to go. Karen, thank you, again for the wonderful meal I really enjoyed it. I will go ahead and make you an appointment for next month. I know you will need one by then. I will show myself out." Bo got up to leave.

"Alright Bo we will see you later." Austin was already enjoying his wife. "Karen, are you ready for bed?" He asked.

"Yes," she answered with her southern accent. "After all, tomorrow is a work day and I know you aren't just going upstairs to sleep."

"No I'm not and neither are you." Austin had love on his mind. That night was as good as all the other times they had made love, if not better. Austin loved being married. His father had always told him when he met the right woman he would want to be married. His father was right.

CHAPTER TWELVE

"Karen I want you to go to work with me this morning. I want my people to meet you right away." "Okay Austin, what do I need to wear; stilts?"

"No, your jeans will do, I'm wearing mine." They both got their shower and dressed. Austin really liked the new life he had now.

"I think we will take our truck this morning." Austin announced over breakfast.

"Austin, do you really like your truck?" Karen asked him one more time.

"Yes Karen I do, so stop worrying about that now. I know there must be something else you can start to worry about."

"Like what Austin?" She asked.

"Oh I don't know, motherhood maybe," he answered.

"Oh Austin I'm not worried at all about that, only because I know that's what you will be doing. She answered. It will be something you did, but you can't control. Our baby will be in me and not you." Karen smiled over at her husband. She was right. If she was pregnant it would be something he had started, but would be completely out of his hands and Karen would be the only person in control other than Bo. That did worry Austin some, but not a lot. He would find a way to be as much a part of it as he could. He was a very smart man and he would find away.

They did take the truck to work and of course several people saw Austin driving it into the parking garage and into his personal parking space, but no one noticed Karen sitting in the truck.

"Mr. Blackburn I see you have gotten rid of your spots car. I would have never thought you would have ever done that in a million years." One of his employees said as he passed the big black truck.

Karen was still sitting in the truck. Austin had just gotten out his side and was on his way around to her side to help her out. He was going to take real good care of his wife whether she was pregnant or not. He was crazy about her and it showed.

"And I see you have even gotten yourself some nice new jeans. They look very nice." The man was really working at buttering up his boss.

"Thank you Roy." Austin answered, that was all he said.

"I just wonder what brought on all of these changes in our boss." Roy thought to himself.

Roy had thought that Austin was going to walk into the building with him when Austin didn't turn in the direction of the elevator. He continued to walk to the other side of his truck. Still Roy thought it was for no other reason than for him to get his briefcase out of the other side of his big truck. Then Austin opened the truck door and out came Karen right into Austin's arms. Roy's mouth flew open, but he didn't say one word. He didn't know who this young beautiful girl was, but he was sure it had to be a woman his boss was involved with by the way he handled her.

"You ready honey?" He asked in a low voice. He didn't want Roy to over hear what he and Karen had to say.

"Yes I guess I'm as ready as I will ever be." Karen was shaking all over.

Austin didn't have his briefcase. He had left it in his office on Friday. He had other plans for his weekend other than work. He took Karen by her hand and they began to walk towards the elevator. Roy had not noticed his employer's wedding band. He was too busy taking in Karen's beauty to notice anything else. Austin had not bothered to introduce Karen to Roy. He would take care of that at the meeting when all of his employees were together.

"Honey let's use the other elevator." Austin wanted to give Roy time to close his mouth and start to wonder who Karen was before he got to the forty seventh floor.

By the time Austin and Karen got up to their floor the whole floor was buzzing with the talk of Austin's new truck. Roy had been a very busy boy.

"Hello Mr. Blackburn do you want me to hold all of your calls until after your morning meeting?" Mary Helen the front desk receptionist asked.

"Yes thank you." He was still holding onto Karen's hand. Everyone noticed right away as they passed them how nice their boss looked in his new dark blue boot-cut jeans. They were not designer jeans like he had always worn before, but instead they were Levis and he wore them with a long sleeve white shirt and new western boots. His new silver buckle and belt was just the right thing to set off the whole look. When everyone thought Austin could not look any more handsome than he had always looked they found out today he could.

When they got to his secretary's office he was still holding onto Karen's hand. "Lisa I don't want to be disturbed." Austin didn't even look Lisa's way until he was about to walk away.

"Yes sir." Again Lisa gave Karen that same ugly look as she had given her on Friday. The day she and Austin were married. This time Austin saw it. Just as he looked down at his secretary he saw her give Karen another mean look.

"Lisa, don't be looking at Karen like that again, you may not like the outcome." Austin still had Karen by her hand.

"No sir I'm very sorry." But she still did it again, and again Austin saw her do it.

"Come Karen before the she wolves get you." He looked over at Lisa sitting at her desk and then back at his wife. As soon as Austin had Karen safe inside of his office he stepped back out to Lisa's desk. He was not putting up with all of the disrespect Lisa was showing his wife.

"Lisa I saw you giving that mean look to Karen again after I told you to stop it. Now do you think I mean it this time or not?" He asked.

"Yes sir, I'm very sorry." Lisa answered, but she did not look as if she was sorry one bit.

"I believe you said that very same thing before. Did you or did you not?" Austin asked.

"Yes sir I did." Lisa wanted Austin to just go on back into his office with his little girlfriend. She knew it would not last for very long, none of them ever did and she didn't see where this one would be any different. She would wait it out as she had done all of the other times. One day she thought Austin would see her as the woman he had been searching for all this time and then all of her waiting would be over.

"Be sure you are at the meeting in fifteen minutes and be sure everyone else is there. Can you do that at least?" He asked.

"Yes sir, Mr. Blackburn." Lisa was mad and it was all due to that young sexy thing that Austin had brought with him into the office for the second time now. Lisa was not going to make life any easier for this girlfriend than she had all the rest of Austin girlfriends.

Austin went back into his office and closed the door behind him. He didn't want Lisa to hear what he and his wife would be saying to each other. He was sure if she could find away to hear what they were saying she would.

"Austin she doesn't like me." Karen said as soon as the door was closed.

"Karen honey she doesn't count. I love you and that's all that counts." Austin was not going to let Lisa or any of his other employees, disrespect his wife. She came first.

"Austin I'm scared to death." Karen didn't want to go to the meeting with Austin and meet all of his employees. She was afraid of what they would think of her.

"As scared as you were Friday in our bedroom that first time?" He asked.

"Yes," Karen answered.

"Oh I don't think you are. After all you do get to keep your clothes on here, at least, maybe in all of the other rooms except this office. I do have a nice leather sofa over there. If my wife and I should decide we need a little more practice we can do it right here anytime we want to and we won't bother anyone." Austin had that look on his face.

"Austin, have you done it on that sofa of yours before?" Karen looked a little upset from just imagining Austin doing that on that same sofa with some other woman. She didn't want to know, but on the other hand she needed to know.

"No, Karen, never, I never mix pleasure with my work and in this office, it has always been just business. That was until last Friday. You will be the first and the only woman to share that sofa with me in that particular way, but Karen I have shared my bed with women before you. I have to be honest, but there will never be anyone else again."

"I know Austin I expected that you had done your share of sleeping around. After all you are a grown man and so good looking who would want to turn you down. In fact I may need to whip me some butts here at your work place if those women don't stop looking at my husband. They must be the man hungriest women in the world and they all want my man."

"Honey you have nothing to worry about. If I had wanted one of them I would not have married you, now would I have Mrs. Blackburn?" Austin already knew what Karen's answer would be.

"No you would not. If you had you would be missing out on all of me," she answered happily.

"So come on and give me a little something to look forward to later." Austin had that look on his face.

Karen looked up at Austin as innocent as she could. "What would that happen to be Mr. Blackburn?"

"You guess." Austin began to kiss her and he was holding her very close he was ready to use the sofa. Then there was a knock at the door.

"Yes." Austin called out. He had almost forgotten about his weekly meeting.

"Mr. Blackburn, it's time for your meeting." Lisa called back at him. She could have used the phone to remind him, but didn't. She was not use to being unable to go right into Austin's office without sometimes even knocking, but he had locked his door when he when back in his office after he had given her the little talk. Lisa decided that her boss' new girlfriend was going to be trouble and she would need to get rid of her as soon as possible the same way she had gotten rid of all of the others.

"Alright thank you Lisa we will be right there. Now we have to go, but there is always later." Austin told Karen while she was still in his arms. And he really meant it.

He took Karen's hand as they left his office and walked down a long hallway to the boardroom. Everyone was sitting around a huge table. Karen had never seen a table as large as this one before. Austin walked them all the way to the other end of the large table where a chair sat empty. He was still holding onto Karen's hand. Seeing that there was not a chair for her, Austin pulled out his chair and took his seat then he pulled Karen down into his lap. Everyone in the room was still watching them.

"Mr. Blackburn I will get your friend a chair." One of the associates said as he started to get up to go and get Karen a chair.

"No, she is just fine where she is." He answered as he motion for the man to sit back down. Karen had one of her arms around Austin's neck. He could feel her body shaking.

"Hello and good morning. Today's meeting is going to be quite short. I have a lot of other things I need to do today so I will make this quick. He took a deep breath and took a slow look around the room at all of his employees before going on with his speech. "This young lady sitting so nicely in my lap is Mrs. Austin Blackburn. She is my wife, if you were unable to figure that out by now. Her name is Karen. I love her very much and if you all want to keep your jobs here with this agency it will do you good to remember she is my wife. That makes her a share holder in this business. She is a big share holder in this company. Meaning she is one of the owners now." Austin stopped talking and looked down at Karen and then he gave her a big smile.

All of his employees just sat there looking at each other without saying anything. They did not know what to say. They never expected their playboy boss to marry, but now the big question on their mind was when did he get married? He had not taken any time off except last Friday and that was not all day, so he would have had to have done it over the holidays they all decided.

"Now that you all have met my wife we are leaving now for the day. We are going back home I will see you all tomorrow." No one moved. Karen got up out of Austin lap and they walked out of the boardroom holding hands just the same way they had come into the room. "Now that will give them all something to talk about for the rest of the day." Austin told Karen as they went back to his office.

After they were all sure Austin and Karen were out of ear shot they began to talk among themselves. No one had a clue as to who Karen was or where she came from. All they knew was she was Mrs. Austin Blackburn and they needed to remember that if they wanted their job. They were sure their boss meant just what he had said.

"Who is she?" One associate asked. "Does anyone know?" "When did he have time to get married?" another asked.

"All I can say is she is a real knockout. He sure knows how to pick a winner." Roy said as he leaned back in his chair at the table. He felt as if he knew more than any of the rest of them.

"Did you all happen to notice he had on jeans today? And did you see that they were Levis?"

"Yes I noticed his jeans right away and I can tell you all he sure looks like a real stud in them. I wish my husband looked that way in anything," one woman answered.

Mary you would think he was a stud in anything he wore. We all know you have always hungered after him."

"Yes I admit I have always had a thing for him. And yes I do notice what he is always wearing, and again yes I would enjoy seeing him out of

his clothes and so would all the rest of you including most of you men."
Mary was one of many who were in charge of bookings.

"I saw him out in the parking garage when he came driving up in
his new big black Ford truck." Roy was happy to be able to tell them all
something they did not know yet.

"He has a truck now? What happen to his red sports car? Do you
think he has gotten rid of it because he has gotten married?"

"Who knows? I guess we will find it all out when he decides to tell
us." Another employee answered. This one didn't seem as concern about
what his boss was doing as the rest of them.

"Now I think his wife was the knockout, she looked like several
million in her jeans." One of the men who didn't feel he was included in
Mary's group of men who would love to see their boss naked, but he sure
would not mind seeing his boss' wife naked.

"I for one think they made a stunning pair," one of the older
employees said.

"I wonder just how long it will last. She looks to be at least ten years
younger than him," one of the younger ladies said. She was hoping it
would be over before the next company party. She had a real sexy dress
she wanted to wear to the next party so she could show off her body to
Austin.

"I wonder where he got her from. I want to get me one just like
her," Roy added. Roy was still trying very hard to be the center of
everything.

"Oh you would Roy," Lisa answered.

"Mrs. Blackburn would you like to try out my nice leather sofa
with me?" Austin smiled down at Karen.

"Austin, are you really serious? You want us to make love here in your
office? What if your secretary comes back and she hears us in here?"
Karen asked.

"Yes I'm serious. I am afraid in these jeans honey there can't be any
secrets and as for my secretary she won't hear a thing." He was ready to get
busy with his wife.

"Okay we will give it a try. After all I want you to look at this sofa
every day and remember why you need to hurry home at night."

"Oh honey I don't need a sofa to remind me of that. Just the
thought of you makes me want to go to wherever you are. But I'm not

turning you down either." Austin answered as he began to remove his and Karen's clothes.

No one knew Austin and Karen were still in the building and in his office making love on his sofa. They all thought he and his wife had left after they walked out of the meeting. However they stayed in his office over an hour. Then they took a shower together in Austin big private bathroom. Still no one had a clue that they were there. After they had redressed they came strolling out of Austin's office. Lisa was back at her desk pretending to work.

"Oh Mr. Blackburn I didn't realize you were still here." She could see his wet hair and she also noticed Karen's hair was wet on the ends. Lisa knew exactly what they had been doing all of this time. She didn't like it at all. Where had Austin found this woman and why had he kept her such a secret for so long. Lisa was steaming, but all of her steam was only targeted at Karen. Lisa knew she was playing a dangerous game and it could get her fired if Austin saw her looking at his wife again the way she had done several times already that day. She decided she needed to be very careful around Austin, but she was not going to stop giving Karen her mean looks. What a waste Lisa kept thinking to herself. What would a handsome successful man like Austin want with a short thing like that young girl no matter how she looked? Sex that's all it was, Lisa decided.

"Austin your secretary doesn't like me at all, but she is in love with you." That statement got Austin's attention right away. Karen told Austin the second they were alone in the parking garage.

"What did you say?" He asked Karen.

"You heard me," Karen answered. "Don't tell me you have never noticed the way she looks at you. I sure have and she doesn't try one bit to cover it up."

"Am I that blind? In that case I don't need her as my secretary anymore. She is going tomorrow. No I'm not waiting until tomorrow. I will do it right now. Come on Karen we have to go back up to my office. I have a little unfinished business to do."

Karen didn't say anything she just got back into the elevator with Austin and in a couple of second they were back on the forty seventh floor.

"Mr. Blackburn I thought you had gone for the day?" Mary Helen the receptionist said as he and Karen were passing her desk on their way back to his office.

"I will be shortly." Austin answered. He was still holding onto Karen's hand. He looked down at her just as she looked up at him. "Karen I love you and only you." He wanted his wife to know there was and had never been anything between him and his secretary except a working relationship as far as he was concern.

"I know that Austin," Karen answered.

As they walked nearer to Lisa's desk she could hear someone coming, but she didn't think it would be them. She raised her head up from her work to see who was there. Her face and her voice displayed her surprise. "Mr. Blackburn I thought . . . ."

"I know what you thought." Austin cut her off. Lisa didn't get to finish her sentence so she just went back to playing like she was working. Austin unlocked his office door and he and Karen went back inside. "Honey will you just take a seat over there on our sofa until I finish this little piece of business?"

"Yes Austin or I could just go back downstairs and wait for you if you had rather do this in private." Karen didn't want to be caught up in the middle of all of it. She knew his secretary would blame her for the whole thing.

"No I want you here with me." Austin didn't want Karen someplace else when Lisa was asked to leave the building. He didn't want them running into each other. Karen turned and went right over to the sofa and took her seat. Austin made a quick call to payroll.

"Betty will you make up a check for Lisa for three months pay and all of her sick time and her vacation pay and then bring it into my office yourself within the next ten minutes. I don't want anyone else knowing about this do you understand me? Bring the check directly to me and no one else. You won't need to stop at Lisa's desk just come directly into my office. I will be waiting for you."

"Yes sir I understand completely." Betty got right to work checking Lisa's record for her pay and benefits. She didn't say anything to the other two women working in that department with her. In less than ten minutes she was walking towards Austin's office with the check in her hand.

"Excuse me Betty, but do you need something?" Lisa asked as Betty started to knock on Austin's door.

"No not from you," she answered as she knocked on the door the second time.

"Come in Betty." Austin called out from behind his desk where he had been waiting for her. Karen was still sitting on the sofa not saying a word.

"Mr. Blackburn I have it." Betty said as she handed the check over to Austin.

"Thank you Betty, now remember not to say a word to anyone." Austin knew if there was one person that worked for him that he could fully trust it was Betty.

"I won't Mr. Blackburn." Betty turned and left the office, but she would have loved to have been there when he gave Lisa the boot and so would more than half of the other employees. Lisa was not even a little liked by the other employees. She had managed to make enemies of everyone that work at the company.

"Lisa, would you please come into my office." Austin said over the speaker phone as Betty passed Lisa's desk.

"Yes sir right away." Lisa answered not knowing what lay ahead of her. Up she went thinking all the time everything she did was so right.

"Mr. Blackburn I tried to stop Betty from coming right on into your office, but she would not listen to me. Maybe you should speak to her about that at next week's meeting."

Austin didn't answer. "Lisa, have a seat." Austin pointed to the chair in front of his desk. She had not noticed Karen sitting on the sofa in the back of the room. In fact Lisa had forgotten all about Karen all together.

"Yes sir I sure will." Lisa took her seat in the chair being very sure to show Austin a lot of her legs.

"Lisa I'm letting you go. I think your attitude is no longer welcome here at my business. I do not like knowing that my own secretary is being disrespectful to me and to my wife. So here is a check for much more than you are entitled to at this time. Lisa you need to take this check and leave."

Lisa reached over and took the check, but she was in no hurry to leave. "Austin, why are you doing this to me? Is all of this because of that little short thing you said you are married to now? I thought I meant more to you than just being your secretary after all these years."

"Lisa you need to get your things and leave." Austin did not like what she was insinuating at all.

"No Austin I have waited years for you and today you tell us you are married to a little nobody! No I'm not leaving she is. I want you and I'm not letting her take what belongs to me. No sir I am not." Lisa sat there without moving.

Karen could hear it all. She felt so hurt. She already had tears running down her cheeks. This woman wanted her husband and she did not mind telling him that she even told him she wanted him to get rid of her so she could have him.

"Lisa, my wife is the most important person in my life, but you are nothing to me. Do you hear me? Nothing, you are nothing to me at all. So if you don't want me to call security you will leave now without any more trouble."

"But why Austin are you doing this to me?" Lisa asked. Lisa was dangerously upset.

"Because Lisa, my wife and I do not want you here anymore." Austin knew the second he had said my wife he had said the wrong thing, but it was too late to take it back.

"She is the one who has caused all of this I should have known." Lisa was already to jump Karen now.

"No Lisa you brought it all on yourself." Austin picked up his phone and placed a call to Mark. "Mark could you come down to my office immediately?"

"Sure right away Mr. Blackburn." Mark was a big man and he was head of security at Austin's company. Security was always a big issue when working with famous and important people.

"Austin you can't do this." Lisa was not giving up yet. She was going to try everything she could to keep her job.

"Lisa you need to go. I don't think we have anything else to discuss. I think I have made myself quite clear. Now you need to gather up all of your personal things and get out." Austin was trying very hard not to raise his voice and to stay calm.

Mark took less than two minutes to get to Austin's office. He opened the door and went in. He had not bothered to knock. "Yes sir, Mr. Blackburn do you need something?" he asked as soon as he was in the door.

"Mark, will you be so kind as to escort Miss Jones from the building and never let her back in it or the parking area ever again. Will you see to that for me?"

"Yes sir, Mr. Blackburn anything you say." Mark took Lisa by her arm and led her out of Austin's office. They only stopped long enough at her desk for her purse and her few personal things. Then Mark took her by the arm again and escorted her to the elevator and then he led her out of the building. Everyone saw her as she was leaving.

"Karen honey I hope she did not upset you too much." Austin wanted to keep his wife out of it, but he had made that tiny mistake himself.

"She did Austin. She is not a nice person at all. I don't understand you ever hiring someone like her to work for you." Karen was shaking all over.

"No honey she isn't a very nice person I agree, but I guess I was just too busy to see her for her real self all these years. You could say I was too close to the forest to see the trees."

"No Austin she did not want you to see the real her. She wanted you to fall in love with her. That was why she wanted to keep her job here even after you told her to leave. She was just not going to give you up."

"Too bad for her is all I can say. I found the woman I love and that is you little Miss Priss and only you." Austin had his arms around his wife.

"Mr. Blackburn I love you too." Karen said as she stood up on her tiptoes and gave him a little kiss.

"Shall we try to leave again? Maybe this time we will have better luck." Austin still had Karen in his arms and so he just started to kiss her again.

"I thought you wanted to go home?" Karen reminded him.

"I do, but not before I get to kiss you as much as I want." They kissed awhile and then they left out of his office and started to the elevator.

"Now I will need a new secretary." Austin said as they walked down the hallway.

"No you won't. I can be your secretary at least until you find a new one," Karen answered.

"You, you want to be my secretary?" Austin asked. He almost laughed. It was hard for him to think of Karen as a secretary. She was so much more to him than just a secretary.

"Yes Austin, me, I was a secretary at the church remember. I'm a good secretary and you won't have to worry about me falling in love with you because I'm already in love with you."

"So you are and you were the good Reverend's secretary for three years. I think I may like having my wife with me all day and knowing that she is in love with me makes it real tempting.

He had one of his smiles on his face. Karen had already learned that meant trouble.

"Now Austin, at work I want you to be my boss not my husband. I want you to treat me as one of your employees and not as your wife while I'm here working. I will be here to work not play. I hope you can remember that for a few hours a day."

"Yes I will, but I thought I was your boss all the time," he answered.

"Well if you thought that you thought wrong. So I hope you do a little better job at work. We don't want anyone else to think the same thing," Karen said as she walked along with Austin.

"I guess I will need to be doing a better job at home too then," Austin teased.

"No you don't. I like everything you do and the way you do it at home," Karen answered.

"So do I and now we will be together all day here at the office and then I will have you all night long at home. I like this married life more and more," Austin answered.

"Austin I am a real good secretary for real. I'm not just saying that I am so you will let me come to work with you every day. You will find it out for yourself tomorrow." Karen had a very serious look on her young beautiful face.

"Oh honey I believe you. In fact you could make me believe anything." Austin was really enjoying married life.

"Austin Blackburn you need to shape up. I won't have another boss like my last one." She was not so happy with her new husband right at that moment.

"No you won't ever have a boss like him again. This one is married to you and I can make all the passes I want and we can use that sofa in my office anytime we want. Mrs. Blackburn I'm not the good Reverend in any kind of way. I don't beat around the bush. When I want something I go after it and most of the time I get it."

"Mr. Blackburn you have sex on your mind way too much," Karen answered.

"Mrs. Blackburn I used to not have it on my mind, hardly at all. Not until I saw you coming across the street to that little coffee shop. Now I can't seem to get it off of my mind." Austin was telling her the truth.

"Mr. Blackburn if I had known such a tall and good looking man was watching me walk across that street I would have given him something to watch." Karen was looking up at Austin.

"Honey there couldn't have been anymore for me to watch. I would have thrown you to the floor the second you walked into that coffee shop if you had shown me anymore. I'm still not sure how I made it though that interview without grabbing you up into my arms and kissing you. Woman you were driving me crazy even then."

"Austin I hope you will always feel that way." She knew that he was everything she would ever want.

"I, will Karen, you can depend on that from me. Now let's get out of this place. We need to go home and be together. I love being married. There is just so much more to being married than meets the eye," he teased her.

"I also love being married Austin, but being married to the right person has a lot to do with it," Karen answered

"Honey you are right. Being married to the right person is the key to the whole thing. For us it's like being on a very good date that doesn't have to end."

CHAPTER THIRTEEN

They went home, but they spent the extra time in their kitchen. Karen wanted to cook Austin another good meal, and of course Bo would be there to eat with them.

"Austin I'm so glad we three got married. Now we have us a wife who cooks the same kind of food I grew up eating. You on the other hand, will need to learn to eat southern food. Such as chicken and dumpling, sweet potato pie, pecan pie and grits. Man I'm in hog heaven and you did it all by marrying Karen for us."

"Now Bo I didn't exactly marry Karen for us. I sort of did it only for me, but I will share some of the goods with you, but not all of them. I hope you know which goods I'm talking about," Austin answered.

"Do you two happen to remember I'm here?" Karen asked.

"Yes we do Karen. Now tell me how things are going for you and big Daddy here?" Bo asked.

"Great," Karen answered. "I'm going to be working for him until he gets a new, old secretary did he tell you?"

"No he did not. Austin what happened to your secretary?" Bo knew Lisa had been Austin's secretary for years.

"I fired her today, she thought I should have not married Karen, but I should have married her instead," Austin answered.

"Did she come right out and say that to you?" Bo could not understand why any woman would do such a thing.

"Yes she sure did and more," Austin answered.

"Then you did the right thing by firing her. Now back to you Miss Karen, I will bring you a pregnancy test tomorrow night. It's new and very reliable. We will test you and see if you are pregnant with our baby yet."

Karen's eyes got as big as two saucers. "You can do that this quick?" She didn't know that it was possible to tell if she were pregnant even before she missed her first period.

"Yes we can," Bo answered.

"Bo that's wonderful." Austin said. "But she is only having my babies not mine and yours.

"See Karen how he can be. He is already trying to take you for himself alone." Bo and Austin both begin to laugh.

You are so right I am taking her just for myself. You need to get your own wife, my friend. Austin said, but he knew his friend was only teasing Karen.

"Karen I should have brought the test tonight, but I walked out and left it lying on my desk, but I won't forget it tomorrow so be ready," Bo told her.

"Austin I'm so nervous, what if we are already pregnant? What will we do?" she asked.

"We will celebrate," Austin answered.

"Yes Miss Karen we will celebrate." Bo was looking right at his friend Austin with a big smile.

"No Bo you will not be celebrating the way we will. Maybe another way, but definitely not the way I have in mind," Austin told his friend.

"Maybe another way, like with cake and ice cream?" Karen asked. "Yes cake and ice cream. I guess that's the only thing I will get. Your husband thinks you belong only to him. Now I wonder where, did he ever get such an idea? Karen if you are pregnant I will put you right on all the pills you will need to take and I will prepare your husband for the things that are ahead for him." Bo knew he could make his friend's life a living hell for the next nine months if he wanted to do it.

"Like what Bo, do you think is ahead for me that I need to prepare for?" Both Karen and Austin were looking at Bo and waiting for his answer.

"You may need to slow down on the sex, for one thing. You don't want Karen to miscarry the baby before she even knows she is pregnant. Another thing Karen may have morning sickness that can go on all day or just for a very few minutes. Now that can last one time or that can go on for months." Bo gave them both a big smile when he finished what he had to say.

"Bo, are you telling me and my new wife we may need to stop having sex after only four days of marriage? Whose side are you on?" Austin asked.

"I'm on both of your sides and yes that is what I'm saying Austin. If you want a baby you will need to be careful is what I'm saying to you both." Bo knew he was going to enjoy being Karen's doctor. He could have his friend jumping through hoops the entire nine months. Austin may be the one married, but he was the doctor and he was the one they both would need to listen too for the next nine long months.

"Bo, are you just saying that because you don't want me to be doing it while you don't have a wife or is it true?" Austin didn't know if his best friend was telling the truth or just messing with him.

"It's the truth Austin; would I do that to you? Well maybe I would, but I wouldn't do it to Karen. Right now is the easiest time for her to miscarry so it's up to you." Bo stopped and looked at them both.

"Bo we will do everything you tell us to do." Karen answered.

"If Karen is pregnant we will stop until you say it's safe, but you had better be telling me the truth or I will have your hide." Austin sure did not want to cause Karen to miscarry, but he didn't like the idea of giving up sex either after only a few days of marriage. However he would if it was necessary.

"Now you are scaring me." Bo laughed. "It's so nice to be able to help an old friend out." Bo was still laughing.

"Oh no, best friend or not you won't need to go that far I can assure you. I won't need any help with that part." Austin answered.

"Austin, don't be mean to Bo. He is only trying to help us." Karen said. She had no idea what the two men were saying to each other.

"I hope that's all he is trying to do." Austin was staring at his old friend.

"I'm sure it is Austin. We want our baby if we are pregnant and we don't want to lose it. Do we?" She asked her husband.

"No honey we sure don't" Austin was still giving Bo a hard look and Bo was still smiling.

"Then be nice to Bo. He just wants to do everything he can to help you out." Karen answered.

"You are really enjoying this aren't you?" Austin asked his friend. "Yes I am." All three of them were still in the kitchen. The two men had decided to help Karen with the clean up after all she may be pregnant already and she needed to be careful.

"I guess there is no need in me hurrying home tonight. After all you two don't have a thing in this world to do." Bo smiled over at Austin.

That night they did not make love. They just laid in bed in each other, arms and did a lot of planning and talking about everything under the sun. They were very happy together, but they were also very anxious.

"This time tomorrow night we will know if we are going to be parents or not." Austin said as they laid in the dark. He could not see Karen's face, but he knew she had a smile on her face too.

"Yes, Austin, and I'm almost afraid to find out. I don't want to find out we aren't. You have worked so hard trying to get me pregnant ever since we got married. She had never felt so loved by anyone.

"Karen I want you to be pregnant, but if you aren't we will keep trying. And if you are and it means, no sex for a while, but our baby will be worth it all. However I don't want you to think I'm only having sex with you to get you pregnant. I love you and I want you all the time. Woman you drive me crazy."

"I know Austin you love me and I'm just as anxious as you are to have a baby. I just want you to know that I will love all of our babies." Karen was young, but she was ready to be a mother.

"And you say we are going to be having eight of them? Honey I'm not sure I will like doing this eight times. Not being able to have sex with you will drive me crazy." Austin had never thought about what couples went through to get their babies born. He didn't really care until now.

"Yes you will be able to do it once we hold our baby in our arms Austin. It will all have been worth it then. We will have a life time to make love and only nine months to make our baby's life. So we need to give him the best chance we can." Karen always made such good sense to Austin when she talked about their babies.

"Karen you are so young and so smart. You just said the words that will make me be able to handle all of this waiting. If it turns out to be just for one day, or the whole nine months we will do it." Austin knew he would do it for Karen their baby and for himself.

"No Austin it's not my words that will make you do it. It's your love for me and our babies that will make us both do it." Austin knew she was right. She was saying what he had thought just seconds ago.

"Yes honey you are right again, it is our love that will make it all work." They were still in each other's arms. Austin started kissing Karen and they wanted to make love so badly, but they didn't. They were going to do whatever Bo told them to do.

"Austin, would you feel better if I slept down in the other room until we knew something?" Karen asked.

"Not on your life." He said as he pulled her closer to him.

The next morning Karen dressed and went to work with Austin. She took right over and started doing Lisa's job the second she sat down at her desk. She started by putting everything in order. Karen felt she would be able to do all the things she had found hidden away in Lisa's desk that she had not attempted to do while she was still there. By the end of the day she would have all the back work done along with all of the things that needed to be done each day. She wanted to be the best secretary Austin had ever had.

"Karen it's break time let's go downstairs and get some breakfast. You need to be eating more." He was hungry and he knew she had to be. They had not had time to eat anything that morning before leaving home.

"Austin will I have time to eat breakfast during my break time?" Karen asked.

"Karen what are you talking about?" Austin had told her they were going to breakfast and now she wanted to know how fast could they eat and be back.

"I'm talking about my fifteen minute break! That's all I get." She answered."

"Karen you and I are going to take as long of a break as we need. No matter what you say you are not an employee here you are my wife. Do you hear me?" Austin did not want to get her upset, but he was not going to let her sit at that desk while he went and had his breakfast. She was going with him every time he wanted her to be with him and that would be all of the time.

"Yes Austin I do hear you, but won't all of the other employees be upset because I'm going to take my break with you," she asked.

"Who cares, what they think, not me. Besides you will not only be taking your breaks with me, but you will be going to lunch with me and going home with me. By the way you are a very good secretary."

"I told you I was. Now I want a raise." Karen looked so serious.

127

"You already want a raise, but I have already bought you pots and pans woman isn't that enough?" he asked her.

"Is all that sex you have already had enough to last you for a life time?" Karen asked?

"No you know it's not." Austin answered. "Well?" Karen asked.

"Well what?" Austin answered.

"Mr. Blackburn I can mess up your computer real bad if you give me any trouble. I know how to do that you know. Do you want me to do that to you?" Then she smiled up at him.

"Alright I will give you a nice raise." She knew he would give her anything she wanted. They were only messing with each other.

"Oh you don't have to do that, I will just tell you later what I want instead of getting paid."

"Okay, so you will be working off whatever it is that you want? And I'm sure we both will end up very happy," he answered. "I'm very sure we will," Karen answered.

They went downstairs to a nice little coffee shop not at all like the one across the street from the church. "Karen, you need to eat all of this."

"I will try Austin, but I doubt I will be able to hold it all." Austin had ordered her the same thing he had order for himself.

"There's no only trying Karen. You need to eat it all." Austin was having no trouble at all eating his food.

"Austin you eat yours and I will eat all I can. Haven't you noticed yet that I'm not quite as large as you, so it doesn't take as much food for me, as it does for you? What is a full meal for me is a hors D'oeuvre for you. So there is no way I will be able to eat all of this food unless you want it to last me for the whole week. Maybe then I will be able to eat it in a week, but not at one time." She was getting full from looking at all the food on her plate.

When they got back to the office Karen went right back to work she was not behind with any of her work nor did she hide any of it in her desk. She even went into Austin's office and took a nap after lunch. Austin took the nap with her. They both lay on the sofa hugged up together.

"Austin, wake up. We have been asleep for two hours. It's a good thing you are the boss or we would both be fired." She just hoped no one had needed him while they were asleep.

"What time is it Karen?" Austin asked.

"How would I know my watch says the same time all day. Give me your arm and I will see." Karen took Austin's arm and pushed up his sleeve and checked the time on his Rolex. "It's already four o'clock Austin. We have not done anything, but eat and sleep all afternoon. If you were not the boss here we both would be looking for a new job."

"Alright let's go home. We have been here long enough." Austin was ready to go.

Karen got her purse and they left. Austin wanted to get home so Karen would be ready to take the test the minute Bo got to their house with it.

It was seven o'clock when Bo got there. They were getting ready to eat. Karen had set the table for three. She knew Bo would be there to eat as soon as he got home from his office and of course he was. It was another great meal.

They were still sitting at the table not say anything. "Karen, are you ready to be tested?" Karen looked from Bo to Austin.

"Yes she is ready." Austin answered. "Karen it will be alright no matter which way it goes." Austin gave her a big hug. Then Bo handed her the test.

"Karen just pee on the stick. It works just like the old test and in ten minutes we will know." Bo then gave her a smile.

In no time Karen was on her way up to the third floor to her and Austin's bathroom. Austin was following behind her. "Karen, do you want me to go up with you?" he asked as she started up the stairs.

"No I will be alright, I will be right back. You just wait here." Austin watched Karen as she went up the two flights of stairs. Then he and Bo took a seat on the forth step from the bottom of the staircase and waited for Karen to come back down.

"Bo, I never expected to be doing this even with a surrogate and here I am waiting for my wife to take a pregnancy test and I'm praying she is pregnant." Austin had changed in so many ways in such a short time, but Bo was not worried at all about him. He knew there was nothing wrong with his friend he had just grown up at last and wanted what every man wants at sometime in his life, a family of his own. Bo wanted the very same thing too. They were not boys any longer.

"Austin it will be alright and I bet she is pregnant." Bo knew with all the love making his friend and his wife were doing they couldn't miss getting pregnant.

It wasn't long before Karen came down with the little stick in her hand. She took a seat between the two men. Austin put his arm around her and pulled her up close to him as they waited. It wasn't long before Bo had his arm around her too.

"Now we wait." Bo said. "It should show up in about ten minutes and then we will know." He gave them both a little smile.

"Well here it comes." All three of them had their eyes on the little stick. "Congratulations, Mama and Daddy in nine months we will be going to the hospital to get our baby." Bo said as soon as he saw the plus sign appearing on the stick.

"Now, Bo my baby is not our baby. If you want a baby you need to get your own." Austin said.

"Oh you know what I mean." Bo was so happy for his friends.

"Yes I do." Austin said with a big smile on his face. He was going to be a Daddy. Karen had not said anything, she was still sitting there. She didn't move. The two men on the other hand were patting each other on the back and laughing a lot.

"Karen honey, are you alright?" Austin asked. She had tears running down her face.

"Karen." Austin sat back down beside his wife and put his arms back around her and pulled her very close to him. "Karen?"

"Yes Austin I'm alright. I was just thinking how close our baby came to not ever existing. How close it came to not ever being."

That got Austin and Bo thinking the very same thing. "Wow Austin your wife is right. When you think how much a few days has changed your lives and mine as well. This is a miracle." Bo just stared at Karen.

"Karen, are you happy that we are pregnant?" Austin asked. "Yes Austin, aren't you?" She had tears running down her face. "Karen the only thing that has ever made me happier was you marrying me. Yes honey I am happy. Now we will do exactly as Bo said for us to do. And . . . . ?" Austin raised his head to look right at Bo, who was watching them both as they still sat on the steps. "If he is lying I will get him later." Bo just gave Austin another big smile.

"I guess you could say I'm going to be an uncle." Bo was almost as happy as they were.

"Yes Bo you can be our baby's uncle, since there are neither uncles nor, aunts on either side of our families." Austin answered.

"Karen you need to let go of every worry or bother you have and you just enjoy the fact that you are going to be a mother. Karen I don't want you to be over doing yourself at anything. This next couple of weeks will be very critical. Until we get you over your first missed period I want you to take it very easy. This is the easiest time to miscarry, mostly because women don't know they are pregnant yet. And they don't know they should restrain from some activities. We will get this baby here because this uncle is taking his job very serious."

"Thank you Bo, I want my baby to be born and to be healthy." Karen was still crying.

"You are welcome Karen. Now let's go back into the den and put you into a nice comfortable chair or maybe into your big old husband's lap. I will go home and let you two have some alone time together. It's not every day you get the news you are pregnant for the very first time. I want my favorite patient to enjoy it all with the man she loves and with the man who so obviously loves her."

"Thank you Bo I will call you tomorrow." Austin said while holding on to Karen's hand.

Bo went home and they went back into the den. Austin took a seat in his big chair and Karen sat down in his lap just the way Bo had told them to do.

"Karen, are you going to work with me tomorrow?" he asked. He wasn't sure if she would want to go now that they knew they were pregnant.

"Yes I am. I had rather be there with you at work than be here alone for the next two weeks while I wait to miss my period," she answered. "Now you know you don't need to work just so you can to go with me every day. You can stay in my office and rest." Austin wanted her with him too.

"Austin there isn't that much for me to do. I got all of the work that needed to be done today out and I got most of the things she had not done and had hidden away in her desk. Tomorrow I will get the rest of it done and tomorrow's work. Austin there was things in her desk that she had not done in months that should have been done the day they were sent to her. What did she do all day besides look at you?" Karen was real glad that Lisa was no longer her husband's secretary.

"She worked I thought." Austin answered.

"Well she didn't, you did her work. She just smiled and flirted with you all day and you paid her to do it." Karen smiled up at Austin.

"Now that I know what can be done in one day, I will know to expect more." Austin said as they continued to sit.

"The next secretary you get will be older and she will know before she even starts her job that you are already taken." Karen didn't want another Lisa working for her husband.

"Yes honey she will know I'm a happily married man. Now we have a lot to think about and it is all wonderful. I can tell you when my parents show up here they will be two happy people." Austin wished his parents would get themselves home. They had been gone long enough he thought. Until he married Karen, Austin had not minded his parents being away having fun, but now he wanted them home.

"I hope so Austin. I would hate to have gone to all this trouble making love with their son so many times and they wouldn't want the results of all my hard work." Karen teased.

"So it was hard work making love with my mother's little boy. I will be sure I let her know how hard you had to work at that little job." This time it was Austin teasing her.

Karen smiled at Austin and then she kissed him. "No not at all. It was my pleasure and you had better not tell your mother anything about what we do in bed."

"And my pleasure as well Mrs. Blackburn and I won't tell if you don't," he answered.

"Austin I'm going to be a mother, me Karen Belmont. Can you believe it?" She was so happy and worried all at the same time.

"No, Karen Blackburn is going to be a mother and Austin Blackburn is the daddy of that baby and yes I can believe it. We have been working at it all weekend."

"Wow I feel sorry for this baby already. He will be kissed and hugged and loved so much he will want to leave home at the age of two just to get away from us." Karen could almost picture them loving on their baby already.

"No he won't. He will love every second of it. Besides at two he will have a sister or a brother by then." Austin answered.

"Do you really think so Austin?" Karen then got another picture in her mind of all four of them.

"Yes I sure do. In fact he may have one of each by his second birthday." Austin was ready to let Karen keep popping them out.

"Now you must be going to have one of those babies yourself." Karen answered.

"No Mrs. Blackburn you will be in charge of having all of our babies. I will just be in charge of getting you with child. I will be the one having all of the fun." He answered.

"Austin I can tell you now, what I want instead of pay." "What does my little wife want?" Austin was almost in a trance from all that had happen to him in the last few days. Not a week, but a few days.

"I want a rocking chair so we can rock our baby or should I say babies." She answered.

"Karen we will get everything you want for our baby." Austin knew if he didn't get it his parents would.

Karen was still sitting in Austin's lap. "Austin I don't want a nursery. I want a bed for our baby in our room. Not down on another floor. I just could not stand that I can tell you right now. I don't know how you rich people do it, but we poor people always keep our babies in the room with their mother.

"I guess honey eight years ago when I bought this house and renovated it I didn't think about getting married one day and having babies. At the time it never crossed my mind that someday I would need a place for a baby."

"That is alright Austin I'm glad you didn't, because eight years ago I had just turned eleven and I would have been too young to marry you then, even if I had wanted to. I was only in the ninth grade. We will work it all out."

"You sure know how to make a man feel old." he teased.

"You know what I mean Austin. I want our babies with us, and I never wanted you having them with some other woman. And I want to be the one having them and taking care of them." Karen wanted to be a real mother to her babies.

"Does this mean you are going to give up your new career as my secretary?" Austin asked.

"No not yet, but as soon as you find a nice older motherly lady to replace me with I will gladly stay home. That is unless I decide I want to go and take my naps with my husband in his office after lunch every day." Karen knew her husband would like that as much as she would.

"Okay, we will start interviewing some women tomorrow. Do you have a certain type of woman you want me to have as my secretary?"

"Oh Austin maybe you need a man secretary." Karen answered. "No, I don't think so." he answered.

"Why?" she asked.

"I just don't want a male secretary." Austin said as he pulled Karen closer to him.

"Okay, just have it your way. Then you can have a woman secretary just as long as she is old and motherly looking."

The next two weeks went by faster than Karen and Austin had expected. Karen's due time came and went and she did not start. Bo told Austin they could continue with the sex now, but not to overdo it. He made that quiet clear to Austin he thought.

"Bo what do you call over doing?" Austin just wanted to see what restrictions his friend would put on him now.

"Oh I would say not doing it more than twice a day." Bo answered.

"Okay, I can live with that for now." Austin answered.

"I would hope so. After all man you are married now and they say your needs for sex after marriage decreases." Bo could only smile at his friend and think what Austin was going to say about that now.

"Who said that crazy statement?" Austin asked. "A survey said it." Bo answered.

"Well nobody bothered to ask me and I'm married." Austin answered.

"Yes you are, all of two weeks and four days and two weeks of it you have not had sex at all. I would say you don't count in this survey. They only ask normal people." Bo smiled over at his friend again.

"It's good to know my best friend doesn't consider me normal." Austin gave his friend a short smile.

"Austin, think about it. You placed an ad in the newspaper for a surrogate mother and you get a cell phone just for that project. You read Karen's one and a half line note and you pick her note out of all of those hundreds of letters you received. Then you get her to call you and meet with you and out of the window the whole idea of a surrogate went, because Austin, you fell in love with your wife while watching her walk across the street. Then you get her to move in with you that same night and you married her the next day and she gets pregnant. What is normal about that whole thing? Not even the fact that she slept down on the second floor and you up on the third floor that first night.

Nobody would consider either one of you to be normal." Bo wanted to really laugh out loud at his friend.

"No I guess not Bo if you put it that way." Austin answered. "Austin there is no other way to put it. That's what happened and now you and Karen are going to be parents and I don't think there could be two better matched people in the world than you two. God sure is the one that put you two together." Bo really believed that God had his hand in this whole situation with Austin and Karen.

"Honey did you hear what our friend said?" Austin and Bo had moved their conversation to the kitchen so Karen could be a part of it. They did not want her to feel left out of anything.

Karen was busy and had not heard what the two men had been saying. "No." She answered as she was putting their supper on the table.

"Honey Bo said we were not normal." Austin had a cute smile on his face.

"So he knows us really well." Karen answered.

"See Austin, your own wife agrees with me." Bo loved this new life he and Austin had now with Karen. It was like being back home in Georgia to him and eating at his parent's kitchen table.

"Sure she does. She knows you are the one who will be controlling the drugs when she goes into labor." Austin laughed.

"Are you two ready to eat?" Karen called out from the kitchen. "Austin when your parents come we will need to use your dining room." Karen said as she finished putting the rest of the food on the table.

"No not mine, but our dining room Mrs. Blackburn. This is your home now." Austin reminded her.

"Okay, it's our dining room Mr. Blackburn that we will need to use when we have real company." She smiled over at Bo and he smiled back at her. He knew he was family and not company when he was at their house.

"Karen, do you like the way your husband has decorated your home?" Bo asked.

"Oh yes it is beautiful. I love it all, especially this big kitchen. I had never seen a kitchen as nice as this one before and one that had been used so little. It's like a brand new kitchen." Karen turned to look at her big kitchen. She loved everything in Austin's house and most of all him.

"Karen if there is something you want to change we can do it honey. None of this has to stay this way. We can move a wall, paint or anything else you want us to do." Austin wanted Karen to be at home in this house.

"Austin I love it all and I think I have already changed enough things in your life at least for awhile." she answered.

Austin put his arms around his wife. "Honey all of the changes you have brought to my life I welcome. My life has only gotten better since you have become part of it. I can only see good things coming from us being together for both of us."

"Oh Austin I love you. Bo you see why I love him so much. He is so sweet." Karen was so happy now.

"Yes he, is a real sweetie, I may start to love him myself." Bo answered.

"No you won't." Austin answered as he gave his friend a little playful punch. "I don't need that kind of love."

"Don't worry Austin you are not my kind of woman. I much prefer your wife to you if you want to offer her to me?" Bo gave Austin a look that said give me a chance please.

"I bet you do. I think we need to find you a wife, so that my wife will be safe around you and you can get that look off your face right now. It won't work." Austin knew his friend was only playing with him and Karen both.

"Don't worry Austin I love only you and I already told you, only you." Austin knew what Karen was saying even without her saying it all. They had such a great connection with each other already.

"See Austin you don't have anything to worry about, but should you come across another woman like Karen, I'll take her." Bo was ready to be married.

"Now you two get to the table and I mean now." Karen had made a roast with all of the trimmings.

"Karen when did you have time to cook all of this?" Austin asked once he saw all the food she had cooked for them.

"Austin I put it all on this morning before we went to work and it cooked all day while we were gone. All I had to do when we got home was to put it together and make us some bread." She was so happy to get to cook again.

Austin was enjoying his new life a lot. He had learned to really enjoy Karen's Southern cooking and Bo could not be happier, maybe a little if he had a wife who could cook like Karen.

"Austin, have you found yourself a new secretary yet?" Bo asked as he waited along with Austin for Karen to get to the table before they took their seat.

"No not yet. Karen is very picky who takes her place. She wants a certain type of woman for the job." Austin was watching Karen as she came to the table and took the chair next to the one he would be using. "Honey, are you alright?"

"Yes, I just feel a little dizzy." she answered.

"Karen you may need to slow down and not do so much at one time. We can order out for food. Austin and I did that all the time before we married you." Bo said.

"Are you two men crazy? I'm dizzy because my sinuses hurt. If it was up to you two I would not move for the next nine months." Karen had never known of two men who were more concerned about one woman in her life. "And Bo we aren't married. Austin is the only one who is married to me."

Both men looked at each other. "But Karen I'm a doctor." Bo answered, but he didn't bother to argue with her about who was and who wasn't married to her. He just felt if Austin was married to her so was he, at least at meal time.

"Yes Bo you are a doctor, but I'm a woman and I know my body and I know my sinuses. Everything that happens to me is not going to be because of my baby. I still have other parts to my body, you two need to learn that soon. And before I forget it Austin I have a dental appointment next Tuesday. I will need some time off to go and have my teeth cleaned."

"How will you get there?" Austin asked.

"I will go with you when you go. I arranged your calendar so that you do not have any appointments at that time or all day Tuesday." she answered.

"See Bo my wife has arranged my life around her dental appointment. I will be very glad to take you for your appointment. Honey that is what husbands are for, they take their wives wherever they want to go and when they want to go."

"Is that all you think I think you are for?" Karen asked Austin.

"No young lady we both know better." Austin patted Karen on her stomach. "Honey, are you sure you are alright?" He had a worried look on his very handsome face.

"No, I feel awful, my whole face hurts. Now does that made you feel any better?" She asked.

"Bo what can I do to help her?" Austin got out of his chair and knelt down beside Karen's chair. He was ready to do anything he could that would help her.

"We will heat a washcloth in the microwave and put it on her face after she lays down upstairs. Austin, take her on up and I will bring the washcloth." Bo was already getting up from the table to go and get a washcloth from the downstairs hall powder room.

"No Austin I will do it, you two go and eat." Karen said as she started to get up from her chair.

"No Karen, I'm the boss and I won't eat while my wife is sick and is taking care of herself. I will take care of you, then I will eat, but you come first. We will go upstairs like Bo said."

"Okay. Austin if you say so." Karen felt so bad she did not feel like arguing.

Austin soon had Karen in their bed and Bo was soon there with a hot wet washcloth to put on her face. "Karen is it too hot?" He asked.

"No Bo, its fine." The heat felt good.

That night they all had supper in the bedroom. Bo had his supper sitting in front of a TV tray and Karen and Austin ate their meal in bed. The men cleaned up the kitchen while Karen continued to lie in bed with the hot cloth on her face.

"Karen I will go now, but I want you to know that was one of the best meals I have had in a long time. Thank you for including me at mealtime." Bo leaned over the bed and gave Karen a little kiss on her cheek. "Karen, are you and your old man here planning to put the baby bed up here in your room?" Bo asked.

Karen and Austin both answered "yes" at the same time.

"Well I guess you two have been making plans already. I will go now. Karen, just keep that cloth hot and soon you should start to feel a little better."

"Bo I'm sorry to have been so much trouble for you and Austin." Karen felt as if she had been nothing but trouble for Austin since they first met.

"Honey you haven't been any trouble for us. If two grown men can't take care of one little girl we are sorry men."

"I'm not a little girl if you haven't noticed." She answered.

Bo and Austin looked at each other. "Oh we have noticed honey. We both have noticed." Austin answered.

"Yes Karen I sure have noticed even if your mean old husband won't hardly, let me near you." Bo answered.

"Bo I believe you will be getting very near me before all of this is over and we plan to have eight babies and besides I thought you said you were going home."

"Yes I did say that, but that was before you told me all about your plan. Wow I will get to know you really well won't I?" Bo was not about to let this opportunity past.

"Austin don't you say it." Karen already knew what was going through her husband's mind.

"Say what Karen?" he asked.

"Don't you play innocent with me big boy. You know what you were going to say. Bo is going to be our doctor. So both of you had just as well, get used to it. After all I'm the one he will be seeing and you know already Austin how I feel about anyone seeing all of that on me."

"Yes sweetheart I know you don't want any pictures of your cootchie when our baby comes." Austin had a silly smile on his face.

Bo busted out laughing. "Only a real southern girl would know what a cootchie was." Bo had not hear that word used since he left the South.

"Yes and Austin and I have already had that little talk." Karen answered.

"Well Karen I will try very hard not to notice your cootchie while I'm delivering all eight of your babies, one at a time for eight years. Austin did you know your wife wanted eight babies and I will get to deliver them all?" Bo had a silly look on his face too now.

"Yes, and if it all goes well we may go on and have a full dozen." Austin answered.

"You two are joking aren't you?" Bo asked.

"No, Bo we aren't. Karen and I both want a large family." Austin was enjoying all of this as much as anyone.

"Three or four children could be considered as a large family these days. You don't need eight to twelve children to have a large family." Bo didn't know if his friends were joking or not.

"Bo I'm the one who will be carrying them and birthing them. All you have to do is deliver them. That won't hurt you at all and you will get paid to do it." Karen said from under the hot washcloth.

"No Karen I may not want to pay Bo to deliver our babies. After all he is getting to see my wife's cootchie. Maybe he should be paying me." Austin said as he smiled over at his best friend. He knew Karen could not see them.

"Now if you two have eight to twelve babies and I get to see Karen's cootchie that many times then I may agree to pay you." Bo was going right along with Austin.

"You two are crazy. Do you two want me to go out and find myself a real doctor not, just a sex starved man playing like he is a doctor?" Karen did not like what they were saying at all. If she did not have her face covered with the washcloth they would see how red her face was becoming.

"See Austin, even your wife knows I'm sex starved." Bo said.

"Yes, but she is not going to be the one who will be getting you over it." Austin answered.

Karen was still lying flat of her back in the middle of the bed. Bo had forgotten all about going on home again. By this time Bo and Austin were laying one on each side of her.

"Do you two men realize I'm a married woman and my husband my not like all of this talk about my cootchie and neither do I. If you two men want me to keep Bo as my doctor you need to grow up."

"You heard her Austin you need to grow up." Bo told his friend. "You too Bo, how do you think I will feel going to a doctor who acts like you two act and on top of all of that my doctor is my husband's best friend. You, both must have graduated from Clown College together. Maybe I need to check and see where you both went to school, that is if you really went at all." Karen looked so serious that it scared the two men a little.

"Karen we are just joking with you honey." Austin didn't want to upset his wife anymore than he and Bo had already done. It may cause him to need to sleep on the sofa in the den tonight.

"Yes Karen we are just joking. I won't look at your cootchie." Bo said.

"And if he does honey I will put his eyes out." Austin answered. "Well that's much better." Karen lifted the washcloth off of her face and smiled at both men. She already knew that would not be the last time the three of them would be having that same conversation.

Then the two men started to laugh again. Karen had no idea at all why they were laughing this time and she was not going to ask. "Austin we need to do something to get Karen to like us again. If we don't she may stop cooking for us." Bo said.

"I sure hope she likes us again, because I'm married to her and it's almost bed time." Austin answered. He didn't care if she wanted to stop cooking. He could just take her out to eat, but he did not want his wife to stop wanting him in their bed.

"Austin I sure hope we, haven't caused her not to want all of those babies either." Bo said as he looked from Austin to Karen to see if she was looking at them.

"You two are still at it aren't you Austin? Karen asked. "You both are trying your best to get me to kick you both out of this bedroom."

"Yes honey we are at it, but we do love you and I'm only trying to get you to kick one of us out of your bedroom." He answered.

"I hope one of you loves me more than the other." Karen answered. "That will help me a lot on deciding if I will kick you both out or just one of you."

"Karen?" Bo answered. "Yes Bo." Karen answered.

"Does it matter which one of us loves you the most and does it matter which one of us stays?" He asked. Karen took her pillow from under her head and threw it at him. "Austin I guess it does matter and I guess you are the one she wants to stay."

"At last you two are getting something right. Don't let me forget to put a big gold star by both of your names tomorrow morning." Karen said.

"I guess you two will want me to go home now?" Bo tried to sound as hurt as he could.

"But remember Bo we are getting a gold star by our names for getting that right so everything isn't all bad." Austin answered.

"Yes Bo we do and don't let your little playmate fool you, it can get all bad if I want it bad." Karen answered. Austin gave Karen a big kiss and then Bo gave her a kiss on the cheek. Then the two men went downstairs.

"Austin you are a lucky man to have me as your friend." Bo said as they went down the stairs.

"Why am I so lucky?" Austin asked.

"Because if I wasn't your best friend I may want your wife, but I know she loves you and only you. You are like a brother to me and I value our friendship." Bo was only telling his friend the truth.

"Yes Bo, I know we are and I'm glad you like my wife, but I'm not sharing her with you. So you can stop buttering me up. She is not something I will ever be loaning out." Austin knew what his friend was telling him, but Austin didn't want Bo to feel as if he wasn't going to ever have the same good life he and Karen were enjoying so much. Austin was sure his friend would find someone to love the same way he loved Karen. It was just a matter of time.

"Well it was worth the try." Bo answered as he went out of the front door. Austin, just smiled at Bo, and shook his head. He soon went back up to the third floor.

"Karen, do you feel like taking a shower with me?" Austin was getting out his underwear.

"Yes I think that would help my sinuses to feel better. I want to feel better before tomorrow. I want to go with you to meet those famous people. I haven't ever seen any famous people before." Karen was still in bed with her face covered with the washcloth.

"Honey you will see a lot of so called famous people. They are everywhere here in the city. They are no different than you or I. They just think they are." Austin answered.

"Oh Austin you are so nice." Karen had never known anyone like Austin or even Bo before. They were so nice and good and they could have everything and they were still good.

"Am I nice enough for you to get into this shower with me before the water goes cold?" He asked.

"Yes I think so." Karen had already gotten out of the bed and was in the bathroom so she dropped her gown and stepped into the shower before Austin had time to say anything else.

All he could do was look for several seconds. "Karen you are too beautiful for words."

"Austin you are making my face turn red." she answered. Karen was not used to all of the nice things he kept saying to her about the way she looked. No one had ever looked at her the way Austin had.

"I can see that." Austin leaned down and kissed her. "Is the hot water helping any?" he asked after a few minutes.

"Yes I think so." she answered as she gave him a little smile. She could see him still looking at her body. She didn't mind at all because she was looking at his.

"Karen I hope we didn't upset you too much by talking about your . . . ." He didn't get to finish saying what he was going to say. Karen cut him off.

"Talking about my, cootchie, was that what you were going to say Austin?" she asked.

"Yes your cootchie." Austin had that smile on his face again.

"Yes you did and that is why I may decide to move back down to the other bedroom." She knew that would not make her new husband happy at all.

"No you aren't moving anywhere. You are just mad at me and you want to punish me a little, but not too much." he answered.

"Yes I am moving. Would you like me to joke around about your stuff?" she asked as she looked down at all of it.

"No I don't think so." Austin knew he would not like that at all. "So why do you think I like it when you and your little friend joke about my cootchie." Karen was being very serious. She wanted to hear what her husband had to say.

"Karen we will not joke about your cootchie again." He knew the minute he and Bo got together again and Karen was with them they would be joking about something and it may well be her cootchie, but he was not about to say that to her.

"Thank you Austin, now are you going with me to see Bo when I go?" she asked.

"Yes every time. I will be right in that room when he checks you." Austin wanted to be a hands on Daddy not just a so called father and he felt it all starts with Karen's doctor appointments.

"Thank you Austin, I want you there with me too." Karen didn't like the idea of going to a doctor at all, knowing what he would be doing, but she would feel a lot better with Austin there with her.

"Honey I want to be as much a part of all of it as I can. After all it is our baby together. You should not have to do it alone." This so called project had turned into something much better than Austin had ever expected.

"Austin, no wonder I love you so much." She was so in love with this man.

"Karen you came into my life just at the right time. I'm very thankful for that gift. God sent you to me and I'm going to take very good care of you and all of the children we will have together."

It wasn't long before they were in their big king size bed making love. Karen was turning into a real good lover with her husband.

"Austin I'm glad we are back to normal." She knew he knew exactly what she was saying.

"Me, too honey. I thought those two weeks would never end, but they did pass faster than I had expected they would. However I'm glad to have them all over and now we are able to get back to our honeymoon. Karen honey you don't need to go to the office and work I could use one of my other employees while I find a new secretary." He did not want her to overdo anything.

"But I want to Austin. I want to go with you all I can, because, before long you will be replacing me with a new old secretary. Besides all the women at your work place are too beautiful and I don't want you to end up with another Lisa. I will just go and save us both from having to get upset. It will save me from getting upset because you have another big tall beautiful woman so near you and it will save you from being upset because I'm upset." Karen was not running any chance that there was another woman working for Austin that has the idea that Lisa had.

"Honey I will need to get another secretary, but there is nothing stopping you from going with me anytime and you can stay in my office with me all day." Karen was lying in Austin's arms. "Now as for all the beautiful women at my work place not one of them holds a candle to you.

"Maybe I will go once in awhile, because if I go too much people may start thinking I don't trust you or maybe you don't trust me." Karen knew how gossip can get started.

"Who cares what other people think, I don't and we both know we can trust each other." Austin just pulled her closer to him and then they went off to sleep.

CHAPTER FOURTEEN

By the next morning Karen's sinuses felt much better and she was her old self again. She saw no need in staying home when she could go with Austin and be his secretary for a few more days. "Honey, are you ready?" Austin asked as he walked into the kitchen.

He was dressed to kill in a new suit that fit him to a tee. Karen was putting chicken into the slow cooker to cook while they were at work. She was dressed in her jeans and a sweater. She always looks good in her clothes although they had not cost very much. "So this is how all these things work?" Austin had never been very interested in cooking at all before.

"Yes it is. You first start by taking them out of their boxes." Karen answered.

"That sounds real complicated to me." he teased. He was amazed at how well Karen could already run their home.

"No it's not and you know it. If it was I couldn't do it." Karen continued to get her supper going. She knew when they got home that afternoon there would not be enough time to cook the kind of meal she wanted to serve her husband.

"Yes you could Mrs. Blackburn. You can do everything." Austin picked Karen up off of the floor and kissed her. "I can't wait until you start to show." He whispered in her ear while he had her up in his arms. Austin was so excited about becoming a parent.

"Sure you can." she answered.

"No I can't. You will be even more beautiful than you are now." All he could think was how much he loved her and to know they were making a baby from that love thrilled his pure soul.

"But Austin I will be rounder than I am tall before it is all over." She was short, but he was sure pregnant women didn't get rounder than they were tall even if they were only a little over five feet tall.

"No Karen you won't. You will be just right. I will love you no matter what size you get." He gave her another kiss.

145

"Austin are you real sure of that, because I plan to get real big."
Karen put her hands together and put them out in front of her stomach
as to show Austin how big she would be.

"Mrs. Blackburn I don't think you will ever be real big." He didn't
care how big she got he would still love her and their baby.

"You say that now, but let's see what you will be saying later." she
answered. "Will you like me so much when I look like this? She puffed out
her cheeks so her face would even look fat.

"Yes I will." he answered. Then he put one of his hands on each side
of her face and pushed the air out of her cheeks before kissing her again.

Once at work Karen decided to call the church and leave them her
new address so that they would be able to send her the last pay check
that was owed to her.

"Lakewood Baptist Church, how can I help you?" The new voice
said on the other end of the phone.

"Hello I'm Karen Belmont and I used to work at the church as
Reverend St. Johns' secretary and I have a pay check due me and I
would like to give you my new address so it can be sent to me." Karen was
so glad that the good Reverend had not answered the phone. She didn't
care to speak to him at all.

"Alright let me get my pen and write it all down. I will be happy
to give it all to the Reverend St. Johns as soon as he gets here this
morning." Karen wondered if the good Reverend was giving his new
secretary the same hard time he had always given her, but she sure was not
going to ask her if he was.

"No you don't need to give him my address you could just mail
my check yourself. You don't need to get him involved with this at all."
This was beginning to upsetting Karen. She did not want the Reverend to
personally know her address at all.

"Well, I will see." the voice answered. Karen didn't have much hope
that the new girl would do as she had asked, but it was worth a try.

"I hope you do, thank you." Karen said and then she hung up her
phone.

"Excuse me Reverend St. Johns, but that was your old secretary on
the phone just then. She wanted to give you her new address so you
could mail her last pay check to her." The new girl was not as beautiful as
Karen in any way. In fact it was his wife who had picked the girl to be his

new secretary just as Karen was going to pick who Austin's new secretary would be.

"Give me that address I will take care of her pay check myself." This was what the good Reverend had been waiting for all these weeks. He knew Karen would call one day about her last pay check and then he would know where she lived.

Once Austin got into his office he got real busy with several of his most important clients. He was going to be busy with some men he had known all his life. They were good friends of his family and they were as concerned themselves as Austin's Uncles or his other daddies.

"Austin is that really your wife sitting out there at your secretary's desk?" the oldest man asked.

"Yes Paul it is. My former secretary had to leave sort of sudden and my wife is a great secretary so she said she would come and work for me until I got myself a new secretary." They could tell Austin did not mind at all having his new wife with him all day.

"With her out there looking so good are you really looking for a new secretary? I would let my wife be my secretary if she looked like yours." Paul said as he looked over at the other man that was there.

"Paul I'm sure your wife is still a very beautiful woman." Austin answered as he looked over some papers that both men would need to sign.

"Yes she is Austin. She is just as beautiful today to me as the day I met her." Paul answered.

"Austin when did you get married?" The other man asked.

"Harry, Karen and I have been married long enough to be expecting our first baby." Austin didn't want to go into all the details of his and Karen's relationship. There were just some things he wanted to only keep between him and Karen and of course Bo.

"Well congratulations son, she sure is a pretty girl. Not at all what we all had ever expected you would marry. She is a lot better than the women you used to date. Boy we all feel like we are your Daddy when we are around you so we hope you don't get offended by anything we may say. We are just old men who have known you all your life and we love you. You really lucked out when you married your wife. She will do you proud."

"Yes sir that's exactly how I feel. I really do love her." Austin had known these men all his life. They had done business with his Dad way before he was old enough to work. Now they were doing their business with him.

Austin had gone to college at Princeton and so had his father and his Grandfather. He was a dark haired six foot and four inch man with a perfect body and he had always been very smart. That made him a very shrewd business man that truly loved his five foot one inch wife. His work had always put him among beautiful women and he grew to know at a very young age that beauty was not always through to the bone. It sometimes was only skin deep and in his business most of the time it didn't even make it through the skin.

"Are we going to take the boy here out to lunch today?" Harry asked. He and Paul had been business partners for over forty years.

"Sure we are and we are going to take his pretty little wife with us. How else will we get to know the girl who stole the boy's heart." Paul answered.

"You are so right Paul." Harry said as he got up and walked out of Austin's office and went to Karen's desk.

"Hello little lady, Austin tells us you are his wife and that you are expecting his baby." Harry wanted Karen to know how much they thought of her husband.

"Yes sir I am on both accounts." Karen smiled and answered. She didn't really know anything about the two men who had been in Austin's office all morning. All she knew was that they were really important men.

"Little lady I'm Harry Sims and I have known your husband all of his life. You have got yourself a good and honest man and I know he will make you a good husband and he will be a very good father."

"Thank you sir, I'm glad you care so much about my husband. I think he is quite wonderful too." Karen looked so young to this older man, but he could see for himself that Karen loved Austin as well. "Honey, just how old are you, if you don't mind me asking you such a question?" Harry was just staring at Karen. He had not noticed until then just how young she looked.

Austin came out of his office and had walked up to Karen's desk before she had time to answer Harry's question. "Harry, are you trying to steal my wife from me?" he jokingly asked.

"No son I'm way too old for all of that and that was never my kind of game. No more than it was your father's game. I was just asking her how old she is." Harry knew Austin is only joking with him.

"She is nineteen years old." Austin was standing next to Karen's chair now and he was holding her hand like a school boy would hold his little girlfriend's hand.

"Your wife is the same age my wife was when we got married. So I know you two are having a very good time together. I can still remember those good old days." Harry had a nice smile on his face.

Yes Harry we are having a very good life together." Austin answered. He loved these two men and they loved him. When he was very young he believed they were his uncles for years.

"Paul meet Austin's wife isn't she a little doll? Look at that big boy next to this little girl. She is going to have her hands full, but I'm sure they both are going to enjoy every second of their life together." Harry knew Austin would never do anything to hurt his marriage no matter how many beautiful women he worked around every day.

Yes Harry I would say Austin sure got himself a beautiful wife." Then Paul turned to Karen. "Hello honey I'm Paul Scott and I have also known your husband all of his life. We are like his other Daddies or maybe a couple of old Uncles. Your husband never has to worry about our accounts. He will always have them. So you just go right ahead and have all the babies you and this big handsome boy want. Your husband can afford all of them and a lot more."

"Yes sir I plan on having a house full of kids. We both want a big family." Karen liked these two older men they seem to care a lot about Austin.

"Karen we are going to lunch now." Austin said as he stood beside her desk.

"Alright I will see you when you get back." She answered.

"No young lady you are going with us." Paul said. Both men wanted to spend more time with Austin and his wife than the few minutes they had spent with them standing outside Austin's office and in front of Karen's desk talking. They really wanted to get to know this young lady.

"After all you do sleep with the boss." Harry added. "Yes she does and very well." Austin answered.

"Austin don't you want me to just stay here? I will be alright." Karen didn't know if Austin wanted her to go with them or not.

"No honey you are my wife not my secretary. You are just here to help me out, but you are my wife first and foremost. So you are going with us. Get your purse and let's go. Someone else will take my calls until we return." Austin was already pulling her chair away from the desk.

"Okay Austin, but I'm not dressed nice like you. I only have on my jeans and this little top." Karen knew all three men were dressed in very expensive suits and they all three looked rich. She wasn't sure she would fit in with the way they looked.

"Yes I know and you look outstanding in them. We will be the envy of all the men in the restaurant." Austin answered.

"Your husband is right you do look like a million. We will be very proud to be seen with you. Were you ever a model?" Paul asked.

"No sir haven't you noticed I'm short. Don't you see everyone here is a foot or more, taller than me. I'm sure I'm the only short person Austin has ever known since grade school." Karen was looking up at Austin all the time she was talking and he was smiling at her all the time.

"Yes honey he is a big boy, but he is a good boy." Paul answered. "Paul you are just a little prejudice I think, but thank you." Austin answered.

"I may be, but every word of it is true isn't it Harry?" Both men had watched Austin turn from a boy into a man and they were very proud of him as proud as if he were their son.

"Yes every word of it. We know it's true because we have known him and his parents for a very long time and now we are even getting to know his beautiful little wife and before long we will know his children too.

As soon as lunch was over and the men did a little more talking, they all left the restaurant. Paul and Harry went their way and Austin and Karen's headed back to work.

Austin they were real nice men. I could tell they both really like you. I hope they will learn to like me. I know they never expected you to marry a woman like me. They thought you would marry one of the tall beautiful model women like your dad did." Karen's voice was telling Austin way more than her words.

Karen hoped Austin was not regretting marrying her, but she knew his life was far different with her than it would have been with one of those tall beautiful women. She hoped his Mother and Father would not be unhappy with her. After all, his Mother was one of those very tall beautiful models and she had given birth to this tall six foot and four inch man that she had married.

Now Karen was worried that her babies would take after her and not their tall Daddy. She was afraid they would all end up short like her. She just knew that would disappoint Austin so very much. "Austin, do you ever worry that our babies will be short like me instead of tall like you?" she asked.

Austin stopped and turned to face her. Then he put his hands on her shoulders while looking down at her. "Karen Blackburn I love you no matter what size you are. Our children will be what they will, but as for me worrying about their height I don't. You are the one person in this world I wanted to have my children. I wanted you to be my wife even more than you having my children. Karen if I had wanted some tall model don't you think I could have settle on one of the women I see every day around here? And settling is what I would have been doing, because my heart would not be in it. I love you Mrs. Blackburn. Do you understand me? Will I need to give you this same little talk again and again? If I do I will be glad to do it, but I hope someday you will believe me and relax and just let me love you. Now let's get back to work so we can go home early."

Karen had not tried to say anything the whole time Austin was talking to her. She just let him talk until he was talked out. "Austin?"

"Yes Karen." He answered thinking she was going to say something about the little talk he had just finished giving her.

"You told me before that you didn't get home until around seven each night, but we have been leaving every day by five or earlier. Why are you now leaving so much earlier? Is it because I'm here with you and you think I need to get home?" They were walking back into the building now.

"No Karen. I just have a reason to get home now where before there was no one there so I just worked a couple of extra hours every night. I'm sure my people like it much better this way. That night Bo didn't come over for supper. He had to deliver a baby and on those nights Bo most of the time had to stay at the hospital until very late or even all night.

"Karen, are you alright with Bo being your doctor? You know you don't have to use him as your doctor if you don't want him. We can get you another doctor." Austin didn't want her to feel uncomfortable in any way around his friend.

They were sitting in the den after they had finished in the kitchen. Karen was watching television and Austin was reading the newspaper. She had not given it much thought until now. "Austin I will keep Bo as my doctor if it is alright with you. After all if I need to I can always kill him. No matter what doctor I use I won't like it when they have to check me or when our baby comes, but you will be there with me and that will make it a lot easier for me."

Austin smiled. He knew they had come such a long way in such a very short time. "Does this mean I can take pictures of our baby being born?" Austin hoped she had changed her mind with some of it.

"No! Are you out of your mind? I may even have you and Bo both hypnotized afterwards so you won't remember any of what you have seen. What am I going to do with you two boys? I know I'm not the only woman you and Bo has ever seen so get over it. Remind me to check your and Bo's papers I want to be sure you two are what you say you are."

"Yes we have seen lots of women, but you are the only one having my baby." Austin answered.

"Yes I am, but I hope after eight, the thrill you and Bo get out of all of this will be over. Not the thrill of us having our babies being over or even us all three being together in the same room when all of our babies are born, but the silly part."

"Karen honey when you go into labor you won't care who sees you. All you will be caring about is getting it over with and who has the drugs." Austin answered. He was almost laughing and he had one of those smiles on his face again.

"Austin that little piece of information didn't help. I hope you didn't think it would." she answered.

CHAPTER FIFTEEN

Another week went by. It was Saturday morning and Karen was in the kitchen making breakfast. Austin came strolling into the kitchen dressed in jeans with black leather chaps and carrying a black leather jacket. Karen stopped what she was doing and watched her husband as he came closer. Her mouth was wide open.

"Karen, close your mouth." Austin told her. He knew she had no idea why he was dressed in this fashion.

"Austin what are you dressed for, it's not Halloween yet?" she asked.

"No honey, Bo and I are going for a bike ride. Do you want to go with us?" he asked. He sure hoped she would want to join them.

"What do you mean by a bike ride? I don't believe your idea of a bike ride is the very same as my idea of a bike ride." Karen could not stop looking at Austin. He looked so handsome, but she could not believe what she was seeing. She knew exactly why men put on cloths like his.

"No I guess maybe not. Bo and I own motorcycles and we take long trips on them every year. We have gone to California and to Alaska on them before." Austin hoped his wife would not feel as if he had hidden his other life from her.

"Austin I believe I need to sit down. I can't believe this. My husband rides a motorcycle." Karen felt so weak all at once.

"Yes Karen your husband and your doctor ride motorcycles." Austin answered.

"Where do you keep your motorcycle?" Karen was still in a fog. "They are all down in the basement garage." Austin answered. He was not going to say anymore than was needed.

"Are you telling me there is a basement and a garage to this house and I didn't know all of that until now?" Karen was in shock again.

"Yes Honey there is a full basement down there and a big garage. I did tell you we had a basement remember the day we were married." He reminded her.

"Yes you did I remember now. But Austin it was our wedding day and I wasn't thinking real clear at the time. Besides I didn't believe you because I had never lived at a house that had a basement before. And you never said one word to me about having a motorcycle. What else do I not know about my wild husband? Do you have any tattoos?" She asked.

"Now Mrs. Blackburn you do know I don't have any tattoos. You have seen all of me so you know there aren't any tattoos on me anywhere. Well do you want to go with us or not?" he asked again.

"Sure why not." she answered. After all this would not be her first time on the back of a motorcycle. Like she had told Austin her mother's boyfriends were always bikers.

"Well then go and get your clothes on and you will need a jacket. It can get cold when we are riding down the highway. Bo will be over in a minute and we will leave." Austin was getting a cup of coffee.

"Austin, are you a good driver? Remember I'm pregnant with your baby." Karen was a little nervous about the whole thing.

"Karen I will take very good care of you. You already know that I would not let anything happen to you or our baby. I love you and our baby. What happens to you happens to me." he answered.

Karen started to go around Austin on her way out of the kitchen to go upstairs, but he grabbed her and pulled her up into his arms. "You never have anything to worry about when I'm taking care of you. Do you understand me?"

"Yes Austin I do, but I can't help my worrying." Karen knew if she could trust anyone it would be Austin.

"I know so give me a kiss and go and get your jeans on. We need to get on the road soon." Austin knew Bo would be over shortly.

Karen hurried upstairs to dress. When she got back down to the kitchen Bo was there having coffee whith Austin.

"Oh don't you two look tough. Who would have ever guessed you do what you do Bo and that my big handsome husband wants to do all he can to keep you in business." Karen was looking both men over real good.

"Well hello to you Karen and don't you look like a biker woman. All dressed in your little tight jeans with your hair pulled back with that bandana and with that tight little tee shirt that shows off your ample breast and look Austin, your wife even has boots. I bet she has a leather jacket." Bo was looking at Karen with a lot of lust in his eyes just enough to upset her a little.

"Yes I do have a leather jacket Bo and you should not be looking at my breast. My husband won't like it."

"Well you don't want me to look at your cootchie and now you don't want me to look at your breast. Where am I supposed to look?" Bo asked.

"I don't know Bo, just look someplace else." Then Karen walked pass the two men as they sat at the table. They both turn to watched her as she passed.

"Karen I found a new place to watch." Bo said.

Karen turned around. "Where have you found to watch now?" She asked. Not thinking where it maybe.

"Your butt," Bo answered.

"Austin hit your little friends."

"No, that's between you two." Austin answered.

"Well I hope this will be all you ever see of it." She said as she stood there.

"Right now it is." Bo answered.

"Bo, don't look at my butt anymore. I may just start looking at yours." Karen said.

"No you won't young lady. You already have a butt to look at and it's mine." Austin answered.

"See Bo you have already upset my sweet husband." Karen answered.

"Are you two ready to go or do you want to stay here and argue with each other?" Austin asked.

"No Austin we are ready to go." Karen quickly answered as she gave Bo one of her mean looks.

"Austin you need to control you wife. I think she may want to hurt me." Bo told his friend.

"Bo I may help her to hurt you. After all I am her husband and her butt belongs to me." Austin quickly told his friend.

"And I am your best friend and I was here first." Bo teased as he looked over at Karen.

"Austin you need to decide who you want to sleep with me or him?" Karen said as she gave Bo another little mean look.

"You sweetheart, I want to sleep with you and only you." Austin said without hesitation. "Bo, will have to sleep all by himself."

"Now I have heard it all, a husband picking his new sexy wife over his very best friend. What is this world coming too? Karen, do you want to sleep half the night with him and half of the night with me?" I think that would be the only fare thing to do. Don't you agree Austin?" Bo had a big smile on his face as he watched Karen.

"No he doesn't think that is a fare thing to do and neither do I. I didn't marry both of you just Austin and if you keep this up I will have Austin to hurt you." Karen was serious.

"Austin how do you plan to hurt me?" Bo asked his friend.

"By not letting you sleep with my wife will be a good start." Austin answered.

"Oh so you want to really hurt your old friend." Bo could not stop laughing.

"Karen, Bo is just teasing with you. He knows I'm not going to share you with him. He just likes getting you upset." Austin put his arms around his wife as he looked over at his friend before he gave Karen a big kiss. Then they all went down to the basement.

"Wow Austin you do have a whole house down here." This was the first basement in a house Karen had ever step foot in and she was so amazed.

"Yes he does Karen. This nice large place down here is where your husband, has all of his wild parties." Bo was really enjoying himself.

Karen turned quickly to Austin. "Do you have wild parties Mr. Blackburn?" she asked.

"No Karen, Bo is just joking with you again. He always tells me that I have the most boring parties he has ever been to in his life."

"Do you Bo? Do you say my sweet husband's parties are boring? If they are so boring to you then why do you bother to come to them then?" she asked.

"Yes I do say they are boring, because they are boring." Bo knew Karen would have a lot to say back to him now, but she had not noticed that he didn't answer all of her questions.

"So you don't want to be invited to anymore of my sweet husband's boring parties. You never answered me when I asked you before why you came if you didn't like Austin's little parties." she asked.

"No I didn't. I want to come to all of your boring parties." Bo answered.

"So they aren't so boring after all." Karen looked over at Austin.

"No they aren't boring at all. I just say that so he doesn't get the big head. You know Karen he has those tall beautiful models here at all of his parties and they are all over him and me the whole time." Bo was looking at Austin. He knew that this would really make Karen mad.

"Bo you are going to get my wife mad at me and you. So, stop talking and get over there and uncover your bike and get it outside and leave my wife alone. She will be riding behind me and I don't want her mad at me. So get a move on it. We need to get down the road." Austin wanted his friend to stop getting his wife mad. He knew sooner or later he would be the one to answer for all Bo had to say.

Karen was right there standing next to Austin. "Austin, tell me which one of these big old bikes is your? The whole room they were in seemed to be full of bikes.

"All but the one Bo is uncovering. That one is his." Austin answered.

"But Austin, there are six of them here besides Bo's bike." Karen had never known anyone who could afford more than one bike at a time and to own six of them was more than anyone she knew could ever even dream of having. She was learning something new about her husband every day it seemed.

"Yes honey there are six Harley's here. I have a thing for motorcycles, Harley motorcycles. What can I say?" he answered.

Karen put her arms around Austin. "Austin I think that is great. Just as long as you don't love them more than you do your little red car or your big old black Ford truck or me."

Austin leaned way down and kissed her." I could never love anything or anybody more than I love you. Not even our babies. You are number one with me." he whispered in her ear.

"Are you two going on the bike or are you going back upstairs for sex?" Bo asked.

"We are getting on one of these bikes as soon as my husband decides which one." Karen answered.

Austin uncovered a big beautiful red Harley. "We are going on this baby today. Karen you will fit just right up behind me and I will be able to feel your legs on me the whole time." Austin answered.

"Oh, Austin if you say so, but my legs aren't very long." she reminded him.

"They are long enough for me." Austin answered as he was giving her the eye.

After they got the bikes out of the garage, they were soon cruising down the interstate. Karen had her chest resting on Austin's back. He could tell she was still a little scared.

"Honey you will be alright. I will take good care of you and our baby." Austin was talking through his helmet radio to her. She just smiled. She knew he would do just what he said.

Three hours later they were making their first stop at a road side diner. It was a real nice little place. Karen could tell it was an eating stop for lots of people by the way the parking lot looked.

"Karen you wait and let me help you to get off." Austin said as soon as they enter the parking lot.

"Austin I don't think my legs will ever be the same." Karen felt all pulled apart.

"Karen you will get used to it in time. We will be doing a lot of this, but not after you start to show or as soon as our doctor friend tells us it's not safe for you or our baby." Austin would not take any uncalled for chances with his family.

Austin lifted Karen off the back of his motorcycle and then he held her in his arms for awhile. "Austin I don't know if my legs will hold me up. They feel real weak right now."

"Well let's just check and see." Austin carefully put Karen down on the concrete. "Honey, how are your legs feeling now?" Austin still had his arm around her after he had put her down onto the ground. He did not want her to fall.

"They feel a little shaky, but I think they will be alright after I walk around a little. Austin I need to go to the ladies' room." Karen needed to go real bad all at once.

"Okay let's go. Bo, are you ready to go inside? My wife needs to use the restroom."

"Yes I am. I'm starving and I could use a burger." Austin had a hold of Karen's hand as they walked towards the diner.

"You two make such a sweet couple. No one would ever guess you won't share your little sexy wife with me." Bo said trying to get Karen all worked up again.

"No I won't. So go right ahead and pout Bo." Austin said as he looked down at his short wife.

The little diner was almost empty. The lunch rush was already over. "You people just take any booth you want. I will be right with you." A middle age waitress said as they walked into the diner.

"Bo, order us a coke. Karen and I are going to the restroom." Austin said as he and Karen went to find the restrooms.

"Alright Austin I will order you two cokes." Bo answered as he took a seat at the first clean booth he came upon.

"You people aren't from around here I can tell." The waitress brought them each a glass of water to the table.

"No M'am we are from New York City. My friend and his pretty wife and I live next door to each other there in the city." Bo was being as friendly as he always was around people.

"So where is your pretty wife?" The waitress asked.

"M'am I don't have one and my friend won't share his pretty wife with me. Have you ever heard of such selfishness in your life and he calls me his very best friend?" Bo sounded so serious.

The waitress just looked at Bo for awhile before she answered. "You aren't from this part of the country are you?"

"No M'am, I'm from Georgia, but I have lived in New York City for years now." He answered.

"What kind of work do you do there in New York City? I know it has to be something that pays a lot for money from what I see." She could tell these people were not hurting for money in any way.

"M'am I'm a doctor." Bo answered knowing what the waitress next question would be.

"What kind of doctor are you?" The waitress asked?

"The best kind of doctor there is I'm an OB GYN doctor." Bo answered with a big smile. He already knew what the waitress reaction was going to be.

"No wonder you don't have a woman. What wife wants her man doing what you do?" Bo just smiled again at the waitress.

"Could we have two cokes for me and my old friend and a glass of milk for his beautiful wife?" Bo asked.

"Yes of course. I will be right back with it all." The waitress hurried away. She wanted to tell the help in the kitchen what Bo did for a living.

Karen and Austin came back into the dining area and slide into the booth across the table from Bo. The waitress came back with the two cokes and the glass of milk. "Who gets the Milk?" she asked.

"She does." Bo answered as he pointed to Karen.

"Are you a doctor like your friend here?" the waitress asked Austin.

"No, I'm not a doctor at all. I'm just a business man." Austin answered.

"Oh, but his beautiful wife here is one of my patients. She's pregnant with their first baby." Bo smiled up at the waitress. He could tell she didn't like this arrangement at all.

"You mean your husband's friend here is going to deliver your baby when it comes?" the waitress asked Karen.

"Yes M'am he is, but he is going to do it blindfolded. My husband doesn't want him seeing me you know where." Karen said as she smiled at the waitress and then back at Austin and then at Bo.

"Young lady wouldn't it be a lot easier if you would just go to another doctor and let him deliver your baby?" the waitress asked.

"Oh yes I agree with you it would, but Bo will be paying my husband to let him deliver our baby and some other doctor may want my sweet husband to pay him for the very same service." Then Karen patted Austin on his arm.

"You mean your husband will get paid by his doctor friend for letting him deliver your baby? Honey you are with two weird men is all I can say." The waitress had never heard of such a thing before in her life.

"Yes M'am I know, but I love this one a whole lot and I like that one a lot so what can I do?" Karen looked so sweet and innocent to the waitress. She could not imagine being married to one man and then letting his friend deliver her baby that would just be too much for her to handle.

"Now could we order three burgers and fries?" Austin asked?

"Yes of course I was just getting to that right now." the very confused waitress answered.

After lunch they got back on their motorcycles and went further down the road. There was a lot of traffic out on the road today and that worried Karen. She had ridden on a few bikes before with some of her Mother's boyfriends, but they only took her, around the block and then back to her house.

"Austin, when are we going to start back home?" Karen asked? She was worried that it would get dark before they could get home if they didn't turn around soon and start back to the city.

"Tomorrow," Austin answered. He knew as soon as he told her they were not going back home today she would be upset and start worrying.

Karen could not believe her ears. Did she hear him right, she wondered. "Tomorrow, did you say tomorrow?" she asked.

"Yes you heard me, tomorrow. We will find a little motel for the night somewhere down the road and then we will ride back home tomorrow." Austin was waiting for her to give him a big pop on his back.

"Austin I can't do that and you know it. I don't have a hair brush or a tooth brush nor do I have any clean clothes to put on tomorrow." Karen was clearly upset.

"Neither, does Bo or me." Austin answered.

"Do you think knowing that makes me feel any better? You two may like wearing the same underwear for two days, but I don't." Karen didn't know what she was going to do.

"Honey I will love you so much tonight you will forget all about clean clothes. Besides I have a tooth brush and a comb you can use." All Austin had on his mind was a night in a motel with his wife. That was something they had never done.

"Do you happen to have a pair of clean panties too?" she asked. "Nope I sure don't. I'm real sorry about that, but that is something I never needed to have with me before on any of my other trips. If you want clean panties for tomorrow you will need to wash out the ones you have on and let them dry over night. Do you get the picture now?"

"Austin Blackburn I think you planned all of this so I would have to sleep without my panties." Karen wasn't too happy at the moment. "Yes I did sweetheart. Now you just lean close to your husband and let him feel you on his back." Karen did exactly what Austin told her to do. He smiled and so did she.

"Bo can you hear me?" Austin asked.

"Yes I can hear you and I heard Karen too. Do you need something?' He asked.

"Yes we may need to stop soon Karen may need to go potty and I don't want to tire her out to much before tonight." Austin answered. "Sure thing Austin, we will stop at the next diner we see." Bo had a big smile on his face. He knew Karen had forgotten all about him being able to hear everything she and Austin were saying to each other.

"That will be great." Austin replied back.

They said very little for the next few miles. Austin wasn't sure if it was because Karen had heard Bo and she knew he had heard their conversation about her panties or if she was just tired. It was another hour before they came upon the next diner.

"Karen we are stopping here at this little diner. You need to rest Honey and I know you need to go potty again."

"Yes thank you Austin I do need to go potty." Karen was so glad to see that diner.

"Honey, always remember to wait and let me help you off. I don't want you to get hurt trying to do it by yourself. There are just too many ways you could get hurt trying to do it by yourself."

"Don't worry Austin I can't reach the ground from way up here so I won't even try." she answered.

Once at the diner the three of them headed right to the restrooms. "See Austin we both have used the restroom and we are already back at the table and your wife is still in there."

"Bo if she isn't out soon I'm going in there and check on her." Austin kept looking in the direction of the restroom to see if Karen was coming. He was about ready to go and check on her when she came out of the restroom door.

"Karen, are you alright?" Austin asked as soon as she got to their table. He sure hoped this little trip was not causing Karen or their baby any trouble.

"Yes Austin I'm just tired." she answered, but she was not smiling any more.

"Bo is she alright?" Austin asked.

"Yes Austin she is. She is just tired from having her legs being straight apart for so long. Like she said her legs are short." Bo could not keep from smiling over at Karen.

They stayed at the diner an hour then they got back on the road. It was past three o'clock in the afternoon now.

"Austin how much farther are we going today?" Karen asked. She knew they had traveled a long way already since they had left home.

"To Canada," he answered.

"Austin I can't go there. I don't have a passport yet and I will need one if we go into that country."

Austin had forgotten all about Karen not having a passport. That would be a show stopper for this trip. "Karen we need to get you a passport. We will do that Monday. Now don't let me forget to do that, you need a passport." Austin answered.

"Austin I'm sorry I messed up your trip. I should have stayed home and then you and Bo could have gone and done what you had planned." Karen felt so sorry for messing up the two men's trip.

"Bo."

"Yes Austin I heard. We will just go another way. We will turn East up at the next road. We will just go East instead of North it won't mess up anything. We will enjoy our ride going east just as well." Bo did not want Karen to feel bad about them not going into Canada. He liked Karen a lot and he knew his friend was so in love with her that it hurts.

"Alright you lead, I'm right behind you." Austin answered. He knew Bo would not be upset. They would just make the trip to Canada another time after Karen gets a passport.

They went east and it was a beautiful ride. They passed beautiful fields and covered bridges. Everything they passed looked so inviting. It was all beautiful country side.

"Austin this is so nice it takes my breath away." Karen wished they could stop for awhile and look at it all.

"Yes it is beautiful and it's always beautiful up here no matter what time of the year it is. Karen we will be stopping soon and getting a motel room for the night. You need to rest your legs some. Are you alright?" Austin was concern about her.

"Yes I am Austin. But if I ever get my legs back together I may never need to separate them again." She answered.

"Oh yes you will." Austin quickly responded.

"I heard that too Austin. You may have just run out of luck. Your wife may have just closed up her business." Bo wanted to laugh.

"Bo I will change her mind and she will open her business up again." Austin answered.

"What are you two boys talking about now?" Karen asked. "We are talking about you Karen who else?" Bo answered.

"Karen, are you getting hungry?" Austin asked. They were coming up on a small community that he and Bo had been by several times on other trips, but they had never stopped there before.

"Yes Austin I am. I feel like I could eat as much as you." She answered. She was still leaning over on Austin's back. It kept her out of all of the wind and she could close her eyes and rest a little.

"Bo did you hear? Karen is hungry, what do you think about that? Do you think she is really as hungry as she said?"

"Yes I did hear her and I'm with her and I'm sure you could use something good to eat yourself. Let's first get our rooms and then let's go and get some good food." Bo was getting a little tired himself.

They rode on and on looking for a sign that read vacancy. They had passed several Motels, but they were all filled. So they kept going farther down the road until they spotted a sign flashing Vacancy. They were ready for a room. It was getting late and the sun was almost down and it would be dark soon. Austin knew Karen would not like riding in the dark.

"Remember Karen to wait and let me help you." Austin said before he stopped his motorcycle, but as soon as it came to a stop he hurried to get off and then he lifted Karen off. "Honey, are you sure you are alright?" He asked as soon as he had her up in his arms.

"Yes Austin I feel fine. Stop worrying so much about me. You will get gray hair from worrying so much and I'm very sure between me and eight kids you will have a head full of white hair in no time."

"She is right Austin you need to relax if you and Karen are going to have eight babies. You need to learn to relax or you will be looking like your children's Grandpa instead of their Daddy." Bo was enjoying all of the conversation that Austin and Karen were having.

Austin didn't say anything he just simply shook his head and thought to himself, how do you relax when your wife is pregnant?

Karen was trying to re-do her hair after she took off her helmet. It was all stuck to her head, but in a few second she had it all looking great again.

"Karen you look fine. I bet you still look better than anyone here." Austin knew he was not just telling her that to make her feel better. He knew it was true.

"Austin you are just saying that because you are stuck with me and you don't want to feel that you are married to the ugly duckling."

"No Karen he is not just saying that to make you feel better. You look beautiful all the time." Bo answered as he took off his helmet. Both men looked very handsome even after the long day's drive.

Karen was still standing in the very same spot where Austin had put her when he took her off of the back of his motorcycle. "Austin come here I need you." She was standing very still she could not move.

"What's the matter honey?" Austin asked as he started towards her.

"I don't think I can move. My legs won't move." she answered."
"What's wrong with her Bo?" Austin asked. Bo could tell now that his friend was going to be worrying about his wife no matter what she did or didn't do. This was a side of Austin he had never seen before.

"She is stiff that's all Austin. There is nothing for you to be upset about. Just pick her up and I will go and get our rooms."

"Alright Bo I will just hold my wife in my arms. That won't be a bad thing to have to do at all. After all I have not been able to hold her in my arms all day and if I hadn't felt her leaning on my back all day I would have been real lonesome. So I will enjoy it. How about you Karen will you enjoy it?" Austin asked.

"Yes Austin I will, but I would enjoy it more if I could feel you holding me. Austin Blackburn I love you." She whispered in his ear. Austin could not resist it any longer he had to kiss his wife. It seemed as if they could not get enough of each other.

CHAPTER SIXTEEN

"Yes sir, can I help you?" the old desk clerk asked when Bo entered the Motel's office.

"Yes sir, I sure hope you can. I need two rooms for the night." Bo said wondering why there were so many people in that small town today.

"Well young man I can't give you two rooms, but I can give you one room with two double beds in it. Will that do? I just don't have two rooms left. Everything is full around here this weekend with that festival going on down the road. It will be this way all week. So do you want the room or not?" the old man asked.

"Yes sir I sure do. We will take it." Bo paid for the room, then, he got the key and hurried back out to where Austin and Karen were waiting.

"Bo did you get our rooms?" Austin asked as soon as Bo got near enough to hear him.

"No, but I got our room." He answered. "What?" Karen asked.

"Hold on Karen. There was only one room left in this whole town and it has two double beds in it. So I took it." Bo answered.

"Well that's alright Bo. We can make it do for one night." Austin would make it work for them.

"Austin did Bo say we all three will be sleeping in the same room tonight?" Karen was still up in Austin's arms. She had both of her arms around his neck.

"Yes honey, but that will be alright because you will be in bed with me and Bo will be in the other bed. At least I hope he will. Now let's go and find our room. Bo what is the number we are looking for?"

"175," he answered.

"Karen I'm going to put you back on my bike and I will push you and the bike." Austin said as he started towards his motorcycle.

"No Austin let me try walking." Karen didn't want him to do all of that for her. She knew he was tired too just like her.

"Honey if you can't walk I will be glad to push you." he answered.

"Austin you are so good to me."

"Karen I'm supposed to be good to you. Aren't you my wife and aren't you pregnant with our baby?"

"Yes" Karen answered. Bo and Austin pushed their bikes as Karen walked along with them next to Austin. "There it is." Karen said as she pointed straight ahead. "It's right in front of us. You don't have to push your bikes too much further."

"Good I'm ready to rest a little myself." Austin said as he pushed his bike into the parking spot that was right in front of their room. Bo parked his bike in the same space next to Austin's bike. Bo opened the door and they all three hurried inside.

"Karen, which bed do you want?" Bo asked while standing in the middle of the room.

"I want the one nearest to the bathroom." Karen quickly answered.

"Okay Austin, which bed do you want?" Bo asked?

"He wants the bed with me. There are only two beds here." Karen answered.

"Yes she is right I do want the bed with her." Austin said as he looked over at Bo.

"Well I was just being nice again Austin in case for some reason you wanted the other bed, I would let you have it and then I would just bunk in with Karen." Bo was smiling again over at Karen.

"No you would not just bunk in with me. Austin is the only one who will ever be sleeping with me." Karen didn't know what she was going to do with these two men.

"Bo I guess my wife has told you." Austin answered.

"I guess so." Bo answered as he winked over at Karen.

"Austin I need to use your hair brush." She wanted her hair brushed now. Just pulling her fingers through it was not enough.

"Alright Karen I will bring in my bag." Both men went out and got the saddlebags off their motorcycles and brought them into the room. "What is all of that?" Karen asked. She watched as both men emptied all of their things out of the saddlebags.

"Oh, you mean all of this?" Bo asked. As he empty his things onto the bed.

"Yes Bo I mean all of that stuff you and Austin have." Karen answered as she watched.

"This little instrument here is my toothbrush." Bo held up his toothbrush for her to see and then he laid it back down on the bed and pick up the next object. "This is hairbrush, my dental floss, and this is my passport." Then he laid them down. "Now these are my clean underwear alone with my, shampoo and my favorite cologne. I've got to smell good as well as look good, don't I Karen?"

"Yes Bo I can see all of the things that you have. Austin do you have these same things in your bag?" Karen was so upset.

"Almost," Austin answered.

"What does almost exactly mean?" Karen asked?

"I have two undershirts in mine instead of only one like Bo and two toothbrushes. I have one for you and one for me. The rest is just like Bo's."

"Austin you planned for me not to have anything here. Like clean under panties." she asked.

"Karen I have already told you what you can do about that tonight." Austin answered.

"Yes you did and I will need to do that. However Mister what do I wear while they are wet?" she asked.

"None!" Bo said.

"Who asked you? I was asking my husband." Karen answered. "You don't wear any, like Bo said. You will be in bed, so why would you need any underwear?" Austin answered.

"I need them when I go to the potty. I need panties to pull down when I go potty." she answered.

"So all you need is something to pull down when you go potting." Austin had a big smile on his face.

"Well yes and no. I also need something on my butt and I don't have a gown either." Karen answered.

"Yes you do Karen. Just like on our wedding night. When you had on my undershirt remember."

"Yes I remember, but I don't remember Bo, being in our bedroom with us then." she answered.

"Karen I'm so sorry I wasn't there then and I missed all of your and Austin's big night, but I'm here now." Bo knew he had just made her mad again.

Karen just looked at Bo for the longest time. "And I'm going to trust you to deliver my precious little baby?"

"Yes you are because you love me and I'm going to be your baby's only uncle." Bo answered.

"Yes you are right I do. So I will need to get you all grown up some way before I need you to do that for me."

"Karen you will be perfectly safe with Bo and me. We both love you in our own way. Me being the one who loves you the most and in a way Bo can't. Do you hear me Bo?" Austin asked.

"Yes Austin I hear you. I will just suffer. If that is what you want me to do."

"Yes you will just suffer. If you think for one minute, I'm both of you men's wife you need to rethink it and in a hurry." Karen was not happy.

"Now that we have done all of our unpacking do you want to go and get something to eat before its gets too late?" Bo asked.

"Yes we do." Austin answered. "Karen, do you need to use the potty before we go?"

"Yes and I need to use your hair brush too. I want to look nice when we go out to eat." She was still a little unhappy with the room arrangement.

Austin gave Karen his brush. She was in the bathroom for only ten minutes. When she came out she looked like a million. She had done it all with only her lipstick and Austin's hair brush. Karen had made herself look as if she had been in the beauty salon all day.

"Wow" Bo said as she walked out of the bathroom and back into the room.

"Austin I'm ready." She said without even looking Bo's way.

"You sure are honey." Austin was ready to just stay in the room and forget about eating.

Karen had her hair down and it was full of curls and pulled back on one side. She had her big hoop earrings on. Austin stood there and looked at his beautiful young wife. "Karen you look so beautiful."

"Thank you Austin. I want to always look good for you. I know you see all of those big tall beautiful women all day and I don't want you to hate having to come home at night to just me."

"Well you sure do look beautiful to me and you will never have to worry about me not wanting to come home to you. Bo, are you sure there isn't another room here?" Austin had other things on his mind other than food now.

"No there is not one other room in this whole town. So I will give you, two hours alone tonight after we get back from eating. If you two feel you need that kind of time."

"Bo what will you be doing? I don't want you out somewhere all by yourself. Austin, tell him, he don't need to do that tonight. We don't need to do anything." Karen felt sorry for Bo and she didn't want him to be lonely. This made Bo feel so good inside.

"Karen I would want Austin to do the same for me tonight if you were my wife." Bo answered.

They decided to walk to a nearby restaurant. It wasn't that far from the Motel and it would save Karen from having to get back on the motorcycle two more times.

As soon as they had been seated at the restaurant Austin and Bo saw a couple of other men they had met several times when they had been out riding over the years.

"Austin, Bo tells us you went and got yourself married." One of the men said.

"Yes Corky I did. This is Karen my wife." Austin was real proud to introduce his wife to his friends.

"Hello little lady, you have yourself a good husband and we can all see he has himself a beautiful wife." Corky had one of those deep voices like Sam Elliott. The kind you could listen to all day and never get tired of hearing.

"Thank you sir I think he is a good guy too." Karen was sitting in the booth as close to Austin as she could get and he had his arm around her holding her there.

"Austin she is a young one and she isn't from around here I can tell." Corky said.

"No Corky she is from Georgia like Bo." Austin answered.

"I can tell she's a keeper. Bo where is your woman?" Corky asked. "I still haven't found one. And Karen doesn't have any sisters." Bo answered.

"And I hope old Austin told you he wasn't going to share his woman with you. I can't really blame him. She isn't something you want to share with anyone not even your best friend.

"That's exactly right my husband is not sharing me with anyone not even you Bo Brooks. And I don't care how much crying he does." Karen answered.

"I guess that takes care of us all as well." Corky teased.

"Yes, Corky you are right. They are even going to have a baby." Bo told their friends.

"Austin you are going to be a daddy?" Steve asked.

"Yes I'm happy to say." The two men congratulated both Austin and Karen.

"Bo are you her doctor?" Corky asked.

"Yes Corky I am, but I can't look. Austin said he would poke my eyes out if I looked."

"Well Bo I can't say I blame him at all. She is one pretty lady and he knows you." They all had a good laugh over what Corky had said.

The two men were sitting at the table across from Austin, Karen and Bo's booth making it easy for them all to talk. After they had finished eating, the two men asked if they wanted to join them in the bar and listen to the band for awhile before going back to their Motel. Steve said that someone had told them that the band was quite good. He knew that Austin and Bo both enjoyed good music.

Corky was a college professor and Steve the other man was a lawyer. No one would have guessed that by the way they both were dressed, but the men had been weekend bikers for years.

"I will be glad to join you, but Austin and Karen are going back to our room." Bo answered.

"So Bo, are you having to share a room like us?" Steve asked. "Yes we got the last room in town." Bo answered.

"So Austin you and your wife are in the room with old Bo tonight?" They all laughed.

"Yes they are and I'm going to give them, two hours alone tonight and then I'm going in and join them." Bo answered.

"Bo, give the newlyweds three hours and you stay here with us and enjoy the music. Then we will walk you home. Our motel is the one next door to yours.

"Alright Corky I will give them three hours. Karen do you hear me? I'm giving Austin three hours alone with you. He will have plenty of time to have his way with you before I get there. So you be sure you save some for me." Bo was already laughing. He knew Karen had not liked what he had said at all.

"Yes Bo I hear you. Aren't you the sweet one? But I can tell you right now there won't be any of me left for you or anyone else ever." Karen answered.

"Yes I am the sweet one Karen. You married the wrong man." Bo got up and went to the men's room.

"Austin you need to find Bo a woman." Karen said as soon as Bo was gone.

"Karen, where do you suggest I look for this woman?" he asked. "Austin, I don't know. Run another ad in the newspaper I guess.

It worked for you it may work for him, but I doubt it. There is always that place where you work. There should be at least one woman there who could put up with him if she tried real hard." she answered.

As soon as Bo was back at the table he had something to tell Karen. "Karen, guess what they sell in the men's room?"

"I wouldn't know. I haven't ever been in a man's bathroom before." she answered.

"They sell edible underwear and I got you a nice pink pair. They are called cotton candy. I know Austin loves cotton candy." Bo had a big smile on his face again.

Karen's face began to turn real red. "Bo what have you been saying to my wife that has her face turning so red?" Austin asked.

"I was just telling her she doesn't have to sleep without any underwear tonight. I told her that I got her a nice pink pair of panties awhile ago when I was in the men's room." Bo took the package with the panties in it out of his pocket and handed them to Austin.

Austin looked at the package and saw what they were. "Honey not only do you have a new pair of panties we will also have breakfast." That did not go over well with Karen at all.

"I may not be sleeping with you either tonight. You and Bo may be sleeping in that other bed tonight. I may be sleeping alone." she answered.

It wasn't long before Karen and Austin went back to the motel. "Bo you need to stop making so much trouble for Austin. You have already made his little wife kick him out of her bed and now he has to sleep with you. I don't think that is the way Austin wanted to spend the night. I know I would not want to be sleeping with you if she was my wife." Steve said. All the men at the table had a good laugh and most of all Bo.

"Austin I need a shower. I feel all sweaty and dusty." All she wanted to do was to get out of her clothes.

"That's something we can do together. I will get you your pretty little gown." Austin got Karen one of his clean undershirts and clean underwear for himself.

"I guess I will wash out my panties so they will be dry by morning." Karen said just before getting into the shower with Austin.

After their shower Austin didn't give Karen time to put on her so called gown. He scooped her up and took her to their bed.

"No need in wasting our time dressing when I will just take it off of you. Karen I have waited all day for you."

"Austin I love you, but I don't know about being in this room with another man." Karen never expected that she and Austin would be sharing a bedroom with Bo.

"Honey it's only Bo." Austin answered. "Oh so he's not a man?" she replied.

"Yes of course he's a man, but he is our best friend. You are one hundred percent safe with Bo."

"I know, but Austin I won't have anything on my butt." Karen did not want Bo seeing here bare butt.

"Then you will need to keep it under the sheet." That was Austin's only solution to her problem.

"I sure will try Austin." Karen said with little confidence.

They made love twice. After all Bo had told Austin he could have sex with his wife twice a day. Three hours later Bo was knocking on the motel room door. Austin and Karen were just getting out of the shower again.

"Come on in Bo." Austin called out.

"I would, but can't. I don't have a key." Bo just stood at the door and waited for Austin to open it.

"Okay I'm coming." Austin opened the door while still wrapped in his towel.

"I see you got the job done." Bo said as he looked around the room for Karen.

"Yes I sure did." Austin answered.

"Where is Karen?" Bo asked when he didn't see her hiding anywhere.

"She is in the bathroom getting her gown on and she is trying to find a place to dry her panties that you won't see." Both men were laughing when Karen opened the bathroom door to come out, but their laughter stop her right at the door. She was carrying her wet panties in both hands.

"Karen put them here on the heater that way when it comes on it will dry your draws." Bo said.

"Thank you Bo, I will if you won't look at them." Bo looked over at Austin and they both smiled.

"He won't look at them honey so come out." Karen came out dressed in Austin's big undershirt and only that, as she carried her wet panties.

"Honey, give them to me and I will put them way over here. That way Bo, can't see your pretty pink lacy almost panties." Austin said.

"Well he sure doesn't need to see them now. You have already told him everything you could about them, but the size and price of them."

"Oh sweetheart Bo didn't hear one word I said. Did you Bo?" "Austin did you say something?" Bo answered. Both men knew Bo had heard every word Austin and Karen had said about her panties.

Karen just looked at the two men. "Like I believe that," she answered.

"I think I will go and get a shower now that you two are out here." Bo got out his clean boxers. By now Austin was walking around the room in his boxers. Austin turned on the television and he and Karen got back into the bed to watch the program that was just coming on.

When Bo came out of the bathroom he only had on his boxers just like Austin. He didn't think anything about it.

"You are only in your underwear." Karen said to him as he walked across the room.

"Yes Karen I am and you are in your husband's undershirt and do I need to remind you that you don't have any panties on or a bra and even after I bought you those nice pink cotton candy panties."

"No Bo, you did not need to remind me about all of that. I know I don't have any on and as for your pink cotton candy panties Austin has already eaten them." Then Karen reached down and pulled the sheet up higher around her.

Early the next morning Karen woke up with her first day of morning sickness. She had to run to the bathroom. She was so sick. All she could do was throw up. Austin and Bo were both still asleep.

"Bo" Karen cried out several times before she woke him. But as soon as he heard her he woke right up. Austin was still sleeping. "Bo" she called out again. Bo got out of bed and went to see what her problem was now.

"What's wrong Karen?" he asked as he entered the bathroom.

"Bo I'm so sick. I can't stop throwing up." Karen was on the floor in front of the commode. She was half way lying on the cold floor and half way with her head in the commode.

"Karen, how long have you been doing this?" Bo felt so bad for her. She looked so pale.

"About a half of an hour I think." Karen answered in a weak voice.

"Let me get Austin so he can hold on to you. I would do it, but you would want to hurt me for doing it later." Bo left Karen on the bathroom floor and went to wake Austin.

"Austin, wake up. Your wife is sick and she needs you." Bo was shaking Austin on the shoulder to wake him. This made Austin jumped right up.

Austin looked to the other side of their bed. "Where is she?" he asked.

"She is in the bathroom on the floor. You need to go in there and hold her up so she can throw up. I would, but she doesn't have any underwear on and she will want to hurt me for seeing her butt."

"Alright Bo I will go. Thanks. Karen you should have woke me honey." Austin said the second he got into the bathroom.

"Austin I didn't know it was going to last this long." Karen was lying flat on the cold floor now. She looked so small and helpless.

"Bo what's wrong with my wife." Austin felt as helpless as Karen. "Welcome to morning sickness my friend." Bo answered. "Morning, sickness," Austin asked? "I didn't really know that there was such a thing."

"Well there is and you have the proof lying right there in front of you on that cold bathroom floor." Bo answered.

Austin got down on the floor next to Karen. "Austin I'm so sick. I can't hold my head up and I feel awful."

"Honey I know. Bo, do something to help her. I love her too much to just sit here and do nothing while I see how sick she is."

"Austin, all we can do now is to get her some ginger ale and crackers and wait until she feels better."

"Ginger ale and crackers; what kind of medicine is that?" Austin asked.

"Austin you, really don't know anything about women and them being pregnant do you?" Bo asked. He had never given it a thought about his friend not knowing anything at all about women having babies.

"No I don't this is my first time at it you know. All I know about it is from what I learned when you needed my help when you were studying for your test." Austin answered.

"I will go and get the ginger ale and crackers. You sit here with your wife. She will need you. After all she didn't get this way alone. You were the culprit in all of this." Bo told his friend.

"Alright I understand, but hurry." Austin couldn't believe how sick Karen was and it was all because of him. All he could think about was what if he had only hired her to be his surrogate and she had to do all of this and work at the church too.

"Austin I need to throw up again." Karen said. That brought him back to the problem they were facing now, but they were facing it together. Not her doing it all by herself.

He pulled Karen up from the floor to the commode and then she started throwing up all over again. "I'm, sorry Karen, I didn't know that all of this was going to happen, from us just wanting to have a baby. This will be the only one we have. I won't expect you to do this ever again."

"No." was all Karen, had time to say before she was throwing up again.

Bo soon came back with the ginger ale and crackers. "Karen, try to take some of this and eat a couple of these crackers. That should help to calm your stomach some." Bo had been through lots of morning sickness with his patients over the years and he knew there was very little to do that would help.

"Alright Bo I will try." But, all she did after eating a few of the crackers and taking a couple sips of the ginger ale was to throw that up.

"Keep trying Karen honey, after awhile it will stay down." Bo felt as bad as Austin. He did not like seeing a woman he also loved this sick.

"Bo is all of this going to hurt the baby?" Austin asked.

"No, Austin she will not throw the baby up. It's in an altogether different place. I can promise you she will not throw it up. She may wish she could, but she won't ever be able to do it. That was one of the things we learned in doctor's school." Bo answered.

Karen was still sick at check out time. "Bo, go and pay for another day. Karen can't ride home like this." Austin was very upset with himself.

"No, I don't think so, but Austin she could be doing the same thing tomorrow morning." Bo told his friend.

"Are you joking?" Austin could not believe what he was hearing. "No I'm not joking at all. Austin haven't you ever been around a pregnant woman before?

Didn't you learn anything from all the studying we did together while I was in school?"

"No, I guess not, but this baby will be mine and Karen's first and our last. I will never let her get this sick again if I can help it." Austin was very serious.

"Karen, do you feel like trying to get home?" Bo asked.

"Yes Bo I need to get home. Austin, will you get me home?" She asked.

"Yes honey, I will get you home. First we will need to get you dressed." Bo handed Austin Karen's underwear from off of the heater.

"Thanks." Austin said as he laid them on the bed. In less than twenty minutes they were outside and ready to leave.

"Karen if you start to feel sick just let me know and we will stop." Austin didn't know how they were going to do this, but he was getting his wife home. Even if it meant he would need to buy another truck and a trailer to haul his and Bo's motorcycles home.

"Alright, Austin," Karen was leaning on Austin's back. She was still real sick.

"Are you okay honey?" he asked again.

"Yes, Austin I'm doing fine." They didn't go the long way home. They hit the interstate right away. In six hours they were home.

"Bo I guess my biking days are over." Austin said when they were at home and putting away their motorcycles.

"No they are not." Karen answered. "You can just go with Bo and I can stay home. Austin you have given up and changed enough things in your life because of me and you are not giving up your bike riding. I like seeing my tall handsome husband in his biker clothes."

"Austin you hear your wife, she loves you and she wants you to still enjoy your motorcycles." Bo could see why his friend had fallen in love with Karen. If he had met her first he would have done the very same thing he was sure.

That night after they had rested Austin ordered a pizza for their supper. "Karen you said no, when I told you this would be our only baby."

"I know, Austin, I don't want this to be our only baby. I want all eight of our babies." She knew how it felt to never have a sister or brother and she did not want that for her own child even thought her child would have both a loving mother and loving father.

"But Karen you could be sick like you were this morning with all of them." Austin wanted her to know this could happen over and over again.

"I know Austin, but I still want them all." Karen was sitting in Austin's lap in their den.

"Karen did you enjoy the trip?" he asked.

"Yes I did Austin. I have never done that before, but next time, pack me a pair of under panties too." He smiled and then he kissed her. "Honey, I enjoyed my bare butted wife."

"I know I felt your enjoyment all night." she answered.

"Oh, so my wife has a sensitive little back side, and she could tell her husband still wanted her."

"Yes I could and that's why I'm going to let you have me now." she answered.

"Now?" Austin asked.

"Yes now, Mr. Blackburn right now." Karen was now over two months pregnant.

CHAPTER SEVENTEEN

"Bo, when will Karen begin to show?" Austin asked. "Austin every woman is different, but I would guess in the next couple of weeks she will be getting a little puffy." Bo answered.

"Are you, two talking about me as if I'm not here in the same room naked with you two men." Karen was up on the examining table.

"Karen you have a sheet on that covers you all over." Bo answered. "Yes I do, but Bo you looked under the sheet." she answered.

"And so did your husband." Bo answered.

"Yes and I don't know which one of you I want to kill first." she told them both.

"Such talk coming from a mother." Bo teased her. "Are you two enjoying all of this?" she asked.

"Yes, Karen we are and we hope you are enjoying it too." Bo answered.

"Bo, I'm going to have my husband pop you if you don't stop embarrassing me." Karen could already feel her face turning red.

"Honey, I would, but he may want to pop me back." Austin answered.

"Alright then in that case, I will just do it myself." Karen just gave Bo a big kick with her foot.

"Austin your wife just kicked me where it hurts. I may never be able to father any babies, all because of this little foot." Bo had a hold of Karen's foot and he was not letting go of it.

"Austin, make your little friend give me back my foot." Karen told her husband.

"Bo gave Karen back her foot." Austin said.

"Okay I will this time, but the next time you kick me I may not be so sweet to you." Karen then stuck her tongue out at Bo.

"Austin did you just see what your wife did to me?" Bo asked.

"Yes, I did, but I have better things for her to do with that tongue other than stick it out at you." Austin answered.

"Now Austin what are you two talking about?" Karen asked. "Honey you will find out in a minute." Austin answered.

"Karen you can get dressed now. Then after you are dressed you and Austin can go to my office." I will be in there waiting for you.

"Alright Bo anything you say." she answered so sweetly. "Austin, are you staying in here with me?" she asked "Yes I am Karen." he answered.

"Yes he, is Karen, he wants to teach you what to do with that tongue of yours." Bo told her.

Karen didn't bother to answer Bo. She was too busy looking at Austin and he was looking at her. The second Bo closed the door behind him Austin had Karen in his arms kissing her. After he finished he said, "Now do you know what to do with that tongue of yours?"

"Yes, keep it in my own mouth." she answered.

Austin just smiled. "No not exactly." Austin said as he helped Karen off of the table.

"I would ask you to turn around while I'm standing here all naked, but what is the use. You would just find a way to look anyway." she said to him.

"Karen you are getting a little puffy."

"Yes I am Austin, is this the first time you have noticed, it. I am almost three months now. That is twelve weeks." she answered.

"Yes you are. I just can't believe in just six months we will have our baby here." Austin could not believe it all yet.

"Austin, are you still glad you married me?" Karen asked.

"Karen, yes I am and you know it. I'm more and more glad I married you every day. Now get your clothes on before we get into trouble." Karen got her clothes on and they were soon in Bo's office.

"Alright Bo tell us what is going on?" Austin said as soon as they had taken their seats in his office.

"Austin, Karen is perfect." Bo answered.

"Bo, I already knew that for myself." Austin answered.

"Now Karen you need to eat a little more. How is the morning sickness, doing now?" Bo sounded just like a doctor.

"It's almost gone I think Bo." she answered.

"Good I will suggest you and Austin go out shopping this afternoon for you some new clothes. Karen, one of these mornings soon you will not be able to get into your clothes." Bo was sitting behind his big desk. He looked every bit the doctor. "Now I'm putting you down for a sonogram next month and a delivery date of December fifth."

"Austin, our baby will be here before Christmas." Karen said.

"Yes and Karen you and Austin will know next month what you are having. Then you will be able to go out and shop for baby things. Now daddy what do you have to say about all of this?" Austin had not commented at all. Getting a due date made everything so real.

"Austin, are you alright? You haven't said anything." Karen asked. "Yes Karen I am, hearing the date that our baby is due made it so real to me. Karen, are you alright?" he asked.

"Yes Austin I am." They were sitting side by side in front of Bo's big desk.

"Are you both alright? You are both too quiet." Bo wasn't sure if this had all sunk in until just now that they were going to become parents. "Yes Bo we are. It's just a wonderful feeling to know when your baby will be born. It is so real now." Austin kept saying. He got out of his chair and knelt down beside Karen and took her into his arms. "Karen you have made me the happiest man in the world in so many ways."

"Oh Austin you are going to make me cry." She had tears in her eyes already.

"Well honey, I feel like I may cry too." he answered.

"Let me get out of here and let you two be alone for a few minutes." Bo said as he got up from his desk to leave.

"Thank you Bo." Karen was still crying. Austin held her in his arms and kissed her.

"Austin it is real, we are really having a baby and next month we will know if it is a boy or a girl."

"Yes Karen we will." They stayed in Bo's office about five minutes before they came out to the front desk to book Karen's next appointment.

"Mrs. Blackburn the doctor has already made you an appointment for the twentieth of next month and we will do your sonogram then. You just go home and relax. In six months it will all be over." The young woman said.

Austin called his new secretary and told her he would not be back to work today. He told her that he was going shopping for maternity clothes with his wife.

"Austin are you really, really, really happy about our baby and about being married to me?" Karen had to know.

"Yes Karen I sure am." Austin wished Karen would just get used to the fact that they were married and that he was happy being married to her. He had no reason under the sun for not being happy.

On their way to the Mall they had a lot to talk about; and there was something that Karen needed to ask, but she wasn't sure how to do it. "Austin," Karen said in an almost whisper.

"Yes Karen," Austin answered without even looking her way. He was keeping his eyes on the road.

"I think we need to be in church. I have always gone to church." She was playing with her hair as she always did when she had to say something that the other person may not agree with. She didn't want to look over at Austin in case he didn't want to go with her to church.

"Alright we will go to church. Which church do you want us to join?" he asked.

"I don't know which church, but I'm Baptist so I want to go to a Baptist church. Austin what are you?" she asked. She had never thought about asking her husband this before.

"I guess I will be a Baptist with you and our children. We will get Bo to go also. If he is going to be our babies Uncle he will need to be in church just like us." Austin answered.

"Yes Austin we all should go as a family." Karen was happy now. She was going back to church and Austin was going with her and they were even going to ask Bo to join them.

"Austin, are you sure you don't mind?" She wanted to be sure he wasn't just saying yes now and when Sunday came he would change his mind.

"Karen I'm very sure. I don't mind us going to Church at all. I have a lot to be thankful for. God has been very good to me. He has blessed me with a good and loving wife and now we are going to have a baby. I have a wonderful job, good parents which I love and who love me and who would give me their last dime. God gave me the best friend a man could ever want to have, Bo. So you see Karen I have a lot to thank the Lord for even if I forget to do it most of the time. So honey I will be very happy to go to church on Sunday with my big family."

"Austin, that makes me very happy. I could not have ever dreamed of having this life. Austin you make me so happy." Karen wished that her mother was a better persons then she could share her good life with her, but she dared not to let anyone from back home know about her new life with her wonderful rich husband.

Austin drove them to a very nice mall that had a very high end mother's to be shop. The type of shop if Karen had not married Austin she would have never entered. She would not have had a need to go there and shop nor would she have the money even if she had the need.

"Austin Blackburn, what in the world is a bachelor like you doing in this shop?" A tall very nice looking woman asked.

Karen was in the dressing room trying on clothes. When she came out of the dressing room she hurried over to Austin to show him her outfit. She did not really notice that the woman was talking to her husband. She just took it that the woman was there buying clothes like her. "Austin, do you like this outfit?"

"That's what I'm doing here in this shop, Martha. Yes Karen I do like that outfit on you." he answered.

"Who is she one of your friend's daughters?" The woman wanted to be as rude as she could be.

"No Martha, Karen is my wife and we are expecting our first child in early December." This woman could tell that Austin was very happy about becoming a father by the way he had introduced his wife.

"Austin this is a shock to me. When did all of this take place? I didn't even know you were going with anyone. When did you get married? I haven't heard about any wedding or was it a shot gun affair?" Martha asked. She knew that was not a nice thing to say in front of Austin's pregnant wife, but she did not care.

"No it was not." Karen answered.

"No Martha, there is no news here. We have been married for several months. My bride and I decided to forgo the big wedding thing with all of the fuss and bother and just go and get married. We are very happy. Things could not be better for me or my wife." Austin answered.

"Well Austin I am shocked." Martha answered.

"Don't be M'am I'm sure there are other people out there you can talk about; but not us we are very happy and we are married." Karen answered.

"Austin just how old is your wife?" Martha asked as she gave Karen a good looking over.

"Martha my wife's age is none of your business. She, has not asked you about your age has she?" Austin asked. Martha didn't even say good bye, she just walked away.

"Austin who was that woman we upset?" Karen asked.

"Just a women I knew a very long time ago." he answered.

"Did you have sex with her? No don't tell me, I don't want to know." She was already regretting asking Austin such a question.

"No Karen I did not." he answered. "So you can just forget about her. I did a long time ago."

"Austin I should not have asked you that question. I just don't know what is wrong with me lately. I want to cry all the time and I want to hit all those tall beautiful women you dated. Lately I just can't do anything right it seems." Karen was in Austin's arms.

"Honey you do everything right. I love you, but we will ask Bo about all of it. He will know if it has something to do with you being pregnant." Austin sure hoped so and that it would end soon. He had noticed how upset the least little thing made her and he didn't want her to feel upset so much.

That night Bo did not go over for supper. He decided to let them have that whole night to themselves, but he did go over the next night.

"Bo, Karen is having some trouble with her moods. She isn't herself sometimes." Austin was trying to put it in a very nice way. He did not want to upset her now by asking Bo about it.

"Oh that's nothing to worry about. It's only her hormones. They will settle down soon and she will be our sweet little Karen once again. She will be a nice sweet Karen who would never think about kicking her doctor." Bo smiled over at Karen.

"No, the old Karen would have never kicked you, but the old Karen was never pregnant either." she answered.

"Now Miss Kicker that's all Austin's fault and not mine. So why haven't you kicked him." Bo said as he was helping Austin to get the food on the table.

"I can't kick my husband for getting me pregnant. I wanted to be pregnant as much as he wanted me to be pregnant, so Bo you are the only one I can kick." Karen saw nothing wrong with her giving Bo a little kick every now and then when she felt like it.

"Okay Karen, but only as long as you are pregnant. The second I pull that baby out of your cootchie, you can't kick me anymore." Bo told her.

Karen walked over to the table and sat down in Austin lap. "Bo my wife is having eight babies so you will have seven more to go. And that could mean again next year she would be pregnant and kicking you again."

"Oh no, not again next year, please don't tell me that now." Bo joked.

CHAPTER EIGHTEEN

A ustin was now getting used to his new (old) secretary. He found that she always got all of her work done and still had time to do a little extra. Karen liked her too. After all she helped Austin to pick her.

Austin was still getting Karen to go with him to his office several days a week, but the days he was going to be out of the office she would stay home and do her house work and cooking. Austin and Karen were as happy as any two married people had ever been.

It was four months after Karen had called the church about her last pay check before she had any response. In fact she had forgotten all about it. It was Tuesday and Karen was at home alone. Austin was going to be out of his office most of the day and Karen had stayed home, she was going to do their wash and give their house a good spring cleaning just like her grandma did every spring back in Georgia. She even had her supper already cooking. Austin had just called and told her he was on his way home. That made Karen very happy. She had missed him all day.

When the door bell rang Karen thought maybe it was Bo coming over for supper a little early. She didn't give it much more thought, but just before she opened the door she decided to check through the peephole and see who it really was before she opened the door. It was none other than the good Reverend St. Johns in person. Now Karen wished she had not started to unlock the door before she checked to see who was at her front door. She was sure that the Reverend St. Johns knew she was there now. He had to have heard the lock click twice.

Karen took a deep breath and asked God to please send Austin home and in a hurry. Then she opened the door. Her hands were already shaking. "Good afternoon Reverend St. Johns I'm surprised to see you at my front door." She was trying very hard to be strong.

"Don't you mean the man's front door that you live with Karen?" he asked in his ugly voice.

"Yes it's his front door as well." Karen was still standing in the doorway. She had not moved.

"Aren't you going to invite me into your house?" The good Reverend asked.

"Don't you mean into the man's house I live with Reverend?" Karen was not giving in to his rudeness.

"Alright then Karen, aren't you going to invite me into his house?" the Reverend asked.

The Reverend had stopped staring at Karen. She had a big loose apron on and he could not see her stomach. "Yes come in. I'm very busy getting our supper ready so I don't have a lot of time to waste." Karen stepped aside so the Reverend could walk past her into the house.

"I can see that everything is nice, real nice and expensive. I knew he had to be rich with that little sports car and the clothes he wore." The Reverend was not in a good mood at all. He did not like losing Karen to this man.

"Reverend St. Johns why are you here?" Karen wanted him to go. She did not want him anywhere near her.

Austin was making his way through heavy traffic. He had decided to put his red Ferrari in the garage and drive his truck to work on Wednesday. That meant he had to go down one block and back up the alleyway to get to their house and garage.

Karen was a nervous wreck. She did not know what to do. She was still praying that Austin would get home soon. The good Reverend was making her very nervous. "Rev. St. Johns would you like to have a seat in the living room?" she asked. She hoped he would say what he had to say to her and leave.

"Yes that would be nice." he answered. Karen led him into their formal living room. The Reverend took his seat, but before he had hardly sat down on the sofa Karen could tell he was up to his old tricks and she was not going to be led into them. "Now Karen you come over here and kneel by me and let me pray for your lost soul."

"Reverend St. Johns why are you here?" Karen asked. She was trying to stay as far away from the good Reverend as she possible could get.

"I came all this way to bring you your last paycheck. I would think you would be more grateful than you are." he answered.

"Reverend St. Johns that was four months ago. I have already given up on getting that check." Karen kept her hands in the pockets of her apron so she could hold the apron out away from her stomach. She did not want the good Reverend to see that she was pregnant.

"Karen you played a good game while you worked at my church and to think all along you had been sleeping with this man. I guess money is what made you jump into his bed. Now I want my share." He was watching her very close now and he was ready to make his move.

The good Reverend was on Karen so fast all she had time to do was to start screaming at the top of her voice. Austin was coming up the basement steps right at that time. He opened the door and ran in the direction of Karen's scream. He reached the living room just as the Reverend pulled Karen's apron off of her.

"You are pregnant!" he said.

Austin was right there. He took hold of the Reverend and pulled him off of his wife. Then he gave the good Reverend a hard hit to his jaw with his fist knocking him to the floor. "Yes my wife is pregnant. Now you get the hell out of my house. You have not heard the last of me." Austin was so angry.

Karen was crying. "Honey, don't cry he will never come near you again." Austin was trying very hard to comfort his wife.

"She's your wife?" the Reverend St. Johns asked.

"Yes and she has been my wife for almost five months. Now you get out of here before I call the police." Austin wanted to hit the Reverend again.

The Reverend St. Johns hurried out the front door. He left Karen's check on one of the little tables he passed on his way out of the front door.

"Karen honey, are you alright?" Austin was holding his wife in his arms.

"I am now, but I was so scared. It was like being at the church when I worked for him all over again. He was coming after me." Karen thought that the Reverend was going to win this time because she would not have been able to get away from him.

"I know honey I heard what he was saying. I came up from the basement and I heard you scream. It scared me so much I started running until I found you. I never expected him to be here in our house." It was as such of a shock to Austin as it had been to Karen.

"I know, now I wished I had not let him into our house." Karen was still shaking.

"It's alright Karen. He needed to find out the hard way, that you are not his. If he ever shows up here again Karen you call the police right away." Austin did not want Karen to see how much he hated the good Reverend.

"Yes Austin I will." Karen was even more afraid of the good Reverend now than she was during the time she worked at the Church for him. "Karen I think, I just saw your stomach move." Austin said as he watched to see if it would move again.

"Yes you did. I felt it moving." she answered.

Austin already had his hand on her stomach waiting for it to move again. "Tomorrow is the big day." he replied.

"Yes it is Austin. Are you ready to hear what we are having?" Karen had forgotten all about the good Reverend as soon as they began to talk about their baby.

"Yes Karen I am. I have never been more ready for anything in my life except for you." Austin was all smiles.

"Austin do you want a boy or a girl?" she asked.

"Karen I don't really care as long as it is healthy and it's ours." Austin was telling her the truth. He didn't really care. He would be just as happy with either a girl or boy.

"Oh Austin I am so glad we are married and I'm not just having my baby and giving it up to you and never getting to see it or you ever again. I don't think I would have been able to have done that even for you."

"Karen you were always going to be my wife. Like I told you before, the second I saw you, I knew I was never going to let you go. Now do you have supper ready? Bo will be here soon. Karen, when did I change from having dinner at night to having supper?" he asked.

"I don't know Austin, because I have only cooked dinner at twelve noon and I have always cooked supper at night. So I don't know what happened to your dinner at night, but if I find it I will sure let you know." she answered.

"Mrs. Blackburn you know that you changed all of that for me. Our children will be having supper at night just like their Mama and Daddy."

Bo came over as soon as he got home. He did not want to miss out on any of Karen meals if he didn't have a reason to miss them. "Bo, do you eat dinner at night or at noon?" Karen wanted to know if Bo was more like her or more like Austin.

"Karen I was raised to eat supper at night and dinner at noon." he answered.

"Thank you Bo, Austin seems to have lost his dinner. He said since I've been married to him I have made supper at night and dinner at noon and he doesn't have any idea where his dinner at night went." Karen sounded so serious.

"Yes that is right Karen. We Southerners know that because our mama's always said don't be late for supper tonight. Not one time did I ever hear my Mama say don't be late for dinner tonight Bo. If she had I would not have gotten back home until the next day at noon." Bo answered.

"See Austin I had nothing to do with you losing your dinner. It was lost all the time. You have just been eating it at the wrong time of the day all these years." Karen gave her husband a big smile.

"You are so right honey. I'm so glad you came along and saved me." Austin answered.

"Now that we have truly blown Austin's mind over his lost dinner, let's eat some supper. Karen it all looks and smells so good. What is it?" Bo asked.

"It's hot chicken salad and pound cake Bo." she answered. "You made a cake?" Bo asked.

"Yes Bo I made a cake." Karen smiled over at him when she answered.

"Karen, if you, knew how to make a cake all this time why did it take you so long to make us one?" Bo loved sweets.

"Because Bo, up until now it was not Austin's birthday. So I had no reason to make a cake. When is your birthday Bo?" she asked.

"My birthday is not until September. Does that mean we won't have another cake until September?" He wanted to know.

"No, but I would wait until I had tasted this cake before I go wanting more if I were you." Karen answered.

"Karen honey it smells wonderful. My wife surprised me again." Austin said as he got ready to go to the table.

"Happy Birthday, Austin I love you. I wanted to have something nice, but I don't know how to cook nice food like you used to eat all the time." Karen had everything on the table. She had put a pretty light blue table cloth on the table with matching napkins. Everything looked great.

"Karen it couldn't be any nicer. I'm a lucky man." Austin was so happy. He never expected to have all of this on his birthday and it all done by his young wife.

"Oh Austin, after this afternoon I'm surprised that you still want me." Karen was still very much upset.

"What happened this afternoon?" Bo and Austin were now sitting at the table.

"Bo, Karen's old boss showed up here this afternoon with her last paycheck. He said he came to get what I had been getting from Karen all these months. I came into the house from the basement and I heard Karen screaming. So of course I came running only to find the good Reverend trying to rape my wife." Bo could tell that his friend was still upset along with his wife.

"What! Did you call the police?" Bo had never heard of a pastor doing such a thing before.

"No, Bo we didn't, but I told him to never come near my wife again. He was quite shocked at that statement and the fact that Karen was pregnant." Austin's voice and the expression on his face told how he felt about the good Reverend.

"Why had he waited so long to bring or even to send Karen her last paycheck?" Bo didn't understand any of this.

"Bo he never gave me a reason why. He just said he wanted what I was giving Austin." Karen had never disliked anyone as much as she disliked the good Reverend.

Bo was shocked that any pastor would ever act in that manner. All of the men of God back in his home town were well respected by their community no matter what denomination they were. They had earned that respect by respecting others and by treating the people in the way God intended them to do.

"Bo you have to remember even preachers are human and sometimes they even fall from grace." Austin said.

"Austin he would have been falling from a lot more than just grace if he had tried that with my wife. You are a lot better man than me. Karen I know it upset you, but don't you worry about that man he will never get near you as long as Austin and I are here we will protect you.

You are very important to me and I won't let you get hurt." Bo was upset too.

"Oh Bo that is so sweet, but I may still need to kick you anyway. Now let's eat." Karen said as she took her place at the table.

They had another great supper that night. They were like a little family. Bo and Austin were still as close as they had been before Karen came into their lives, but now they had her and she made both men happy in their own way.

"Austin your wife sure cooks great. Are you sure you won't share her with me?" Bo winked over at Karen.

"Yes Bo I'm very sure I won't be doing that with anyone including you. Karen have you seen any woman in church we could get Bo married off to without too much trouble? I need him to have his own wife as soon as possible." Austin said.

"No, but I haven't been really looking for him a wife. He seemed pleased at just sharing your wife with you Austin." Karen turned around to Bo. "Bo do you really want a wife or are you just joking? If you really want a wife we will go out one Sunday after church and get you one from off of one of those corners where those working girls hang out. Do you have twenty dollars?" she asked. They were all three cleaning off the table and putting the food away.

"Thanks a million Karen. I didn't know you cared so much for me. But all joking aside, Karen if I could find a woman exactly like you I would marry her just as fast as my friend married you." Bo was serious.

"Would you really Bo?" Karen asked.

"Yes I would Karen I honestly would. You have made my friend here into the happiest man I know and even though we thought we both were already pretty happy you have managed to make us even happier. I want that same exact happiness for myself. So do you have someone hidden away for me?" Bo asked.

"No not yet. But I will start looking. I want you as happy as Austin and me. Bo I love Austin so much and I'm sure there is some woman out there that would love you just as much." Bo put his arms around Karen and held her close to him. He even gave her a little kiss on her cheek.

"Bo, now don't you be forgetting that's my wife you have in your arms and that you are kissing. I'm still standing near enough to you to give you a good pop if I need to." Austin said.

"I won't forget because you won't let me and she won't let me forget either. Between the two of you I can't forget it for a second no matter how hard I try." Bo had that playful smile on his face.

"Bo tomorrow is Karen's appointment and you will do the sonogram on her." Austin was getting excited.

"Yes that's right. It has been a month already. I bet you two are excited. I know I am. Funny how all this has affected my life so much as well. I guess when you care about two people as much as I care about you two it will do that to you every time."

"Yes Bo it will. Just wait until it's your baby you are waiting to come into this world." Austin answered.

"Austin I would love to be doing what you are doing right now." Bo answered.

"You mean sleeping with Karen?" Austin asked.

"Why yes Austin. What else are friends for? However this time I was thinking more on the lines of having a family of my own. I see how all of it has changed you and how you look forward to getting home at night just so you can be with Karen."

"Yes Bo you are right I can't wait to get home at night now. Just knowing Karen is here waiting for me makes every second that I'm away seem longer. Bo my friend you need a wife. I can tell you they are a very good thing for a man to have around the house." Austin answered.

"So you think I'm a thing?" Karen asked.

"No sweetheart you are my, everything." Austin gave Karen a little kiss.

"Karen, are you worried about tomorrow?" Bo asked.

"No, I'm just excited about it." she answered with a big smile. "Karen I haven't had time to tell you how cute you look in your little maternity clothes. You look almost as cute as you looked in Austin's undershirt."

"Thank you Bo they are a lot more comfortable than my other clothes. Bo you need to forget how I looked back then, but on the other hand maybe you both need to remember how I looked then because I will never look that way again."

"No Karen we aren't worried about you not looking that good again. We know you will be looking even better after your have our baby. Bo answered.

"Yes Bo I know she will. But she looks great now even though she needs these new kind of clothes. The other day she was still trying to wear her old jeans, but she could not fasten them around her waist. So she left the zipper unzipped. She tried very hard, but they would just not stay up. I found my wife standing here in our kitchen with her jeans around her ankles."

"Karen Blackburn is that anyway for you to be in the kitchen when you are cooking our meals? Which one of us were you waiting for?" Bo asked.

"Now Bo, I was not waiting for any one and least of all you. I was just in the kitchen working. I didn't expect my jeans to fall all the way off of me. I thought they would stay up." Karen's face had turned a little red.

"So your husband came into the kitchen and found his beautiful young wife ready for him?" Bo was giving Karen a hard time.

"No he did not. I wasn't ready for anything. I was working. They just fell off, that, is all. Is that all you two men ever think about?" she asked.

"Karen we used to not think so much about it at all. You are the one who has put it on our minds so much now." Bo answered.

"Bo, I'm not supposed to put it on your mind at all. So just get it out of your mind right now. Do you hear me? I'm not yours; I'm married to Austin and only Austin. This is no joint deal. There is only two people in our marriage do you understand that Bo Brooks?" Karen was still getting all red in the face.

"Austin isn't she something when she gets so upset." Bo was grinning from ear to ear.

"Yes she is Bo, but I won't be able to save you if she decides to kill you for teasing her so much." Austin answered.

Karen stomped her foot and walked out of the kitchen. She did not know how she would ever win when these two men were together.

"Austin I guess you won't be getting your birthday gift tonight." Bo said as he and Austin watched the door of the kitchen to see if she was coming back.

"Well let's just clean up the kitchen and maybe she will have changed her mind by bed time." Austin answered. The two men got busy and got the kitchen as clean as Karen would have done it.

"I heard you Bo and you don't know what you are talking about. I got a pretty gown to wear tonight for Austin's birthday. So now Mister what do you have to say about that?" Karen asked as she waited for the two men to come strolling out of the kitchen.

"See Austin you are still getting your birthday present after all." Bo was smiling over at Karen.

"Honey you won't need to put on your pretty gown tonight to make me happy." Austin answered.

Karen was sitting in Austin's big chair in the den just waiting for him to show up. She could see and hear everything the two men were saying and doing in the kitchen.

"Karen how did you make this pound cake have such a hard crust on top? Bo asked.

"Bo I was just lucky. Just like Austin will be tonight, but not you." she answered.

See Austin she is just rubbing it in more and more. She knows I will go home all by myself and get into my big bed all by myself, but does she care? No not one little bit." Bo gave Karen a sad look. "Karen"

"Yes Bo." she answered.

"Did I tell you about the cameras I have in my examine rooms. It makes a very good close up of my patients'—." Before Bo could finish telling Karen his lie she was in the kitchen.

"What did you say?" she asked with both of her hands on her hips.

"I said did I tell you about my cameras?" Bo was not backing down. He had her going and he loved every bit of it.

"No! You did not. Austin did you hear what your little best friend just said? He has made pictures of my cootchie. What are you going to do to him?" she asked.

"Yes honey I heard it all and he is lying to you. There can't be any cameras in those examine rooms." Austin answered.

"Are you very sure Austin?" Karen was looking from Austin to Bo and aback again.

"Yes Karen I'm very sure. Bo, tell her before she kills both of us." Austin said.

"Karen I was just joking with you. I was just seeing what you would say and what you would do." Bo was laughing at her.

"Well Bo I will just show you." Karen pulled out the water sprayer from the kitchen sink and sprayed Bo all over.

Bo stood there soaking wet. "Karen did you enjoy doing that to me?" he asked.

"Yes Bo I did." she answered.

I also enjoyed doing something." Bo answered and then he smiled down at her.

"What did you enjoy doing, Bo?" Karen asked.

"I enjoyed examining you last month." Bo said with a big smile on his face. That just made Karen even madder.

"Austin, do something with him. He isn't supposed to say things like that. He isn't supposed to enjoy examining me. Now I won't ever go back to any doctors." Karen was almost in tears.

"Karen, don't say that honey. You will need Bo." Austin answered. "Austin he looked." she answered.

"Yes Karen he did, but someone was bound to do that sooner or later. Bo is your doctor and that is his job." Austin didn't know what else to say.

"Yes, but he said he was not going to look. And he did." She was still upset.

"I lied to you Karen." Bo answered.

"Bo, don't go and make her any madder than she is already. I have to live with her and it is my birthday and I have not gotten my present yet." Austin pleaded with his friend.

"Oh Karen I didn't see anything I promise you." Bo was already trying to make up with Karen.

"Bo, I don't believe you now. How am I ever going to have a baby now?" she asked.

"Karen, I'm your doctor and I'm also yours and Austin's best friend, but if you want some other doctor I will understand." Bo felt so bad about upsetting Karen now.

"No I don't want another doctor. Do you think I want every doctor in New York City looking at my cootchie? No you have already looked so you will have to be my doctor, but I don't want to hear anything about it. Do you two big boys understand me?" She had her hands on her hips again.

"Yes Mama we do." They both answered.

"Does this mean my friend Austin will still get his birthday present tonight?" Bo asked.

"Yes Bo yes and tomorrow night too. Are you happy?" Karen asked.

"No I'm not, but I'm sure Austin is real happy and that's all that counts to you. Don't forget tomorrow we will find out what we are going to be having."

"Yes Bo we will." she answered.

"What do you want us to have Bo?" Karen asked him.

"Oh Karen I just want a big twelve pound baby. How about you Karen what do you want?" Bo asked.

"Are you trying to be funny?" Karen asked? She was not happy with the thought of having a twelve pound baby.

"Yes he is Karen. He will not let my wife have a twelve pound baby or I will put the hurt on him myself." Austin answered.

"Karen I will not let you have a twelve pound baby. That may hurt just a little." Bo said as he gave her another big smile.

"That may hurt? You know as well as I do that it will hurt whether I have a twelve pound baby or a five pounder." Karen knew Bo was still trying to upset her.

"Karen I'm not going to let you hurt, don't you know that by now?" Bo answered.

"Yes I do Bo, Austin won't let you. Will you Austin?" Karen said as she smiled up at her husband.

Austin had his arms around Karen. "No sweetheart I won't let him let you hurt."

The three of them went into the den and watched television for awhile. Karen sat in Austin's lap the whole time. She gave Bo a few mean looks all during the rest of the evening.

"Bo tomorrow we will know what we are having won't we?" Karen asked after she had cooled down some.

"Yes Karen we will and if I can't see what sex it is we will do it again later." He wanted to make Karen happy again.

"Again, when?" she quickly asked.

"In just awhile after you move around some. That usually will make the baby move into a different position. That helps us to see if it's a boy or a girl. Bo explained.

"How do you know if it's a boy or if it's a girl?" Karen asked.

Bo looked over at Austin. "Karen are you serious you don't know how I can tell if it's a girl or boy?" he asked.

"Yes I'm serious as I can be." she answered.

"Austin I think you need to explain the birds and the bees to your wife before bed time tonight."

"Karen, Bo can tell if it's a boy by his winky." Austin answered. "And if it's not a boy there won't be a winky."

"Oh will he have one of those already?" she asked.

"Yes Karen if it's a boy, but not if it's a girl like Austin said." Bo answered.

"Alright I just didn't know our baby would have all those parts already. I do know the difference between a male and a female. I knew right away Austin was no girl and when he took off his clothes I was very sure I was right." She answered.

"Good I was very worried about old Austin." Bo said.

"Well Bo you need to stop worrying about Austin and start worrying about yourself." Karen said as she still sat in her husband's lap.

"Why should I worry about myself? I know what I am. I have a winky just like Austin." Bo answered.

"Bo I was not talking about your little winky." Karen answered.

Bo was sitting in the big chair on the other side of Austin with a table and lamp in between them. He could see Karen very well.

"Austin I said I had a winky just like yours and your wife called my winky little. She must have been peeping at me."

Karen sat straight up in Austin's lap. "No I have not. Austin, tell him I have not ever peeped at his little winky."

"Karen Bo knows you have not seen his winky. Bo she has hardly seen my winky let alone looked at yours." Austin had his arms around Karen holding her into the chair.

"Austin that's not funny. Look at me I'm pregnant with your baby and you are telling Bo I haven't ever seen your winky. I have many times, you just didn't know it." she answered.

"Karen it is alright for you to see my winky. I think I have seen all of you and that's how it is supposed to be. Honey I love you and I want us to know each other inside and out."

Karen had her arms around Austin's neck now. "Austin I love you more every day." And then she turned to Bo, "Bo, I'm sorry I don't know if your winky is small or not, but if it's like Austin's then it's perfect."

"Well thank you Karen I have never had such a compliment before in my life." he answered.

"You are welcome Bo." Karen smiled at Bo and then she kissed Austin. Bo soon went home and Karen and Austin went upstairs to their bedroom.

"Karen, do you want to take a shower with me tonight. I will let you see my winky." Austin teased.

Karen was getting out their clean underwear and she was going to turn down their bed. "Austin I have seen your winky before so you won't be showing me anything I haven't already seen. I'm your wife, I will shower with you and I will look again."

"I'm glad my wife will be looking, because I sure will be looking at her." he answered.

"Austin I'm not thin anymore. I'm fat now." Austin could tell this was bothering Karen a lot.

"No you are not fat Karen you are pregnant and that makes me very happy. I just wish my parents would get home before their grandbaby arrives. It would be nice if I could introduce my new wife to them."

Karen got her clothes off and got into the shower with Austin. "Austin what if your parents don't like me?"

"Karen they will love you and if they don't I will take time to check and see if those people are my real parents. Because I know my parents will love you because I love you. So stop worrying so much."

After their shower they went straight to bed. "Karen, what in the world, are you doing? Austin could see that she was really working on something.

"Austin I'm putting this pillow near my stomach so our baby will have a pillow to lie on." she answered.

Austin was near the middle of the bed right next to her. Karen placed the little pillow where she wanted it and then she laid back down.

"Karen I don't think the baby knows about pillows yet." Austin said as he watched to see what else she may do.

"He does now." she answered. "He?" Austin asked.

"Yes he does know now." Karen answered. her.

"Karen do you think it's a boy that we are having?" he asked.

"Yes I do Austin, because I ordered a boy." Austin just laughed.

"So what are we going to name this boy?" he asked.

Karen was lying in Austin's arms she had her hands up on her stomach. "I don't know, maybe we will name him after his Daddy." "What do you want to name him Austin Jr.?" This took Austin off guard. He had not given it one thought about them naming their baby after him if it turned out to be a boy.

"Yes that's the name of his Daddy isn't it?" she answered.

"Yes we know that for sure. So you want him to be named after me." Austin felt so loved by this young woman that was his wife.

"Yes Austin I do, don't you?" she asked.

"Well yes. I do if it's a boy. I think every man wants a son named after him." Austin remarked.

"Well I can tell you it's going to be a boy. You just wait and see if I'm not right. He will be a big boy just like his Daddy. Sweet, loving, generous and caring making his parents glad he is their son." Karen was rubbing her stomach as she talked.

"Karen if it's a girl will you be disappointed?" he asked.

"No because it's a boy. I won't need to be disappointed." she answered while still rubbing her stomach.

"Okay Mrs. Blackburn, I hope you are right. Now I want my birthday present." Austin turned over to face his wife.

The next morning they didn't need to get up so early. They had time to make love again before getting into the shower. Karen made them breakfast and by their appointment time they were waiting anxiously at Bo's office for their name to be called.

Bo came out into the waiting room dressed in his white doctor's coat. He was a very tall good looking man standing just a hair shorter than Austin. Austin's hair was very dark and Bo's was a medium brown with sun highlights all through it. He was a good looking southern man.

"Karen, are you ready?" Bo asked. She and Austin were sitting on a little love seat sofa.

"Yes I'm ready Bo. Austin, are you ready?' Austin just gave her a smile and helped her up off the sofa and then they went into the back with Bo.

"Karen all we need to do today is to check your stomach and do the sonogram. You won't need to take anything off. Just get up here and raise your top high enough for me to see. Austin can pull your pants down some, just enough so, I can put this cold jelly all over your stomach and then we will see what you have in there." Bo knew they both had to be a little nervous.

"Bo, you will see he has a little winky just like you and his Daddy." Karen said then she let Austin pull her jeans down some for Bo.

"So Karen you think it's a boy?" Bo rubbed Karen's stomach with the jelly before he started the test; because he was sure after all he was going to be this child's only uncle.

"Karen you and Austin watch the screen. See there is your baby. Right there and now let see what it is."

"Austin there he is. He doesn't look like anyone in my family I know so Austin he must take after your family." Karen said as she watched the screen.

"Karen's right he does take after your side of the family." Bo answered.

"What?" Austin still could not believe it.

"Austin you have a son. There is his little winky right there and that's his long legs. There is no doubt about it you have a son. Karen, how do you feel?" Bo was as happy as Austin.

"Happy." That was all that Karen could say at that time. Bo could tell she was going to cry. Today he didn't want to upset her anymore than necessary.

"I will make a few pictures for you of your son. That way you can have one for your desk at work Austin and Karen can have one at home and of course Uncle Bo will want one. We will make the proud Grandparents one we can't leave them out." Bo knew Austin's parent would go crazy over their grandchild.

"Thank you, I think I'm still in shock. I'm going to be a father to a son." Austin was beside himself.

"Yes Austin you sure are. In less than five months you will be carrying this big boy around yourself and giving Karen a well deserved brake." Bo was still checking the screen to see if there was anything he should be concerned about.

"I will be glad to do that Bo." Austin turned right back around to check on Karen. "Honey, are you alright?" he asked.

"Yes Austin I am. Now do I get up from here?" Karen asked?

"Yes, but let me wipe some of this jell off of your stomach first. Austin would you like to get it off from down there?" Bo point to the lower part of Karen stomach.

"Yes Bo I will be glad to get it from way down there." Bo smiled over at Austin.

"Karen you do know I see a lot of big stomachs in here." Bo asked.

"Yes Bo I do know that, but that's not all stomach down there. And I still can see over my stomach right now and I can see you Bo." She answered.

"Yes Karen you can see over it for right now, but next month will be an altogether different story. Now I need to feel your stomach and see how your son is doing." Bo was now pushing around on Karen stomach.

"He is doing fine." she answered.

"Now Karen you be still and let me be the doctor here. I want to be the one to give you all the good news. Yes he is fine Karen. Now you can go back shopping and get all the boy things you want. Austin, are you going to take Karen out to lunch and then go shopping? You did come in your truck today didn't you?"

"Yes we did Bo. We wanted to be prepared." Austin said as he finished wiping the last of the jelly, off the bottom of Karen's stomach.

"Good. She is ready to go. Karen, check at the desk for your next appoint. It will be your last monthly appointment. You will need to come back every two weeks for awhile. Then it goes to every week until your son is born." Bo was being a doctor again.

Austin was dressed in jeans and a nice pull over knit shirt with a collar. Karen had on her jeans and a white top. They looked like a model couple.

"Bo, don't you forget supper tonight." Karen reminded him.

"Yes Karen I will be there, after all we still have cake." he answered.

"Yes we do Bo and when it's your birthday we will have a cake again." Austin helped Karen off the table.

"See Austin you were right she can be a good little girl when she wants to be." Bo said.

"Yes I know Bo. She can be a very good girl." Austin answered.

"What are you two saying now?" Karen asked.

"Nothing sweetheart," Austin answered. Then Austin and Bo smiled at each other.

"I hope the other seven are all girls so I won't always be out numbered." Karen said as Austin helped to get her pants back into place.

"No, you don't. We need a few boys mixed in there with our girls." Austin answered.

"Then you two big boys need to start being a whole lot better or I will be ordering only girls from now on." Karen sounded very serious to Austin.

"Bo Karen can't do that can she? Austin had a worried look on his face. He could already see himself and little Austin Junior living in a house full of little Karens."

"Maybe, some scientists, say a woman can decide which she wants a boy or a girl by the food she eats and a lot of other things. So Austin it would be in your best interest to talk her out of having seven girls if you can." Bo wanted to laugh, but his friend was very serious and he knew it.

"Bo I can tell you right now I will be trying to sweet talk her out of the rest of our children being all girls. My son and I won't stand a chance. He will always be at all of his sisters' mercy."

"Yes he will and Karen will be right there helping your girls." Bo answered.

Karen finished pulling her top down over her stomach and picked up her purse and was ready to leave the little room. She wanted to leave Austin and Bo standing there. However before she was able to get out of the door Bo had one more thing he wanted to ask her.

"Karen when it's my birthday will I get the same present that Austin got last night?"

"I don't know Bo do you have twenty dollars to pay the girl from the corner yet?" Karen answered.

Austin and Bo followed Karen out front to the appointment desk. "Margo, would you please be sure you give Mrs. Blackburn an early afternoon appointment. She will always need to get here in time to get back home before it's too late for her to cook supper for Austin and myself." All the time he was talking Bo never even looked Margo's way.

"Yes Dr. Brooks whatever you say. Mrs. Blackburn, will one thirty be good for you or will that be too late for you to get your meal cooked?" Margo asked.

"Yes that's fine. I can always put supper in the slow cooker." Karen answered.

"Yes you can. After all women always have more than one job to do don't we?" Margo answered as she put Karen's information into the computer.

"Margo Wilson, are you married?" Karen had not seen a ring on Margo's hand.

"No M'am I'm not. I have never been married. Why?" she asked. "I was just wondering. Do you have a boyfriend?" Karen wanted to know if this sweet girl was available.

"No M'am I don't. I've only been here in New York for six months and I don't trust a lot of people yet." Margo was another shy girl like Karen.

"I know how you feel. Where are you from?" Karen asked.

"Ohio, my daddy is from there. My mother died four years ago and I lived with my grandparents up until I came here. My Dad is in the Navy and he is gone a lot out to sea."

"How old are you?" Karen hoped Margo didn't think she was being too noisy.

"I'm twenty two. I got out of school and went to community college for two years and then I worked at a doctor's office in my grandparent's home town for two years. One day I decided I needed to come here, so here I am." Margo had not stopped working the whole time she was talking with Karen.

"Oh you are so right you did need to come here and I know why." Karen answered.

Margo was a little older than Karen, but they were about the same height and weight. That is if Karen was not pregnant.

"Margo, would you call me one night. I have a real nice man I would love for you to meet." Karen hoped this would not scare Margo away.

"Sure Mrs. Blackburn I will call you. I would love to meet a nice man. A person can get real lonely living here when they don't know anyone."

Bo and Austin did not hear Karen's conversation with Margo. Margo had only been working at Bo's office for five months, but he didn't know her, she thought. Bo's office manager had hired Margo, after the last girl had quit, to get married and move away with her new husband.

Margo was a pretty light brown haired girl with blue eyes. She was also short like Karen. She was five foot one inch tall. Karen felt with all of her heart that this was the perfect person for Bo.

"Karen, are you ready." Austin asked as soon as he and Bo had finished talking.

"Yes Austin I am now." Bo kissed Karen on her cheek. "Bo you hurry over tonight. I want to show you our new baby bed."

"Karen I didn't know you already had your baby bed?" Bo answered.

"We don't yet, but we will by tonight." she answered.

"Austin I guess you are going shopping. Did you drive your truck again today?"

"Yes Bo I did. I have learned to do that every time Karen and I come to the doctor. Her doctor is always telling her to go and shop for something. He must be going to help support her shopping habit that he has helped her to acquire."

Austin and Karen left Bo's office to go and buy a baby bed and a rocking chair. Next month it would be something else Bo will tell Karen she and their son will need. Austin was very sure so he will be driving their truck again to Karen's next doctor's appointment.

CHAPTER NINETEEN

"Karen there must be a hundred beds in this room. How do we decide which bed will be the best for our baby?" Austin asked.

"Austin we will ask which beds are the best and then we will chose one of them." Karen didn't know anymore about buying a baby bed than Austin.

A salesperson soon came over to give them some assistance. "Hello may I help you?" she asked.

"Yes you may. My wife and I need to purchase a baby bed and we want a good one not a piece of junk. We want a well built bed that will last for more than just one baby." Austin was sure the saleslady had heard this story before.

The saleslady could already tell this man was used to only the very best. "Yes sir I understand completely. Is this your first baby?" she asked.

"Yes and we are going to have eight. So you understand our need for the best bed." Austin answered.

"Goodness you sure will need a good strong bed." The saleslady could see how handsome Austin was and thought the woman is very smart to keep his interest at home where it belongs. She also could tell that this man would want the best bed they had even if this was going to be his and wife's only child. He just looked the type who demanded the very best of everything every time.

"M'am we are having a boy this time, but I want a bed that will work for both girls and boys. I'm sure we will be doing it again next year." Karen added.

"Yes I'm very sure you will." The saleslady said. She had no doubt at all what Karen had said would be true.

"Austin isn't that the same woman we saw at the Mothers to be Shop last month over there looking at those beds?" Karen had hoped that she would never see that woman again, but here she was again.

Austin turned in the direction Karen was looking. He wanted to see who Karen was talking about. "Yes it is Honey."

"Austin, why don't you go over and speak to her. I hate for your friends to think I'm causing you not to be their friend anymore."

"Alright Karen I will go, but only because you want me to go." Austin left Karen with the saleslady and he walked as slow as he could over to Martha. Hoping all the while she would leave before he got over to her, but of course she did not.

"Hello Martha, are you getting a baby bed today also? My wife and I are here shopping for our baby bed." Austin was there, but his heart was not in to it. He had rather be over with Karen looking at their baby's bed.

"Well hello Austin I'm surprised you came over here to speak with me at all. Where is your child bride?" she asked.

"She is over there looking at a bed like I said before. She sent me over here to apologize to you for being so rude to you the last time we met."

"Yes Austin, you were rude, but I can understand why. After all you have been living with that child and that sure has to be a lot of pressure on a man your age." Martha was not being any nicer today than she was the last time they had met.

"Martha my wife is not a child. She is very much a woman and she is just right for me in every way. I'm very sorry I interrupted you." Austin turned before Martha had time to say anything and went back over to where Karen was looking at a pretty dark wooden bed.

"Austin, do you like this bed?" She asked as soon as he was near enough to see the bed well enough.

"Yes Karen I do. I think it would go very nicely with our bedroom furniture." he answered.

"Yes that was exactly what I was thinking. It would fit right in with what we have in our bedroom. I like it a lot, but Austin it really cost lot of money." Karen whispered.

"How much money does it cost?" he asked?

The saleslady told Austin the price of the bed alone. Austin didn't blink an eye. "Alright we will take it. If my wife wants this bed, that's the bed we will get. Now we need a few more things, such as a changing table and a chest for our son's clothes. Karen, can you think of anything else that we need for our son while we are here?

"Yes Austin we will need a rocking chair. Our baby will need to be rocked to sleep at night." Karen knew babies all like to be rocked.

"M'am, then we will need two rocking chairs." Austin answered. "Why will we need two rocking chairs Austin?" Karen asked. "Karen honey we will need one up in our bedroom and one down in our den. Neither you nor I need to be downstairs in the middle of the night rocking our baby. Especially when we could just do it right in our bedroom. So Miss, do you have rockers?" Austin asked.

"Yes sir we sure do." The saleslady was more than happy to make the commission on all the things Austin and Karen wanted for their son.

Austin and Karen took the bed home first, but it took three trips to get the rest of the things they had bought.

"Honey Bo can help me to put the bed together tonight while you are cooking supper."

"Austin if you don't know how to put our baby's bed up I can do it. I've put lots of beds together before at the church.

"Karen I think I can do it. I will read the directions very careful and then I will give it a try. I'm sure between Bo and me we will be able to do it."

"Alright, but you will still need me before it is over." Karen answered.

After the third trip they had it all home. Austin put the truck into their basement garage. He would need Bo's help to get the chest from out of the back of his truck.

"Karen I hope we won't need to replace anything except for maybe the mattress. Austin was walking bent over like an old man. "I think I have pulled every muscle in my whole body doing all of this for our son."

"Austin I will keep that all in mind when I'm in labor trying to push our baby out of my cootchie." Karen answered.

"Alright Karen I got the message. You are right honey. This is nothing compared to what you will be doing. I understand that completely."

Austin pulled Karen into his arms and started kissing her. "I'm very glad to have you for my wife even if you do put me in my place quite a lot. Woman have you ever noticed how much larger I am than you?" he asked her.

"Yes I noticed that the first day at the coffee shop, but I decided I would love you anyway." she told him.

"You decided you loved me that first day?" Austin wasn't sure he had heard her right.

"Yes Austin I did the second I laid eyes on you. I wanted to be your wife. But I wasn't sure you even wanted me as your surrogate let alone to be your wife. I saw how you looked at me as if to say I was way too short for a man like you." Karen had him where she wanted him even then.

"Yes I did do a lot of looking at you. I was looking at your perfectly shaped body and your breast. Man you looked good in that sweater. I wanted you right then." he told her.

"Austin Blackburn you were not looking at my breast all that time." Karen's face was turning red.

"Yes I was Karen. I could not keep my eyes off of them. They were so sexy looking and you looked so innocent. The two just did not go together I thought at the time." Austin admitted.

"Well maybe I should have just flashed you with them." she answered.

"Maybe you should have and then I would not have let you sleep on the second floor that first night." he told her.

"Maybe Austin I didn't want to sleep on the second floor that first night, but now you won't ever know." Karen gave her husband a beautiful smile.

"Karen, honey, I know exactly what you would have done if I had told you to come up stairs with me that first night." Austin knew she was buffing.

"What do you think would have happened?" she asked.

"What do I think you would have done? You would have run as fast as you could to that bedroom and closed the door and locked it." he answered.

"Are you sure Austin? I didn't lock or even close that door that first night. I wanted you to marry me and I was ready to do anything to get you interested in me." Now she had Austin thinking. It didn't really matter now if the door to her bedroom had only been left opened by accident. Austin will never know.

"I remember that night well. I laid up there all night just thinking about you and wanting you. Now you tell me you didn't close your bedroom door and I could have came down those stairs and gone into that bedroom." Austin looked so disappointed.

"Well Austin that is something you will never know now." Karen just smiled at Austin making him wonder.

"No I won't, but one night later I had you in my bed as my wife. And there is no one, who can ever come between us now." Austin was very sure of at least that one thing.

"No, Austin not anyone, but this little fellow," Karen was patting her stomach.

"Yes he may come between us for now, but never in a bad way." Austin answered.

"No Austin never in a bad way." Karen felt as if she was the luckiest woman in the world.

"Karen you are even more beautiful pregnant than you were that first day I saw you."

"Oh you mean that one day I wasn't pregnant that I knew you." she answered.

"Yes I guess one day was all it was because you have been pregnant every day we have been married. Karen I had you pregnant the first time we made love." Austin wondered if Karen felt used because of that one reason. After all he did go to meet her the day before to get her to be a surrogate for him.

"Yes Austin isn't that great? We have been three almost all the time we have been two." she answered.

Austin knew that some women may feel a little odd being pregnant their whole married life. He thought how lucky he was to have Karen and that she seemed to be happy with being pregnant their whole marriage.

"Karen, are you really glad you are pregnant? You know we haven't really had a normal married life."

"Why would I want a married life if it's only going to be normal? Why would I want anything less than what we have together? After all it is our marriage and no one else's." she answered.

They talked a little while longer while they were still down in the basement. "I think we need to get upstairs and you need to get our supper ready woman. Bo and I will eat and get busy with putting up that bed. I think we will do it better if we eat first."

"Austin we need sheets, a bed shirt, blankets and all of those things before we can put our baby into his beautiful new bed." Karen was so happy.

"Yes we do. I had forgotten all about all of those little things. You can go with me to work tomorrow and we will go shopping again after lunch. Remember Bo said for you to start eating more." Austin reminded her.

"If I go with you tomorrow I will need to put something in the slow cooker again." Austin and Karen were in the kitchen now. "Austin what time is it?"

Austin glanced down at his watch "six thirty, why honey?" "I was just wondering if Bo was hungry yet."

"I will call and check and I will tell him to get right over here." Austin went into his office and called Bo on his cell phone. He had laid it down on his desk when he took the mail into his office earlier.

"Hello." Bo answered.

"Bo we are home, Karen has supper almost on the table. If you have not changed your clothes yet, then do it, before you come over. I need your help. I have a basement full of baby furniture and I need to put a baby bed together tonight." Austin knew he could always count on his best friend.

"So daddy, you are getting ready to bring that boy home already?" Bo asked.

"Yes, Bo I am and I could not be happier. Bo, don't get me started. Karen and I just had a good talk while I unloaded some of the truck. She is so wonderful, I will tell you all about it later, so come on before supper gets cold."

"Alright Austin I'm coming now, I have already changed my clothes. Open the door I'm standing on your stoop now."

"Then why don't you just use your key?" Austin asked as he hurried to the front of the house to open the door for Bo.

"Austin you look just like a daddy." Bo said as he walked in.

"You mean, they all look like they are going crazy all the time?" Austin answered.

"Yes, just like you. If you think this is hard on you, think how Karen must feel. She is married and pregnant by the man she met one day and married the next. Her life has changed right along with her body. All you, did, was to get a beautiful woman to marry you and you even get to sleep with her every night and sometimes when it isn't even night." Bo wished it was him who was going so crazy.

"Yes Bo I agree with you one hundred percent. Karen has had the most to get used to, but she has done it all. I really do love my beautiful young wife." Everyone that saw them knew that they were truly in love with each other.

"Spoken like a man in love. If only Karen would find me a little woman like her, I could be as happy as you are my friend." Bo answered.

Austin and Bo went to the kitchen where Karen was. She already had the table set.

"Hello Bo, are you ready to eat and then build me a baby bed?" She asked.

"Yes M'am, your happy husband and I will get you a baby bed built and ready before you need it." Bo answered.

"Bo I didn't like the way you said that at all." Karen began to wonder if these two smart men knew anything about real work.

"Well Karen you aren't dealing with your average men. You only have us." Bo answered.

"Austin, Bo doesn't know how to do anything either. So I will show you two big boys how to put a baby bed together right after supper. Now sit down and dig in." She told them.

"Yes M'am, Austin are you going to let your wife put us down like that and us sitting right here at the table with her?" Bo asked.

"Yes Bo if she can put that baby bed together I sure am, because you and I have no idea how to do it, but I'm pretty sure we will learn before the night is over." Austin had a big smile on his face, but Karen failed to notice.

After supper they all three cleaned up the kitchen. Karen got after them to get with the job. "I'm having a baby in a few months. We don't have forever to get this done. Do you two understand me?"

"Yes Karen I know you are having a baby I looked under the sheet remember." Bo answered.

"Austin where is your tool box?" Karen asked. "Where is my, what?" Austin asked.

Karen could not believe her ears. Her husband did not know what a tool box was. "You know the thing you keep your tools in. Things like a hammer, screwdriver, pliers, and those sorts of things." Karen looked shocked at Austin. She had never known a man who didn't own a tool box before.

"Karen honey, don't look so disappointed I have a tool box. Honey I was only teasing you." Austin went to the basement and got his tool box. "Karen, Bo and I can put the baby bed together. We have just been pulling your leg. Who do you think did all the renovation in our two homes? Bo and I did it all." Austin answered.

"You and Bo did all of this? Austin I'm so relieved. I wasn't sure I could do it all by myself. I love you." Karen said as she gave him a big hug.

"Karen I would have never let you do it all by yourself." Then all three went down to the basement. It was like another house down there. It was furnished with very nice furniture, but not in the same style as the rooms upstairs.

"How many trips, did it take you to get all this furniture home Austin?" Bo asked as he looked the room over that was full of boxes. "Bo it took three trips and now we need to get it all upstairs."

Austin was still tired from unloading most of it, but he was not going to say one word. No not as long as Karen was standing there with them. Austin had not worked that hard since he and Bo had finished their homes and that had been a few years ago.

"All of it?" Bo asked.

"Yes all of it goes to the third floor except for one of the rockers and it goes into the den." Austin was already up on the bed of his truck getting ready to unload the chest.

Bo looked over at Karen. "Karen would you like to change bedrooms and you and the baby sleep down here at night in the basement. Austin and I could make you a real nice room all girly the way you would want it down here and we would not need to move all this big old heavy furniture up three flights of stairs."

"No she doesn't want to change bedrooms. She is sleeping in our bedroom and so is our son. So Bo, stop talking and start lifting." Austin said from the bed of his truck.

"Karen what do you say?" Bo was still waiting for Karen to say something back to him.

"Bo, do what my husband said. Start lifting. I'm not sleeping anywhere my husband doesn't sleep. Do you get it?" she asked.

"Yes M'am I do. Austin, would you sleep down here with your wife and son?" Bo was still teasing Karen.

"Bo, I would if it was necessary. However, it is not, so I think you need to just stop talking and start lifting." Austin gave Bo a little friendly hand jester to get him going.

"Well it was worth the try." Both men got a good laugh from all of it.

Karen was there waiting and watching as the two men took the big box off the back of the truck with the chest in it.

"We need to get it all out of these boxes first. Then it will be much easier to manage." Austin said as soon as it was off the truck.

"Austin do you want me to do something?" Karen asked as she stood watching her husband working.

"No Karen I do not." Austin answered. "You are already doing something." Austin and Bo both smiled over at Karen. Karen smiled back at Austin. You could see the love in the look they exchanged with each other.

"Karen when are you going to find a woman like you for me? Then I could buy a truckload, of baby things." Bo said.

"Soon Bo, very soon, I will have you married." Karen answered and then gave him a big smile.

Bo looked from Karen to Austin wondering if he knew something he had not told him yet.

"I don't know anything about that Bo." Austin answered without even being asked.

After they had it all off of the truck and out of the boxes they began taking it all upstairs.

"Which rocker do you want left in the den?" Bo asked.

"It doesn't matter Bo, they are exactly alike." Austin answered.

"Yes they are. I can see that now. Karen, now tell me who do you have in mind for me?" Not knowing who Karen had in mind for him was killing Bo.

"Oh Bo, just wait and see you will love her. You just want to take the fun out of it all." Karen answered.

"You mean there really is a "her?" Bo asked. He want it to be a certain her, but if it wasn't he would just deal with that when he had to.

"Yes Bo there really is a "her". I would not tease you the way you and my husband seem to like teasing me. I'm much nicer to the two of you."

"Karen, if you would find me a girl like you, I would marry her and have me a baby and I would never tease you again."

"Bo I love you and Austin and I know if you two could not tease me you would not be yourselves. So don't say that, I would hate to see you explode from trying to be so good."

"Oh Karen I would delivery all of your babies for free if you would find me a woman to marry." Bo was as serious as he could be.

"Austin did you hear Bo? He said he would delivery all our babies for free. We can have all the babies we want now." Karen was smiling over at Bo.

"Good, then we will go ahead and have all the rest of those babies if they are going to be free." Austin answered.

"What do you mean by all the rest of those babies?" Bo asked. Bo had never heard his friend say anything about wanting more than one child, but he felt Austin's mind had changed because of Karen. The man was in love and that made all the difference in the world. Now he had a need to want to share his self with her and their children.

"Oh Bo we would just have the whole dozen. There would be no need stopping at eight if we can get the other four for free as well." Austin had a big smile on his face. Bo could see how much Karen had changed him into a family man already and Bo thought it was very becoming of Austin.

"Oh I see you want to turn this basement into bedrooms too." Bo wished he was making jokes about having a family too.

"Maybe or we could move or even just buy the house on the other side of us and make it a part of this house and you could do the same Bo on the other side of you." Austin suggested.

"Then you and I could start renovating all over again. Karen, are you sure you want me to see your cootchie that many times?" Bo asked.

"After the first time Bo you won't be that fascinated with it so much because my husband will be right there with us." Karen said as she watched Austin.

"Austin did you hear her? She has decided to let you see her cootchie after all." Bo knew Karen would change her mind again before it was all over at least a dozen times.

"Yes Bo it sure seems like it." Austin answered.

"Austin, don't you get too excited about seeing my cootchie. It may scare you so bad you may not want us to have the rest of our babies." Karen still did not feel completely comfortable with the whole birthing thing.

"Karen you know that won't stop me from wanting you and from us having the rest of our babies. You are beautiful and I love you so much that even seeing your cootchie won't change my mind." Austin had that smile on his face again.

"Austin you say that now, but wait a couple more months and you may change your mind; when I'm as big as a house and you can't get your arms all the way around me anymore."

Austin stopped what he was doing and went over and put his arms around her. "Karen you will always be beautiful no matter how large you get and I will always love you. After all it's only our son growing inside of his mother and I'm the man that caused it all."

"Austin I want you to cause all the others too." she answered.

"I will honey. We will have all the babies we want as long as you want them and Bo says it's safe for you to have them." More and more Austin was feeling like a real family man and he loved that feeling. He was very sure his Father had that very same feeling about his Mother and him.

"Karen I will keep a very close eye on you and if you and Austin want all eight or even all twelve of those babies I will help you get them all here." Bo was a very good doctor and he would do just as he said.

"Thank you Bo. That is very sweet of you." Karen looked so sweet and beautiful to both of the men. She may be Austin's wife, but Bo was not blind.

"You are welcome Karen. That will give me more times to see you." he answered.

Austin and Bo got the baby bed put together once they had it up on the third floor bedroom. It was a beautiful bed. It changed Austin's bedroom from looking like it was still a bachelor's bedroom in a family looking bedroom.

"Austin it's so beautiful I think I'm going to cry." She could not Help but to think she could have missed out on all of this.

"Oh Karen it's alright." Austin gave her a big hug. Then he asked her if she wanted the baby bed there or someplace else?

"I love it right where you have it. I don't want our little boy too far away from me and I want the changing table at the foot of his bed. That way I will have his diapers handy all the time."

"Where do you want his chest and the rocker?" Austin asked as soon as he and Bo had them up in the room.

"I like them both right where they are." Karen answered. You did good Austin it's beautiful, I love it all." The room looked just as beautiful as before, but in a very different way.

"Yes it does look like we are in the baby business now. Karen we need to get our son some clothes. We can do that tomorrow after lunch." Austin was now even more anxious than before for his parents to get back home. He had so much to show them and to tell them. His life was changing a little more each day and he loved every little bit of it. He had found the woman he loved and had married her. Now they were going to have their first child in just a few months. All of that was what he wanted so much to share with his parents.

"Yes Austin we do need to get things ready. He will be here before we know it." Having the baby bed made it seem even more real to Karen and she knew it did the same thing to Austin.

"I'm so glad you two found each other. Do you hear how much you two are alike? Austin when we bought our homes we never thought we would be doing all of this baby stuff." Bo said.

"Yes I know Bo. Karen and I are a lot alike and you are right we sure did not give babies or wives a thought when we bought and renovated our houses, but now that is all I think about." Austin still had Karen in his arms.

"Well if that's all you two are going to do tonight let's go back down to the kitchen and have some cake and I will make you two some coffee," Karen said as she looked over the room one more time. It was so beautiful she wanted to jump up and down, but she was very sure that would give both of the men a heart attack.

"That sounds good to me." Austin answered.

After they had finished having their cake Bo decided to go home. "I'm going home so you two can play house some more. I will see you tomorrow." He gave Karen a kiss on her cheek and Austin walked him to the front door. "Austin who has Karen got for me?"

"I have no idea. She has only been to work with me, to church and to your office. So I'm as surprised as you. So I guess we both will find out together." Austin was sure if Karen had someone for Bo she would be a very nice woman.

"Do I need to be sure my good suit is clean and I have good sheets on my bed?" Bo asked.

"That may be a good idea. Now, good night Bo, go home." Austin said as he started to close the door. "I have a wife waiting for me."

Soon Austin was back in the room with Karen. "Honey, who do you have for Bo?"

"Oh Austin you will have to wait just like Bo and see who it is when he does. I don't want you to know before Bo knows because you will go straight to him and tell him. I know you two big boys. I will tell you this much; I know God sent her here for Bo. Like God sent you to find me. I just need you to trust me on this."

"I do trust you Karen. You should know that by now."

CHAPTER TWENTY

The next morning Karen went to work with Austin again. She just lay on Austin's sofa while he worked at his desk and made several phone calls. At noon he stopped working.

"Karen wake up it's time to go." He was patting her on her shoulder to wake her.

"Austin did I fall asleep? I seem to be getting a lot more tired than I used to be."

"I guess being pregnant has a lot to do with that honey."

Austin took Karen to lunch and then shopping. After supper that night the phone rang and Austin answered it. "Karen it's for you."

"Oh it must be her." Karen said as she took the phone from Austin and gave him a little smile. Bo and Austin looked at each other.

"So she is real." Bo felt so good knowing this.

"It sure looks that way Bo." Austin gave his friend a big smile. He wanted his best friend to have as good a life as he was having.

Karen went into the den with the phone and took a seat in her new rocking chair. She did not want the men to hear what was being said between her and Margo. "Margo I'm so glad you called. I was hoping you would call soon."

"Mrs. Blackburn I wanted to call last night, but I decided to wait until tonight. I didn't want to rush you." Margo sounded so sweet and she was as lonely as Karen was before she met Austin.

"Margo I know just how you feel. Margo would you like to come to our house this coming weekend. You said you didn't know anyone here and you could come and stay with us over the weekend and meet this wonderful man. I think he is almost as wonderful as my Austin." Karen wanted Margo to want Bo so bad.

"Oh Mrs. Blackburn, I don't know. I don't want to be any trouble for you after all you are pregnant." Margo would love to go some place for a weekend she had not been anywhere at all since she got into the city. Like it had been for Karen all those years she had worked at the Church she didn't have any place to go other than to work, but Margo didn't mind that at all she got to see Bo on those days. The weekends were the days she did not like, only because she had to wait two whole days before she would be back to work and could see Bo.

"Margo my name is Karen. I'm only nineteen years old so just call me Karen please." This surprised Margo.

"Karen you are only nineteen years old? Your husband must be somewhat older than you?" Margo asked.

"Yes he is, but I love him so much and he loves me the very same way. You know we want eight babies. We told Bo we want twelve so now he is worried that he will have twelve of our babies to delivery. I like to make him worry." Karen had to laugh a little after telling Margo her little secret.

"Wow that is a lot of kids, but I would want a lot of them if I had a husband like you do Karen." Margo answered.

"Margo you could just come over here Saturday morning and bring your clothes to stay overnight." Karen hoped she was not rushing her new friend too much, but she felt very strongly that Margo was the woman for Bo.

"Alright I will do it. I'm already excited about it. It has been a long six months being alone." Margo felt real good about having met Karen. She hoped things would turn out as Karen wanted she said.

Karen gave Margo their address and then they hung up. Karen took the phone back to the kitchen and put it away. Karen was not telling Bo or Austin anything about her call. She was sure if she told Austin who Margo was it would not be any time before he would be telling Bo.

"Karen was that Bo's woman you were talking with so long on the phone?" Austin asked.

"Yes Austin it sure was. Now I need to finish up in here." Karen said knowing the suspense was killing the two men.

"No, you need to tell me about my woman." Bo was right in her face.

"No I don't because there is nothing to tell you yet. When you need to know I will tell you. So just wait and see." Karen just gave Bo one of her sweet smiles. "Austin will you help me to take all of these tags off of our babies little clothes and the rest of his things?" She was not going to say anymore about her call or her caller.

"Sure sweetheart I will be very happy to help." Austin answered.

"So, will I." Bo said. "Austin did you two leave anything in the stores?". Bo asked his friend after seeing all the bags of baby things sitting around the room.

"Just a very little," Karen answered. "Our son is very special just ask his Daddy." she answered.

The next morning Karen got Austin off to work and she started to do their laundry and all of the new baby things. She wanted to have them ready to use. By noon she had it all finished. She took it easy for the rest of the day, but she had supper ready when Austin got home.

"Karen honey I'm home." Austin called out as he came into the house from the basement.

"Austin I'm in the living room." Karen called back. She was cleaning it and their big formal dining room. "Austin, do you mind if I clean up your office some?"

"No why would I? After all it's your house too. Now come here and give me a big kiss. I missed you all day." Karen was up in Austin's arms in no time. Her feet were not even touching the floor." Karen I don't believe we will be able to do this anymore. Your stomach is in the way and I'm afraid I may hurt you and our baby." Austin could clearly see how sad that made Karen. I think I will need to start holding you like this instead." He put one of his arms under her legs and his other around her back and picked her up in his arms.

"Oh Austin this makes me feel like a bride again."

"Yes you are my bride and you will always be my bride." He answered.

"Yes Austin your bride with a big stomach." Karen answered as she rubbed her stomach.

"So!" Austin answered.

"I'm glad I was your bride so I could be the one to get this big stomach." Karen said exactly what Austin wanted to hear.

"Good now let's go and eat, I'm hungry. Bo is delivering a baby and he won't be here tonight." Bo had always given Austin a call when he would not be home at his regular time so Austin would know where he was in case of an emergency and Austin had always done the same. It was just their way of being safe.

"Oh that's nice. One day it will be our baby boy that he will be delivering." Karen answered.

"Yes, but not tonight." Austin knew Karen was glad of that too.

Saturday morning Karen got up early. She wanted her house to look spotless when Margo got there. She had even made her homemade chicken salad to serve at lunch time and homemade toastie. She wanted their first luncheon to be wonderful in more ways than one.

"Karen why are you up so early?" Austin asked.

"Austin we are having company this weekend." Karen was already in the bathroom doing her hair and putting on her makeup and Austin was still in bed.

"We are having company, who?" He had not heard about them having any company this weekend at all.

"Bo's, woman that's who is going to be our company." Karen answered. "She is coming this morning and she will be staying overnight. I hope that's alright with you? I'm sorry I just forgot to check with you first to see if it was alright for me to invite someone to your house."

Austin was still lying in bed while they talked. "Yes it's alright. Honey this is your home as much as it is my home. You can invite whoever you want. So Bo's woman, will be here this morning." Austin was almost as anxious as Bo to meet this mysterious woman.

"Yes Austin and I want to have Bo over for lunch to meet her. Then we will see if they go together as well as we do."

"Karen I hope you don't get disappointed." Austin knew that most of the time blind dates just do not work out. He had been on a few of them in his life and he was always happy when the evening was over.

"I won't be Austin you just wait and see. I picked a girl like me because Bo is like you. If it works for us it will work for them as well."

"Are you sure Karen?" Austin still had his doubts.

"Yes Austin I am. Bo wants a wife and she wants a husband. That is half of the battle." Karen had come back to the bedroom and was sitting in bed with Austin. In fact she was sitting on top of Austin.

"Mrs. Blackburn this could be very dangerous if you get my drift." Austin said as he looked her over.

"Yes I do and if I didn't want you I would not be sitting right here on top of you." she answered.

"Oh you came here to me." Austin stopped just looking at his wife and reached up and pulled Karen down on him and started kissing her.

CHAPTER TWENTY ONE

M argo rang the doorbell at eleven o'clock on the dot. Karen
and Austin were all ready for her. Karen still had not told
Austin where she had met Margo. She wanted to wait and
see if Austin or Bo would recognize her.

"Come in Margo let me have your bag." Karen said as she held the
door open for her new friend.

"No, you are pregnant let me carry it." Margo said.

"Hello Margo, I'm Austin, Karen's husband. I don't believe we have
ever met." Margo looked over at Karen. Karen just smiled. "No I don't
guess we have." Margo was not going to say anything. She would wait for
Karen to tell her husband where he had met her.

"It's nice meeting you Margo." Austin shook Margo's hand, but he
had no idea at all who she was or where Karen had met her.

"Austin, will you take Margo's bag to that room we both like so
well." Then she smiled up at him.

Austin knew the room Karen was talking about. Karen's old room,
the room she had stayed in that first night. While Austin was gone up
to the second floor with Margo's bag, this gave the two girls time to do a
little talking.

"Margo I have not told Austin anything about you. I didn't want
him to be informing his friend anything about you." Karen was not
even telling Margo who she was there to meet either.

"Oh I understand. If he didn't like me he wouldn't want his friend to
like me either." Margo didn't really understand at all.

"No not at all. I just didn't want them to know anything. He and
his friend are too close for me to tell Austin anything I didn't want his
friend to know and especially if it's something concerning him." Karen
answered.

"Karen who am I going to meet?" Margo asked. She was just as
anxious to know as the two men.

227

"Just wait and see. I can tell you he is very handsome and smart. And he will make you a good husband." Karen was keeping her fingers crossed.

"A good husband, I wish." This was getting better and better all the time Margo thought.

"Margo, do you cook?" This was something Karen was sure that would be important to Bo.

"Yes I do. Even though I'm, not Italian I do cook a lot of good Italian meals." Margo was old school. She believed the way to a man's heart was through his stomach.

"Do you cook southern?" Karen wanted to be sure she had gotten Bo the right woman.

"No, but I wished I did." She didn't, but she was willing to learn. That still made her a good candidate for Bo.

"Margo if I teach you to cook southern will you teach me to cook Italian?" That was something Karen would love to know how to cook.

"Sure that would be fun." Margo really liked Karen a lot even in this short period of time she could tell that they would get along real well.

"Margo, will you please excuse me, I need to speak with my husband." Karen wanted to go and find Austin she could use his help now.

"Sure I will just sit here and wait until you get back." Margo was a little nervous, but it was a good kind of nervous. The kind you feel when you know something good is going to happen.

Karen left Margo sitting in the den while she went to go find Austin. It was time to put her matchmaking into motion. When she found him he was upstairs in their bedroom. "Hello honey, are you and Margo having fun?" He asked. He hoped he could get Karen to tell him more about this woman she had for Bo to meet.

"Yes we are and we are going to have even more fun." Karen was not going to slip and tell Austin anything she didn't want him or Bo to know yet.

"Honey did you need me for something?" He was sure she did or she would not have left her guest downstairs waiting.

"Yes I do. Austin, why don't you go over to Bo's house, and tell him to dress in his tight little jeans just like you have on and tell him to come over here for lunch. Now I don't want you to say one word to Bo about Margo. Do you understand me Mr. Blackburn? Not even her name. Now if you don't think you can do that I will go over to his house myself."

"Yes Mrs. Blackburn I understand you perfectly. I will do just as my little five foot one inch wife tells me to do." Austin then gave Karen a little kiss and they both left their bedroom and went back downstairs. Karen watched Austin as he went out of their front door.

Then she hurried back to the den where Margo was waiting. "I'm so sorry, but I had something that Austin needed to do for me. Margo if you don't mind while we are waiting we will get lunch on the table. I'm sure both of our men will be here shortly."

"You mean the one you want me to meet?" Margo said. She already liked having him referred to as her man.

"Yes that would be him. Now Margo, don't looked shocked or anything like that when you meet him. Just go along with what I say alright?" Karen was so sure that this was the woman for Bo.

"Yes Karen I will do just as you say. I want to find someone so badly to love and to love me. I want to get married and have a big family someday. Just like you." Margo even had that same look on her face that Karen gets when she talks about have children.

The two women got the table set and Karen took all the food out of the refrigerator that she had prepared earlier. She wanted this luncheon to be the best it could be for so many reasons.

"Karen this all looks beautiful and you did all of this yourself?" Margo asked.

"Yes I did." Karen answered. She was so proud of the nice dishes of food she had made. They were nothing fancy, but it was all very delicious food. Things her grandmother and her teachers had taught her to make.

"I can't wait until we start cooking together. I can already tell you will have a lot to teach me." Margo already really liked Karen in every way.

"Oh Margo it will be fun. I made pink lemonade for us. Do you like lemonade?" Karen knew everyone in the South loved lemonade, but she was not sure about the people from Ohio.

"Yes I do." Margo quickly answered.

As soon as Austin rang Bo's doorbell he was there to answer it. "Bo Karen said for you to dress in your tight little jeans like me and come go over to our house for lunch. I have been ordered to say just that and no more." Austin stopped talking and waited for Bo to ask him that one important question.

"Austin is she there?" Bo asked.

"Bo I can't say anymore or my sweet little wife will be upset with me, but if I were you I would get my jeans on and get over there as fast as I could." That was all Austin could safely say.

"Alright I will do it, because I think she is over at your house right this minute." Bo had a big smile on his face. He only hoped Karen had picked the right woman.

"Alright Bo, maybe she is and maybe you will like what you see." Austin didn't want to say too much and have Karen mad at him.

Bo didn't waste any time getting redressed. In less than ten minutes the men were walking in the front door of Austin and Karen's house.

"Honey we are home." Austin called out as soon as he opened the front door. He wanted Karen to know they were there just in case she had some dramatic way she wanted Bo and Margo to meet.

"Austin we are in the kitchen come on back here." Karen called out.

"Karen, do I look alright to meet this man?" Margo was no different than any woman who was meeting a man for the first time.

"Yes Margo, you look so beautiful it scares me." Karen answered. "Oh Karen, you're the beautiful one, everyone can see that so easily." Margo had never seen anyone as beautiful as Karen in Bo's office before. She was real glad that Karen was already married and that Bo was only her doctor. She had already forgotten what Bo had said when he told her to make Karen's next appointment, but doctors are always saying things to their patents that they don't really mean. They are just being nice to them.

"Hello ladies." Austin said as soon as he came into the kitchen. Margo had her back to the door so she was not facing the two men when they came into the kitchen.

"Bo I would like you to meet Margo Wilson." Karen said so sweetly.

Bo pretended he did not recognize who Margo was when he got his first glance of her, but he was so glad it was her. He liked everything he saw. He had a big smile on his face. A lot like the one Austin wore all the time when he is with Karen.

"Margo, meet Dr. Bo Brooks." Karen said. Margo smiled and stuck out her hand for Bo to shake. She didn't know if he recognized her or not.

She was so happy it was Dr. Brooks that Karen had her come to meet. She could not have been any happier.

"Margo it's nice to meet you." Bo held on to Margo's hand a long time. He was looking her over just like Austin did Karen that first day.

"Bo would you and Margo, like to sit here?" Karen was pointing to the other side of the kitchen table.

"Yes Karen we sure would. Margo, are you from around here?" Bo asked not wanting her or Karen to know he knew exactly who Margo was.

"No not really I moved here six months ago." she answered.

"And it has taken this long for us to meet?" Bo answered. "Karen, tell me why has it taken you this long to introduce us?" he asked. Bo was still playing it as cool as he could.

"It just has. Now Bo, ask Margo where she works?" Karen wanted this to work for these two nice people so badly.

"Margo, where do you work?" Bo asked.

"I work for a doctor." Margo was brokenhearted that Bo had not recognized her at all. She was one of his employees and he didn't even know her she thought.

"Oh that is nice. What's his name? I may know him." Bo had a hold of Margo's hand again and he was not letting it go.

"His name is Dr. Bo Brooks. Have you ever heard of him before?" Margo asked.

"Yes I do believe I have. Margo, are you saying you work for me? Where do you work in my office?" He was still trying to play it cool.

"Dr. Brooks I work up at the front desk. Dr. Brooks I'm sorry I didn't know it was you I was coming here to meet. I'm so sorry I will leave now. I don't want to be any trouble." Margo was close to tears and she didn't want Bo to see her crying.

"No Margo, there is no need in that at all. I don't want you to leave. I want you to stay. I want to get to know you." Bo really liked this girl and it did not start today.

"But Dr. Brooks I work for you." Margo answered.

"So what's wrong with you working for me? Can't I enjoy being with you even though you work for me?" Bo asked.

"I guess so. I don't really know." Margo answered.

"Bo, Margo did not know it was you who I wanted her to meet." Karen said. She did not want to cause Margo any trouble and she sure didn't want her to lose her job.

"Karen it is alright. I'm just surprised I haven't met her before." He lied.

"Dr. Brooks you have met me. You have even talked to me several times, but you just never looked at me." Margo answered sadly.

"Margo he's looking now." Austin said as he gave Karen a little kiss on her cheek.

"Yes Margo I'm really looking now. Karen when did you meet Margo?" Bo asked.

"The other day when I had my appointment at your office I met her at the front desk when I was checking out." Karen answered.

"You mean she had been working for me all those months and I never noticed and you see her and here she is?" Bo was still playing it cool.

"Yes sir, and here I am." Margo did not know if Bo was happy to see her or if he would fire her on Monday when they went back to work. This scared her a lot.

"Margo can I be honest with you?" Bo asked.

"Yes Dr. Books, you can be honest with me. I think I can take it." Margo was ready for anything she thought that he may say to her in front of his friends.

"I want a wife. I told Karen to find me one like her and I would marry her right away." Bo was still holding back how he has been feeling about her all these months.

"You want a wife like your friend's wife?" Margo asked? "Yes I do." Bo answered.

"How do you know if another woman will be like her?" Margo asked.

"Margo, you are like me aren't you?" Karen asked.

"Yes I guess in a way we are a lot alike Karen and I. We both want the same things in life, but will any woman ever be what you would want or will she be just a substitute for Karen?" Margo needed to know Bo's answer.

"Margo I'm not in love with Karen. All I meant by being like Karen was she wants nothing more than to be a good wife to my best friend

Austin and a good mother to their children and that is what I want in a wife too.

"What are they Margo? Those things you want in life." Bo asked? "I want to be married to someone who will love me and I will love and who will want a large family. I know that don't fit into a lot of men's lives, but that is what I want." she answered.

"Margo that's what I want in my life too." Bo answered.

"But Dr. Brooks you don't know anything about me." Margo was so scared that she was not at all what Bo would want.

"Margo my best friend is Austin. He met Karen on Thursday afternoon after five o'clock and married her the very next day. I don't know two happier people in this world. All because they both wanted the same thing and was willing to do what it took to get it. Karen got pregnant the day they got married. That's what I want to do. Do you understand what I'm saying?" Bo hoped he was making himself clear to her.

"Yes Dr. Brooks I do." Margo was hoping Bo would see all of that in her. After all she had spent six months working for him and looking at him every chance she got. She still thought he had never noticed her.

"Margo do you think you could learn to love me?" Bo asked. Margo looked up at Bo as if there was no one else in the room. "Dr. Brooks, could you learn to love me?" she asked.

"Yes I believe I have already started loving you." And that was no lie. Bo was still holding her hand.

"Now Margo, answer my question, could you learn to love me?" Bo was looking Margo in the eye while he waited for her answer.

"Dr. Brooks I have always known I loved you. I have been doing that for months now. So that is something I don't need to learn to do at all. I already love you." she answered.

Bo smiled a very big smile. "So we are already ahead of the game. Karen you did real well. I want this one." Bo answered.

"Bo, are you serious?" Karen asked.

"Yes Karen I am. Austin is the happiest man I know. He took a chance with his heart and so am I. Margo will you marry me?" Bo asked.

Margo started to cry. "Is that a yes or a no?" Bo asked.

"It's a yes if you are very sure this is what you want, because I'm only doing it one time." she answered.

Bo grabbed Margo and gave her a big kiss. "Margo you are fired for being married to the boss."

"But we aren't married yet." she answered.

"We will be. Now Austin, where can we go to get married today?" Bo asked.

"I don't know off hand, but we can get on the internet and find you a place." Austin answered.

"Alright let's do it." Bo was ready to marry Margo today. "Are you all going to eat my lunch or not?" Karen asked.

"Yes Karen we are. I will get my lap top and we will find Bo and Margo a place to get married today." Austin hurried into his office. "Margo, are you alright with all of this?" Karen did not want Margo to be pushed into anything she did not want.

"Yes Karen I am for some very odd reason I am. I'm perfectly happy with it all. It is as if this was all supposed to happen." Margo was not just a love sick young girl she knew exactly what marriage meant. Her parents had a very good marriage and she wanted hers to be just as good.

"I told you the other day it was. Do you remember?" Karen asked. "Yes, I do. Now what are they doing?" Margo was still sitting at the kitchen table.

"Margo my husband and Bo are looking for a place where you and Bo can go today and get married. When they find it you and Bo will get married just like Austin and I did, but you have had all those months to love Bo so it won't be that odd after all." Karen hoped that Margo was as in love with Bo as she said she was.

"No because I have dreamed about it enough. I always thought the wait would be worth it in the end." Margo answered.

"Margo you are like me. I thought the very same thing." Karen was right.

"Karen you were a virgin too?" Margo asked.

"Yes I was and I'm very glad I was." she answered.

"Bo will be so glad. Just let him find it out for himself." Karen told her.

"I will because I just don't think I would be able to tell him something like that yet." Margo was as shy as Karen.

"Margo, do you want children right way?" Karen hoped she would.

"Yes I do. I want a lot of children. I was the only child and I never had anyone to play with. It was very lonesome some of the time." Margo was remembering some of those days when she spent so much time alone.

"Margo I was an only child too." Karen told her.

Bo and Austin came back into the kitchen with Austin's lap top. "We can fly to South Carolina and get married today." Bo told Margo.

"Are we going to do that?" Margo asked.

"Yes, we will leave here at two and get there at four, get married and fly back here and be home by two or three o'clock tomorrow morning. How does that sound to you Margo?"

"It sounds wonderful to me Dr. Brooks." Margo had not realized she had called Bo Dr. Brooks.

"Wow that's even faster than us." Karen answered.

"No not really Karen we have six months on you and Austin. I just want to get married today. Monday Margo will stay home and play with you all day and with me all night." He gave Margo a big smile. She even smiled back at him.

"Bo you don't have rings." Karen remembered Austin stopping and buying their wedding rings on their way to the courthouse.

"Yes we do Karen. I have my Great Grandmothers rings. I will go and get them now. Margo, would you like to go with me and see our home?" Bo just wanted to get her alone for awhile.

"Yes Dr. Brooks I would." Margo was anxious to see if Bo's home was as nice as Austin and Karen's.

"Margo, I'm Bo. If I'm going to be your husband you need to stop calling me Dr. Brooks." He had to laugh. He could just hear her calling him Dr. Brooks while they were in bed making love.

"Yes Bo I can do that." she answered.

"Margo, I will make you and Bo a lunch to take to the airport. You can eat it on the way and Austin and I can drive you there. Can't we Austin?" Karen asked.

"Yes sweetheart we can." Austin was willing to do anything to help his friend.

"Austin we will be right back. Karen did I say thank you and that I love you today?" Bo asked.

"Yes Bo, I think you did." Karen answered.

Bo took Margo by her hand and led her to the house next door. "Margo I hope this isn't too fast for you." Bo didn't want Margo doing something now and later regretting it.

"No I don't believe it is Bo. I'm just surprised at you wanting to get married so quickly and without even asking me any questions." Margo answered.

"Karen has already done all of that I'm very sure and if she is happy I know I will be." Bo already knew a lot about Margo from her personal file.

Bo unlocked his front door. "Well here it is Margo, home sweet home." He said as he held the door open for her.

"Oh, Bo it's beautiful. It's a lot like Karen's and her husband's place." Margo was so happy.

"Yes Austin and I did all of the renovation ourselves. We worked on our houses for two years before we had them finished." Bo was very proud of the work he and Austin had done.

"Where did you live during those two years?" Margo was looking around the place she would be calling her home.

"We lived in Austin's basement. Let me get those rings before I forget. You just go ahead and look around. After all you are home sweetheart." Bo was almost as happy as Austin now.

Bo went upstairs to his safe and got his great grandmothers rings for Margo. Margo, went into several of the rooms, she could not believe she was going to marry the man she had been in love with for the last six months.

"Karen she is a very good match for Bo." Austin was very pleased with Karen. "No wonder he fell in love with her so quickly."

"Yes Austin she is perfect for Bo and he will be her very first too." Karen said.

"Does he know that he will be her first?" Austin asked.

"No, he doesn't, but he will soon find it out I'm very sure. Austin, she is an only child like us and she is short like me and she cooks and she is beautiful. What more could Bo want."

"Karen she may be all of that, but my wife is all of that and more." Austin answered.

"Austin I love you, but I hope Bo is feeling the very same way about Margo." She hoped it was not just what the people back home called surface love.

"Karen, stop worrying. I'm very sure Bo is on cloud nine. Didn't you see how he looked when he left here with her? I think our friend has been keeping a secret from us." Austin was already thinking that his good friend had his eye on Margo all the time and he had just not said anything.

Bo and Margo didn't need to stay away very long. They needed to get to the airport if they planned to be married today.

"Margo before we go back over to Austin's and Karen's house I want to kiss you if you don't mind?" Bo had waited a long time to kiss this woman and he was not going to wait another minute.

"Bo if you don't hurry up and kiss me I'm going to kiss you." Margo answered.

That was all it took for Bo to know he had him a Karen too. Austin would not be the only one with a big smile on his face anymore.

"Come here woman I need you." Bo was so relieved it was Margo Karen had found for him. He had waited long enough to be with her. It was driving him crazy not having her. Now he did and he was not going to waste one minute of it.

"We are back. Are you two ready to take us to the airport?" Bo asked as soon as he and Margo got in the door.

"Yes we are. Let's all go and get into the truck and get down the road." Austin answered.

"Austin did you get our tickets all ready?" Bo asked.

"Yes, they are waiting for you at the counter." Austin said as he got ready to help Karen into their truck.

"Karen I want to sit back here with Margo. So you will be stuck up front with your husband. I'm sure Austin wants it that way too." Bo said as he gave Karen a big smile that said you did good girl.

"Yes I do. This little woman is my life. I want her as near to me as she can be." Austin answered.

"Margo wait and you will see that Bo will be the same way about you I know." Karen knew Bo was like Austin in many ways.

"I am already. Thank you Karen." Bo said from the back seat. "Good then Margo will be pregnant by tomorrow and you all will have a little girl for our little boy." Karen answered.

"Karen I will try just for you." Bo answered.

"I'm very sure you will be trying." Karen answered him back.

"Bo, how does it feel to know you have someone to take care of besides yourself now?" Austin asked.

"Austin it feels wonderful and to think she was in my office all this time." Bo still had not said anything to them about having feelings for Margo for the last six months. "Margo you should have just popped me and gotten my attention. We have wasted almost half of a year. Think about all of the nice times we could have been having all this time." Bo was smiling big.

"Now you tell me." Margo answered. They all four laughed. "Karen, you did good girl. I'm very happy with Margo. I can see us being just as much in love with each other as you and my old friend Austin." Bo turned his head to look at his future wife. "Margo, are you happy?" he asked.

"Yes I am Bo I'm very happy." She had just enough time to finish what she was saying when Bo kissed her again. Margo never dreamed everything would work out so well. She had managed to get the man she had fallen in love with and she had not needed to do anything, but show up at Karen's house.

Bo and Margo ate their lunch in the back seat of Austin's truck on their way to the airport. It was all very good except they were so excited about everything that was happening that they really didn't get to enjoy how good the food tasted that Karen had prepared for them. Sort of like a bride groom feels at their own wedding reception.

They were getting to the airport just in time to check in. There was no time for long goodbyes. "We will see you when you get back." Austin said just before driving away.

"Austin, do you think they are alright?" Karen asked.

"Yes Karen I do and like I said before I believe Bo has been keeping a secret from us. I think he has been looking at her the whole time that she has been working for him. He didn't say anything to her because he was her boss."

"I do too Austin, because he took hold of her hand the second he saw it was her and he didn't let go of it." Karen had noticed that right away.

"I think my friend had eyes for Margo all along, but he just did not know how to go about getting her. Now he doesn't have to keep his secret anymore, he has her. My, little wife, took care of that for him." Austin gave Karen a nice smile.

Once inside the airport Margo wanted to be sure Bo know what he was doing. "Bo, are you really sure you want to marry me?" she asked.

"Margo yes, I want to marry you. Margo honey I need to tell you something before we go any farther." Margo looked up at Bo she didn't know what to expect. She was a little scared to find out what he wanted to say. "Margo I have been looking at you at my office for months, but I didn't want you to know or anyone else. You came to work for me just before Austin married Karen. The second I saw her she reminded me of you. Both of you are short and beautiful." Bo told Margo the story of how Austin met Karen and how they ended up married.

Margo had never heard of anyone doing that before. "Now that's a love story. I hope we have as good of a marriage as they have." Margo had a good feeling about everything now. After hearing Karen and Austin's story she knew she and Bo could do it.

"Margo we will if that is what we want. Karen is right there for Austin and he is always there for her. She even goes to work with him some days because he misses her so much."

"Bo what kind of work does Austin do?" She had not heard anyone say what kind of business Austin had, but she knew from all they had that it had to be something very important.

He and his Dad own one of the largest Celebrity promoting businesses in the world. So he is involved with beautiful people all the time. Yes rich, tall, and beautiful people. Yet he found his love in Karen, all five foot one and a half inches of her. Austin is a very wealthy man and Karen has no idea as to how wealthy her husband is. She doesn't know how important he is at all. To her he is the man she loves and the father to her baby. His father is his only partner. He and Austin's mother are on an around the world tour at the present. They don't even know their son is married, let alone the fact that he is going to be a daddy. They will be crazy in a very good way about all of this when they get home."

CHAPTER TWENTY TWO

Their plane landed just a little later than scheduled. They were married and got back to New York around one o'clock Sunday morning.

"Mrs. Brooks, are you ready to go home?" Bo asked.

"Yes Bo I am." Margo answered. It was two o'clock before they got home. Austin and Karen were asleep next door.

"Bo all my things are next door at Karen's." Margo was worried that she would not have anything to change into.

"Maybe not honey. If I know our friends they will have your things at our house waiting for you." Bo was right. Karen and Austin had even changed the sheets on Bo's bed and had it all turn down and waiting. Margo's bag was sitting on the long bench that sat at the end of Bo's king size bed. Everything was cleaned and polished.

"Bo, this is beautiful, I have never been in a man's bedroom before. I never thought they looked anything like this." Margo was very impressed.

"You have never been in a man's bedroom before?" Bo asked.

"No Bo never, nor have I ever been with a man. This will be my first time. I know nothing about making love. So I hope you know something about it and I'm very sure you do."

"That is great honey. That's just the way I wanted it to be."

"Bo I'm not as young as Karen, but I'm sure I'm just as scared as she was. My knees are already jumping."

"Margo, don't be afraid. I'm your husband now and we will ease into it all. We will start with a nice warm shower."

Bo could tell Karen had been in the bathroom as well. Everything was perfect. She had nice clean towels hanging out and everything was shining like a honeymoon suite. This made Bo really realize how much he meant to both Austin and Karen.

"Bo do you mean you want us to take a shower together?" Margo asked.

"Only, if you feel that you want to do it Margo?" Bo didn't want to rush her anymore than he had already and he felt he had already done a lot of that for one day.

"I will after all we are married now and I want us to always share everything. I don't want you to think I'm not willing to share everything with you."

"Margo we are always going to share everything." Bo could already tell they were going to be happy together.

They took a nice long shower Bo could not have been more pleased. Margo was happy about being Bo's wife. Bo thought his new wife was beautiful with her clothes on and without them. Margo was real pleased at how her new husband looked as well.

"Margo I don't want to rush you, but I do want you in every way."

"Bo I think it's a little too late to be worrying about you rushing me now. I think we have already rushed into a lot. Now we need to slow down and enjoy the rest of our life together. I'm not going away and I hope you feel the same. I will be a good wife and I think you will be a good husband and I want you too." she decided to add at the last second.

"Margo I feel that very same way too."

"Bo I never want to make you sorry you married me that would be the last thing on earth I would want for you."

"Margo I hope you are never sorry either." Bo leaned down and kissed his new wife. He knew now how Austin felt every time he was near Karen.

"Bo, why did you want to get married so fast? We could have dated." Margo asked.

"Yes we could have done that, but why should we waste all that time when we would have ended up married anyway. I would have wanted you with me every time I took you back home. I used to watch you at the front desk and wonder if you would date me. Now I know."

"Yes I guess you do know. Bo, there will be a lot of upset women in your office Monday morning."

"Why?" Bo asked.

"Because Bo, I was not the only woman working in your office that is madly in love with you. There are several women working at your office that want you." Margo knew because she had heard several of them talking about what they would do if they would ever get him.

"Margo, don't tell me who they are I don't care. You are the only woman in all my years of being a doctor I have ever even looked at. The rest of them have just been wasting their time, but I don't think they need to know this was our first date."

"No I don't think so either. I would prefer they believe we have been dating all along." Margo answered.

"Then that's what we will say to them Monday." Bo kissed Margo again. He liked having a wife. "Margo, are you ready for bed?" he asked.

"Yes Bo, I'm ready." Margo had on her big tee shirt gown. This reminded him of Karen the weekend they went out on their motorcycles.

"Now that's some gown." Bo said the second he saw his wife dressed for bed.

"Yes it is. I didn't know I was packing for my wedding night, but it would not have made any difference, this is my gown and this is what you get like it or not." Margo then gave Bo a big smile.

"And it's such a big gown." Bo teased.

"Yes they say one size fits all. I will be able to wear this gown forever." Margo said with another big smile. She hoped Bo understood what she had said.

"Well it will do for now." Bo was in his boxers. Margo got into bed and Bo got in beside her.

"Bo I hope you don't expect too much. If you do you will be sadly disappointed."

"Margo we will be perfect, but I first need to know if you want children right away or not?"

"Why not Bo if you do, I do." Margo answered. She wanted Bo as happy as his friend Austin.

"Alright we will not worry about protection then." Bo answered. "I'm nervous Bo." Margo could feel herself shaking.

"I know you are honey, but you don't have anything to worry about. We are married and I'm sure your father, will aim at me and not at you." Bo answered.

"Bo my father doesn't even own a gun." she answered. "Wow that sure takes a load off my mind." Bo answered.

They made love. Bo was so tender and loving towards Margo. He made her feel so loved. Everything he did was to make her relax and enjoy it along with him. He wanted his wife happy.

"Bo you made it so nice. I never dreamed it could be so nice." Margo was surprised at how much she enjoyed their love making even thought it was her first time.

"Margo it should always be that way." Bo answered.

CHAPTER TWENTY THREE

The next morning Bo and Margo slept in. It had been a long night. After all they had spent it getting married and making love.

"Austin, do you think they made it back home last night?" Karen asked as she sat in bed.

"I don't know Karen we will just have to wait and see, but in the mean while I can think of something for us to do while we wait." He had that look on his face.

"Well if that is what you want to do it had better be in a hurry. We need to get ready for church." Karen answered.

"Well then lay down woman so I can do just that." But of course they did not do it in any hurry. They never did it in a hurry.

"Austin I do love you so much. Even when you make me do all of this." Karen knew every day what a lucky woman she was.

"Karen honey I'm so glad you do, because it makes being married so much better. Now if you didn't love me I would have to be spending a lot of time convincing you to love me. And what do you mean by even when I make you do this?"

Karen just laughed. She knew he was well aware that she loved making love with him as much as he loved doing it with her. "Now get up Austin we need to get our shower and get dressed and I don't mean any messing around in the shower either. Do you understand me Austin?"

"Yes M'am I do. I have said I do a lot since I met you little lady." "Yes you have and Austin it has worked for you and for me every time. You say I do and then I do it with you."

They showered and dressed for church. But today Karen was not happy in her clothes. "Austin do you think I look big in this dress?"

"Karen, do you want to look big in that dress?" he asked. He was not taking a chance at saying the wrong thing. He knew women often asked question that get men in trouble when they answer them too honestly.

"No, why would I want to look big?" Karen quickly answered. "Okay then you are good. It doesn't make you look big at all."

Austin was not going to say the wrong thing to Karen for sure. He had learned a long time ago not to do that when answering any woman's question about how she looked in her clothes. He would leave all of that to someone else.

As soon as church was out they hurried home. They both wanted to see if Bo and Margo had gotten back from South Carolina and find out if they were married. It was after two o'clock when their door bell rang.

"They are here, Austin go and open the door." Karen was so anxious to hear what Bo and Margo had to say.

"Yes Karen I will." Austin was just as anxious as Karen to find out if Bo had married Margo. So he hurried to the front door.

"Well how did it go?" Austin asked as soon as the door was opened.

"Austin, meet my wife, Mrs. Bo Brooks." Margo was standing at Bo's side.

"So you two did it?" Austin was real happy for his friend. He knew that marrying Karen was the best thing he would ever do.

"Yes we sure did and we did it all." Bo said with a big smile on his face.

"Margo, don't listen to those two men." Karen said as she led Margo to the kitchen. "They all have a one track mind and it's always on sex. You would think at their age they would have gotten over it some."

"Yes, but Karen aren't we glad they haven't." Margo answered.

"Yes Margo we are, but they don't need to know that little bit of information they would be using it against us all the time. I want Austin to always want me. Margo is everything alright?" Karen asked.

"Yes Karen, it could not be better. I'm going to call my grandparents today and tell them about us getting married and I will write my daddy and tell him. Karen Bo had already noticed me at work. He even remembered my first day there. Karen he even liked me back then." This Karen could tell made Margo feel a lot better about everything.

"So Margo he was just acting like he didn't know who you were?" "Yes that was what he was doing. Karen I'm so glad you asked me to call you. There is no telling how long we would have gone without saying one word to each other. Now I have the man I love and he loves me." Margo was beaming.

"Margo I'm so glad it all worked out this way. I knew you were like me and that is what Bo told me to look for in a woman for him." Karen and Margo were hugging when Austin and Bo came into the kitchen.

"Karen did Margo tell you?" Bo asked.

"Yes Bo she did. She said, you were already wanting her before Austin even met me. So Bo, what took you so long to get her?" Karen asked.

"I was chicken." he answered. They all laughed.

"Well Bo my good old friend you are all hooked now just like me." Austin had a big smile on his face too.

"Yes Austin, just like you. We both got caught by little short girls and we love it all. Now all we have to do is wait for them to make us daddies." The thought of being a daddy made Bo even happier.

"Bo, have you and Margo decided to start your family right away too?" Austin asked.

"Yes Austin we have decided there is no reason to put it off. My wife doesn't need a doctor. I can delivery all of our babies. Austin between Karen and Margo I think I will be very busy delivering babies for both of us."

"Bo does Margo want a large family too or did you even bother to asked her?" Austin asked.

"Yes she does Austin and that makes me very happy."

"Bo, would you two like to join us? We were just going out to eat. Karen needs to eat more. Her doctor said for her to do that at her last appointment." Austin reminded Bo.

"That sounds good to me Austin, but first let me ask my wife." Bo answered with a big smile. "Honey would you like to join our very good friends when they go out to eat?"

"Yes, Dr. Brooks that would be nice. After all we do need to eat sometime today." Margo didn't think she would have enough energy to make love again if she didn't eat something soon and she was very sure her new husband would have that on his mind again today.

"Alright we will go. My wife needs food and so do I. Where are we going?" Bo asked. He felt as if he had used up all of his energy too.

"Karen wanted to give the Italian place another try. So far we have been there twice and she hasn't eaten a thing there yet. So we are going again. They say the third time is a charm."

They all went out the front door and got into Austin big black Ford truck. Bo gave it a long looking over. "Austin I think I need to get me one of these trucks. Margo honey, how do you like this truck?"

"Bo it's big, but it's great." she answered.

"Austin I think I'm going over to the Ford place and get a big truck like this." Bo had been sold on Austin's new truck for some time now. After all he was from the South.

"Margo, Karen told me a Ford truck does something to a man. It makes a man feel like the man he thinks he really is and the women who drive Ford trucks know they are women with power right under their foot. Now Margo how do you feel about Bo feeling like the man he thinks he is?" Austin asked.

"I love it. Because I think he is that man too. So if Bo wants himself a big he man truck I want my big he man husband to have it." She answered.

"Spoken like a real bride. Thank you so much Honey." Bo gave Margo a little kiss on the cheek.

"Karen do you drive this big truck?" Margo asked.

"No Margo, I don't drive at all. I have never learned to drive." Karen answered.

"I do Karen so I can drive us anywhere we want to go and I can teach you to drive too." Margo had been driving for years.

"Margo I don't know if I'm smart enough to learn to drive." Karen answered.

"Yes you are Karen. Margo, Karen finished first in her class at the old age of sixteen. Now she is an old married woman and expectant mother at the very old age of nineteen." Bo answered.

"Hello Mr. and Mrs. Blackburn how are you today? I see you are expecting a little one. How is married life treating you?" Gino asked as soon as they walked into the restaurant.

"Yes we are expecting a baby boy Gino, and as for how married life is treating us we love it more and more every day. These are our good friends, you already know Dr. Brooks and this beautiful young lady with him is his wife Mrs. Margo Brooks." Austin answered.

"Very nice meeting you Mrs. Brooks, are you two newlywed also?" Gino asked.

"Yes Gino as a matter of fact we are. We got married yesterday." Bo had that big smile on his face again. He and Austin were both grinning. Their wives wanted to kill them both. It was as if they had a big sign on their back saying we get sex from our wives all the time.

"Oh so you are really newlyweds. I will give you Mr. and Mrs. Blackburn's favorite booth it's, way in the back and very private." Gino gave both wives the once over. He liked what he saw every time he looked at Karen and Margo was nice too. "I never had to accommodate these two men before with a nice quite out of the way booth until they met you two ladies." Gino just could not stop looking at the two women or stop talking.

"Thank you Gino we do appreciate it." Austin said as they followed Gino to the back of the restaurant as he continued to talk to their wives all the way to their booth.

"Austin we have been here three times now and I haven't had any food yet. So please let me have something today. I promise I will eat it all and I will make love with you all night." Karen was as hungry as all of the rest of them today.

"Alright Karen, that's a deal. Bo you heard her, she is going to make love to me all night for the price of a meal." Austin loved being married. It sure was a lot better than any date he had ever had.

"Yes Austin I did and I think I should be getting the same deal from my wife. How about it Margo, do I get the same deal?" Bo asked. Margo's face started to turn red. "Margo is that a yes?"

"Bo, don't you be asking me something like that while we are around other people." Margo was still a little red.

"Alright honey I won't. I will just believe you will do it." Bo answered.

"Yes you can do that, but if I should change my mind I will let you know." Margo then gave Bo a big smile.

"Austin I believe we have two very shy wives and I do believe they have two husbands that like it that way."

As soon as they were seated in their booth the girls went to the restroom, together of course as all women do. "Karen I do love Bo, but I just don't know what to say to him when he asked me about having sex with him in front of Austin. I can feel my face turning red every time. How do you handle that with Austin?" Margo sure needed Karen's help.

"Margo I had to learn to handle Austin and Bo and you will need to do the very same thing. We will just give our husbands what they want every time they want it and they will be Daddies a lot of times for wanting it so much. Margo we have very good husbands and if they want to make love with us all the time then we should be happy it's us they are wanting and not some other woman." Karen had given Margo very good advice.

"I agree with you Karen. I guess all of this is just so very new to me. Karen I want to thank you for taking my bag over to Bo's house and for all the nice things you did. I know you did them because Bo didn't have time to do them himself." Margo just could not get over how nice Karen was.

"You are welcome, but I didn't do it alone, Austin helped." "Karen Bo said you go to work with Austin sometimes."

"Yes I do. I sleep on his nice leather sofa and he takes me to lunch and sometime shopping and sometimes we even make love on that leather sofa. I love my new life with Austin. I never want to go back to my old life ever again." Karen was a very happy woman.

"Austin I wonder what has happened to our wives?" Bo was not used to having a wife and he had never paid much attention to how long his dates took in the restroom before. In the past with most of his dates he didn't care if they had taken all night in the restroom or if they had even decided to leave without telling him. He was just not that much into any of the women he had dated all those years.

"Bo they are in there talking about us and comparing us to each other. They both think they got the better husband, but you and I know we got the best wives." Austin and Bo were both watching for their own wife to return to the table.

"Yes Austin we did. I'm so grateful to Karen for seeing that Margo was the right woman for me. I just don't know how she did it."

Austin knew he would not be the same man today if he didn't have Karen to love him and him to love her. He knew his friend would be feeling the very same way in a short while.

After the girls got back to the table they ordered their meal. They all got the same thing except for one thing Karen got a different dressing on her salad. They all seemed to have enjoyed the meal very much.

After they left the restaurant they drove over to the Ford dealer. It did not take long for Bo and Margo to pick out a new Ford truck. They picked a nice big blue one. It was like Austin's except for the color. They even used the same salesman that Austin and Karen had used.

Austin isn't that our salesman over there?" Karen asked.

"Yes honey I do believe it is, but I have forgotten his name." Austin answered.

It's Moody, Austin, remember?" Karen answered.

"Yes I do now, but what I remember most is the way he kept looking at you." Austin then gave Karen that look.

"Well Austin I don't think you will need to worry about that this time. I'm very sure he won't be looking at me. Not with this big stomach." Karen was looking very pregnant today.

"Margo maybe we should have waited until you had a big stomach sticking out before we came here then Mr. Moody would not have had his eyes popping out of his head so much from looking you two over." Bo and Margo went inside with Mr. Moody to do up the paper work. Karen and Austin left them there waiting to drive their truck home.

"Austin what do you want to do?" Karen asked as soon as they got home, but she really didn't need to ask.

"Guess?" he answered.

"Guess, did you say guess?" Karen asked.

"Yes I did Mrs. Blackburn so guess." Austin answered.

"I know what you want. So get upstairs while I'm in the mood." she answered. Karen was already going up the stairs.

"Karen, are you in the mood? What brought that on I wonder?" Austin asked.

"You, you always bring that mood on and especially when you are wearing those tight jeans of yours. I take one look at you and I get in the mood. I love you so much Mr. Blackburn you sexy man." she answered.

"I love you too. So let's get upstairs before you change your mind. I may need to stop wearing anything, but my jeans if they affect you this way." They made love for two hours that afternoon.

Bo and Margo wasted no time getting home after they had finished at the Ford Dealer. They went straight upstairs to their bedroom. They were so in love.

"Bo, do you think, Austin and Karen, know what we came home to do?" Margo asked.

"Sure they do and they came home to do the very same thing. Didn't you see how Austin, kept looking at Karen. He was ready to get her back in bed all day. He sure loves that woman and Margo I want us to love each other the very same way."

"We will Bo just give us time."

CHAPTER TWENTY FOUR

T he next morning Bo did go to work, but Margo stayed home. She and Bo were going to her apartment after work to get all of her things and move them over to Bo's house. Margo loved her new house and her new husband. In just one weekend she had change her whole life.

Karen stayed home and cleaned. Austin was going to be very busy with several people and Karen did not want to be around all those tall beautiful people while she felt so big and fat. She told Austin before he left for work not to let any of those tall beautiful women get near him. He was taken. He told her not to worry he had exactly what he wanted and it came in a small package with a bonus.

Margo decided to do some cleaning as well. Later in the morning Karen called over to check on Margo. She wanted to be sure Margo was alright and to see if she needed anything.

"Hello."

"Margo its Karen, are you alright?"

"Yes Karen I am. I'm so happy. Bo is so wonderful just like you said he would be. I knew I felt a lot for him all those months, but I did not realize how strong my feelings were until we got married. I guess I have just let all my feeling go now because I have him."

"Yes Margo you do have him now. What did your grandparents say about you and Bo getting married?" Karen hoped it would all be good.

"They were all excited because I had told them so much about him over the last six months."

"Oh that's nice. I haven't told anyone in my family that Austin and I are married. I don't have anything going with them. I left there and I have never been back." Karen did not want to ever get involved with any of her family again.

"Karen I'm so sorry. I wished you had a family like I have." Margo felt real sorry for her new friend.

"No Margo I have a much better life with Austin. He is so good to me. I love him so much and we both are so excited about our baby boy. I hope you have a baby soon." Karen was already making plans for both of their babies so she needed Margo to get pregnant soon.

"I do too. Bo wants me to get pregnant right now. He is just like Austin. He wants a big family." Margo was happy that Bo wanted lots of children and so were her Grandparents.

"Has Bo told his family yet? I bet they are as happy as your grandparents." Karen asked.

"How did Austin's parents take the news of him getting married?" Margo felt that they must have taken it very well.

"They don't know we are married or anything else." Karen answered.

"Boy I would hate to be you when they find out about you and their son being married." The second she had said it Margo wished she could somehow take it all back.

"No Austin said they would be fine with it, but I'm not so sure. Margo I need to go and lay down for awhile are you cooking supper for Bo tonight?" Karen got talking again and forgot that she was going to rest some before starting her supper.

"Yes I thought I would give it a try. Do you need anything from the store?" she asked.

"Oh are you going to walk down the street to that little store?" Karen asked. She had often done the same things for her and Austin.

"Yes I thought I would, do you need anything?" Margo asked again.

"No, but I will walk with you if you don't mind." Karen answered.

"Oh Karen I would love to have you walk with me." Margo wasn't sure of the neighborhood yet even though she had only seen really nice homes in it. She was glad to have Karen walk with her.

"Okay I will meet you out side." They hung up and Karen then called Austin on his cell phone.

"Hello sweetheart how are you feeling today?" he asked.

"I'm fine Austin. I'm going to walk to the store with Margo and I didn't want you to worry if you called here and I didn't answer the phone." Karen was putting on her shoes as she talked to Austin.

"Karen you be careful I love you." He was very busy today and he didn't have much time for anything except business.

"I love you Austin and I will be careful. Goodbye." When Karen came out of the door Margo was already there waiting for her.

CHAPTER TWENTY FIVE

When Bo got to his office that morning he had a meeting with all of his employees. He wanted to stop any gossip that may come up about him and Margo.

"Dr. Brooks we are all here except for Margo and she is out and we have not heard from her yet. That is so unlike her." Bo's office manager said as they all begin to gather for the meeting.

"That's alright. Thank you all for taking the time to come in here. I just wanted to tell you all I got married this past weekend." Bo could hear the air being sucked out of the room.

"Oh Dr. Brooks we didn't know you were involved with anyone. Who did you marry and do we know her?" one of his nurses asked.

"Yes you all know her. Margo Wilson is my wife." Bo didn't say anymore. He wanted to hear what they all had to say about him and Margo being married.

"Margo? Our little Margo is your wife?" one of the nurses asked. "Yes, Margo is my wife. So she will not be back here to work. We will need to replace her as soon as we can." Bo saw no need in telling his employees anymore.

"Congratulations doctor Bo." several said as they all began to leave the room.

"Thank you all." Bo wanted to go right to work. He had his wedding band on so they could all see it.

"Doctor I'm so surprised. I didn't even know you knew her." one for the other woman who worked up front with Margo said.

"Well I must have, after all we are married." Bo answered.

The rest of the morning Bo could hear his employees talking about nothing, but him and Margo. He could also tell some of the women employees were not that happy about Margo stealing his heart. One even had nerve enough to ask him if he had to marry her.

"No my wife and I did not have to get married. Why would you ask me such a question? I do not want to hear one more question as to whether we had to get married or not. I married my wife because

I love her. Do you all understand me? If you don't please resign today because your service will not be needed here any longer." As soon as that was said Bo walked away from the small group that had gathered in the hallway outside of his office. He was not pleased with some of his employees at all.

After he had finished with several of his patents and was back in his office he decided to give Margo a call, but she did not answer. He just left her a message. "Hello honey it's me I'm working and I miss seeing you here. I may need you to come and sit so I don't miss you so much during the day. I love you, by the way, it's me Bo your husband."

After getting back from the store Margo played the message over and over again. She loved hearing Bo's voice. It made her smile and before long she was dancing all around the house. She went from one room to the other dancing.

Karen went home to lie down, but not before she called Austin to let him know she was back home from the store. "Hello sweetheart I, guess you are back home?" Austin was sitting at his desk getting ready for another meeting.

"Yes I am and I think I need to lie down. Austin I don't feel very good." Karen was getting sicker by the second.

Austin stopped what he was doing and was walking out of his office. He was going home to check on his wife. He did not like the way she sounded. Something was wrong and he knew it. "Karen just lay down on the sofa in the den don't try climbing the stairs. I'm already on my way home. Now I want you to go into the den while I'm still on the phone and you lay down. I will stay on the line so you won't be all alone." Austin was truly worried.

"Austin, please hurry I feel like I really need you." Karen started to cry.

"Karen lay down right where you are on the floor I will be there soon. Don't you even try to take another step." Twenty minutes later Austin was coming up the basement steps. He found Karen on the floor. He called Bo as fast as he could.

"Dr. Brooks an emergency call from Mr. Austin Blackburn on line five. He said there was something wrong with his wife and he sounds very upset."

Bo answered the phone as quickly as he could. "Austin what is the matter with Karen?"

"Bo she is laying on the floor and she is sick. What do I do?" Austin was hurting. He did not want anything to happen to his wife or his son.

"Austin call 911 and I will meet you at the hospital." Bo left his office in a rush. He did not want Karen to be losing her baby.

Austin called 911. Karen was so sick she could not raise her head. Within minutes the ambulance was there to take Karen to the hospital. Austin was going to follow them in his little red car.

Margo saw the ambulance and hurried over to see what was wrong. She never expected to see Karen being carried out of the house to the ambulance.

"Margo, Bo is on his way to the hospital do you want to go with me and ride back with him?" Austin was ready to get into his car.

"Yes Austin let me do that. Austin what happened?" Margo could not understand all of this happening so fast. She had left Karen less than an hour ago and she seemed to be fine then.

"Margo, Karen called me when she got back to the house from going to the store with you. She said she was so sick she had to lie down on the floor. She was not even able to get into the den to the sofa. I don't know what is wrong. I called Bo and he is meeting us at the hospital. Off they went right behind the ambulance. "I should have ridden in the ambulance with Karen." Austin was so upset.

"Austin she doesn't know you aren't there with her. Those people are taking such good care of her right now. You would only be in their way." She hoped that would make him feel a little better.

"Yes I guess you are right. I would have just been in their way. I just love her so much. I can't let anything happen to her." Austin never said anything about their baby. At that time all he cared about was Karen. She had to be alright.

Bo was waiting at the door of the hospital when the ambulance got there. Austin parked and ran into the hospital and Margo came running in right behind him.

Bo had already gone in with Karen. She looked so pale and her blood pressure was up. Bo got right to work getting Karen's pressure down and running several test on her to see what was causing her all this trouble.

In a short while Margo and Austin were permitted in the back to see her. "Bo what's wrong with Karen? You have got to help her. I can't lose Karen I love her." Austin was taking all of this very badly.

"Austin we are not losing Karen or your son. There is something causing this and we will find it. You just relax. Come in here and stand near her bed and hold her hand. Let her know she is not alone. Margo honey I'm glad you came with Austin. Bo had not even noticed Margo being there until then. He leaned over and gave his wife a quick little kiss as he hurried to the other side of Karen's bed. Bo was going to test her blood. He even drew it himself.

"Karen, honey I'm here with you sweetheart. I love you so much." Austin had tears in his eyes. Bo had never before seen his friend so upset.

"Austin, she will be alright. Bo will do everything for Karen." Margo hoped she was telling him the truth.

"I know he will Margo, but this is my wife and I can't do anything to help her. I feel totally helpless." Austin had tears running down his face. He had to wipe them away with his hand several times.

"Yes you can Austin. You can pray for her and your baby." Margo was very strong in her faith.

"Yes I can do that, thank you Margo for reminding me." Margo left so Austin could talk to God about his wife and baby. Austin began to pray from his heart as tears ran down his face.

"Austin its food poison, that Karen has. She had eaten something that was bad." Bo said as he came back into Karen's room.

"What did you say Bo?" Austin asked.

"I said Karen has food poison. I will pump her stomach and with this IV she will start feeling better and so will your son. They both will be alright. Austin I will need to keep her over night. Austin I would not let something happen to Karen I love her too." Bo was working as fast and as hard as he could.

"Yes I know Bo, but she is my wife." Austin stayed in the room while Bo pumped Karen's stomach. She was awake. Austin saw tears running down her face. He wiped them all away.

"Karen your throat will be sore for a few days. Other than that you and your son will be fine. So stop your worrying. That big boy is fine. In fact both of your boys are doing fine now." Bo smiled over at Austin.

Karen stayed in the hospital overnight and so did Austin. He was not leaving her side. He got her a nice gown and robe with matching slippers along with some underwear from the gift shop plus two dozen red roses. They had just gotten Karen in her bed when Austin came in with her things and the roses.

"Austin you got me roses. I've never had anyone to give me roses or any other flowers before." That made Austin sorry he had never sent Karen any flowers before. Not even the day after they were married or when they found out that she was pregnant.

"Oh honey I should have sent you flowers a hundred times. I'm so sorry." Austin hated that it had to take something as bad as this for him to give his wife flowers.

"It's alright Austin you have given me something a lot better than roses." she answered.

"Yes, but I should have sent you roses for him too." he answered. "Oh Austin I love you and I don't need flowers from you to know you love me. You prove that every day by the way you treat me." Austin kissed Karen again and again. He knew he would never regret marrying her.

"Karen I have something else for you." Austin held up the big bag.

"What is it?" She asked.

"I got you a gown, robe with matching slippers and some underwear." he answered.

"Oh Austin see what you do. All of this is roses to me." she answered. Austin thought Karen had a way of always making him feel good by the way she appreciated everything he did for her.

"Now let me help you to change out of the rest of your clothes before Bo and Margo get back here." Austin took off Karen pants, bra and panties and then he put her gown on her. I got you another pair of panties for tomorrow morning I knew you would want another clean pair to wear home." He smiled at her and she smiled back. "That will save me from having to wash them out and hanging them out to dry." "Austin I would not let you wash out my dirty underwear." Karen told him.

"Why not you wash mine all the time?" he answered.

"That's different I'm your wife and I use the washing machine to do it." she quickly told him.

"Karen I would do it for you and more." Austin would not have one reservation at all about hand washing out his wife's panties.

"I know that, but I don't want you to do that for me." Karen looked down at her new gown. "Austin this is a beautiful gown it must have cost you a fortune."

"Karen it did not cost a fortune." he answered.

"Maybe not to you Austin, but to me it did." Karen loved the gown. It was very beautiful and so lady like.

"Honey you can have anything you want; my money is yours." he answered.

"No Austin it is not. You had all of that money before you met me and it had nothing to do with me."

"Karen it has everything to do with you. I worked hard all those years so I would have money for my family. You are that family."

"Oh Austin you see why I love you so much. Even before you met me you were thinking about our future. Not many men would have thought to do that for a family they did not have yet."

"Yes Karen I was thinking about you for a long time and you were thinking about me because, you waited for me and only me." Austin wanted his wife to know she had done her part too.

"Austin I love you and only you, so how could I have done anything with anyone, but you? Austin is Bo sure our son is alright?" Karen was still worrying about how her being sick may have affected their baby son.

"Yes honey he is alright, but if you want another sonogram to see for yourself we will get Bo to do another one." Austin would do anything to ease his wife's mind.

"Can we Austin? I just want to see for myself that he is alright." Karen wanted to see her son and see that he was still where he should be and doing what he should be doing at this time.

"I will ask Bo for one when he gets back here." Austin was sitting on the bed beside Karen when Bo and Margo returned carrying three large bags of food.

"Karen, how are you feeling?" Bo asked as soon as he was back in her room.

"Oh Bo I feel so much better. You just can't believe how much better I feel. I thought I was going to die there for awhile." Karen was so happy to be feeling so much better even if she was still not perfect yet.

"You look better, little girl you had us all worried." Bo was glad Karen had thought to call Austin when she got so sick. He would hate to think what would have happened if she had not made that call, but he was not going to tell her that now.

"I'm so sorry. I felt so bad all morning, but I thought it would soon go away. I even went to the store with Margo hoping the fresh air would help. Oh Margo you didn't get to cook your meal for Bo. I'm so sorry Margo." That upset Karen too.

"Karen it's alright Bo and I will just have it tomorrow night. Karen you are much more important than any meal I could have cooked for Bo tonight." Margo went over to the bed and hugged Karen. They both knew they were going to be very good friends.

"Karen what did you eat yesterday that we all did not eat?" Bo needed to know this in case it was something he needed to inform the Health Authority about.

"Bo I don't know I thought I ate the same thing as all of you. But none of you are sick or at least I hope you aren't."

"No Karen you didn't. You had a different salad dressing than all of us." Austin remembered her not wanting the same dressing that the rest of them were having.

"Yes Austin you are right I did at the restaurant yesterday. Could that be what has caused all of this?" Karen asked.

"Yes I do think so. I will give the restaurant a call right now." Bo got on the phone and talked to the manager of the Italian restaurant where they had all eaten at on Sunday.

"Karen we won't go back to that restaurant again." Austin felt real upset. He had taken Karen there three times and the first time she ate she got food poison.

"No Austin the food is great. It was most likely only the salad dressing I ate. All of the other food I had was the same as you three had too and you three say you aren't sick."

By ten o'clock Karen was asleep. "Bo why don't you and Margo go home I will be here with Karen and if I should need you I will give you a call." Austin had taken a seat in one of the chairs in Karen's room and he was ready to stay the night there.

"Alright Austin we will go, but if you need me I will come back. Otherwise I will see you two by eight o'clock tomorrow morning." Bo was tried and he was ready to go home, but if Karen had still been sick he would have stayed there with her and Austin all night. She was more than just his patent.

As soon as Bo and Margo were in the elevator and alone he gave her a big kiss. He had missed her all day. Not having her at his office to look at during the day made his day seem very long. "Bo you could have stayed with them I could go home in a cab."

"No you are my new wife and we have things to do tonight." Bo answered. "Karen is fine. She will be up and ready to go home by tomorrow morning. I'm only keeping her here over night as a precaution."

"Bo, how did it go at the office today?" Margo asked.

"They were all surprised, but happy for us." Bo thought it better not to say what some of his employees had said. He decided to keep all of that to himself. He did not want his wife to feel that she was not liked by his office workers only because he had married her and not one of them.

"Bo is Karen really alright?" Margo was real concern about her new friend. Karen had already become her best friend.

"Yes honey she is and she will be her old self in just a couple of days. Her throat will be sore that's all." Bo was glad to know his wife was this worried about Karen. It only proved to him that he was right. She was the right woman for him.

"Bo this afternoon when they took her out of their house she looked so pale. Austin was so afraid. I know he thought he was losing her and their son."

"I know honey he loves her just like I love you." Bo held on to Margo's hand as they walked out into the parking garage.

"Bo do you really love me?" she asked. She just loved to hear him say that he loved her.

"Yes Margo I have for some time. I was just waiting for Karen to make her move. I have loved you for months. That's why I had you moved to the front desk instead of letting you stay where you could have been better used. I wanted you where I could see you all day."

"So you really did see me there."

"Yes I saw you every chance I could Mrs. Brooks. Sometimes I even made up reasons for going out to the front desk with my patents."

"Bo I was so much in love with you and I thought you didn't know I existed. When Karen invited me to meet someone I had about given up hope. I was so happy when it was you I had come to meet. I almost passed out."

"Margo I was so happy too and I was not letting you get away. I had to do the same thing as Austin; he let his heart lead him and that is what I did."

That night Bo and Margo made love again and again. "Mrs. Brooks you are exactly what the doctor ordered."

"I sure hope so because I'm all you ever get. There are no second tries. The buck stops with me. Do you understand that Dr. Bo Brooks?"

"Yes M'am you have made it very clear, but you are all I will ever need Mrs. Brooks." Bo was a happy man. He kissed his wife again.

"Bo, are you ever going to tell your parents about us? Or are you going to wait and let them just show up here one day and find you surrounded by four or five children? Then they will ask you, who are all of these people? Then you will answer, oh, didn't I tell you about me getting married ten years ago to Margo. I'm so sorry I thought I had said something to you about her and our children"

"Margo, don't look so worried. My parents will love you. I just thought we would do it all at one time." Bo answered.

"Do what all at one time?" Margo did not understand.

"Tell them we are married and pregnant all at one time." Bo thought that would be a wonderful surprise for his parents. They would be wild about Margo and they would go pure crazy if they knew they were going to be grandparents as well. That was something they had always wanted for their only son. They wanted him to have a good life with a woman he loved and that loved him. The children would just be a part of their love.

"Yes, but that may not be right away." Margo hoped she didn't end up disappointing Bo.

"So we will do it when it happens. There is no big hurry." Bo didn't want Margo to feel pressured in any way.

CHAPTER TWENTY SIX

"Margo would you like to go into the office and get checked?" Bo asked.

"Bo Brooks I think you have checked me enough." Margo had not thought about him doing that too.

"I know, but this time I mean a real checkup. Like with a doctor. You need to know if everything is alright and if it's not we can take care of it." he answered.

"Oh you mean go to that person that I used to work for and let him give me a checkup?" Margo loved just looking at her husband, and he undoubtly loved looking at her.

"Yes I mean him. You could come in after hours and no one would know that you came for a checkup if you didn't want them to know." Bo did not want to embarrass his new wife by her having to come during regular hours for a checkup and all of his employees know what he was doing with her.

"Okay I will do it, but only after all of your office help has gone home." Margo felt a little too shy to go back to Bo's office yet.

"Margo, just take a cab to my office tomorrow. Then we can come back home together."

"Bo, are we really what you want? I mean you and I being married. Is that what you want?" Margo had to make sure before she went any further into this marriage.

"Yes Margo it is." Bo answered.

"Bo you could have had any woman you wanted." Margo still could not understand why this tall handsome, well educated, rich man would want her for his wife.

"Yes I could and I do. I have the one person I want and it's you Margo Brooks. You are the woman I want." Margo began to cry. "What's wrong honey did I say something wrong? Did I say something that upset you?"

"No Bo you said everything right. I still can't believe I have you as my husband. I prayed and prayed. I was ready to give up, but something kept

267

my hopes up even when Karen asked me to call her. I wasn't sure how close you were to Austin and Karen. I just kept praying that it would be you and it was."

"Honey I was just about to fire you and then ask you out all in the same sentence." Bo shocked Margo with his statement.

"Fire me?" Bo had his arm around her. He could feel her trying to pull away.

"Yes fire you. I needed you to need me." he answered.

"Bo I needed you for the whole six months, but I needed my job too. What would I have done if you had fired me?" she asked.

"Margo you would have married me, that's what you would have done. You don't need that job now so let's go to sleep. It's after one o'clock. Woman you have worn me out." Margo kissed Bo and then she lay back down beside him.

Austin got up in bed with Karen. "Austin have you got enough room?" she asked.

"Yes honey, but none to spare." Karen lay in Austin's arms with one of her arms by her side. It still had the needle in it. "Karen, are you feeling better?"

"Yes Austin I felt so terrible I didn't know what was going on or what to do, but to call you."

"Honey you did the right thing. Now you are over it and we will go home tomorrow morning and later we will go over to Bo's office and he can do another sonogram on you. You will see our baby is alright for yourself."

"Oh Austin I love you and our little baby boy. I'm so glad it wasn't something else." Austin was glad to hear the relief in Karen's voice.

"Honey so am I." Austin could not have ever imagined feeling this way about a woman and an unborn child. Love had changed everything in his life. He was so thankful. They slept just the way they were all night. The next morning Bo was in their room before they woke up.

"Good morning sleepy heads." Bo looked every bit the doctor. Karen opened her eyes. "Good morning Bo."

"Karen, how are you feeling this morning?" Bo asked as he began to check her out.

"I feel like I may pee my pants that's how I feel." she answered. "Alright then go to the bathroom. Austin, help her with that pole."

When Austin got out of bed he only had his boxers on. He took Karen into the bathroom and in a little while they both came back into the room. Bo was putting something in his little laptop computer.

"Karen let me finish checking you out and then I will get that needle out of your arm so you can go home." Bo told her.

"Bo, Karen and I need another sonogram. We need to know our son is alright. We need to see him." To Bo Austin sounded as worried as Karen had been.

"Alright we will do another sonogram. Bring her into my office around five and we will do one. Now that you are going to my office this afternoon Margo needs a ride there. She was going to get a cab, but since you are going there she can just ride with you two. She needs a check up, but she didn't want to do it while all of my employees were there."

"Sure she can, Bo you can take care of both of our wives today." Austin answered before Karen could say anything.

"Karen, lie back down and while your husband gets his pants on and I will take this needle out of your arm. Austin did anyone come in during the night to check on Karen?" Bo asked.

"I guess not I didn't hear anyone." Austin answered.

As soon as Bo had the needle out of Karen's arm she went back into the bathroom to do her hair. She wanted to look nice when she left the hospital to go home.

"Austin did Karen sleep all night?" Bo asked.

"Most of it, but we did not do anything if that is what you are asking." Austin answered.

"No I was just wondering if she slept alright, but the other bit of information was nice to know you let her rest last night." Bo just smiled at his friend knowing he had spent most of his night making love with his wife. "Now you two get out of here. Go home and rest. I will see you at my office later and don't forget my wife." Bo told them.

On their way home Austin stopped at a small restaurant and got two take out breakfasts. "Karen I want you to eat every bite of your food. You are way too thin. I want you and our son healthy. You are not fat, you are pregnant. Do you understand me little girl?"

"Yes Austin I understand." Karen ate most of her breakfast. Austin ate all of his and the rest of hers.

"Now let's go upstairs and get in the tub. We both need a bath."
"Austin, aren't you going to take a shower?" Karen asked.

"No I'm taking a bath with my wife and then we are going to bed.

You can decide what we do from there." Austin answered and then he gave her a big smile.

Karen started up the stairs, Austin was right behind her. She still had on her new gown, robe and the matching slippers that Austin had gotten for her the night before from the hospital gift shop. "Austin, I will get out our underwear if you want to start the water for the tub?" "Anything you say honey." When Karen got to the bathroom with their clean underwear and another clean gown Austin had just finished shaving. "You ready?" he asked.

"Yes I'm ready." Karen took off her gown and underwear to get into the tub. Austin was right there to help her.

"Karen you are beautiful. Our son has only enhanced your beauty."

"Austin, would you be saying all of that if you were not married to me?" Karen asked.

"Karen if you were not my wife you would not be pregnant with my son yet. Nor would you be bathing in our tub with me." he answered.

"No I would not, but that did not answer my question." she replied.

"Yes now I have said it and because I am your husband and I can look at all of you. That is one of the privileges a husband gets with marriage." Austin answered.

"But Austin do I just look alright to you or do you look at all of those very tall women around you all day at work and wish you had married one of them instead?" Karen was sitting in front of Austin in the tub.

"No Karen never I don't love any of them. That is why I was going to get a surrogate to have my baby. That was until I saw the woman I wanted that day more than anything to be my wife. Sweetheart that was you."

"Austin I looked at you that day in the coffee shop and saw a movie star type of man. Then I looked at me and saw a smirf." she answered.

"Karen there is nothing wrong with being short. I will confess at first I didn't know about wanting a short woman. Soon I learned I love a short woman. Now I know you make me feel more like a man than any tall woman ever could. Karen Blackburn you are my wife and I live only for you." Then he pulled her close to him and kissed her.

Austin and Karen spent the whole day together. Austin called his office and had all of his appointments changed to the next day. He wanted to stay home and be with Karen.

"Karen, where would you like to go on vacation? Bo and I usually go off on our motorcycles for at least a couple of weeks a year, but now that we are married I'm sure those types of vacations are over."

"Austin, they don't have to be over. I can stay home and you and Bo can still go on your vacation as always." Karen did not want to be the one to cause trouble between Bo and Austin in anyway.

"No way, sweetheart. We will just have to come up with some solution. I'm sure Bo and I are smart enough to come up with something."

"Austin I didn't marry you to change everything in your life." Austin was sitting in his recliner in the den and Karen was rocking in her new rocker.

"Well honey I married you to change your life. I only want you to have room in your life for me and all of our children. If that's not changing your life what is? Karen I want you to change my life. If I had wanted it to stay the same I would not have gotten married, but I did get married and to you. So change anything in my life you want to change. That is how much I want you in my life." Austin answered.

"Austin Blackburn you are the best husband in the world. You should get an award for being such a wonderful husband."

"I know. That's exactly what I was going for." he answered. "You are teasing me aren't you?" Karen asked.

"Yes I am Karen, but I do mean every word I said. I want our life together to be what my, little wife wants it to be."

"Austin what if Margo and I go in the truck with a trailer and you and Bo ride your motorcycles some and ride with us some. And if Margo wants to ride with Bo some you could put your motorcycle on the trailer and you could drive the truck and ride with me some."

"Karen I think that will work. I will talk with Bo about it tonight." Austin was happy that his wife had come up with a way that they could all enjoy their vacation.

"Austin you don't think Bo will want to go off on a honeymoon with Margo instead of going off with us, do you?" Karen didn't know if

Margo would want to go on her first vacation as a married woman with her and Austin.

"I don't know." That made Austin remember that he had never taken Karen on a honeymoon either. The only trip he had taken her on was when they rode his motorcycle to Maine and she had morning sickness.

"Karen we didn't take a honeymoon trip. Did you think I just didn't want to take you on a honeymoon?" he asked.

"No Austin I didn't. I just thought we went right into being married and not just living together. I never thought we needed to go someplace else to be alone. We were already alone. No Austin I have a honeymoon every night when you get home from work and even sometimes we have a honeymoon on your sofa when I go with you to work."

"Karen that's the way it was with my Mama and Daddy and it still is. They may be in their fifty and sixties, but they still have a very good marriage. I will always want that for us and we will have as many children as you want, but Karen we are going to have the cleaning people here twice a week. I do not want you doing anymore housework. In fact we may have them here every day after the baby comes. I don't want you run down from taking care of me, the babies and this house."

"Austin I'm not going to argue with you. I feel tired all the time now." She had been looking a little tired to Austin, but he had not said anything.

"Karen, have you told Bo that yet?" Austin asked.

"No I thought it would go away soon." she answered.

At Four thirty that afternoon Margo came over. "Come in Margo, you look so nice and slim." Karen said as she looked at herself in the mirror as she passed it. She looked anything, but slim and she still had several months to go before Little Austin would be born.

"Karen I wish that I looked like you." Margo said. She knew Karen could only see how beautiful other women looked right now that was not big with a child.

"I know Margo, but all I see is nice beautiful tall thin women around my husband all the time, and look at me. I wonder why he would ever love me." Karen was feeling a little sorry for herself today.

Austin had heard what Karen had said. He didn't like her feeling this way at all. "Karen I love you and only you. Because you are the one I want to love. Well hello Margo. Are you ready to go?"

"Yes I think I am. I'm a little nervous." She told Karen.

"Margo you will be alright. Bo is your husband so it won't be like having some stranger checking you. If he does anything you don't like just don't have sex with him tonight. Then the next time you need a checkup he won't do that again."

"Karen I don't think Bo being my husband helps any. I'm still nervous, but I will keep what you said in mind."

Austin drove them to Bo's office. The last of the patients were leaving. "Hello Margo congratulations. I never suspected you and Dr. Bo were seeing each other." Margo didn't answer, she just let it go. "Your husband is in his office if you want to go on back. You do remember where it is, don't you? Mrs. Blackburn, Dr. Bo has room three set up for you. I'm going now. I will see you next time."

"Good bye." Austin said as the employee left.

Margo went down to Bo's office. She knocked on the door and waited for him to ask her in. "Yes" she could hear Bo say.

"Bo it's me Margo." she answered.

"Come on in Margo." Bo got up out of his chair and came around to the front of his desk so he could kiss his wife. "Margo, are Karen and Austin here?"

"Yes they are. Karen is already to see her son again." Bo was holding his wife close in his arms. He could hear her heart beating.

"You smell good." he told her.

"Thank you sir, I wanted to smell good for my doctor so he would not look at anything he shouldn't." she answered

"Oh but don't you sound a lot like another one of my patients. She wants me to do it all with my eyes closed. I hope you don't have that same idea."

"I think my doctor could be speaking of my good friend Karen. She is a lot like me I think. Maybe I should have the same idea as Karen and ask my doctor to close his eyes too while he is checking me."

"Come here woman and let me check a little of you right here." Margo was already in Bo's arms, but he still pulled her up a little closer to him. "You do know I miss seeing you up at the front desk every day. It's a little lonely here now, but when I start thinking about what is waiting at home for me I start smiling. I bet my staff knows exactly what I'm smiling about."

"Bo I'm sorry you are so lonely. Would you like for me to come back to work? I will if you want me to." Margo answered.

"No honey I will have to learn to be here without my wife." Bo answered.

"Just as long, as you, don't find someone else to look at during the day." Margo said while Bo was kissing her on the neck.

"I won't honey I can tell you that right now. I don't ever want to lose my wife. Now that I have just gotten her where I have wanted her for six months I want to keep her there. Right here in my arms." Bo kissed Margo one more time. "Honey I need to go and see about Karen. Do you want to go and see their little boy with me?"

"Bo, do you think they would mind me being in the room with them and seeing their son?" Margo didn't want to intrude on Karen and Austin at all.

"No, Come on, that little fellow will be calling you Aunt Margo so you may just as well meet him today." Bo took Margo by the hand and they went down the long hall to the room where Karen and Austin were waiting. "Hello Karen how are you doing this afternoon? A lot better than yesterday I hope."

"I feel fine Bo." Karen answered.

"Bo my wife is lying to you. She is tired and she can't get going anymore." Austin answered.

Bo could easily tell this was worrying his good friend. "Austin it's all because of you." Bo answered.

"Me, what do I have to do with it?" Both Karen and Bo looked at Austin at the same time. Karen had her mouth wide open. "What do you have to do with it?" Karen asked.

"Yes, that's what I want to know. What did I do?" Austin asked again.

Karen pointed to her stomach. "This is what you did Mr. Blackburn if you don't recall." she answered.

"Yes Austin you got your wife pregnant and you keep her up all night making love with you. I know Austin because I have been doing the very same thing with my wife and I'm all worn out and it hasn't been a week yet. You and Karen have been going at it for five months. I'm not at all surprised that she is worn out. You should be worn out too."

"Alright, Bo it's all my fault. From now on I will only make love with my wife half the night until our son is born." Austin answered.

"Yes because after he gets here you won't get to do it ever again." Both Austin's and Karen's mouth flew open when Bo said that to them. "What!"

"Just kidding," Bo said as he winked at Margo who was standing over in the corner of the room. "Now let's have a good look at our big boy. Karen, lie down and close your mouth. Austin will find a way to make love with you. After all it will take that to get all the rest of those babies here."

"Bo, don't make my wife's face turn so red. It may not be good for her or me." Austin said as he held onto Karen hand.

"Oh so you noticed that too." Bo said.

"Yes I did. It makes me feel good knowing she can still turn so red even after she knows we have seen so much of her." Austin answered.

"Margo, don't listen to them. They like playing doctor and up until now I was their only patient." Karen said from the examining table.

"Karen I hate to tell you, but that did not help me to feel any better. I don't want to be anyone's patient except Bo's." Margo was still standing in the corner. She was almost too afraid to come out of it.

"See Bo, Margo doesn't want anyone, but you. Isn't that sweet of her?" Karen asked.

"Yes it is. Thank you Karen." Bo said as he started the sonogram. "You are welcome Bo any time." She answered.

"There he is. See Karen look at your son. He is playing with his toes and there is his little winky just like his Daddy's. Oh no I maybe wrong he may have a bigger winky than his Daddy's." Austin didn't say anything, but he did give his friend the evil eye.

"Bo he is cute isn't he?" Karen could not get over how much he already looked like Austin.

"Yes Karen he is just like his mother. Austin what do you think about your son?" Bo asked.

"Bo I love him, but I'm thinking over how I feel about my good friend right now." Austin answered.

"Austin, don't get upset with Bo, for saying our son's winky is larger than yours. Bo knows your winky is the same size as his." Karen told her husband.

"Karen I won't get upset with him as long as you don't mind that my winky is as small as Bo's. I only know I love you and our baby son with all of my heart."

"Oh Austin that is so sweet, see Bo how sweet my husband is." Karen started to cry.

"Now honey, don't cry. See our son is doing great. He is right here." Austin touched Karen's stomach. "Can you feel him right there?" he asked.

"Yes Austin I can. Austin can you feel him too?" Karen asked.

"Yes Honey I sure can. My son is right in there." This really touched Austin's heart. He knew this was all very real. This young girl was giving him a son. Austin was thirty five now and his nineteen year old wife was doing this all for him and no one else. He couldn't be happier. Maybe a little more if his parents would only get themselves home.

"Austin what's the matter?" Karen asked.

"Nothing, Honey and everything," Austin said as he wiped the tears from his eyes. "I just can't get over being able to see our son so clear while he is still inside of you Karen."

"Bo, tell Austin if our son could be inside of him some of the time I would let him." Karen said.

"Austin do you want your son inside of you for a while? Your wife is willing to let you carry him around some now."

"No I don't think so and Karen doesn't either. She is just saying that because she knows it won't happen." Austin looked down at Karen lying on the table. He could not help, but to smile. He was so proud.

"Austin is right, I don't. I want his Daddy to love me so my little Austin is just where he belongs right now."

"Karen, I would love you if we could never have any babies. I just plain love you. It has nothing to do with you being pregnant. I fell in love with you way before you got pregnant."

"Yes you did Austin a whole day." Bo answered.

"Bo did it take me that long to get her pregnant?" Austin asked. "Yes Austin you were slow." Bo answered.

"Bo, are we through?" Austin asked.

"Yes we are for now. Austin, are you going to clean up your wife's stomach for me while I take my wife to another room?" Bo asked.

"Yes I will be happy to do that and then we will go. I will use my key and lock you two in. Will you be alright here by yourselves?" Austin asked.

"Yes we will, who knows what we may do?" Bo took Margo down the hall to another room.

"Bo, are you sure I need this done?" Margo wasn't so sure anymore after she saw what the guys put Karen through.

"Margo if you would rather have another doctor do it, I will understand." Bo did not want to do anything his wife did not like.

"No Bo you are my husband, if I can't trust you who can I trust." she asked.

"Alright then let's get to it. Take off everything and put this sheet over you." Bo handed Margo a nice clean white sheet.

"Bo, turn around." Margo told him.

"You want me to turn around so I don't see my wife naked?" Bo asked.

"Well I guess that is sort of silly after this week. So don't turn around just unfasten my bra for me." Margo started taking off her clothes while Bo stood and watched.

"I will be glad to undo everything." Bo had a big smile on his face.

"Bo will you lock that door?" she asked.

"Yes if it makes my wife feel better, I will lock the door." Bo went over to the door and locked it. Then he told Margo she needed to slide a little more to the end of the table. Margo slid to the end of the table just like her husband told her to do. "Good, this will be a little uncomfortable." Bo said as he started to examine his wife.

"How do you know it is just a little uncomfortable?" she asked.

"I don't. I only say it because they told us to say that in Medical school." Bo answered.

"And what school did you say you went to?" she asked.

"Oh it was no school I just took a quick course online." Bo answered.

"Did they tell you in that online course that your patients may not believe that one word "little?" Margo asked.

"No they said if nothing else works for us to just smile." Bo answered.

"Well you can just wipe that smile right off your face and get this thing over with. I'm not going to lie here with my legs in these things and with your head under that sheet much longer."

"Margo I see no reason why we can't get pregnant right away. When was your last period?" Bo asked.

"Last week." Margo answered.

"So next week it could happen. Margo, would that be alright with you?" Bo asked. He wanted to be sure that was what she wanted too.

"Yes Bo it would if it's alright with you." Margo wanted to start as family with Bo as much as he wanted one with her.

"Oh honey it has been alright with me all week. I'm really looking forward to being a daddy after all these babies I have delivered for everyone else. I want to do the same thing for us."

"Alright Bo we will do it." Margo was ready to be a mother as long as Bo was ready to become its father.

"Margo, are you sure?" Bo asked again.

"Yes Bo isn't my husband my doctor. I won't have the worry other women have. My husband will be the doctor seeing all of me and not some other person. So yes I want a baby with you so stop asking me if I want to get pregnant. The answer is yes."

Austin drove Karen to a nice restaurant where they had dinner. They wanted a nice quiet evening out. Austin did not want Karen hurrying home to cook them an evening meal. "Karen, how does your throat feel?"

"It's alright now Austin. I'm just so happy about seeing our little boy. Austin he is so cute isn't he?" Karen had a big smile on her face. "I had no idea people could see their babies so well before they were born.

"Yes he is very cute. I could not be more pleased. Karen you are doing a very good job of carrying our little boy. I want to thank you for doing that for us."

"Mr. Blackburn it's my pleasure. I'm only glad I'm married to you and not just carrying him to give him to you. Austin I don't know if I would have been able to have given him up even to you. Somehow I would have gotten you to let me be your baby's nanny. I would not have just walked away from you or my son."

"Karen I would not have asked you to do that for one minute. All of that surrogate business went out the window before we spoke the first words to each other in the coffee shop. I was going to have you and our baby."

"Oh Austin I'm so glad."

"Now I want you to stop thinking about something that was never going to take place. I'm just thankful I did it so we could meet." Austin pulled Karen into his arms and gave her a long kiss.

"Are you ready to go home? You know we have to get right to it tonight." Austin didn't mind going home at all and going to bed a little earlier.

"Yes Austin we do. So let's go home and get to it as you said." "Woman you know there will never be any just getting to it with us ever. I love you too much for that to ever be our way of making love." "Yes Austin I know and I love you so much too." Karen knew her husband had only been joking with her.

CHAPTER TWENTY SEVEN

"Karen I have to fly out to Los Angles, tomorrow for a few days and I need you to go with me. Do you think you are up to a trip?"

"You are going to California?" Karen had never known anyone who had ever been to California before.

"Yes and you are going with me if you are up to it." Austin answered.

"Yes I'm up to it." she quickly answered.

"Then we will need to go home and pack tonight." Austin had made many quick trips to places before. He never thought anything about leaving on short notice. It was something he had done since going into business with his father. It was his way of life up until now that is.

"Austin, when will we leave?" Karen was so excited. She had never been anywhere except with Austin and Bo on the motorcycle trip and when she came from Georgia to New York and that was her first big trip ever.

"Tomorrow morning." Austin answered.

"Mr. Blackburn, just how long have you known that you were going to California?" Karen asked.

"I have known since yesterday, but you were sick and I didn't want to go if you were not able to go with me. I'm sorry if this doesn't give you much time to prepare." Austin answered, but yesterday after Karen had gotten sick he wasn't sure if he would be going anywhere.

"Austin you know I don't need time to pack. I can do that in no time. I can't wait to go. I haven't been to many places and none before coming here and to go to California. It doesn't seem real." Then she gave Austin a big thank you kiss.

"So my wife is alright with having to make this trip with me?"

"Yes I think it's wonderful. Where are our suitcases? We need to pack." Karen was ready to pack as soon as they got home.

Austin went into his closet and got out his largest piece of luggage. They both began to pack. Austin knew he was going to enjoy this trip more than any of the trips he had taken previously.

"How long will we be there?" Karen asked. She wanted to be sure that she packed enough clothes to last through the whole trip.

"We will fly back home on the weekend, so pack for four days. That should do it." he answered.

Karen got it all done and was sitting on the bed while Austin gave Bo a call to let him know they would be gone for four days. Karen was so excited about the trip. It would be her first airplane ride.

The next morning they got up early and Austin drove them to the airport. The traffic was already very heavy. "Austin I've never been on an airplane before. I thought that would be nice for you to know when I'm stuck to the ceiling of the plane and you can't get me off of it."

"Karen there is nothing to it. Just relax and pray the pilot read the map right." Austin answered.

"Austin they have to be able to read a map right to drive an airplane? I can't even read a map when I'm sitting in a chair here on earth and they expect pilots to do that while they are driving an airplane way up there in the shy?"

"No Karen I was only teasing you. Now I don't want you to worry I will be with you all the way." He had never heard anyone say what Karen had just said and it was all so funny to him. He only wished he had been able to laugh.

"I'm not worried, I'm excited, but Austin it must be costing you a lot of money for me to go with you for those few days. I could just stay home and wait for you to get back here."

"It won't cost that much and I had rather pay it than be missing you the whole time I'm in California." Austin knew he would be miserable the whole time he was there if Karen stayed home.

"Oh Austin, that's so sweet. Would you miss me? No one has ever missed me before." Karen answered.

"Well I would and I would not like it so you are going with me everywhere I go." Austin did not mean just this one trip. He meant forever.

"Austin I may not always be able to go with you. After I get farther along they won't let me fly with you."

"I know so I won't be going either. All of that business will have to wait or my father will go and handle it. My mother won't be pregnant and she will be able to fly." Austin had Karen in his arms.

"Austin you can't do that. I can stay home and you can call me every night. In fact in a couple of months you may not want to be seen with me at all."

"Never, Karen that will never happen I will always want to be with you. I want everyone to know you are my wife and it's my baby you are carrying."

"Austin I wonder if all husbands feel that way about their wives when they get really big?" She sure hoped so. It would be awful to be married to a man who didn't want to be with his pregnant wife.

"I don't know Karen, but they should. Their wives didn't get that way all by themselves. It took them both to get her pregnant and the men should appreciate their wives for going through all of it to give them a family."

The next morning they went out to the airport and then a few hours later they were in California. "See Karen it wasn't bad at all was it?"

"No Austin it was great and we are here already. I can't believe we got up in New York this morning and now we are way out here in California." Karen felt as if she was living a dream.

"Karen we will rent a car to use while we are here. I want to take you to all of the places you want to see. Right now I will take you to the hotel and then I will go to work."

"Already Austin, but we just got here." Karen wanted to be with her husband some.

"Yes I'm afraid so honey, but that will give you time to rest. Remember you are still pregnant."

"Oh I don't think I will have any trouble at remembering that for awhile yet. He has been giving me some very big kicks all day and I think he is just getting started." she answered.

Austin and Karen stayed in California until Sunday. Then it was time to fly home. "Karen I hope you enjoyed the weekend." Austin said as they sat in their seats on the plane.

"I did Austin it was like a honeymoon for three, me, you and our little Austin." Karen, said as she rubbed her growing stomach.

"I guess it is different for you Karen because I am finding it a little different for me now."

Karen's face went almost white. She was so afraid Austin's, feeling about her were changing. After all she was not thin anymore. She was all puffy and her stomach was growing larger every day. She was not that young pretty girl he had met at the coffee shop anymore.

"Karen, take that look off your face right now. I know exactly what you are thinking even without you telling me. You think I don't feel the same about you now. You think that I feel like the new has started to wear off now that you are growing larger each day with our son inside of you. You are wrong. I love you even more because you are willing to go through all of this for us to have our son. I just meant I need to take better care of you like when we make love we need to be very careful. I do not want to hurt you or our son. I want you to know I will always think you look beautiful pregnant."

"Austin I don't know how I would stand it if you didn't like the way I look." The rest of the trip home Karen had her head over on Austin. He was holding onto her while she slept.

"Karen, wake up honey we are landing. You need to get your seatbelt on now." Austin helped her to get it under her stomach.

It was very late by the time they got home Sunday night. "Karen tomorrow I want you to stay in bed all day. You are over five months and after this past weekend you need to rest some. I will get up and go into my meeting and then I will come back home. And when I do I want to find you still in bed. Do you understand me little lady?"

"Yes Austin I understand." she answered.

CHAPTER TWENTY EIGHT

The next morning Austin got up and got ready for work and left Karen in bed, but as soon as he was out of sight she got up. She wanted to get the things done she didn't do last week because of being sick and going to California with Austin. She had big plans. She wanted to get her kitchen rearranged so it would fit her better and she didn't have a lot of time left in which she would be able to do it herself.

It must have been around eleven o'clock when while in the kitchen in between her loads of wash she heard the front door opening. "Austin is that you already?" Karen started towards the front of the house. She had on one of her big aprons with sweat pants and a top.

"Hello, she said to the two people standing in the front hallway. "Hello, I'm Mr. Blackburn's father." A tall man in his early sixties answered. "And this beautiful lady here is his mother. I guess you are his cleaning girl? We will just go up stairs and put our things away. We have been out of the country for some time now and we haven't seen our son in several months. What did you say was your name?" Mr. Blackburn asked.

Karen was just standing there she didn't know what to say or do. These were her new in-laws. These two people were Austin's parents. She just could not imagine what they were going to think about her. She had never seen such a good looking couple before. They were both very tall, beautiful and well educated. Everything she was not.

"My name?" Karen repeated.

"Yes dear what is your name?" Austin's father asked once again. "Karen, Karen Blackburn." Karen managed to say. Her knees were shaking so hard she didn't know if they would hold her up much longer.

Austin's mother looked over at her husband. "Blackburn did she say Blackburn Maxwell?"

"Yes M'am I'm Karen Blackburn." Karen repeated again.

"Do you just happen to have the same last name as us or is there something new in our son's life?" Austin Mother asked.

"I am Austin's wife, if that's what you mean by something new in his life?" Karen answered.

"You are our son's wife?" Both of Austin parents had big smiles on their face. "Oh that's wonderful." They both grabbed Karen's hand and started shaking it. "When did, all of this take place?" They both wanted to know.

"We have been married for over five months now." Karen answered. "Let me call Austin and let him know you are here. He will be so happy, I know."

"Yes do that we can't wait to see our son. So you are his wife. You sure are a cute little thing." Mr. Blackburn told her.

Karen hurried into Austin's office to call him. She left his parents standing in the hall. "Austin you know those two people you told me about and said they would show up here one of these days."

"Yes, I remember Karen." Austin said with a big smile on his handsome face.

"Well they are here." she answered.

"That's great! Honey how do you like them?" Austin asked. Austin's Dad took the phone. "She loves us son. What do you think and we love her too. She is a little doll. Just the kind of wife you needed. She is wonderful. We are so glad you had the good sense to marry her. Now son I'm going to give the phone back to your wife."

"Thanks Dad, tell Mom I said welcome home and hello." "I will son." Austin's Dad handed Karen back the phone. "Hello." Karen said.

"Karen I gather you have not told them anything about us having a baby yet?" Austin asked.

"No Austin I haven't, but I think when I take off my apron they won't have any problem telling that for themselves. So I'm just not going to take it off. I'm leaving it on until you get home. Then you can tell them yourself. So when will you be getting home?" Karen felt a little nervous.

"I am already on my way, honey don't worry about them. I'm in the parking garage getting into our truck as I speak."

"I love you Austin, please hurry."

"I love you Karen, see you in a few minutes." Austin hung up his phone and started his truck. "Dad is going to love you and he will be getting himself a truck." Austin thought to himself as he patted the dashboard of his big black Ford truck. He drove straight home and parked right out in front of their brownstone.

"Mr. and Mrs. Blackburn, could I get you some lunch? Austin is already on his way home." Karen told them as she tried to be a good hostess to her new in laws.

"Now Karen you don't need to do that. We can all just go out and get some lunch and talk after Austin gets here."

"I guess I need to change my clothes if we are going out. Will you please excuse me, I'll hurry right back." Karen kept on her big apron and hurried up to the third floor. She didn't want Austin's parents to know she was pregnant yet.

Now what am I going to wear that won't be too motherly? Karen picked a pair of jeans and a pretty white top. She did her hair and makeup and put on gold hoop earrings, a pair Austin had gotten her over the weekend in California. She could not have looked any better. She heard the door open as she was coming down the stairs.

"Austin, son you look wonderful, married life sure agrees with you." His Dad told him as soon as he was in the door.

"Yes. I know. Where is Karen?" Austin's eyes kept searching for Karen all of the time he was speaking with his parents. "Spoken like a real husband." his Dad answered.

"I'm up here Austin." Karen was standing at the top of the stairs. She came slowly walking down.

"Mom, how are you? We have been looking for you two for the last three months. What took you so long to get home?" Austin asked.

"We were enjoying ourselves son. We didn't know that our only child had gotten himself married. If we had known that we would have come home sooner. Imagine the surprise we had when we walked in and found Karen here. At first we thought that she was your cleaning girl."

"No Mom she is not that. She, is my wife, we have been married five months." By now Karen was standing next to Austin. "Mom and Dad, we want to tell you that you are going to be grandparents."

"What? Karen is pregnant? But she is so small." Mrs. Blackburn was shocked, but happy.

"No Ma'm I'm not small anymore. I have a big stomach." Karen answered.

"How far along are you?" Austin's mother asked while still gazing at Karen stomach.

"Five months now." Austin answered. "Son, you didn't?" his Dad asked.

"No we did not. We got married so that we could. We did it all the right way. We just cut out all those months of dating and waiting." Austin was even glad to have it all over with now.

Austin's mother then hugged her son and then she hugged Karen. "Austin she is just a little doll."

"Yes Mom she is and I love her and we are having a boy." Austin felt so proud.

"What? You already know that now?" That news did make Austin's Mother happy at least.

"Yes, Bo told us and we saw him. We even have pictures of him." Karen said just before going into Austin's office to get the pictures off of Austin's desk that was already framed. She wanted to show it to Austin's parents.

"I hope you didn't forget to get us one of these pictures to frame." Mrs. Blackburn said.

"Let me see my grandson. Oh Austin he is so wonderful and he is ours." Mr. Blackburn was as excited as his wife about their grandson if not about their new daughter-in-law.

"Yes he is all ours." Austin answered. He had a big smile on his face.

"Son, you must be excited. Oh what a foolish question I know you are." Mrs. Blackburn said while looking at the small picture of her first grandchild.

"Karen you got pregnant right away." Mr. Blackburn was not as friendly as his wife towards Karen.

"Yes Dad, she did, the day we got married." Austin answered. Karen popped Austin on the arm. "You were not supposed to tell them that about me. What are they going to think of me now?

"Karen they know we had sex after we got married. How else could you have gotten pregnant?" Karens face was red. "Karen, don't be embarrassed. That is a part of marriage, the best part for most." Austin wanted his little wife to feel better.

"Now let's go and get something to eat." Mr. Blackburn was already showing his wife to the door.

"Karen you haven't given me a kiss yet." Austin said as soon as his parents were not so near.

CHAPTER TWENTY NINE

"**O**h Austin I don't think your parents really like me. I think they are just pretending that they do, because they don't want to upset you." Karen was in Austin's arms. He kissed her before answering her.

"Karen they do like you I know my Mom and Dad and even if they didn't that would be just too bad, because I love you."

"Austin I don't want to come between you and your parents." Karen had a sad look on her face. All she could see now was Austin and his parents breaking up their relationship and it would be all because of her.

"Karen you haven't and now let's go outside and give them the next shock, our new truck." Austin felt that they were on a roll now so why stop now.

"Son, are we going to walk or are we getting a cab?" Maxwell knew his son's car sure would not hold all of them.

"Neither Dad, we are taking our truck." Austin answered.

"Your, truck, son you sure have been busy changing a lot of things in your life. Is this also something to do with your new wife?"

Austin stopped walking and turned to face his dad. "Dad, I hope you don't mean that the way it sounded, because I don't want to choose between you two and my wife. Karen is my wife and she would win. You two need to understand that right now."

"We do son, I did not mean anything bad. I was just asking if all of these changes came about because you have a new wife and a baby on the way." Maxwell did not want to have any hard feelings between him and his son. They had always had a perfect relation before.

"Yes, it all has to do with that, but I'm the one who chose to make all of these changes. I love Karen with all of my heart and she is pregnant with my son." Austin was still facing his Dad and they were eye to eye with each other.

"Austin don't get upset with your Dad, he just can't understand why you would choose me when there were so many beautiful women you could have chosen." Karen was standing right there and she had heard it all.

"No Karen, there was no one, but you for me. I didn't want any other women. I only want you and you will always be the only one I want." Austin was openly upset with his parents.

"Son, give us another chance and please forgive us for being so narrow minded. We can see how much you love Karen. Karen, will you please forgive us too? We, only want the best for our only child, you can understand that I'm sure."

"Yes and Karen is the best for our son." Mrs. Blackburn said. "Karen is just a little doll just like I said before. My best friend when I was growing up was a sweet small girl just like Karen and she was the best friend I ever had. Austin, son, I'm very happy for you and for myself. I have a daughter at last and I'm having a grandson. I hope this won't be my only grandchild." Austin's mother was very pleased with her new daughter-in-law. Even though she knew she would have to do a little work at convening Austin's Father of it.

"No Mom it won't be. As a matter of fact we are planning to have eight babies." Austin answered hoping this would not shock his parents as much as all the other things they had found out since just getting home.

"Eight, but I hope not all at the same time." Bridget said while looking shocked again.

"No, we are going to do them one at a time." Austin quickly answered.

"Good, I guess Bo is going to be Karen's doctor? What does he think about his best friend being married?"

"Mom, Bo is married too. He got married last weekend." Karen didn't know if that was a good thing for them to hear right now or not.

"Both of you boys got married?" Austin's Mother was shocked once again.

"Yes Mom we did. Both of our wives are short and we both have new Ford trucks." Austin never expected his parents to act this way.

"Wow, Maxwell did you heard that? Both boys are married and they both have big Ford trucks and they did all of this while we were gone."

"Mom, you and Dad were gone a year and a lot can happen in one year." Austin answered. He did not want his parents blaming Karen for all of the things he had done. He was happy with his new life and he thought his parents would have been happy for him.

"Yes I can see that for myself." They all four were in Austin's truck on their way to eat.

"Son, this is a real nice truck. I had no idea trucks looked like this inside. Maybe you will let your old man drive it some while we are here."

"Yes, I will be glad for you to drive it. Then we will take you to the Ford dealer and you can get one for yourself." Austin said making Karen smiled to herself. She was remembering how Austin had acted the day they got their truck. He wasn't so sure he wanted to be a truck man at all. Now he knows he is.

"So you are telling me that's all it takes and I will be wanting one of these trucks?"

"Yes sir I am." Austin said as he drove down the crowded street. "Did you get rid of your Ferrari?" Austin's Dad asked.

"No way, I still have my baby." Austin answered making Karen wonder if Austin's car meant more to him than he had said and he had sure said enough.

"What does Karen drive, not his big truck I hope." Maxwell asked.

"She doesn't drive anything."

"Karen don't you know how to drive?" Maxwell asked. "No sir I don't. I never learned to drive." Karen answered.

"Austin took drivers education in school when he was sixteen. Didn't you have that in your school?" Bridget asked.

"Yes M'am' we did, but I was too young to take the class." Karen answered.

"Karen just how long have you been out of school?" Bridget asked.

"Three years now." Karen slowly answered.

"Mom, are you trying to ask Karen her age in around about way? I will tell you she is nineteen years old." Austin answered. He knew this would shock both of his parents.

"What, Austin your wife is a teenager? Do you know that son?" Maxwell could not believe what his son had done.

"Yes, I know. I have already been told that by Bo. Then he asked me for my wife." Austin answered.

"Well that's Bo for you." Mr. Blackburn answered.

"Karen you were sixteen when you graduated from high school?" Bridget asked.

"Mom she finished first in her class and there were one hundred and thirty five of them not just two." Austin was very proud of his wife even If she had finished last in her class. He loved her.

"So we got ourselves a genius and a daughter-in-law all in one." Bridget answered.

"No M'am I'm not a genius. I just studied a lot and never went out on any dates ever."

"Karen it's alright just as long as you married our son because it is so easy to see you love him as much as he loves you."

"Yes M'am I sure do." Karen wanted to get to the restaurant. She needed to be near Austin.

"Son," Maxwell said.

"Yes Dad," Austin was pulling into the restaurant parking lot at that time.

"How long did you two know each other before you got married?"

"Oh let me see, we met on Thursday after work and we got married on Friday at lunch time. Now Dad, don't say anything. I did what I wanted to do. I married the woman I wanted to be with the rest of my life." Austin answered.

"Son, I didn't say a word. If you and Karen are this happy you did the right thing."

"Yes, we did. I will tell you all about it one day." Austin looked into the back of his truck to see how Karen was doing. She was back there with his Mom. "Honey, I will get you out. You just stay right there until I get there. Don't you, try getting out by yourself."

"Alright Austin I will wait. Anyway I don't think I could do it by myself." she answered.

CHAPTER THIRTY

They all had a nice lunch and they did a lot of talking. The older Blackburns were happy for their son and overjoyed about becoming grandparents. When they got back home Austin and Karen showed Austin's parents all of the baby things they had bought.

"Karen this is a beautiful bed it looks as if it was made to go with Austin's bedroom suite."

"Yes M'am' it sure does." Karen answered.

"Mom it's not my bedroom alone anymore. My wife shares this room with me. So it's Karen's bedroom suite too." Austin thought they had gotten over all of this back in the restaurant.

"Oh honey, I'm sorry. I didn't mean anything by that at all. I'm just so used to it only being Austin's."

"But Mom, it's not just me anymore and it won't be long before there are three of us. And then we plan to have another baby as soon as we can." Austin answered. He was sure this would also shock them.

"Austin you may need to give Karen a little break there somewhere, after all she is just a child having a child."

"Mrs. Blackburn I'm not a child and I haven't been a child in many years. I will be alright. Austin takes very good care of me and we love each other." Karen was sitting on the very edge of their king size bed.

Austin's mother was sitting in the rocker. "Karen I can tell you are all grown up, but you are still so young and our son is thirty five years old. He is old enough to take good care of you and all of the babies you have for us, but honey your body will need to recover from each baby before Austin gets you pregnant again so give yourself time. We love you already and we will love every one of our grandbabies. You are very special to us." Then Austin's mother turned to him. "Austin what can we buy for our grandson?"

Austin was there listening to his Mom. "Ask Karen what she wants for little Austin." he answered.

"You are going to name him Austin?" Mrs. Blackburn had a big smile on her face.

"Yes we are, I love Austin for a name and I love your son Austin. So we are naming him after his daddy." Karen was smiling too.

"That's wonderful, I love that name too. That's why I named my son Austin."

"And that's why I'm naming our son Austin after his daddy." "Karen what does your family think about you being married to a man Austin's age?"

Austin and his father had gone back downstairs. Karen was alone with Austin's mother now. He and his father wanted to go out to the truck. "Mrs. Blackburn my family doesn't know that I'm married. I haven't seen or heard anything from any of my family, since I left home three years ago to come here." Karen answered.

"Yes, but honey you was only sixteen years old then." Mrs. Blackburn could not imagine letting Austin leave home at sixteen. She didn't even want him to leave home to go off to school, but he did.

"Yes M'am', I was, and I left the day I graduated and I came here and got a job as secretary at a church and that is where I was working when I met your son. Then we got married and now we are expecting our son." Karen wanted so badly for her in-laws to like her, but she didn't think it would ever really happen.

"Karen you are a God—send. I was almost afraid that Austin would never get married. Now I'm going to be a grandmother and to think there will be seven more after this one." Bridget truly did like Karen she just hoped that someday Karen would believe her.

"Yes that is what we are hoping for."

"Karen, aren't you a little small for having eight babies?" Bridget asked. She was concern about all the hard work Karen would have each day doing for a family of eight children. She sure knew she would have never been able to handle that many children at any age or size.

"No, I don't think so and I'm not having them all at once. I think I'm just right for having all of Austin's babies. Mrs. Blackburn if you don't like me you can say it to me. You don't have to act like you like me because you don't want to hurt my feelings. I know you want Austin to think you like me, but you don't have to pretend around me. It is alright I didn't expect you to like me. I know you wanted a tall beautiful woman for your son just like you, but I'm not that and I do love your son and if that is not enough for you and your husband, I'm truly sorry. I don't know what else to do except to leave and I don't plan on doing that at all."

"No you are not going to do that ever. You are going to stay right here and make my son happy, just like you are doing. Karen I may have thought that is what I wanted for my son, but it's plain to see that he has what he wants and that is you. So I never want you to ever feel that we don't love you. You are a beautiful woman even if you are a little short doll. Come here and give me a hug."

"Oh Mrs. Blackburn I do love your son Austin." That was all Karen could think to say.

"I know honey, just like I love his father. I, had this very same conversation years ago with my mother-in-law, but you stood up to me way better than I did to her. So we are going to be the best of friends, because my son is very important to me and his father."

"Yes, M'am," Karen answered.

Once Maxwell had his son alone he had a few more question he wanted answered. "Austin did you know that Karen was so young when you got involved with her?"

"Dad I want to stop you right now before we both say something we'll regret. I did not get involved with Karen, I got married to her. Then we had sex and not before, but even if we had it's no business of yours or Mom's, but because I don't want there to ever be any questions about my wife. I will tell you that Karen was a virgin. She proved it to me the day we were married, afterward and not before."

"Alright son you don't need to make it any clearer. I get the picture. You married her because you love her."

"Yes Dad that's it." Austin was running out of ways to tell his Dad that he loved his wife and that was the only reason he had married her.

"Son, we are just concerned about your welfare." Austin's dad was looking right at him.

"Well don't be where Karen is concerned. She is everything to me and that is not going to change."

"That's good son, that's the way it should always be. Now let me drive your truck. You say I will want one of these?"

"And you say Bo is married and he has a truck too?" Maxwell could not get over all of the changes in his son life and Bo's as well.

"Yes he is and she is a short girl too." Austin answered. "Well I hope he is just as happy as you and Karen are."

"Yes, I think he is. He has a big smile on his face all of the time now." Austin and his dad took a nice long drive giving his dad a good taste for a truck.

"Son, you are right, I do like this truck." Maxwell was now wondering how he could get Bridget to like a truck.

"Dad Karen said that it does something to a men when they drive a Ford truck, she says, "IT MAKES A MAN FEEL LIKE THE MAN HE THINKS HE IS AND IT LET'S A WOMAN KNOW SHE IS A WOMAN WITH POWER RIGHT UNDER HER FOOT."

"I sure believe every word of it." Maxwell was falling in love with his son's Ford truck.

The two women were still up in Karen and Austin's bedroom. "Karen let me see your maternity clothes." Bridget has always been into fashion after all she had been a model before marrying Maxwell.

"Alright, but I don't have many." Karen answered.

Mrs. Blackburn and Karen walked into Karen's closet. "Karen is this all of the clothes you have?" Bridget was shocked at how few clothes Karen had.

"Yes but, it's enough, I have five new outfits that Austin bought for me, when I couldn't get into my regular clothes anymore."

"Karen, did my son take you shopping to buy any clothes before he took you to get these five outfits?" Bridget asked.

"Yes M'am, I got two pair of new jeans. I didn't need anything else. I had some clothes that fit me then."

"Honey, come with me." Bridget took Karen's hand and walked her over to Austin's closet. "Honey look at you husbands closet. Do you see something different here?" she asked.

"Yes M'am', he has real nice things and all I have is jeans and tops. Oh no, I bet Austin must be so embarrassed to have me meet his friends."

"No, Karen my son is not like that, but you do need more clothes. So while your mother is here, you and I will go shopping and our husbands can tag along. Someone will need to carry our things. Now let me see your lingerie."

"My lingerie?" Karen asked.

Karen went over to the dresser and opened her one drawer. "Is this it?"

Bridget asked?

"Yes M'am," Karen answered.

"Karen what am I to do with you? My son is a very wealthy man and you have nothing. He needs his mother to talk to him."

"No, no Mrs. Blackburn it's not Austin's fault. I don't go anywhere so I don't need anything." Karen answered. She didn't want Austin to get upset over all of this. He has already been upset enough today, because of her she thought.

"My son knows better than this." Karen was almost in tears when Austin came back up to their room.

"What's the matter Karen?" Austin asked as soon as he got into their bedroom.

"Nothing, Austin nothing," Karen kept saying.

"Mom, what is the matter with Karen, and why is she in tears?" Austin was not at all happy with the way things were going.

"Austin she is upset because of you." Bridget answered.

"No Austin, I'm not upset with you at all. I love you." This only upset Karen more.

"Well then what is the matter? One of you two needs to tell me." Austin looked from his Mother to Karen and waited for one of them to answer him. "Austin, look at your wife's closet then look at yours." Bridget answered.

"Yes, so?" Austin asked.

"Son, your wife has nothing. She doesn't even have a set of clothes for each day of the week. Did you know that she only has five sets of clothes and look here this is your wife's underwear and gown drawer, she, has it all in one drawer. Now all of the other drawers are full of your clothes. Your wife has one drawer and it is one of the smallest drawers in this room. I bet she doesn't even have a drawer in your bathroom."

Austin turned to his wife. "Karen do you have a drawer in our bathroom?" Austin waited for Karen to answer.

"No, I keep my brush and lipstick in my pocket book."

"Austin, son you need to do better towards your wife." Austin, looked at Karen, he had not given it a thought that Karen had nothing.

"Yes dear, your, bras, panties, slips, gowns, those sorts of things."

She just always dressed in **her** jeans and top, because that is all that she had and now the five maternity outfits which was one dress and four pair of pants and four tops.

"Karen have you worn the same dress to Church every Sunday?" Austin asked.

"Yes," Karen answered. She did not want Austin to get mad with her about her clothes.

"Why have you worn the same dress every Sunday?" he asked, but he already knew the answer.

"Because son that's the only dress your wife has that she can fit into, where on the other hand you have a closet full of clothes." Bridget was not going to let her son get away with this.

"No, Mrs. Blackburn I don't want Austin spending all of his money on me. I won't be pregnant much longer." Karen was getting real upset.

"Karen you are only half way and if you are planning to get pregnant again right away you will need good clothes and lots of them."

"Austin, tell her no." Karen was in Austin's arms now. "Austin, please don't spend any more of your money on me. You have already spent too much because of me. You have already spent money for rings and all that. Now you have already bought all those baby things and a truck for our baby to ride in so please Austin, don't spend anymore of your money on me. I don't need any more clothes. I have more now than I have ever had." Karen had tears running down her face.

"Karen honey, why are you crying?" Austin didn't like to see his wife this upset over nothing; as he saw it.

"Austin I just don't want you to be upset when you don't have money for something you want because you had to buy things for me."

"Karen I'm not your mother and I want you to have everything you want and more. My Mom is right you do need a lot of things. Tomorrow we are going shopping. So Karen, don't be upset. I love you sweetheart."

"Austin your wife has no idea how wealthy you are. Son you need to sit down with her and go over it all with her. If she is the women you want for the rest of your life you need to tell her everything. Do you have a new Will to protect Karen if something should happen to you?"

"No Mom I don't, but I will." Austin knew he needed to do that right away. Karen was his wife and she was having their baby. All of this made Austin feel very proud.

"Son, you need to call your lawyer and have your Will updated right now. Don't put it off. Do like your mama said." Maxwell was realizing how wrong he had been about Karen.

"I will Dad right now."

CHAPTER THIRTY ONE

Austin went down to his office. "How could I have forgotten to do that he asked himself?"

"Pete its Austin, are you busy?"

"No not this very minute Austin. It has been a while since I spoke to you last. Did you ever find yourself a surrogate?"

"No, but I did get married five months ago." Austin answered. "What? I can't believe this. You got married, who to?" Pete was as shocked as his parents had been earlier.

"I married Karen Belmont. I'm very sure you don't know her." Austin was certain of that.

"So you decided to do it the old fashion way and marry her to get yourself, an heir."

Karen was still in their bedroom and she had decided to call Margo. When she picked up the phone and put it to her ear she heard Pete saying," decided to marry her to get yourself, an heir. Then I guess you will be divorcing her as soon as she gives you a baby and taking your heir." Karen quickly hung up her phone. She didn't wait to hear what Austin had to say. "No Pete I got married to a woman I really fell in love with and I need to get my Will updated. I want it to include her and our son."

"You have a son already?" Pete was sure this had to have been a shotgun wedding for sure.

"No not yet. Well yes, but he has not been born yet." Austin was so happy to be able to tell his friend he was married and he loved his wife and that they were having a son.

Karen was upset. In fact she was so upset she got her old bag out of her closet and packed all of her old things in it, but only two sets of her new maternity clothes. She picked up her pocketbook and walked out of Austin's house without being seen by anyone. She didn't know where to go. All she knew was she had to go somewhere away from Austin. If he had been lying to her all this time about loving her and he was planning to take her baby and divorce her as soon as she gave birth to their son she needed to leave as fast as she could. She would not give up her baby, but she was sure Austin was powerful enough to take his son from her. She had to get away even though she loved Austin. If he did not love her she could not stay. Leaving was all she could do.

She decided to go down the street and go back up their back alley and go into their basement and stay until she knew what to do. After all, the basement was very large with lots of rooms. She could hide there for awhile.

"Mom have you seen Karen I can't find her anywhere." This was beginning to worry Austin.

"Austin, she was still upstairs when I came down. She was going to give Bo's wife a call."

Austin went up to their bedroom. He saw the phone lying on the floor. He knew something was wrong. Karen's closet door was open. Austin could tell most of her things were gone and so was her pocketbook. He went running down the stairs. "Mom where is Karen?" Austin asked once again.

"Son, I have already told you she was still upstairs and was going to call Bo's wife and tell them we were home."

"She is gone Mom, Karen is gone." Austin was in a panic he needed to find Karen.

"Austin, tell me how do you know for sure that she is gone?" Bridget asked. She wanted to help her son, but she didn't know where to start. "She took her old clothes and her pocketbook. Mom I have to find my wife." Austin was going crazy.

"What do you think made her want to leave? Do you think it had to do with us?" Bridget asked.

"No Mom, I think she overheard what Pete said on the phone." "What did he say that would cause Karen to leave? Son she is pregnant."

Austin told his parents the whole story. "Well I don't blame her at all, if I had heard that I would leave too, if I were Karen. Now let's go and find her. Where do you think she would go?"

"Mom she has no one, but me. We need to find my wife. We have done nothing all day, but upset her with all those questions about me being taken in by her. If anyone was taken in it was Karen. She is nineteen years old and I'm thirty five don't you two know, I'm an adult. I chose to marry Karen. I wanted her for my wife because I love her and only her. Now she is out there somewhere pregnant and with no place to go.

Do you two realize what could happen to her and my baby? I don't think I have ever been this upset in my entire life and it all came about today. Karen was just in the hospital last Monday. She doesn't need to be getting upset." Austin began to cry.

"Son, get a hold of yourself. She won't do anything crazy she loves you and that baby too much to do any harm to herself." Mr. Blackburn told his son.

"No we have already done it to her. Can't you, two understand I love my, short beautiful wife. What is wrong with her being shorter than me? I love it that way. I feel like it's my job to protect her, but I have driven her away."

"Austin let's sit down and decide where she could have gone." Bridget was as upset as her son, but she was trying very hard not to let it show.

"Mom she has no place to go. She has only me."

"No son she has us too." Maxwell did not like this at all.

"But Dad she doesn't know that yet. She doesn't even know she has me right now. All because I used our house phone to call Pete about my Will."

"What's wrong with that son?"

"Nothing it was what she heard that was wrong. I'm going to call Bo and see if he thinks she will be alright." Austin soon had Bo on the phone.

"Bo," Austin quickly said.

"Yes Austin is there something wrong with Karen?" Bo asked. "Yes she is gone."

"What!" Austin told Bo what had happened. "Austin she is in the house some place. Karen would not do anything to harm your baby and we both know that or sure. She loves you man. Now go and find your wife. You go by yourself, and you search every inch of your house from top to bottom."

"Alright Bo I will. Thank you I needed to hear that Karen loves me."

As soon as he hung up the phone he sat down with his parents to tell them of his plan. He was going to start with the basement and work his way up to the first floor and then the second and last the third.

"Son let us help you."

"No Dad I need to find her and talk to her. I need to prove to Karen that I really do love her and I would never divorce her and take our baby son from her. I have a lot to prove to my wife. I want you two to just stay right here and pray she is in our basement."

Austin went down the basement stairs. He didn't say a word. He went from one room to the other searching for Karen. He had searched half the basement when he heard Karen crying in the bedroom he had used while Bo and he were restoring their homes.

"Karen," Austin said in a soft voice. "Karen," he then repeated.

She raised her head off the pillow. "Austin, I won't just give you my baby."

"Karen no one is going to take our baby from you. Karen I love you with all my heart. Honey you only heard what Pete my lawyer said. You didn't hear what I had to say. I told Pete I married the woman I loved and we are having a baby boy together. Karen I'm never going to divorce you. I love you way too much to lose you."

"Austin how do I know you aren't just telling me all of this so I will stay until I have our baby and then you will tell me to leave."

Austin took Karen into his arms. "Honey I need you to believe me because I'm telling you the truth. Haven't we been honest with each other from the very start?"

"I thought so Austin, but now I don't know. Your parents don't believe I'm good enough for you and neither do I. They think I got pregnant to get you to marry me."

"No Karen they don't. I told them the whole story. They know if there was any tricking being done it was on my part and not yours."

"Yes and that's what scares me. What if our whole marriage is no more than just a trick so you could get you a baby?"

"Austin," A voice called from the door. "Bo we are in here."

"I see we have found our lost wife." Bo said while still standing in the doorway.

"Yes, but she doesn't trust me anymore. Bo, tell my wife I love her." Austin had tears in his eyes.

"Karen, Austin does love you. I know right now it doesn't seem like it because everything is so messed up, but Austin is my best friend and I can tell you your husband loves only you and he is never going to divorce you. He would rather die than to lose you Karen."

"Bo, I love Austin, but I'm not smart like he is so I don't know what to believe."

"Karen do you trust me?" Bo asked hoping she did still trust one of them.

"Yes" she slowly answered.

"Then believe me when I say your husband loves you. It was Austin's love for you that made me go and marry Margo. I want to love her the same way Austin loves you."

Austin was still sitting on the side of the bed holding on to Karen. He hoped Bo was getting through to her. He did not want to lose his wife or his son.

"Austin I'm sorry I left, but I could not let you just take my baby." Karen was still crying, but not as bad as she was when Austin first found her in the basement.

"Karen it's our baby and we will be having this baby right here in your stomach together a long with seven others." Austin wanted his wife back.

"Karen, are you alright? I mean do you have any pain?" Bo asked. "No Bo I'm fine." Karen answered.

"Then I'm going to leave and let you two, makeup and I do mean makeup. Austin, you make your wife feel she is loved by you." Bo went back upstairs to see Austin's parents. They were still waiting in the den.

"Bo is everything alright?" Mrs. Blackburn asked. "Yes M'am it will be soon." Bo answered.

"Bo, Austin said you got married just last weekend." "Yes sir I did." Bo answered.

"I hope you dated your wife longer than Austin did." Maxwell said.

"No sir I did even less. We married the same day we meet." Bo answered.

"Good heavens what is the matter with you two men. What did your parents say about all of this?"

"They don't know yet, but they will say I'm a smart man for not letting Margo get away from me. After all I am an adult and I don't need my parents' permission to do anything, the same goes for Austin."

"Yes you are right you two man are adults and we trust you both with everything else so why not trust you to know who to love and when to marry. Karen is a sweet girl and we are lucky to have gotten her for our daughter-in-law. Is she alright Bo?" Bridget asked.

"Yes, she is now that Austin is with her. He is down there right now proving to her how much he loves her. So I wouldn't go down there if I were you. They may be very busy. Your son needs this time to prove he really loves his wife in every way." Bo took a deep breath. "Austin does love his wife. I hope you two know that already."

Mr. Blackburn was sitting in Austin's big chair. Bo was standing right in front of him.

"Well I'm going home and see my wife. I may want to prove my love for her too."

Back down in the basement Austin was busy with his wife. "Karen I don't know how to make all of this up to you. All I know is I love you more than my own life. All I want to do is hold you in my arms and never let you go."

Karen was still lying on Austin's basement bed. Austin slid down on the bed so he was lying next to her. "I love you so much honey." Austin said as he began to kiss his wife and she was kissing him back. He knew she wanted him as much as he wanted her.

Austin didn't even bother to close the door the rest of the way. He was sure Bo had told his parents they were busy and not to come down to the basement that they would be up later.

CHAPTER THIRTY TWO

T wo hours later Austin and Karen came up the basement stairs together.

"Mom, are you and Dad ready to go and get something to eat?" "Yes Austin we are. Karen, please forgive us for saying those things that upset you so much. We really do love you already and we are very glad our son married you as soon as he did and didn't give you time to think it over because if he had we could have lost out on having you as our daughter. We are so happy that you are going to give us a grandbaby soon."

"Thank you Mrs. Blackburn. I do love Austin and we are both giving you this baby." Karen was sitting on the sofa next to Austin. He had his arm around her.

"Austin my bag is still down in the basement."

"That's alright honey I will get it later when we get back. I love you Karen don't you ever scare me like that again. You almost gave me a heart attack."

Karen turned to look at him. "Austin I never wanted that to happen, but I just did not want to lose my baby or you."

"I know Karen and you are not going to lose either of us. Now are you ready to go eat?"

"Austin is my hair messed up?"

"Now let me see. It looks like you have been . . . ." Austin leaned very close to her and whispered. "It looks like you have been letting your husband have his way with you."

"Austin Blackburn, do you mean your parents know what we were doing down in the basement all of that time?

"Yes Karen I'm afraid so honey." Austin had a big smile on his face.

Karen began to slide closer and closer to Austin. "Karen if you get any closer to me we will be making love again."

"Austin, don't talk so loud your parents will hear you."

"Karen my parents aren't sitting in those chairs anymore. They have gone upstairs to get ready for us to go out to eat. Do you want to redo your hair now?"

"Yes of course I do, but I don't have a brush." she answered. "Here," Austin had taken his comb out of his pocket and handed it to her. "Use my comb and I will help you. Tomorrow we are going to buy you everything

"Yes you have Austin. I just don't need a lot of things. I would not know what to do with any more than I have already."

"Karen, there are a lot of things you need. You just don't know it because you have never had them. Tomorrow I'm going to change all of that for you. You will have everything a woman wants and needs. Karen you are the woman of this house and I want you to start feeling like you are. Do you have any idea how much I am worth by myself?" "No, but I know you work very hard for us to have what we have.

I haven't thought about how much money you are worth. I know you have this house, but I don't have any idea what it's, worth. I know you have a little red car that cost three hundred and fifty thousand dollars, so I guess your house is worth that much too and you have a new Ford truck that cost sixty five thousand dollars and you paid for all of it when we got it, but that's all I know."

"Karen I'm worth by myself not counting my parents money, but all by myself I'm worth over three hundred and seventy five million dollars. Karen, do you have any idea how much money that is?"

"No, but I know it's a lot, but I don't see what that all has to do with me?"

"Karen it has everything to do with you. We are married and what I have is yours. My money is your money. That was what I was doing on the phone. I was talking with my lawyer about getting my Will updated to include you and our son. Do you see how much I love you and our son?"

"Yes Austin I do, but I don't want your money, I just want you." "Honey you already have me hook, line and sinker." Austin was kissing Karen when his parents came back into the den.

"Are you two ready to go and get something for dinner or do we need to go back upstairs and wait another two hours?" Bridget asked.

"Yes Mom we are ready to go and get some supper." Austin answered.

Austin's mother just stared at him. "Supper when did you, start having supper young man?" she asked her son.

"Oh Mrs. Blackburn, that's, all my fault too. I cook supper at night and I guess I have made Austin take up another one of my unsophisticated habits. We always had dinner during the daytime and supper at night. I'm so very sorry I will not say supper anymore. Austin I'm so sorry that's all I seem to be saying today." She didn't know what else to do, but to keep her mouth closed as long as his parents were there.

"Karen," Austin said. He knew his wife was upset again and this was their home and not his parents. "Karen you can say supper at our house because we will be having supper at night and dinner at noon. This is your home and we will be doing it your way. This is not my Mom's house it is ours. I'm very sure my parents can survive having supper at night when they come to visit in our home with us.

"Yes Karen, we will be very happy to have supper with you and our son and soon our grandson." Bridget answered. She didn't want to be the one to cause any hurt towards her daughter-in-law ever again.

"Thank you Mrs. Blackburn, but I don't have to say supper or anything else at all. I will just sit here and be quiet."

"No Karen, it is as Austin said this is your home and in the South the people have supper and you should have it your way here in your own home."

"Are we all ready to go? I'm ready to drive my son's big truck again."

"Oh Mr. Blackburn isn't it a joy to drive a Ford truck? All you need to do is put on a pair of tight jeans and a long sleeve white shirt with a pair of boots and get into your big Ford truck and you will become a different man."

"Karen do you own a lot of stock in the Ford Company?" Maxwell asked.

"Oh no sir, I don't own anything. I just know how all the men back home feel about their big Ford trucks."

"Maybe the Ford Company needs you to do their advertising for them. You sure know what to say."

"No sir, I already have a job. I'm Austin's wife and that is a full time job."

"Yes it is and I like it that way. Mom you get up front with daddy I want to sit in the backseat with my beautiful wife."

"Austin, all I can see is that you need now some good country music. Then you will have it made."

"Yes Dad I think so. Tomorrow while we are all out shopping I will pick up some and you can do the same." Austin smiled down at Karen. He knew Karen loved country music and he liked it too. Maybe he didn't care for it as much as she did, but he loved it now.

Everyone enjoyed their meal. They all danced a little. "Austin, your parents sure love each other and they love you so much that they are willing to put up with me. I hope we will feel the way they do about each other when we have been married as long as they have."

"I'm very sure we will." Austin said as he danced Karen around the floor.

"Austin I'm sorry I don't know how to dance very well. All the dancing I have ever done was with my grandma and we were not good at all."

"Karen you dance well enough for me. After all you are pregnant." "Austin you are used to women who have taken all sorts of lessons to do things and I have never taking any lessons that were not given to us in school, but I do know how to two step and line dance. I bet Bo knows how to do that, but I'm very sure you don't."

"Yes Karen, he does and I think maybe it's time I learned. After all I want to be the one dancing with my wife." Karen smiled up at Austin and thought she could not have asked for a better husband.

Austin's parents were really into their dancing. They had danced all over the world and next week they were going back home after being away for a full year. They were ready to go home to their country estate. They hoped that before they left Austin and Karen's house, things would be as loving as it was before they got there and changed everything. "Bridget we sure messed up things at our son's house. We almost cost him his wife. I feel as if I stepped over my bounds several times while talking with our son today. He told me Karen was a virgin when they got married."

"Maxwell, why on earth did our son feel that he needed to tell you something that personal what did you say to him?" Bridget and Maxwell were still dancing.

"I made the mistake of asking him if he had to marry her because she was pregnant with his baby. He told me no. That she had never been to bed with him or any other man until they were married. They both wanted to have a baby right away so they didn't wait. Bridget, I think we both have said and done things we would not have said or done if we had come home and found him married to a tall beautiful woman like his mother as he said. I, believe he is right, we would have accepted it all without any questions. Instead he married the woman he loves and we tried to pick it all apart. Trying to find some reason for it and trying to find a reason for not liking our new daughter-in-law. We wanted to blame her for tricking our thirty five year old son into marrying her, but we were wrong Karen did not trick our son. They fell in love and did what they needed to do. They got married just like we did all those years ago. I think our son found the same love with Karen I found with you all those years ago and we are still in love today."

"Yes Maxwell you are right. Our son got himself a wonderful little girl and I love her. She may not be tall, but she is just right for us and our son. Besides we are getting a grandson in just four months. Maxwell I never dreamed of ever being a grandmother. I just never allowed myself to want that for myself. I was afraid we would never have any grandchildren. Austin sure surprised us."

"Yes he did and would you look over there at them. I have never seen our son so happy. He has someone he wants to do for and he wants her with him all the time. Work is not the only thing in his life anymore. He has a family to take care of now and I do believe they will have all eight of those babies."

"Why not, our son can afford them and if he can't he can have our money."

"You are right honey. That's why we worked so hard all those years, so our son could have everything he needed."

"Mom, are you and Dad ready to go? Karen needs to get home and rest some. Bo told me I could not keep her up all night long making love, she needed to sleep some. So if you two are danced out we will go as soon as daddy gets back to the table."

"Of course we are ready to go. We sure don't want anything to happen to our new daughter in law and our grandson. Karen I just can't wait to be a grandmother. You have done the one thing I never dreamed of ever getting."

"Thank you Mrs. Blackburn."

"Karen, call me Bridget or Mom or anything other than Mrs. Blackburn."

"Oh I didn't know that was wrong too." Karen thought she had done it again.

"No Karen it's not wrong. My Mom just wants you to call her something more loving than Mrs. Blackburn that's all." Austin explained.

"Oh, you mean like Mom." Karen asked. "Yes," Bridget answered.

Karen didn't answer she wasn't sure she would be able to ever do that. She had only called her own mother mom a few times in her life. Only because her mother wanted to be called Joyce by her instead of mom or mother or mama.

"Here comes your Dad now. Maxwell, are you ready to go. Our son needs to take his wife home. He is not through playing with her for the night." Bridget said.

Maxwell smiled at his wife and son, but he didn't look Karen's way he was sure that would embarrass her. "Yes by all means, let's get him home so he can play."

Austin and Karen got into the backseat again. "I feel like I'm on a double date Maxwell and the couple in the backseat is having all the fun." Bridget told her husband. He just laughed.

"Don't worry honey we will be having just as much fun as they are in a little while."

"I can hear you and I don't want to picture that in my mind." Austin said from the backseat.

"Son, I think your mind is only picturing what you will be doing with your wife not what I want to do with your mother. And I hope when you get my age you will be just as excited about Karen as I am about your beautiful mother. You will feel like you are the luckiest man God has ever put on this earth to have your wife."

"I know I will Dad and I'm glad my parents still feel that way about each other."

"And we are glad you found someone you will love when you get our age and older."

Austin had one arm around Karen so he just pulled her closer to him and kissed her. "See Karen you have nothing to worry about. You are stuck with all of us."

CHAPTER THIRTY THREE

The next morning Karen was up early. She had cooked them all a big southern breakfast and had it ready when they all came downstairs.

"Karen, that was a very good meal you cooked for us. I can see my son will need to hit the gym again if he eats his wife's cooking every day." Maxwell just could not keep his foot out of his mouth.

"Karen, why don't you have a cook and a housekeeper?" Bridget asked.

Karen glanced over at Austin before she answered. "I didn't know I needed them. I thought I did the cleaning of Austin's house good enough and cooked good enough, but I guess I don't. Austin I didn't know I was not doing anything good enough."

"Karen you do everything very well. You have kept our house cleaner than it was ever kept before, even though I had a woman who came in every week to do it. Mom I have already told Karen we will be getting a woman to do the cleaning and cooking when she gets a little farther along. Did you know Karen was doing our washing and ironing."

"No Austin, she doesn't. You have your wife doing all of that?" Bridget wanted to pop her grown son.

"Yes she does and every night when I get home she has a delicious meal waiting. She even worked at the office a few weeks for me and she still did all this same work."

"Austin you did not marry Karen for her to be your maid and I want you to get her some help. She is already too far along to be doing all of that work. You are a grown man and if you can't do all of what she is doing and do your job then why do you let her do it?"

"Son, what did Karen do at the office?" Austin's Dad didn't know that there had been any changes at the office. Austin had not said anything to him about it.

"Oh Mr. Blackburn I didn't do anything that would mess up anything. I just worked as Austin's secretary until he got a new one."

"Son, what happened to Lisa?" Maxwell asked. "I fired her." Austin answered.

"Why? She was a beautiful girl." Maxwell said.

"Yes and she made faces at my wife and she was not doing her work."

"So who do you have now?" Maxwell always thought Lisa was a nice girl.

"I have Mrs. Meeks now. She is a very good and efficient secretary. She gets all of her work done each day. Unlike Lisa, who hid it away in her desk and never did it." Austin answered.

"Karen, have you ever done anything like being a secretary before?" Maxwell asked. He was trying to justify why his son would allow his wife to play at being his secretary even if he was in love with her. Business was business as Maxwell saw it.

"Yes sir, I was a secretary for three years at a church." Karen answered.

"Three years?" Maxwell asked.

"Yes sir. Three years like I said before." Karen answered again. "Daddy, Karen is a very good secretary. She even takes shorthand.

When was the last time you found anyone who could do that lately." Austin asked.

"I don't know, but I do know I've always missed that when it became old fashioned. How did you learn to do shorthand Karen?"

"I learned to do it in school. I was too young to learn to drive so my business teacher taught me shorthand instead. She said I may never get to use it, but if I ever did I would be glad I knew how to do it. And she was right and I have always used it."

"Well young lady you are full of surprises. Now let's go shopping." Bridget was in the shopping mood and she was already to go.

CHAPTER THIRTY FOUR

They shopped all day long, but before dark they were home. Karen and Austin were in their bedroom putting away the things they had purchased. "Austin I did not need any of these things."

"Yes you do Karen. You didn't even have perfume and I had not even noticed." Austin was so ashamed of himself for not seeing how little his wife had and his mother had to be the one to show it to him.

"Well then did I really need perfume if my own husband could not tell if I used it or not?" Karen asked.

"Yes Karen every woman needs perfume. It makes them feel good." Austin answered.

"Oh so that's why I don't always feel good. I thought it was from morning sickness. And it was from me not having any perfume all that time. Austin I may not even be pregnant. This may be from me not having perfume too." Karen was pointing to her stomach.

"No Karen that is from me. We can't blame that on you not having perfume."

"No I guess not. Austin will having perfume make my life better?" She asked.

"No, but it will make life smell better." he answered.

"Austin Blackburn, are you saying I stink?" She did not like this at all.

"No because you always smell like lavender. I always thought that was a real nice smell. I didn't know it was just from your soap. I thought it was from your perfume."

"Austin does it matter if it was from soap or perfume just as long as I smelled nice and I was clean?" she asked.

"No Karen, it doesn't because you always smell so good. I want to be with you all the time. Karen I like that yellow gown of yours a lot so wear that one tonight so I can have fun taking it off of you." Austin said.

"Austin then why do I need to put it on if all you are going to do is take it off of me?" she asked.

Austin pulled Karen close to him and then he bent down and whispered. "Because I like taking all of your gowns off of you every time you put them on."

"Oh well, Mr. Blackburn then I guess I need to tell you I like it when you take them off of me." Then Karen gave him one of her sweetest smile.

"Karen Blackburn I'm so glad you do because I will always be taking them off." Austin knew that was exactly what he would always do.

"Yes so am I. If taking my gowns off of me makes you happy I will just wear two gowns to bed so you will have twice the fun every night." She told him.

"No you don't need to go that far. One will be enough. Now let's get our shower and get into that bed before it gets too late. I sure do not want Bo coming over here and telling me that I'm keeping you up to late. He may tell me I can only make love with you on certain nights just to be a little mean to me."

Karen was ready to take her clothes off, but she wanted to first let Austin see her new underwear. "Austin, do you like my new granny drawers?"

"Your, what?" Austin asked.

"My, new underwear!" Karen took off her jeans and showed Austin her new very high waisted underwear.

"Wow those are some serious underwear." He had never seen a woman in anything like that before.

"Yes they are and they are what I will be wearing from now on until our son is born. Nothing else comes even close to covering my stomach. All my other underwear just rolls down under my stomach and I don't feel like I have anything on anymore."

"Karen I guess these big ones are what you will need to wear then. I can always take them off of you too." Austin didn't mind doing that at all. "And when you get them off of me you will feel like you have really done something." Karen was looking at Austin while holding on to the waist of her big granny drawers.

"Karen you look like Humpty Dumpty in that underwear." He was almost laughing.

"Yes, Austin I do, and I'm only going to get bigger every day." She gave her big underwear a little pull at the waist.

That night Austin made love with his wife, but they were not the only Blackburns making love in the brown stone that night.

"Austin did you ask you parents if they wanted to go to church with us this morning?" Karen was already doing her hair and putting on her makeup.

"No, but I will go down to their room and ask them."

By the time Austin had gotten back to their room Karen was dressed in one of her new maternity dresses. She had done her hair in curls and had pulled one side back with a little comb. She looked so pretty. She even had little high heels on today for church. She came out of her closet all dressed just as Austin came back into the bedroom.

"Karen, you look so beautiful." It made him stop and stare at her for a few seconds.

"Do I Austin? Now put this picture in your mind. My big granny underwear, are underneath all of this."

"Oh Karen that is a picture I could have lived without." Austin was making all kinds of funny faces at her.

"Austin do my granny underwear bother you that much?" she asked.

"No Karen I was just kidding you. I know you have to wear things that are comfortable for now, but one day you will be wearing your little under panties again. That's the day I'm looking forward to already."

"Austin, are your parents going with us?" Karen asked. She knew he had already forgotten about why he had gone downstairs. She guessed the thought of her big granny drawers drove every other thought out of his head.

"Yes they are and they are already dressed."

"Good we will be a whole family today." That made Karen very happy.

"Yes Karen we are, two generations almost three." Austin answered.

They all walked out of the front door just as Margo and Bo came out of their front door on their way to church too.

"Austin I see you have your whole family going to church this morning." Bo said.

"Yes Bo I do have the whole bunch going." Austin answered.

"I guess Margo and I will see you there. Karen you're real pretty in your new dress and you have your hair done up so pretty." Bo wished Margo was pregnant like Karen, but he felt sure they would be soon.

"Thank you Bo, if you only knew how awful the rest of me looked under this pretty dress."

"I could give you a quick little check up and see for myself." Bo answered as he gave Karen a little smile. He knew that would get her going.

"No Bo, you cannot, you and Austin play doctor enough without me giving you both more time to play." Karen answered.

"Now Bo don't you go and get my wife mad before we get to church. She may not let me hold her hand while the preacher is talking." The men had a good laugh over that as they always did after one or both of them had done something that may make Karen mad with one of them or even both of them.

"Hello Margo, I'm glad to see you going to church with Bo." Austin could already see what an impact Karen had made on all of their lives. "Thank you Austin. I always loved going to church on Sunday.

It just seems like the right thing to do. Karen, are you doing alright?" Margo asked. She didn't want to ask too much in front of Austin's parents, but she sure would like to know how things were going between them all.

"Margo I'm doing great now that I have met my in-laws. They are real nice people. A little on the tall side like their son, but I'm very sure I will change some of the future Blackburns height. Now I would like you to meet Austin's mother and father they are the other two tall people here. Margo it seems that you and I are the only short people in town."

"Hello, I'm Bo's wife I guess you already know that though."

"Yes we heard you two had gotten married. Congratulations, to you both Margo," Bridget said.

"Karen that is a beautiful dress you have on and your makeup and hair looks really nice. You look like a model yourself."

"Yes a big fat model." Karen said as she glanced over at Austin. "No you are not fat Mrs. Blackburn, you are pregnant." Austin wished his wife would just accept the fact that she was as beautiful pregnant as when she wasn't.

"Austin you love me so you only see what you want to see." Karen answered.

"Karen I want to see all of you all of the time and that is not fat it's my son." Austin was helping Karen into the back seat of their truck.

"Dad, get up there and drive. Mom you get up there with him. I'm sitting back here with my beautiful wife. You know where our church is at. It's the big Baptist Church three blocks down and two blocks to the right."

"Yes son I know it well." Mr. Blackburn quickly turned to his wife. "Bridget how do you like Austin's big Ford truck?"

"I like it a lot." she answered. She had no idea where all of this was going.

"Karen, tell your mother in-law what a man who drives a Ford truck needs." Maxwell wanted his wife to hear what they would soon be wearing.

"Alright, I will, if you really want me to Mr. Blackburn." She could not tell whether, he wanted his wife to know he wanted to get some jeans or if he was only making fun of her. "A man needs a pair of new tight Jeans that are boot cut with a long sleeve white shirt and a pair of western boots."

"So Maxwell, do you and Austin have new jeans and white shirts with boots?" Bridget asked.

"I don't Bridget, but I'm very sure Austin has a lot of new tight jeans and I'm pretty sure he has boots to go with his new look as well."

"Karen, tell Bridget the rest." Maxwell seems to be on some kind of a roll, but Karen wasn't sure if he was being nice or just still making fun of her.

"Yes sir" Karen told her mother-in-law her little Ford slogan.

"Well I do say our little daughter-in-law should be working for the Ford Company. Austin, do you like your truck?" Bridget asked.

"Yes Mom I really do. At first I didn't think I would, but that was before I drove it. One time is all it took. I hardly drive my Ferrari at all anymore, but Karen won't let me get rid of it. She said that was to be my only reminder of my bachelor days."

"She is right son. You should keep it. If only so your son can have it one day." Bridget did not want her son getting rid of all of the reminders of his days before Karen. He may regret it one day she felt.

"Yes Mom, but I may need more than just one if I'm going to give them to my sons." Austin was giving Karen the eye. She knew what he was saying about having more than just one son and the other seven children being girls.

"Where do we park son?" Maxwell asked as soon as he had the church in sight.

"Dad there is a big parking lot in the back." Austin answered. Maxwell drove around to the back of the big Church. "Son, you need to help Karen. This is a long walk for her."

"Mr. Blackburn it's not that far to walk, I can do it. After all I'm just a kid." Karen smiled up at Austin.

"Yes you are just a kid having a kid." Austin was only reminding his wife what his mother had said yesterday after finding out Karen's age.

"Austin Blackburn, I'm more than just a kid, I'm your wife. I had hoped you would have known that by now."

Austin was helping Karen out of the truck now. "Yes Karen I know that very well. Today you look like a grownup woman. You look so sexy I could hardly stand just sitting next to you."

"Austin your parents will hear you." Karen did not want her in-laws hearing all of the things their son wanted to say to her all the time.

"I don't care who hears me. I still want you Mrs. Blackburn." Austin leaned down and kissed Karen right there.

"Austin Blackburn we are at church not the drive-in."

"No we are not in the church yet, we are still in the parking lot. So I can kiss you all I want." he answered.

"Austin your parents are right ahead of us and they can hear everything you are saying. Oh here comes Bo and Margo. We can wait and they can walk in with us." Karen was so glad to have Margo there. She hoped this would give her in-laws someone else to question for awhile other than just her.

"Yes let's wait" Austin said. "That will give me more time to mess with my wife before we get into church."

"Austin, behave yourself or I will get your Daddy to do something with you." Bridge said as she and Maxwell walked just ahead of their son. Karen was sure she would be the one they would blame for all of their son's bad behavior.

"Yes Mom, but I will still do all I can with my wife even in Church." Austin answered.

"Karen honey, I can tell you have your hands full being married to our over sexed son." Bridget said. This really surprised Karen. She was not being blamed at all for Austin's behavior.

"Mom is that any way to talk about your son to his pregnant wife?" Austin asked.

"Yes it is. All I'm trying to do is to explain to Karen she is always going to be pregnant. I can tell it already and I don't think you will be stopping at eight babies either."

"Mrs. Blackburn it's alright I love your over sexed son and he is the one who will need to put up with me, every time I'm pregnant and it will not always be pretty."

"Son, I think these females are ganging up on us men." Maxwell replied.

"You think so dad." Austin answered.

CHAPTER THIRTY FIVE

After church everybody went out to a restaurant to eat lunch. "Austin, I see your dad has your key. Is he going to be buying a truck now?" Bo asked.

"Bo, I sure think so they both love it." Austin was pretty sure that both of his parents were sold on getting a truck.

"Why not, it isn't like they can't afford to buy anything they want." Bo answered.

"Mrs. Blackburn, are you happy about having a grandson?"

"Oh yes Margo, I'm overjoyed and they are naming him after his father." Margo could tell that Austin's mother was happy, but she wasn't so sure about his dad.

"Oh Karen, that's nice." Margo thought that Karen would want to name her baby Austin. Because she loved her husband so much.

"Bo we need to talk about our vacation." Austin wanted to tell him about Karen's idea.

"Yes Austin we do now that we both have wives."

"Yes, but I think we can still do our same vacation with them. It will just take making a few little changes and you and I both already know we sure don't want to go anywhere without our wives. So here's our solution. We can take one of our trucks and we put a trailer on the back of it to carry our bikes and we can drive some and Margo can drive the truck if you and I want to ride our bikes at the same time and then one of us can drive awhile and we can be with our wives." Austin said as they sat at the big table.

"Yep we can do that. I really think that would work and I would like us to go by my parents and let them meet Margo." Bo said wishing that they had more news for his parents other than just getting married.

"Are you boys going to still ride your bikes on vacation?" Maxwell asked.

"Somewhat, we were just saying Mr. Blackburn, we could take one of our trucks and get a trailer for our bikes and then we could ride our motorcycles some and ride in the truck with our wives some."

"That would work. I bet the girls would even ride with you some." Mr. Blackburn said forgetting about Karen's condition.

"Yes, I'm sure Margo will, but not Karen she cannot get on my bike until after our son is born. I won't have it." Austin was not letting Karen on the back of anything right now.

"Well son I didn't expect you to let Karen and I'll bet that Karen would not even want to." Maxwell, knew that he nor Bridget would want Karen on a bike right now.

"Yes she would if she wasn't this far along. We took a little weekend trip before she started showing and she got her first days of morning sickness while we were on that little trip. Dad I didn't think that I would be able to get her back home, she was so sick. So I never want to go off again on any trip with just my bike."

"Son, being married changes a lot of things for a man you will learn. You can't just make plans that don't include Karen anymore. That is if you plan to stay married and happily." Maxwell knew what he was talking about.

Everyone was talking and having a nice time at the restaurant, but afterward they were ready to go home and get into more comfortable clothes, especially Karen.

Taking the truck and a trailer for our bikes is a good idea. He even said something about going down to Georgia to see his parents. He wants them to meet Margo. He is hoping that she will be pregnant by then I know."

"I hope so too Austin, I would like one other fat person around me at least." Karen said as she tried looking at herself in the full length mirror in their bedroom.

"Karen Blackburn, do I need to tell you again that you are not fat, you are pregnant." Austin only saw how beautiful his wife was and all she saw was how thin every other woman was that she saw.

"Austin I know that, but I'm still bigger than any of you and I'm only five months pregnant and I still have four months to go." Karen was happy about being pregnant, but she never expected to get so large so soon.

"Yes, four months. You can do it honey. Now do you want me to undo the back of your dress?" Austin asked as he started to take off his shirt.

"Yes I do, I just want to put on my gown and rest a little if that is okay with you." She felt a little worn work today. She guessed some of it was from all of the stress from meeting her new in-laws for the first time.

"Sure I will take off my clothes and we both can do a little resting." Austin said, but he already had that look on his face.

"Austin, I really do mean rest." Karen knew Austin well.

"Alright, we can just rest if that's all you want to do." They both got into bed.

"Austin it's not just all that I want to do. It's what I need to do right now, later will be different. Now can you just lay down here beside me and behave yourself?" Karen looked over at Austin waiting for his answer.

"I will try, but I can't promise anything." Austin still had that look on his face. The one that Karen had learned that meant he would be up to something soon.

"I bet if I would give you a big kick and send you flying right out of this bed you would learn to lay down and behave yourself." Karen thought she may just need to try that sometime.

"Now would you do such a thing to your old sweet husband?" Austin asked. Not believing she would ever do such a thing to him.

"Yes in a heartbeat. Do you feel like finding out if I would?" Karen asked. She was lying in Austin's arms now.

"No, but aren't you tempting me just a little by lying here almost naked and so close to me?" he asked.

"Austin Blackburn, I have on my gown and my granny underwear. I'm very sure none of this would turn anyone else on if they saw me."

"Maybe you aren't suppose to turn on anyone else, but your husband." Austin answered. "Maybe because he knows what you really look like when you aren't pregnant and that's what got you pregnant in the first place."

"Oh so that's how this all came about and all the time I was under the impression it was because my new husband was so horny he could not help himself."

"You are right I couldn't help myself. Now are you ready to give in or not?" Austin asked.

"No, I meant what I said Austin. I need to rest some. If you don't behave you are going to be picking yourself up off the floor because I'm

ready to give you a big kick. Right now you are just pushing your luck."
Karen knew he did not believe she would kick him.

Austin was not about to give up. He was in the mood and he was
not wanting to take no for an answer.

"Alright big boy you asked for it." Karen gave Austin such a big kick
that he landed on the floor beside their bed.

"Karen you really did it." Austin said as he lay on the floor.

"Yes I did. I told you I would and you just would not listen. So you
just had to be shown. Now are you ready to get up here and behave so I
can rest some until we both are ready to play your game?"

"Yes I will get back up there and wait." Austin never dreamed that she
could kick so hard that he would land on the floor.

"Good boy." Karen helped Austin up off the floor and they both got
back in bed. They even fell asleep for over an hour.

"Karen I bet I have a big bruise from that kick you gave me." Austin was
trying to make her feel bad for kicking him out of their bed.

"Yes you may, but you will listen the next time I tell you I'm tired." she
smiled and said.

"Yes I will. Otherwise my little pregnant wife may kill me with her
little foot." Austin was soon over his fall and was ready to try again.
Karen soon gave in and Austin got his way.

"Mom did you and Dad lie down and rest awhile?"

"Yes we did, but we heard an awful sound from up in your room just
after we got to our room. What fell?" Bridget asked.

"Me," Austin answered. "Karen literally kicked me right out of our
bed." Austin looked so innocent.

"Why?" Bridget asked. At first Bridget thought Karen should not
have done her son so badly, but she thought it over for a few seconds and
then she quickly changed her tune. "What were you doing that you didn't
need to be doing?" She was still looking her son right in the eye.

"Mom why would you think it had to be all, my fault? Don't you
think Karen could have done something that caused it?" Austin was
doing his best to look innocent.

"Son, I know your, Daddy and you are exactly like him. Do I need to
say any more?" Bridget waited for her son's answered.

"Well I'm not going to tell you and neither is Karen. You will just have
to always wonder." Austin looked over at Karen when he said all of that
to his Mom.

"You don't need to tell me I can guess. Karen would you like to go for a little walk?" Austin's mother gave him a little smile. "We will see."

"Yes Mrs. Blackburn I would enjoy that very much. Austin, are you going with us?" Karen asked.

"Yes if you want me to go and if you won't kick me again. I will be glad to go walking with you." Karen stuck her tongue out at Austin. "Woman, do you remember the last time you did that what happened?"

"Yes I do," Karen answered.

"Do you recall what happened to you then? Well that same thing can happen to you again." Austin had that smile on his face again.

"Only if I let it happen." Karen answered.

"Now my wife thinks she is in control of everything." Austin said kiddingly.

"She is." Bridget quickly answered.

"Right now she may be, but she won't always be pregnant." Austin was giving Karen the eye.

"She will be if you two are planning to have eight babies. Now do you want to rethink that decision?" Bridget asked.

"No M'am we do not. Austin will just have to get used to not having his way all the time." Karen was giving Austin the eye now.

"Are you saying I get my way too much?" he asked.

"Yes I do, but not anymore or you will find yourself on the floor more often and I may even be on that floor with you." Karen answered.

"Now that sounds a lot better." Austin could not resist kissing his wife.

"Dad, are you going for a walk with us?" Austin asked.

"Sure your Mom will need someone to be with her while you paw all over your wife." Maxwell answered.

They walked for an hour before going back to the brown stone. "Austin I think I'm going over to the Ford dealer tomorrow and look at a truck for your mother and me."

"Dad I will be glad to drive you and Mom over to the dealer. Are you planning to buy a big truck like Bo and I have?" he asked.

"Yes we are. Your Mother and I decided we could use a big truck around our place. I guess we will need to get a few new pair of jeans and a couple of long sleeve shirts. We sure don't want to lose out on the true affect you get from driving a big Ford truck." Maxwell had a big grin on his face.

Monday Karen got up early and had made a big breakfast. She wanted Austin to have a good breakfast before going off to work. When Austin's Daddy and Mama came downstairs they were all excited about breakfast.

"Karen we could smell your cooking all the way up to the second floor and I expect Austin could smell it up on the third floor as well. It smells great, when do we eat?" Bridget said as soon as she walked into the kitchen.

"Thank you Mrs. Blackburn anytime now." Bridget had given up getting Karen to call her anything else except Mrs. Blackburn.

As soon as breakfast was over Austin drove his parents to the Ford dealer then he was going on to work. "Dad, I'm going on to work if you should need me to come back just give me a call."

"Son, before you go give me a check. I will need one to pay for our truck."

"Alright I have one right here." Austin reached into his suit coat pocket and handed his Dad the check. "I was sure you would need one." Austin went on to work. He was sure his parents would find the truck they wanted.

"Hello Mr. Blackburn, here are your messages." Austin's secretary handed him a stack of them. "Everyone of them wants you right now." She told Austin.

"Thank you Betty I will get right to it." Austin went into his office to start making his calls. He spent the rest of the morning on the phone then he called Karen.

"Karen honey has Mom and Dad gotten back yet?" he asked.

"Yes Austin they have and they have already gone home. They wanted to drive their new white truck." Karen was still busy doing her housework.

"So they got them one and its white." Austin was not surprised at all. His Dad had always bought all of his cars in white.

"Yep they did and they even got new jeans and shirts for both of them. They are really taking to having a truck very serious." Karen and Austin both laughed.

"Now tell me how my wife is doing?" Austin was sitting behind his big desk with his feet resting on top of it.

"I've been busy changing all the bedding and doing our wash. Other than that I have just been sitting back and eating Bon Bons."

After they hung up Austin had his secretary to call a cleaning service. He was not letting Karen do anymore house work no matter how much she protested. He was going to put his foot down. She was his wife not his maid.

CHAPTER THIRTY SIX

T
he next week Margo decided she was going to teach Karen how to drive. "Margo what am I going to learn to drive in?" Karen asked.

"Bo's car and Austin's car that is what we will use. You can drive them both and they will not miss the gas then." That day they started out in Bo's Jaguar. Margo got it out of the garage and then she began Karen's first lesson.

"Margo, are you sure I'm not going to wreck Bo's car?" Karen was a nervous as she could possibly be.

"I'm sure we are going to just drive up and down this long alley until you gain confidence in what you are doing. Then we will go out on to the street." Karen didn't have any trouble at all learning to drive Bo's car. In no time at all she was driving Bo's car everywhere. By the third week of her lessons she was driving Austin's Ferrari as good as he could. She could shift the gears without any trouble and she could down shift like a pro.

"Today Karen we are going to get your driver's license as soon as our husbands gets off to work." Margo told Karen.

"Okay Margo, I will be ready, you come over and we will go." While they were at the drivers license office Margo got her new license with her new last name and address. Karen passed her test both written and driving. Both girls were so excited. Karen had used Bo's car for her test.

"Karen, are you going to tell Austin that you have your driver's license now?" Margo asked.

"No not yet I want to surprise him." Karen wondered when would be the best time for her to tell him.

"I'll bet he will be shocked." Margo teased.

"You are right he will be." Karen answered. "I'm not a little girl anymore, I'm over six months pregnant and I may need to drive my children to soccer practice one of these days." For the first time in

Karen's life she didn't have to depend on any else to take her where she needed to go.

"Karen I'll bet that you will be driving them more than just one day." Margo laughed.

"I'm sure I will, I know Austin won't be able to do everything for our kids and work so it will be up to me to do my part."

Later that day Karen, decided to go to the little store down the street and she knew that she would not be able to carry her bag back, so she decided to drive Austin's Ferrari. It just so happened that Bo and Austin decided to come home early, because the next day the four of them were starting their vacation together.

When Austin opened the garage door all he could see, was the empty space where his Ferrari used to sit. He stopped and immediately checked to see if his and Bo's motorcycles were all there. The only thing missing was his baby, his red Ferrari. He immediately called the police and reported it stolen.

Margo had gone to return some books to the library. Austin told Bo to check his garage. Bo did just that and everything was there. It didn't take long until the police called Austin to tell him that they had his car and the person who had stolen it. They told him he needed to come down to the station and fill out some paperwork. Austin called Bo and got him to ride down to the Police Station with him so that he could drive his car back home.

When they got to the police station they were told by the officer that the person who had taken Austin's car said that she was his wife.

"No, my wife doesn't even know how to drive." Austin answered. Austin was furious. He wanted to get his hands on this person and pull them apart and if they had done anything to his baby there would not be enough people in the Police Station to pull him off of this person.

"You know the girl is even pregnant and she is still out stealing cars." The police officer said while shaking his head.

"What? She is pregnant?" Austin asked. This got Austin wondering.

"Yes she is about six or seven months I would say and she is a real beautiful woman. I just don't get it sometimes." The policeman said as he shook his head again.

"That's my wife, Karen is my wife." Austin answered wondering how in the world this could have ever happened. Karen doesn't drive.

"Okay, I will bring her out so that you can identify her." The officer left the room to go and get Karen.

Austin and Bo stood there waiting for Karen to come out. 'Bo, how could all of this have happened? Karen, doesn't even know how to drive and especially my car?" Austin asked.

"It beats me." Bo answered.

It wasn't long before the officer came back in with Karen. She was so relieved to see Austin. She still had all of her groceries in the bag.

"Karen what happened?" Austin asked.

"What happened is that I got arrested, handcuffed and brought here in a police car. Then I got finger printed, my picture made and then put into a cell. Your wife and our baby have been in jail. Austin don't just stand there do something." Karen was so upset.

"Mr. Blackburn is this young lady your wife?" The officer asked . . . . "Yes sir, she is." Austin was so relieved, but he was still in a fog about what had happened. "Karen, how did you get my car out of the garage and all the way down to the grocery store?"

"I drove it out like I have been doing for the last month. If you had not come home so early you would not have noticed that it had been driven at all." Karen didn't know whether to cry or be mad.

"But honey you don't know how to drive." Austin was more confused than Karen.

"I do now." Karen answered. "At least I did, but I may not drive ever again after this." she answered.

"How did you learn to drive?" Austin asked.

"Margo taught me in Bo's car and yours." Karen answered.

"Bo our wives have been doing this all behind our backs." Austin was so relieved that it was Karen who had his car and not someone else.

"Yes they have. I only hope that is all that they have done." Bo said. Margo had her own little secret that only she and Karen knew right now. This was something not even Bo knew yet.

"Bo we will need to go to the impound lot and get my car. You drive it home." Austin was still a little shaking from thinking some had stolen his baby.

"No Austin, I will drive your truck and Karen can drive your car and you can just ride with her." Karen thought that Austin was going to faint right there in the Police Station.

"Man it's only a car and Karen is your wife and she is pregnant, so let her get it home for you. After all she did get it to the store all by herself." Bo had a big grin on his face. He wished he had his camera with him. He would have liked to have been able to take Austin's picture when he told him to let Karen drive his car home and him just ride with her.

Austin drove to the impound lot. "Karen, get in and drive us home and let me see what you can do." That was all it took. Karen turned the key and off they went.

"Austin which way is home?" He told her and she drove them to the back alley and right into the garage. Bo was already there waiting.

"It sure didn't take you two long to get here." Bo was smiling.

"No it didn't, she didn't have any trouble driving at all. Karen how long have you been driving?" Austin wasn't sure if all of this had really than place or if he was in some kind of bad dream.

"A month," she answered as she handed Austin his keys. "Are you mad at me?" she asked.

"No I'm not mad, just surprised that's all." Austin answered as he put the keys into his pocket.

"I'll bet you were mad when you opened that garage door and your little pride and joy was missing."

"Yes Karen I was, I almost had a heart attack." Austin answered. "Did you miss me?" Karen asked.

"No I didn't worry about you not being here, because Bo said that Margo had gone to the library and I thought you were with her. I guess I was wrong."

"Yes you were because I was in jail for stealing a car." Karen answered.

"Karen, are you mad at me?" Austin asked.

"I don't know yet, I'll tell you later tonight when we are in bed and you want me for something." she answered.

"Karen honey, how can I make this up to you before bedtime?" Austin asked.

"Now Austin that is much better." she answered.

"Does this mean that everything will be alright in our bedroom tonight?" he asked.

"Of course Austin why not, I do love you and you do love me right below you loving your little red car, your job, you motorcycles and your house. Oh I almost forgot Bo and your parents."

They were in the kitchen now and Karen was getting her little bag of groceries put away. "Karen Blackburn I hope you don't really believe that for a second. If I had not thought you were at the library with Margo, I would have been in a panic from not seeing you. Honey I do not care more about that car or anything else or anyone else than I do of you. How can I convince you of that honey? Just tell me how? Do you want me to sell my car?" he asked.

"No! I do not. I like driving your cute little car." she answered.

"So you like driving it, then you just started doing that any time you want."

"Austin, I'm almost too big for it. I'm sure I have done my driving of your car for now. All I wanted to do was to go and get us some snack food for our trip tomorrow and I ended up in jail."

"Karen I did not know that you had learned to drive. Do you have a driver's license?" Austin asked. He could not still believe all that had happened.

"Yes I sure do and I'm a good driver." she answered.

"Yes, I saw how good you are. Karen do you want me to just order us a pizza for supper tonight?"

"Yes Austin, if you want to." They had an early supper and went to bed. They were going to leave by eight o'clock Saturday morning.

"Austin quit messing around and get to it. It's getting late and we have to get up early." Karen said.

"We don't have to get up any earlier than we always do, so lay back down here and enjoy it." About that time their baby kicked Austin. "I think Karen our son takes after his mother. He likes to kick me too."

"Did you feel him when he kicked Austin?"

"Yes honey I sure did. I know it must hurt when he kicks that hard."

"Austin, I think I'm getting used to it, because if he doesn't kick I start to worry." Karen answered.

"Well honey I think he is doing great and he has a very good mother carrying him."

"Austin I hope so, I've never done anything more important than carrying your baby."

"Karen it is our baby." They were soon asleep. Karen had her head on Austin's pillow and her stomach resting on her little pillow.

CHAPTER THIRTY SEVEN

"Karen, don't forget to get our three pillows. Just drop them down the stairs and I'll take them out to the truck." Austin told her.

"I'm going now to help Bo get the trailer hooked up and get our bikes onto it. Don't you try to carry anything down the stairs do you understand me?"

"Yes Austin I do and I will do just as you say."

Margo still had not told Bo that she was pregnant, nor had Bo even thought about her being pregnant. He had so much on his mind. He had forgotten all about the fact that he could be getting his own wife pregnant. Margo was already almost two months along.

It took an hour before they were all settled into Austin's big black truck. Karen was up front with Austin. Bo and Margo were in the back seat.

"Bo I need to talk to you." Margo sounded so serious.

"Okay, Margo is there anything wrong?" Bo had his arms around Margo.

"No I don't think so." she answered.

"So tell me Margo what's on your mind?" "Bo I'm pregnant." Margo answered.

Bo didn't say a word. He acted as if he did not understand what Margo had said. Karen and Austin were talking and they had not heard Margo.

"Bo did you hear me? Did you hear what I said?" she asked.

"Yes Margo, I heard you." This was not the reaction that Margo had expected.

"Well Bo I guess there is something wrong. I thought that we wanted a baby, but I guess I was very wrong." This hurt Margo so much.

"Wrong Margo honey, it couldn't be any better news. I love you and we are going to have a baby. Austin I'm going to be a daddy just like you." Austin was shocked.

337

"Bo, why haven't you, said something about Margo being pregnant before now?" Austin asked.

"I didn't know, she just told me." Bo answered.

Austin looked over at his wife. "Karen did you know?"

"Yes Austin I did, I've known for almost two months." Karen answered.

"What?" Austin didn't understand any of this.

"Bo why didn't you know your wife is pregnant, aren't you that kind of doctor?" Austin asked.

"Yes Austin I am, but it never occurred to me that Margo was pregnant." Bo was still in shock.

"Bo aren't there a few little tell tale signs that can help a man to know if the woman he sleeps with and makes love to every night is pregnant?" Austin was going to kid Bo a lot about this.

"There should be, but only if you aren't so caught up with sex." Bo answered.

"Bo Brooks is that all I am to you? Free sex?" Margo asked. "No Margo, I didn't know it was free." Bo answered.

"Well it's not anymore." Margo pulled away from Bo and slid to the other side of the truck.

"Margo I love you and I'm just shocked. I could not tell that my own wife was pregnant." Bo could tell he was in trouble.

"Bo, don't get too upset over it. You never had anything to let you know that I was. We got pregnant just like Austin and Karen did. I never had my period after we got married and started having sex. You know all of that free sex that you have been getting every single night since we got married." Margo answered. Bo still had a shocked look on his face.

"Bo I need you to tell me that you want our baby and I need you to do it before we get any further down this road, because if you don't I'm going to ask Austin to stop and I'm getting out. My baby and I will walk right out of your life. Bo I don't care how much I love you. I will not live with you if you don't want our baby."

"Margo I want our baby and I want you. I just can't understand why I didn't realize that you never had your period since we've been married." Bo began to wonder what kind of doctor he was.

"Bo I didn't know that you just didn't. Maybe because you didn't care that I wasn't having my period. I don't know anything else to say."

"Margo, please understand that I want our baby very much and I want you very much, and that you have just made me very happy. Now Austin can't strut around being the only new daddy, I'm going to have a baby too."

"Bo did you marry me just because Austin married Karen and now we are having a baby just because you didn't want Austin to have a baby and not you?" This was as upsetting to Margo as Bo's first reaction had been.

"No I had already decided that I wanted you before Austin even met Karen. I just didn't know how to go about getting you and then Austin met and married Karen. I decided that I could do the same thing if I could ever get the nerve to speak to you instead of at you as you so delicately put it. I wanted you Margo and I want our baby more than you can imagine. So please don't ever say that you will leave and take our baby because you don't think that I love you. Margo Brooks I'm crazy about you.

"Oh Bo I do love you so much that I would die if I could not be your wife anymore." Margo looked a little sad, hurt and mad all sat the same time.

"Margo you will never have to know how that feels, because we will always be married." Bo took his wife in his arms and kissed her again and again. Austin and Karen never knew what had taken place between Margo and Bo in the back seat of Austin's truck. Later in the morning they stopped for breakfast.

"Bo, do you want to ride your bike with me for awhile?" Austin asked.

"Sure I do, just let me tell Margo." Bo answered.

Austin went back to check on Karen, he had just helped her back into the truck. "Karen, are you alright with me riding my bike for awhile?"

"Yes, just as long as you do it in front of us where I can see you and know that you are alright." Karen's door was still open so Austin leaned in and whispered. "I love you Mrs. Blackburn." Then he held her for awhile in his arms. "Honey I love you and we will be very careful so don't you worry. We will only ride for a couple of hours then we will stop so that you and Margo can get out and walk around. After all Bo and I have both got pregnant wives to take care of and we want to do that job well."

Bo and Austin got on all of their leather and then unloaded their bikes. Margo got into the driver's seat. Bo gave her a big kiss and hug. "Margo I'm so happy."

"Thank you Bo I needed to hear you say that to me." Margo answered.

"I know honey, I'm so sorry that I didn't react the way that I should have. I just could not understand how I could miss the signs that my wife is pregnant, I am an O.B.G.Y. N. doctor after all, but you can believe that I am happy. I can't wait to hold my baby."

"Our baby Bo!" Margo answered. "Do you know a good doctor that I can use?"

"Yes, I do as a matter of fact. It's daddy." Margo could tell now that Bo was happy with her and with their good news.

"Margo we are going to ride right in front of you and Karen so stay close enough that no cars can come between us. The speed limit is seventy so we will be right on it."

"Alright, Bo I will not let anyone get right near my man." Margo answered.

"Or my man either." Karen said. She was in her usual seat the front passage seat.

"Margo," "Yes Austin," "Go ahead and adjust your seat and mirrors now. Bo and I will ride for a couple of hours and then we will find someplace for us all to rest. Karen, if you need me for anything honey you have Margo blow the horn."

"Alright, Austin we will be alright. I love you." Karen was happy to be a big part of this man's life.

"Now Karen, give me a kiss. Margo, don't forget that you have a trailer back there so don't be changing lanes too quickly." Austin reminded her.

"Austin I won't forget. Karen will remind me." Margo answered as she looked over at her very pregnant friend.

"Yes she sure will." Austin answered. Then he turned his attention to his wife. "Karen I love you and I wish you would be sitting on the back of my bike, but I am even happier with you sitting here with our little fellow."

"Austin I am too. I love you now get up there so that I can watch my tall handsome husband's backside while he rides his big bike."

"Now will you two men go and get on your motorcycles so we can get on the road?" Margo said as she took one more look at her handsome husband. Both men hugged and kissed their wives one more time.

"At last, maybe now we can get on down the road. I thought they would never get on their motorcycles and ride. It is almost as if we are forcing them to ride their motorcycles." Margo could not help, but to laugh.

"I know our men love us and they are feeling lonely because we aren't on their bikes with them, but they will get used to it before this trip is over I'm sure." Karen answered.

"Karen, are you feeling alright?" Margo asked. "Yes I'm fine I'm just big." she answered.

"So that is what I have to look forward to myself?"

"Yes Margo, but you won't mind it at all. Austin is so good to me and Bo will be the same way." Karen knew Bo was just as happy about being married as Austin was and now that he knew he was going to be a Daddy he would be even happier if that was possible.

"I know Karen. I have never seen two men so much alike." Margo answered.

"You know they have been friends for years. Longer than we are old." Karen answered.

"Oh! So that is why they are so much alike. They have shared a lot of their life with each other so there is a lot of history between them." Margo was driving right behind the guys.

"Margo, aren't they handsome on their motorcycles?" Karen asked. She thought Austin was the most handsome man on earth.

"Yes Karen they are. Who would have thought that you and I would be the two women who would wind up with those two handsome studs." Margo was driving just the way that Bo and Austin had told her to drive. "Karen did you call your family and tell them that you were going to be in Georgia?"

"No Margo I'm not going anywhere near them. I don't want any of them showing up at Austin's front door wanting money, so I'm all the family that I will ever have other than Austin and our children." Karen knew that her mama and at least one of her boyfriends would find their way to New York and ring their door bell one day if they knew she had married and her husband was Mr. Austin Blackburn.

"I don't blame you at all for feeling that way. My father said that he was going to come to see us at Christmas, but Bo may want to go to his parents for Christmas. I haven't told him about my Daddy wanting to come at Christmas yet."

"Margo I'm going to tell you something and I hope it doesn't upset you because I love you like a sister, but you need to stop keeping so much from Bo. He is your husband and you should be sharing all of this with him as soon as you know it because, one of these days it may hurt your marriage. Secrets in marriage just don't work." Karen stopped talking. Margo still had her eyes on the road, but she didn't say a word for a long while. Karen was afraid she had said to much and that she had just lost her only friend.

"Karen don't worry I'm not mad at you. You just told me the truth and sometimes the truth is very hard to take. I don't want to lose Bo. I love him so much and tonight I'm going to tell him about my daddy wanting to come for Christmas. Then if he still wants to go home to his family for Christmas I will just stay in New York and have Christmas with my daddy."

"Margo, Bo won't go to Georgia for Christmas. I can tell you that right now." Karen answered.

"Karen I do hope that you are right." Margo wanted them to have the first Christmas of their marriage together.

"Austin what do you the think the girls are talking about?" Bo asked.

"Oh! Bo they are looking at us and thinking how lucky we are to have them." Austin answered.

"Austin I almost blew it this morning when I made Margo so mad about the baby until she was ready to ask you to stop the truck and she was going to get out and leave me." Bo was still somewhat upset at himself about the way he had handle Margo's news.

"Why, because you didn't know that she is pregnant?" Austin asked.

"No Austin not because I didn't realize my own wife was pregnant, but I didn't act happy about the news that she was pregnant." Bo answered.

"So why didn't you act happy Bo?" Austin asked.

"I was so shocked I could not react. I just could not understand how I could miss the fact that my own wife is pregnant." Bo still sounded a little out of it to Austin.

"Well Bo you just aren't the doctor that you think you are is all that I can say. So maybe you should start selling trucks or something like that for a living." Austin joked.

"Oh! Is that the only words of encouragement that my best friend has for me?" Bo asked.

"Yep, I guess you failed that part of sex lessons." Austin just had to laugh.

"I must have Austin." Bo answered.

"Bo if I had not called you about Karen's time I would have slept through this whole pregnancy thing myself. I knew nothing about a woman's period or being pregnant. You know that for yourself. It has never been a part of my life until now and it is the same with you. You knew to be alert at the office, but at home you were just being a husband and not a doctor. That's all that it was so be happy now and don't worry about not knowing Margo was pregnant. She could have told you that she missed her period just like Karen told us." Austin did not want his best friend to feel bad about something that most men are as guilty of as he himself was.

"You are right I just need to go with it now and get ready to be a father." Bo was feeling much better now.

"That's right we are going to be daddy's you and I. Who would have ever thought that, would ever happen to us." Austin answered.

"Not me Austin." Bo quickly answered.

The men were really enjoying their ride. Several cars loaded with women had passed them and had flirted with them. Austin pointed back to the truck every time sending the flirting girls away.

"Karen, are you getting tired?" Margo asked.

"Yes Margo my legs are stiff and I need to walk around for awhile I think." Karen answered.

"Do you want me to blow the horn so that Austin will pull off?" Margo asked.

"Margo let's wait a few more minutes, it will be two hours soon and they will pull off then I'm sure." Karen didn't want to take anything away from the two men's vacation. She felt that she had already done enough of that for this year.

"I, hope so, I can even tell that you are getting uncomfortable." Margo was getting worried about her friend.

"Yes I am, but I have enjoyed looking at my handsome husband's back side the whole time. Margo aren't they both handsome?"

"Yes Karen they are." Margo answered. She had been enjoying the same thing Karen had.

"Look at Austin in his jeans with those long legs, he is just too much." Karen was so in love.

"Well, Well, Well, Miss Karen has the hots for her husband." Margo was so surprised to hear Karen talk about her husband in that way.

"Yes I do in a very big way." Karen pointed to her stomach.

"Bo I believe we need to be pulling off the road soon. I have been watching Karen in my mirror and she doesn't seem to be doing well right now." Austin began to worry a little. He hoped this trip was not too much for Karen.

"Austin there is a rest area coming up in two miles. Will that do?" Bo asked.

"Yes it will." Austin answered.

"Karen, how are you doing?" Margo was worried about her friend.

"Margo I'm doing okay I saw a rest area sign and I know Bo and Austin saw it too. I have seen Austin watching me for the last forty five minutes. He knows that I need him." Karen answered.

Karen had gotten to the point where she was ready to scream. Every spot on her was hurting. "Karen, the men just turned on their turn signals so we are about to go off the road." Margo wanted Karen to know she didn't have long to wait.

"Good Margo, because I really do need to pee now." Karen answered.

"I will just follow them. They will know where they want us to go." Margo kept following the men. It wasn't long before Bo motioned for Margo to park. The guys parked and began taking off their helmets even before getting off of their bikes. Austin hurried to Karen's side of the truck and opened her door.

"Karen, are you alright?" He asked as soon as the door was opened.

"Yes Austin I'm alright as far as I know." she answered.

"No you are not. I saw you and I know when the woman I love is not alright." Austin did not believe her for one second.

"Austin my legs are tired of sitting that is all." Karen answered. "Alright let me get you out of this truck and then you can go to the bathroom. Afterwards you and I will walk all around this lot."

"Oh! Austin I missed you so much, but I have liked looking at you all that time." Karen answered.

"I saw that." Austin was unfastening Karen's seat belt. Margo was out of the truck and she and Bo were already hugging and kissing.

"Karen, aren't you going to give me a kiss?" Austin asked. "Oh! Yes Austin I will give you a big kiss." she answered.

"Are you going to let me make love with you tonight?" he asked. "Yes." Karen quickly answered.

"Well that didn't take you long to decide." Austin kissed Karen again and then he walked her to the restroom. "Karen I will be right here waiting for you when you come out. Be careful and if you need me holler and I'll be right in there."

"Alright, Austin, but I'm fine. I love you and I'll see you in a little while." Karen needed to get into the restroom now. She didn't have any more time to waste. Austin went into the men's room and Karen into the ladies' side. Austin was back and was waiting when Karen came out, but she was worn out. He could tell. "Karen, are you alright?"

"No Austin I'm not I need to sit down." Austin picked Karen up into his arms and carried Karen back to the truck. Austin began to call out when they got near the truck. "Bo, open the truck Karen needs to sit down."

Margo and Bo were just on their way to the restrooms. "What's the matter Austin?" Bo asked.

"Karen needs help there is something wrong." Austin was getting upset.

"Alright put her into the back seat." Bo got his bag out of the back of the truck. "Karen, are you in pain?" Bo asked.

"Yes I have pain in the bottom of my stomach." she answered. "Alright I need to check you. Austin, get Karen up in that truck and get her pants off."

"HOLD IT." Karen yelled. "What do you mean you want my pants off and you're going to check me?" she asked.

345

"Lay down Karen and don't get so upset you will only bring on the pain more if you get upset and we don't want it to come on any more than it is." Bo was doing his best to calm her.

"Karen, please do what Bo says for you to do. I will be right here honey." Austin was holding onto her.

"Do you two think that makes me feel any better?" she asked. "Karen all I'm going to do is feel your stomach, but the jeans have to come off. I'm very sure that you have on some big old thick granny drawers." Bo smiled and said.

"Yes she does" Austin said as he un-did Karens jeans and slid them off of her just as she had another hard pain.

"My stomach is in a big knot." Karen called out in pain.

"Yes Karen I can see that. Austin set on the seat and let Karen put her head in your lap. I'm going to rub her stomach so that your son will relax a little. He is in a big knot from Karen sitting too long in the truck, so we need to stop every hour and let her lay on the back seat and Austin you can rub her stomach like I'm doing right now." Bo was a good doctor and he loved Karen and did not want her to be in any pain.

"So I'm alright and our son is alright?" Karen asked.

"Yes Karen you are, but you need to do what I say. You are seven months along and you could go into labor if you don't listen." At this point Bo needed to be very serious with her.

"She will do everything you say Bo. I can promise you that." Austin answered.

Yes Bo I will even if I have to—." Karen didn't get to finish her sentence.

"Be checked by me." Bo answered.

"Yes even that, if it is for our son." Karen answered.

"Well you don't need that yet, but we will be a lot more careful with you and your son from now on during this trip. Now I'm going to the restroom. You and Austin stay here and rub your stomach very lightly like I was doing. That's all he needs and after he is all relaxed I want you and Austin to take a walk all around this place, but Karen put you jeans back on before you get out of the truck and before I forget to tell you, you have very nice legs." Bo smiled and said.

"Austin, pop him." Karen told her husband.

"Karen tomorrow you and I will ride in the truck. Bo and Margo can ride Bo's bike. I need to take care of you. You are very important to me. I want to be right here with you in case you should need me."

"Austin I don't want to mess up your vacation. You and Bo have already changed too much of your vacation just because of me. Austin why don't you just put me on a bus going back home and you go on with Bo and Margo and have fun. I will get back home and I'll be alright."

"NO! Are you out of your mind? I would never do that to you. You are staying right here with us. Bo has already said you and our son were both alright. We will just take it slower. Karen you are on vacation with your doctor. He will be with us the whole time, so you are staying right here with me on this back seat young lady. Do you understand me?"

"Yes Austin I understand."

"Now let's get your jeans back on your butt."

"Yes Austin, I'm not used to you wanting me to put my jeans on me. It's usually you wanting to take them off of me."

"Well sweetheart that will come later." Austin helped Karen to get redressed and then they went walking.

"Karen, are you getting tired yet?" Austin asked. They had been walking for awhile and he didn't want her to overdo.

"No." Karen answered.

"Are you getting hungry?" Austin asked. "No not yet." Karen answered again.

"Karen, are you mad at me honey?" Austin asked. "No." Karen answered once again.

"Then why aren't you talking to me?" he asked. "I was thinking Austin that's all." she answered.

"What was it you were thinking about honey?" Austin hoped it wasn't something too upsetting.

"About you and Bo and about what you were going to do to me back there in the truck." Karen didn't seem to be too happy over what he and Bo may have needed to have done.

"We weren't going to do anything, but help you honey." Austin answered.

"I know, but I didn't want you to do all of that for me." she answered.

"You didn't want me to help you?" Austin had a worried look on his face now.

"No I didn't want both of you to help me. I only wanted you to do the helping. After all I knew it wasn't our baby coming." she answered.

"I know honey, but Bo only wants to be sure our baby gets here and you both stay here. Karen you need to realize that both of us will be there when our son begins to come and you will be glad that we are there." Austin hoped he could convince his wife of all of this before little Austin decided to come into this world.

"I know Austin it's just that I'm not used to men knowing so much about me. I'm still getting used to sleeping in your house let alone in your bed, but I don't want to be any other place." Karen answered.

"I know honey, but you will get used to it all one day. I love you and I know that all the things a woman goes through to have a baby has to be hard to do sometimes. All you need to remember is Bo and I love you and we only want to do what is best for you and our baby."

"I know Austin, but I think it's harder now that Bo is married to Margo. I feel odd letting her husband know so much about my body." Austin wanted to laugh, but he knew women felt a lot different about personal things than men. "Karen maybe you need to talk to Margo and see how she feels about you being Bo's patient now that she is married to him." Austin felt that Margo would not see any problem with Karen being Bo's patient. At lest he hoped she didn't.

"Yes Austin I think I do need to have that little talk with her and I believe you need to have the same talk with Bo." Austin didn't answer, but he knew he would be doing just that as soon as he and Bo were alone.

Austin was still holding Karen's hand when they came walking back to the truck. "Karen, you aren't still upset are you?" She gave him a little smile. "No Austin I'm alright. You and I are always going to be alright. You are my husband and I love you." Austin just pulled Karen into his arms and kissed her. He didn't care who could see them at the rest stop nothing was going to stop him from showing his wife that he loved her.

The men began to load their motorcycles on to the trailer. "Karen, are you feeling better now?" Margo was truly worried about her new friend.

"Yes Margo I sure do, but need to ask you something very important while our husbands are busy loading up their bikes on the trailer." Margo could tell Karen was worried about something.

"Alright Karen what is it you need to ask?" Margo waited to hear what she had to say.

Karen looked over at her friend. "Margo, do you mind if I'm one of Bo's patients?" Karen was almost holding her breath while waiting for Margo's answer.

"Good heavens no, Karen why would I? He is your doctor and if I can't trust Bo and you who in the world can I trust. Karen, don't worry about being Bo's patient. I know it is hard on you, but I'm good with it." Margo gave Karen a big hug.

"Margo I didn't want you to be upset with me." Karen answered. "Karen I know Bo is a good doctor and you are my very best friend.

You prove that to me all the time. Bo would be so hurt if you were not his patient. So you let Bo do whatever it is he needs to do to get our daughter's husband born. Do you hear me women?" Margo began to laugh.

"Yes I do Margo and you sound just like Austin, he is always saying "do you understand me woman?" Thank you I just didn't know if I could stand going through letting one more person check me out." Now both women were laughing.

"Yes, it is really personal isn't it? I'm glad Bo is my husband that helps a lot I can tell you." Margo answered.

"Austin thinks he is a doctor right along with Bo when it comes to getting his son born." Karen told Margo.

"Karen that is so cute. Austin sure does love you and your baby a lot." Margo could see the way Austin helped Karen all of the time.

"I know Margo and sometimes it makes me feel bad when I kick him out of our bed for messing around with me so much." Karen answered with a smile on her face.

"Oh girl I bet it does." Margo said.

"No not really. I just like to see his face when I do it." Karen was laughing.

"Girl you are bad." Margo decided she may do Bo that same way one day soon.

"I know Margo, but at seven months what else can I do? I know he loves me, but the man is sex crazy." That was the only way Karen felt she could describe her husband.

"No Karen he just loves his hot wife a lot." Margo answered.

"Yes you are right. Well here they come. Don't they look like something in all that leather?" Karen asked.

"Yes, Hot." Margo answered.

"Bo I want to ask you something before we get into the truck." Austin said as they worked with their motorcycles.

"Sure Austin is it something to do with Karen?" Bo asked.

"Yes, she is worried now that you are married that your wife may not want her to be one of your patients."

"Why should Margo care who my patients are? I was Karen's doctor before I married Margo. Austin if you or Karen, feel you want another doctor I will understand, but you don't need to get another doctor on my or Margo's account. Karen is my patient first. Her and your son's welfare is the most important thing." Bo answered.

"Bo, Karen and I only want you to be her doctor not only with this baby, but with all of our babies. We just don't want you and Margo to have any trouble between yourselves because of us." Austin never would have thought in a million years that he would ever be having such a conversation with his best friend.

"Don't worry Austin there won't be any trouble. I will speak with Margo about all of this the first chance I get." Bo felt sure Margo would see it all as he did.

Austin was watching the two girls and saw them hugging each other. "I think Karen has already done it by the way our two wives are acting right now." Austin answered.

Bo raised his head to look at their wives. They were hugging and laughing. "Yes you are right they have already settled it and I'm still your wife's doctor." Bo answered. He was very pleased that Karen had talked to Margo and everything was settled.

"Yep I think so friend." Austin answered.

After they had finished with their motorcycles Austin and Bo went up to the cab of the truck where the two girls were sitting. "Girls are you ready to hit the road again?"

Bo and Austin had taken off their leather and now they only had on their tight jeans, shirts, boots and sunglasses, but they still looked like two handsome studs to their wives.

"Bo you drive for awhile I'm going to sit in the back with my sexy wife and rub her stomach." Bo looked at Karen and smiled.

"Bo Brooks you can just wipe that big smile off your face. Austin isn't going to be doing any more than that I can promise you." Karen answered from the back seat.

That made Bo laughed right out loud. He knew his friend, but he didn't say a word. He just kept on laughing.

"Austin, you tell Bo you aren't going to be messing around with me in this back seat." Karen was as serious as she could be.

"Well honey I don't know if that will be the whole truth or not. I may try to do a little messing around with you. After all I've hardly been near you all day and that can be mighty hard on a man my age." Austin answered.

Karen just looked at Austin. "When did you start talking like that?" she asked.

"When I got married to a little southern girl," Austin answered and then he smiled and winked at her.

"Austin I wonder if our son is going to be just like you?" Karen asked.

"He will be if he gets a sexy little wife like his mother." Austin answered.

"Austin do you still think I'm sexy?" Karen wondered if he would think that was another one of those trick questions that wives like to ask their husband.

"Yes Karen I sure do. Just looking at you turns me on." Austin was already getting that look in his eyes.

"Are you sure it's not just your accomplishment that turns you on now?" Karen asked as she looked down at her stomach.

"Well yes maybe it does, but the rest of you, has me wanting it to be time for bed all the time." he answered.

"Austin Blackburn what are you going to do when I can't have sex before and after little Austin is born?" Karen was sure she would not enjoy that time any more than Austin would.

"I will just suffer." he answered.

"Well, start suffering it will be good for you to learn how before you are forced into it." Karen answered.

"How can that be good for me and why would I need to learn to suffer until I have to suffer?" he asked.

"It will teach you to control what's in those tight jeans of yours." Karen answered.

"Oh is that all you are worried about, what's in my tight jeans?" Austin said and then he just smiled at her.

"No I'm worried about all of you. I know what you can do." Karen hoped her husband would never get tired of her and want some other woman.

"Yes you do, if anyone does." Austin pulled Karen into his arms and started to kiss her. She just could not resist him any longer. She wanted him as much as he wanted her.

"Mrs. Blackburn tonight," Austin whispered to her. "Yes Austin tonight," she answered back to him.

Later Karen laid her head down on Austin lap and he began to rub her stomach. "Karen our son is becoming a big boy. Bo, how much larger do you think Karen's stomach will get?" He had never seen a stomach as large as hers was already before in his life. The women he had always been around spent a lot of time and money trying to keep their stomach as flat as possible.

"Austin, Karen still has two full months to go and that is when your son will be doing his most growing. He will weigh anywhere from eight to ten pounds." Bo answered.

"Are you kidding that much and Karen will have to have him?" Austin answered.

"Yes wasn't that the idea when you put him into her." Bo asked. "Yes, but I didn't think about him being born at that time. I had a lot of other things on my mind then." Austin answered.

"I thought about it Austin. What goes in has to come out." Karen answered.

"Karen I will do everything I can to help you when it comes time for our son to come out." Seeing his little wife like this made him appreciate her even more.

"I know you will Austin because if you don't I will kick your butt right out of our bed when I get back home from having Little Austin. Do you want me to do that?"

"Never Karen, I don't want to ever go to bed at night without you." Austin leaned way down and kissed Karen on the top of her head.

"Neither, do I Austin." Austin was trying to pull Karen up so he could really kiss her.

"Do I need to be looking for a motel room for you two back there?" Bo asked.

"No Bo we have decided to wait until tonight." Austin answered. He would not have minded at all if Bo had found them a motel, but he was real sure it would make Karen and Margo both mad. They would not like it at all if anyone even thought that their husbands had stop at the motel just to have sex with them.

"Good because it is only lunch time and I'm ready to eat. Margo honey, are you ready to eat some lunch?" Bo asked as he drove down the long highway.

"Yes Bo I am and I'm very sure Karen needs to eat something." Margo was still worried about Karen.

"Yes I do. I'm eating for two you know." Karen had heard what Margo had said.

"Yes honey we know. We just wondered if you knew it." Austin answered.

"Austin I sure do know it. See he is wiggling right now." Karen took Austin's hand and laid it over her stomach.

"Bo our son is moving around like crazy." Austin was afraid something was wrong.

"Good he is suppose to do that my friend." Bo answered.

CHAPTER THIRTY EIGHT

Before long they were sitting in another little diner. It was similar to all of the other diners they had ever stopped at. "You folks need a little more time to check the menu?" The waitress asked.

"Yes just a little more time thank you." Austin answered. Farther away from New York the harder it got for him to order from a menu. He just did not recognize the names of the food.

"You folks aren't from around here are you?" The waitress asked. "No we are from New York City." Austin answered.

"Then you all are big city people." The waitress was looking them over as if they had just landed there from Mars.

"Kind of you could say, M'am, he is, but the rest of us moved there from different places." Bo was pointing at Austin.

"You aren't a Yankee I can tell." The waitress told Bo.

"No M'am I'm not. That young pretty lady and myself are from Georgia." Bo was pointing over at Karen. "This pretty one here is from Ohio and like I said that big guy over with that pretty lady is the big city boy."

"Is that one there yours?" The waitress asked? She was pointing to Karen.

"No M'am that one is the big city boy's. This cute one here is my wife and we are expecting a baby in seven months. Now Austin is my best friend and he and this pretty woman here, are going to have their first baby in two months. They are so in love." Bo gave Austin a silly little smile. Austin knew he was being setup by his friend for something, but he wasn't sure what it would be.

Then it came right on cue. "Did he have to marry her?" The waitress asked.

"No M'am he wanted to marry her. In fact he could not wait to marry her." Bo answered. He wanted to burst out laughing, but he didn't.

"He looks like he would be one hot stud." The waitress answered.

"Yes M'am we both are, just you ask our wives." Bo said.

"I don't have to I can see that for myself and since both of your wives are pregnant I know they let you both have your way with them." The waitress looked at Margo and then Karen and then to Austin. "You two guys have got yourself two smart young wives. They know how to keep you two coming home at night I can already tell."

"Yes M'am our wives sure do know how to do that and we are real glad about it." Bo answered.

Austin was smiling as he listened to his friend talk. He had always been fascinated at how Bo could talk to waitresses at all types of restaurants and they would spend a lot of time talking to him because they enjoy it.

"Karen I want you to eat a big meal and you too Margo. It's not too early for you to start doing the same thing Karen is doing." Bo told the two wives.

"Yes Bo I will eat for two, but remember I will never eat as little as Karen eats. So do you want to rethink all of that just a little?" Margo asked.

"Margo you eat all you want and if it gets to be too much I will tell you that you are getting too fat and then I will duck. Because I'm sure you will be throwing something at me." Bo was all smiles.

"Yes Bo I will you can count on it." Then Margo gave Bo a little kiss.

After lunch they switched places. Austin drove and Karen sat in her usual seat right next to him. Bo and Margo got into the backseat. It was their turn to make out now. "Do I need to find you two a motel room now?" Austin asked.

"If you want to it's up to you." Bo answered. Austin kept on driving.

"Bo this trip is a lot different from the ones we used to take." Austin remarked.

"Yes Austin it is, but I like this way of vacation a lot better, don't you?" Bo didn't want either of their wives to feel that they had taken their husband freedom away.

"Yes I sure do. Who would have thought two little girls could have made such a big change in our lives. Tonight when we go to bed I won't be sharing in a room with you Bo. I will be sharing a bed with my wife instead."

"Austin you do like the changes that I have made in your life don't you?" Karen asked.

"Yes Karen, I'm a lot happier than I ever thought I could ever be." He answered.

"Bo, tell Margo how happy you are now that you have her." Karen said from the front seat.

"Karen I don't have to, she already knows." Bo answered.

"Oh are you trying to embarrass me?" Karen's face started to turn red.

"No Karen he is trying to embarrass me and he is very happy I can tell you both." Margo said.

"Yes Karen I am very happy." Bo said and then he kissed Margo. "Karen don't you wish we were still in the back seat?" Austin looked over at his wife and asked.

"No because it can be very dangerous for one of us." s he answered.

"Honey, tell me how could it be dangerous, you are both already pregnant. So what can we do that we haven't already done?" Austin asked.

"We could do it back there." Karen pointed to the back seat. "Oh so we could." Austin began to smile.

"Austin Blackburn don't you go and get any idea about us in that back seat. It won't work." Karen answered, but she knew it was too late he was already thinking about it.

"I won't Karen." He lied.

"I don't believe you one little bit. I can see it in your eyes already." Karen just looked at him.

"You can, so how are we doing?" Austin had a silly grin on his face.

Karen cut her eyes back over to him. "Mr. Blackburn we always do great." she answered.

Just before dark they stopped at a real nice motel. There they got connecting rooms. The men thought their wives would like that better than them being separated from each other. "Margo don't you think it's a lot of fun traveling together like this?"

"Yes Karen it is and I like that our rooms are connected. It will make it easier for us to visit with each other." Margo answered. When

Margo said that the men knew they had made the right decision about the rooms.

The girls, were busy getting things out of their suitcases they would need for the night. "Girls would you like to go to the bar and dance a little tonight?" Bo asked.

"Bo, will Karen be able to dance?"

"Yes Margo she can dance as long as I'm there to do the two step with her." he answered.

"Oh Bo will you dance with me" Karen asked?

"Sure as long as Austin and Margo don't mind." Bo answered. "We don't mind at all," Margo answered.

"No Bo I don't mind just as long as you return her to me after the dance." Austin answered.

"Austin I will never leave you. I will be right in your sight all the time." Karen answered.

"I know that honey and I will be watching you all the time. Then I will try to dance the next dance with you if you want to give it a try with me."

"Austin, I would love for you to learn to Two Step. Then we could do some line dancing together. It's all very easy. I learned to do it when I was young."

"Did you learn that in the sixth grade too?" Austin asked.

"No Austin I didn't learn that until I was in the seventh grade." Karen answered.

"Margo do you line dance and do the Two Step?" Karen asked.

"No Karen, but I will learn right along with Austin. I'm sure you and Bo will be able to teach us how to dance tonight, but Karen, please be real careful when you are out on the dance floor."

"I will Margo. Your daughter needs my son for her husband. So I will be very careful. Besides Austin would have a fit if I were not careful."

"Yes you are right Karen I would."

They soon closed the door between the two rooms so they could each have some private time before getting ready to go out for the night. Each couple took a nice long shower. Afterwards Austin and Karen lay down on their bed. They were very sure Bo and Margo were doing the very same thing in their room.

"Karen you try and rest some before we go out to eat."

"Austin, are you really going to let me rest or is this just a trick to get me into bed with you?" Karen asked.

"No it's not a trick yet." he answered.

Karen didn't bother to put on her gown she just had on her granny drawers. "So aren't you going to put your gown on now?" Austin asked.

"Why" Karen asked?

"Because, honey you always sleep in your gown." Austin answered.

"Oh so I do, but I'm not sleeping now Austin I'm just resting." Karen answered in a very soft voice.

Austin began to smile. "So we can mess around a little?" he asked.

"Yes a little," Karen answered. Austin took her into his arms and then he started kissing her.

"Bo, do you think they know we are in here making love?" Margo asked.

"Yes because Austin is in there doing the very same thing with his wife." Bo answered.

"You, think so even as far along as Karen is?" Margo knew almost as little as Austin and Karen about having a baby.

"Yes they can still make love. They just have to be careful and I'm very sure Austin is being very careful with his wife and baby. He loves Karen so much and they both love that baby. Margo I feel the very same way about you and our little girl."

"Bo do you think we are going to have a little girl?" If they did it would make Margo very happy.

"Yes I do and I'm happy with that aren't you?" Bo asked.

"Yes I want a girl so badly Bo. I want our little girl to love little Austin and I want them to get married one day." Margo and Karen had their children's life all planned.

"Yes Margo that would be nice. Now all we will need to do is to have seven more babies to marry the rest of Austin's and Karen's children." Bo wondered what his wife would think about doing that now. Maybe they needed to spend a little more time talking and a little less time making love Bo thought for only a split second then he decided that would come soon enough.

"Bo, do you think we could?" Margo asked.

"Margo, would you want that many babies?" He was totally surprised. He knew she wanted a large family, but that many.

"Yes why not." she answered.

Bo just laughed. "Austin will never believe this."

Two hours later they were back in the shower. "Austin I have soap in my eye." Austin began to help Karen. "Hold still honey and I will help you to rinse it out."

It wasn't long before Karen had another problem. "Austin now my stomach is in a knot again." "Do you want me to rub your stomach too?" "No Austin I can do it myself." she answered.

"Austin," Karen was looking up at her husband.

"Yes Karen." He answered wondering what her problem could be now.

"Do you think I'm getting too big to take a shower with you?" Austin didn't need any time to think it over he just answered. "No why would I think that, aren't you still my wife and didn't we do this together?"

Karen smiled and answered. "Yes we did, but I have not noticed your stomach getting any larger just mine."

Austin looked down at Karen. "Karen do you know your stomach hides a lot of you from me when we are in the shower when I look down at you now?"

"Austin you are trying to make my face turn red aren't you?" she asked.

"Maybe just a little, but Karen we are married and we will share our showers anytime we want to always." Austin never thought he would love anyone the way he loves his wife.

They soon got out of the shower and got somewhat dressed. It was a very nice motel suite. Nicer than any hotel or motel room Karen had ever stayed in except for the one they stayed in while in California.

"Austin I want us to share everything not just showers. I don't want us to have any secrets from each other ever." She was still thinking about Margo keeping secrets from Bo.

"Karen I agree. We should never keep things from each other no matter what."

"Austin, are you talking about me learning to drive?" Karen didn't know if he was happy or not about her knowing how to drive.

"Well I may let you get away with that one. After all you did land in jail." Austin let out a little laugh.

"Austin, don't remind me of that. I will never forget that awful day and it was only yesterday." she answered.

"Karen I'm glad you learned to drive." At last he had said it. "Now I am too." she answered.

Austin, what are you going to wear tonight?" She didn't want to dress before she knew what he would be wearing.

"Do you need to ask?" he answered.

"Your jeans and white shirt," Karen answered.

"Yes, Mrs. Blackburn and you can wear your jeans and white top." That was another thing Austin never thought he would do.

"We will be like twins, but in our case triplets." Karen answered as she started to get dressed.

"No we will be like a husband and his pregnant wife." Austin answered.

Austin picked Karen up in his arms and danced her around their room. "Austin you dance so well I'm surprised you don't already two step." She was holding on to Austin as they went around the room.

"Karen that was always Bo's, thing not mine, until I married you. Now I find myself needing to learn it so I will be the man dancing with my wife and not my friend."

"Austin I'm not that good at dancing. I only had my grandma to dance with so you know you don't have anything to worry about. You will be dancing in no time and a lot better than me I can already tell." When Bo and Margo had finished dressing they just knocked on the door that separated the two rooms. Austin hurried and opened the door. "Did we disturb you two?" Bo was grinning.

"No we are ready to go if you are." Bo was dressed exactly like Austin. He had a white shirt, jeans and boots. "I see we are dressed alike." Austin said as he looked over at his friend.

"No Austin I have a bigger belt buckle than you and I have my name on my belt and you don't. People are going to think we are a part of the band because we look so good." Bo said.

"Good because I would not want to walk around all night with your name on my belt. I don't think the world is ready for two Bos." Austin answered.

"Austin, stop teasing Bo." Karen said and then she gave Austin a big pop on his arm.

"Yes Austin, stop teasing me before your wife gets upset with you." Bo loved teasing Karen, any time or any place.

"No I won't just get upset with him I will just kick him right out of our bed." she answered.

"No she won't because I won't let her do that anymore." Austin was still rubbing his arm. He was acting like she had really hurt him.

"Oh! So she has already done that before." Now Bo was really laughing.

"Oh yes she has done that before. When my wife says no messing around she means just that and she proves it." Austin was smiling at Karen.

"Yes I do, but you still don't believe me do you?" Karen asked.

"Yes honey I believe you, but I still feel the need to try." Austin answered.

"Yes I know you feel the need to try because I feel your need." Karen said just as Austin kissed her.

CHAPTER THIRTY NINE

They picked a nice bar and grill to eat at. It had good food and live music, a real country western band.

"Austin this is really a nice place. It's so clean and I like my food too." They were sitting in the small dining room.

"Karen I'm glad because I want you to start eating more." Austin along with Bo thought Karen was too thin.

"Austin I am eating more. Can't you see that?" But it was not Austin who answered her.

"No, none of us can see that and I'm your doctor." Bo answered. "Yes I know Bo, but I am eating more." Karen kept trying to convince them.

"Well we will see at your next weigh in." Karen just turned and looked over at Margo. "See what you have to look forward to."

Margo smiled. "Yes and I can't wait because I will eat, Karen." "That's my girl." Bo said as he watched Margo take another bit.

It was not long before they were all finished. "Karen, do you want to go to the ladies' room?"

"Yes Margo of course I do. I always want to go there for some unknown reason." Karen answered.

"Girls we are going into the bar and get a table before the place gets full." Austin wanted Karen to be sure she knew where they would be.

"Thank you Bo." Karen said as she and Margo left the table to go and find the rest room.

After paying their bill the two men went into the bar. The band was just starting to play. The second they walked into the room two women in their late twenties spotted them and they really liked what they saw. "Fran, do you see what I see?" One woman asked the other.

"Yes I do. It's like looking at heaven on earth. We need to get our claim on those two before some other girls do." Fran and Faye were regulars at the bar and they knew everyone who came to the bar.

"I want the tall one." Faye quickly said. "Which one would that be?" Fran asked.

"The dark haired one he looks just like a star." Faye could already see herself in Austin's arms.

"So does the other one so I will be very glad to settle for him." Fran said, but she didn't see any settling being done Bo was as handsome as Austin.

"I bet you will. Now let's get to the restroom so we can get back out here before anyone else tries to claim them for themselves." Faye said.

"Yes we may get real lucky and take them home with us." Fran answered.

Austin and Bo found a table near the door like they said they would do. The two women were still talking about Austin and Bo when they got into the restroom. Margo and Karen were each just coming out of their stalls and the two other women went into them. While all the time they were still talking about Austin and Bo.

"Fran they look so handsome in their tight jeans with those long legs. I wonder who they are? It's for sure they aren't from around here or we would already know them." Faye said.

"Yes and I hope they aren't just passing through." Fran wanted these two handsome men to stick around for awhile. She was sure then that she and Faye could get to know them real well.

Margo and Karen washed their hands. At first they did not realized the two women were talking about their husbands. Then when the two women said something to each other about tight jeans and long legs Karen realized the two women were talking about Bo and Austin. She looked over at Margo with two big eyes. "What is the matter Karen?" Margo asked.

Karen pointed to the stalls and said "Listen."

"Oh I understand, we need to get to our husbands before they do." The two wives left the restroom.

"Yes before these two women try to take our place. I don't want any women taking my long legged husband." Karen may have been seven months pregnant, but she was still the prettiest woman in the place with Margo coming up a very close second.

Bo spotted their wives as they came up to the bar door. "Austin there's our wives now. I will go and get them." Bo got up and hurried to Margo and Karen. "Hey you two pretty ladies we have a table over here."

"Bo it's dark in here." "Yes Margo it is. That is why I came to the door to help you. Austin is waiting at the table. Karen, watch your step. There are two steps right in front of you so give me your hand."

"Yes Karen let Bo help you. Austin would die if you fell." Margo said.

"I know, so Bo, give me both of your hands. I can't see a thing." Bo held on tight to Karen. He didn't want anything to happen to his best friend's wife either.

"Austin it is so dark in here. I don't see how we will be able to do anything in the dark." Austin could not help himself he had to smile.

"Karen I can think of a lot of things we can do in the dark, but your eyes will adjust soon and it won't be that dark to you anymore and you will be able to see everything in here."

"Yes you are right Austin I can already see a little better." Karen took the seat next to Austin. He pulled her chair right next to his. He wanted to be able to hear her and touch her whenever he wanted. Bo had done the same with Margo's chair. These two handsome men loved their two pregnant wives.

It wasn't long before the two other women came into the room. They stood up at the door until their eyes adjusted to the darkness before walking out into the room. There was an empty table right across from the two couples' table. Because Austin and Bo had pulled their wives' chairs so close to them they were not seen at all by the two other women as they took their seats at the nearby table in such a way that they would be sure that Bo and Austin would get a very good view of them. They were both very tall slim girls with lots of makeup. They turned several times in their chairs to glance in Bo and Austin's direction while still not noticing the two wives at all. The band started to play a nice slow number.

"Karen should we give it a try?" Bo asked. "Yes let's do." Karen answered.

All of a sudden the two girls from the other table turned towards the two men. "Hey do you two good looking guys want to dance?" Fran asked.

Austin looked over at Bo and then back again at the two women. "Are you talking to us?" he asked?

"Yes of course, do you see any other tall good looking guys in this place?" Fran asked.

"Well, miss I will tell you the truth I haven't been looking for any." Austin answered.

"Well do you and your friend want to dance?" Fran asked again. "Well I was just about to——." Austin didn't get a chance to get it out of his mouth before the women were standing up waiting for Bo and Austin to dance with them. Bo stood up and took Karen's hand and walked her out by the two women's table as they stood there.

"She's with you two?" Both of the women asked at the same time. "Yes both of our wives are with us. That is my wife over there at the table and this pretty lady here is my friend's wife." Bo answered. "Why are you two tall handsome men married?" Fran asked.

"We are married because we love our wives and we want to be married to them always. We both are going to be Daddies soon." Bo said as he held on to Karen's hand and led her out to the dance floor.

"I would be pregnant too if I was one of them." Fran said to Austin.

"Well you aren't them and we are both very pleased with what we already have and we are keeping them and they sure know how to keep us very happy." Austin then turned his attention to the dance floor where Bo and Karen were doing the Two Step.

"Karen you are a very good dancer. I have always told you that, but of course you never believed me." Bo said while he and Karen danced.

"Yes Bo you have told me that many times." Karen answered. "Now girl if you had not married Austin look at all the fun we would be missing." Bo had a big smile on his face.

"Yes Bo you are right. We would be missing out on a whole lot and especially me. I wouldn't have a home, husband or baby on it way." she answered.

"Or me as your friend and doctor." Bo quickly added.

"That's right, but without Austin I would not need a doctor. Bo I'm sure glad I do need you." Karen could not think of any other way she wanted to spend her life.

"I am too Karen." Bo pulled her close into his arms and danced her around the floor.

"Austin I think we could do that." Margo said as she sat there with Austin watching her husband dance with her friend.

"Yes I believe we could. I'm getting a little jealous too sitting here watching your husband holding my wife in his arms while he is smiling so big." Austin didn't know he could feel this way.

"I know what you're saying Austin. I think he is doing it on purpose so you and I will get up there and dance with them." Margo answered.

"Well all I can say is it worked because I can't wait until Bo returns my wife to me." Austin could not take his eyes off of Karen. Even pregnant she was still so beautiful.

"Well I'm sure they will be back soon the music has stop." Margo was ready to learn to dance anyway her husband wanted her to dance. "Yes here they come now." Austin was already pulling Karen's chair out for her to sit in.

"Austin, please try dancing with me. I know you can do it." Karen started saying even before she got back to their table.

"Yes Karen I will. Bo you didn't need to enjoy dancing with my wife so much?" Austin told his friend.

"Yes Austin I did and I also enjoyed holding her close too." Bo loved to joke with his friend.

"Margo he didn't I can tell you because little Austin kicked him several times." Karen answered.

"Good Karen, or should I say thank you little Austin because that will save me from having to do it to him myself later." Margo answered.

Bo took Margo's hand. "Honey I was just messing with Austin. I knew he was over here having a cow because I was out there dancing so close with his wife."

"Well what about me?" Margo asked. "Margo, were you jealous too?" Bo asked. "Yes Bo I was and I still am." she answered.

"Oh I guess Karen and I were better than we thought." Bo smiled and said.

"Now Dr. Bo Brooks I want you to dance with me." Margo told her husband.

"I sure will Mrs. Brooks. Do you want the same attention?" Bo asked.

"No I want more. I'm married to you." Margo answered.

"Okay I will be glad to give my wife more." Bo said as they went back out to the dance floor, but this time with his own wife. Austin and Karen were right behind them.

"Do you see those two good looking men's wives?" Fran asked her friend Faye.

"Yes I do and it makes me sick. Why would they want to waste their time with two short things like those two?" The two women were watching the two couples very close and the more they watched the madder they both got.

"Faye I think we still could get to know them. You see how pregnant that one is. I bet he would enjoy a nice change from her." Fran said as she put on some fresh lipstick.

"Fran I would not doubt it. Let's just go right up there and cut in on their dance." Faye was as bold as her friend Fran when it came to men.

"Alright Faye let's do it." Fran answered as she put her lipstick away.

The two women walked to the dance floor one went to Bo and the other to Austin. One was going to tap Karen and the other was going to tap Margo on her shoulder.

"Hey, I'm cutting in." Fran said as she tapped on Karen's shoulder. "No I don't believe so. My wife is not leaving my arms. So I suggest you go someplace else and do you shoulder tapping." Austin answered.

"Austin," Karen said in a soft voice.

"Yes Karen." Austin answered while trying to avoid the other woman all together.

"Don't let me go." Karen answered.

"I'm not honey, there is no way I'm dancing with that woman. I'm a married man and I'm here with my wife and that is you Karen." Austin danced Karen off out of the woman's reach. Bo did the same thing. After the dance they went back to their table. The two women were back at their table too.

"Are you really married to those two short things?" Faye asked. She was still mad.

"Yes we are married to our wives and they are not short things. These beautiful pregnant ladies are our wives and we love them and they are staying our wives. I just don't understand why you think we need to explain it all to you two." Austin was getting a little upset himself by now.

"I just don't get it." Faye answered.

"Well, Miss you don't need to get it. It's our business and not any of yours." Bo answered as he took Margo's hand to his lips and kissed it. Austin already had Karen in his lap and he was kissing her.

"Ladies we are taken. Go try some place else and leave us alone." Austin then turned back to kissing Karen. The two women soon left.

They danced a few more dances. "Bo I'm ready to go if you are. I have something else I want to do." Austin said.

"Me too Austin and we can't do it here." Bo answered.

"Nope we sure can't. So let's get out of here." Austin helped Karen up out of his lap and they went back to the motel.

"Bo let's go and check on our motorcycles and trailer before we go to our rooms. Do you girls want to ride with us?" Austin asked.

"Yes we do. We don't want to take any chance that those two tall girls aren't around here someplace." Karen answered.

"Karen it would not do them any good. Bo and I already have what we want for the rest of our lives and that is you and Margo." Austin was so in love with his wife.

"I'm so glad, but we will still ride with you just in case those two women don't understand all of that." Karen answered.

"Yes Karen I agree with you." Margo said as she sat in the back seat with Bo.

"Margo those women didn't have a chance with us. We only like short girls don't you know that by now?" Bo answered.

"Bo Brooks you only love one short girl and that is me." Margo answered.

"That goes for you too Austin. I saw how those two looked at you and Bo." Karen didn't like those looks at all.

"Well honey people will always look at other people, but that don't mean they get what they look at. Nobody is taking you from me or me from you." he answered.

"Yes Margo it's the same way with us." Bo answered.

"Bo there's our bikes." Austin said as they pulled up near them. "Yes all nice and pretty. Do, you want to be alone with them for awhile so you two, can give them a big good night kiss." Karen asked.

Margo busted out laughing. "Karen they probably would if we were not here with them."

"Yes we would. We have a big thing going on with our motorcycles. They are our other women." Austin answered.

"Are you serious Austin?" Karen asked.

"No Karen you are the only one in my life I want to ever kiss." Now Austin could not imagine ever wanting to kiss another woman.

After they had checked everything they saw that it was all okay. Then they parked the truck right up next to the trailer. Then they all walked back up to the front of the motel. Austin carried Karen in his arms most of the way. She was tired and he didn't want her getting any more tired than she was already. He had plans for that night and she would need to be awake.

Margo and Bo were walking just ahead of them. "Bo I need to talk to you when we get back to our room." Margo sounded so serious.

"Margo is there something wrong?" Bo asked.

"No not with me or our baby and I hope not with you." she answered.

Bo didn't know what it could possibly be. He didn't want to question his wife in front of Austin and Karen. He would wait until they were alone in their room.

"Bo what time do you want to get up tomorrow morning?" Austin asked as they walked along together.

"Seven will be alright. We aren't that far from Georgia. We should be at my parent's house around two thirty or three tomorrow afternoon." He answered.

"Alright we will be ready." Austin said as he held on to Karen.

As soon as they were in their room Bo was ready to hear what Margo had to say. "Margo we are alone now tell me what is wrong?" This had worried Bo the whole walk back to their rooms.

"Bo my father wants to come and visit with us at Christmas." Margo held her breath and waited to hear what Bo would say.

"Okay that's good." Bo answered.

"But Bo you wanted to spend Christmas with your family in Georgia. So if you still do it's alright I will just stay at home and be with my Daddy and you can still go to Georgia and be with your family."

"No you will not. You are my family and if your father is coming to our house for Christmas we both will be there to have Christmas with him."

"Bo, that makes me so happy. I didn't want us to spend our first Christmas apart." Margo felt so relieved.

"Neither do I honey." Bo answered as he pulled Margo into his arms and he started kissing her. He was so glad that it wasn't anything awful that she had to tell him.

Karen and Austin got ready for bed right away. "Austin, were you really jealous when Bo and I were out there dancing tonight?

"Yes I was." he answered. "I found myself looking at my beautiful pregnant wife in another man's arms and I knew that was something I could not stand to see happening ever again."

"But Bo and I were not doing anything, but dancing." Karen answered.

"I know Karen I'm not talking about you just dancing with Bo. I'm talking about another man ever loving you and making love with you."

"Austin I already told you that I could not ever do that with anyone else. It's just way too personal to do with someone else. The thought of that makes my skin crawl." Karen answered as she made an awful face.

"Well that is the nicest description of making love I have ever heard. It almost makes me not want to do it ever again, but only almost. Karen I'm happy you feel that way because I don't want you to every do it with anyone else, but me." Austin was ready to stop talking and get down to business.

"You don't have to worry about that." Karen was still making that awful face.

"Karen you don't make a face like that when we are making love I hope?" Austin asked.

"No Austin never, but the thought of someone else makes me sick. Austin, are you telling me you have never looked at me when we are making love? I've looked at you a lot of times." she answered.

"Yes Karen I've watched, but I was just wondering if you make faces like that when I was not looking."

"No Austin I never have and I won't ever." She knew with Austin she would never need to make a face. He was her dream man and she loved him.

"Karen let's stop talking and get down to business." Austin pulled Karen close to him.

"Honey this is getting harder and harder to do." Austin wasn't sure what to do tonight, but he was sure he was going to doing something.

"Yes it is Austin, but I bet you will find a way." Karen answered. "Yes I will Karen." Austin answered.

CHAPTER FORTY

B y nine o'clock the next morning they had eaten breakfast and where back on the road. Bo and Margo were riding Bo's motorcycle. Austin was driving his truck and Karen was sitting next to him.

"Honey, are you alright?" Austin asked.

"Yes Austin I am. Little Austin is wiggling all around. He is a busy little boy like his big old Daddy." Karen was rubbing her stomach and watching little Austin move around.

"Karen, Bo and Margo are staying with his parents for a few days. I thought you and I would enjoy that time by ourselves in some nice hotel not too near to Bo's parents house."

"Whatever you say Austin we both know what you want to do don't we?"

"Yes we do, don't we? He answered her back. "I want some alone time with just you Karen and our big boy. Karen do you realize two months from today our son is due?" Austin had a big smile on his face.

"Yes Austin I do. I just hope I don't act like a little girl when it all starts to happen."

"You won't honey I will be right there with you." Austin didn't care if she acted like a little girl. He knew it was going to be a very painful thing she was going to be going through.

"Yes you will. I plan to be holding on to you. That reminds me when we get back home we have those birthing classing to join."

"I had forgotten all about them." Austin answered.

"No, you had not. You were hoping I had forgotten about them. Austin we need to do them. I don't know anything about having a baby except it comes out where I wished it didn't." That made Austin smile. "I see you smiling. You wouldn't be smiling if it was your cootchie it was coming out of mister." Karen answered.

"It is my cootchie that our son will be coming out of Mrs. Blackburn." Austin still had that smile on his face.

"Sort of, but you won't be feeling it like I will." Karen answered as she rubbed her stomach.

"No I won't, but I will be feeling bad for you just the same."

"I know you will because I will be squeezing your hand so hard you will be in pain right along with me." Now Karen had a smile on her face.

"So you are going to be sure I have some pain too." Austin answered.

"Yes I am. You aren't going to just sit there while I do all of the work."

"Karen if I could do it for you I would. So if you want to scream, kick me, and hit me, it will be alright with me. After all I did do this to you." Austin answered.

"No Austin we did this together. You and I did it. Not one of us, but both of us together. We both want our baby so it's just as much my fault as it is yours and I'm very happy to say and I'm just as happy to be pregnant with our little Austin, who may not be so little, when he is born."

"No he may not. By the way Bo thinks our baby is going to be one big boy." Austin was still smiling.

"Hum, I wonder which one of his parents he is taking after, his big Mama or his little Daddy. Maybe he will come here walking and we won't need to teach him to do that one little thing." Karen answered.

"Maybe, but I doubt it. He will however come crying and hungry. Karen, are you going to breast feed him?" Austin asked. He didn't remember her saying if she was or not.

"Yes and that will be another thing you will have to help me to do." Karen answered.

"I can't, I don't have the same equipment as you." Austin did not know how he could help her do any of that.

"No you don't, but we will have a breast pump and you can help me with it."

"So you are telling me we need to get one of those pumps?" He had heard of a breast pump before, but he didn't remember where he had heard of it.

"We sure do if you don't want me to be leaking all over the place after Little Austin is born. We can freeze it you know and if we have more than we need we can donate it to other babies to use." Karen had already checked into that program

"That is real interesting." Austin said. He had never heard of that before, but he didn't know a lot about having babies at all.

"Austin, I just want to do everything I can to give our son the best start in life I can." Karen loved her husband and their baby so much. They were her whole life.

"Karen I'm so proud of you." All Austin could think about was how proud Karen was always making him.

"Let's wait and see how proud of me you are when my boobs hang down to my knees and then you hate how I look." she answered.

"Karen," Austin was driving right behind Bo and Margo while they rode on Bo's motorcycle. "I will never hate how you look."

"After all I want those babies too and you have to use your body to get them here." He never wanted his wife to feel she was not beautiful to him. "My body won't change Karen because we are having children, but yours will and I am the one who will be helping to change it. I really love you."

"Oh Austin I needed to hear you say that, because I wanted to ask you if my boobs were getting any larger?"

"I don't think so I thought that you already had large boobs. I do remember that from the coffee shop. I saw them the second that I saw you. You were sexy then and you are still sexy today."

"Austin, you're sexy too and I'm not the only one who knows that. Margo and I heard those two women last night in the bathroom talking about our husbands. We knew they were talking about you and Bo when they said you had long legs and tight jeans. Austin you make my heart flutter every time I see you and when you have on your tight jeans, boots, white shirt and sunglasses. I feel like jumping your bones." Karen had a cute little smile on her face.

"Well! Mrs. Blackburn I should always dress like that if it makes my wife want to jump my bones. I'm anxious for you to get un-pregnant so that I can do it all over again." Austin answered.

"I bet you are. Austin I'm not as innocent as I was seven months ago. I have learned a lot from my handsome husband. I know what he likes."

"Karen, do you really mean that?"

"Yes I do Austin I want us to have a very good sex life. I want you to want to come home every night."

"Karen I promise you I will."

Karen and Austin talked about everything. They were so good together.

"Austin I need to stop. Little Austin is knotting up. He wants his daddy to rub his mama's stomach some."

"Okay sweetheart I will let Bo know." Austin flashed his headlights on and off several times before Bo noticed them. He gave Austin the thumbs up and he left the interstate with Austin right behind him.

"Honey we will go to the rest room first and then you and I will get in the back seat and you can put your head in my lap and I will rub your stomach until our son relaxes."

"Thank you Austin. He can really make my stomach hurt. It gets so hard and it feels like a big cramp."

"I know it hurts honey, I'm sorry."

"No don't be sorry Austin. I love our little Austin. He is just doing what he wants to do. I just don't have a lot of room for him to play in." "I know that. I can see it. Now you sit still and I will come around and get you out." Austin parked and hurried over to Karen's side of the truck. He even unfastened her seatbelt.

"Honey I'm just going to lift you out. I don't want you to do anything, but breath."

"Austin will it be alright for me to pee" Karen asked? "Yes this one time." Karen smiled at her husband.

"Austin, how is Karen doing?" Bo was quite concern about Karen, but he didn't want either one of them to know.

"Bo she has another big knot in her stomach."

"Well we will load my bike and I will drive and you and Karen sit in the back and you can do your job."

Margo was with Karen now. "Margo how did you like riding on the back of Bo's motorcycle?" Karen could already tell she liked it by the look on her face.

"Karen I loved it. I have never had so much fun. Did you like it when you rode with Austin?"

"Yes I did. I like being right there with him so none of the woman who pass us will think he is available, but I won't be doing that again for awhile. I will just have to be content for now having Austin's baby. And Margo I am."

"Well I would sure think so. Karen, you will be back there real soon leaning on his back."

"Yes I will. He said he likes to feel me leaning on his back. I do love Austin." Karen was all smiles.

"Karen, girl, the whole world can see that both of you are in love with each other."

"Oh you think so. Well I'm so glad because we are." Karen had stars in her eyes from just thinking about her husband. "Margo did you have your talk with Bo?"

"Yes Karen I did and you were right. He is staying home Christmas. I feel so much better. Bo is so good Karen thank you. I love him so much and I know he is just as in love with me."

"Are you nervous about meeting his family?" Karen could see Margo was rubbing her hands together nervously.

"Yes Karen I am. I feel like a cat walking into a room full of rockers."

"Don't be, Austin said Bo's family were real nice people and that his mother and sisters will love you and I'm sure his father will too." The two girls were still in the ladies' room. Now they were doing their hair.

"Now I think I need something to drink how about you Margo?" Karen asked as they worked with their hair.

"Yes I could use a bottle of water. Karen, Austin is going to say you have just emptied it and now you want to fill it back up again."

"I know, but he will just have to get use to it. I will be doing that for another two months at least." Karen answered.

Both men were at the trailer working with Bo's bike. "Bo I think we have it up here good now. It's not going anywhere." Austin said.

"I hope not Austin. I, wonder what is keeping our wives?" Bo was still worried about Karen.

"Who knows, women just take longer." Austin answered.

"Yes Austin they do, but they are worth it wouldn't you say?" Bo had a smile on his face from just thinking about Margo.

"Yes at least our wives are worth it Bo." Austin knew Karen was worth everything to him.

The two men were ready to go to the restroom themselves now before they got back on the road. They went to the restroom and were back waiting at the truck. It was another five minutes before the girls came out.

"Karen what takes you two so long in the restroom every time?" Austin asked.

"Austin it takes me awhile just to get my seat cover made and sometimes if falls into the commode before I have time to sit down on it and then I have to start over again. Then I have to get all my clothes down. All you do is walk in and aim. Then after I use it I have to redress you don't, you just zip up." Karen answered.

"Karen I think we have adjusted to married life real well. My little wife don't mine one bit telling me how much easier it is for me to pee than her."

"No I don't. Now I need something to drink." Karen was standing right in front of Austin when she said all of that.

"Honey, you just got through getting rid of what you had in you and now you want more." He thought she would not want anything to drink for the rest of the day to keep from having to go pee so much, but he was wrong of course.

"Yes I do. I need to have something else to drink now." Karen was hot and she wanted something cool to drink.

"Now what would you like to fill up on?" he asked. "I want some orange juice." She answered.

"Margo, do you want something to drink?" Austin asked. He knew they all needed something. It was hot.

"Yes Austin I would like a bottle of water thank you." Margo was glad she was not as far along as Karen now. She didn't think she would be able to handle this trip if she was.

"Bo do you want something while I'm going?" Austin asked.

"Yes I do. I will have a coke, but I will go with you. I don't want you to mess up my order." Bo joked.

"You are right I would mess up your order for sure." Austin joked back at his friend. They were always doing or saying something like that to each other.

"Austin, don't let Bo say that to you." Karen was looking at Bo. "Karen he is just joking. He didn't mean it." Austin answered.

"Yes Karen, I was just joking with your little husband. You won't need to save him from me this time." Karen then gave Bo a mean look.

"You want to stick out your tongue at me don't you, but you are afraid to because you already know what could happen to that tongue of yours." Bo teased. He loved to tease Karen more than anyone.

"Yes I do, but it won't always stop me." she answered.

"Good, go ahead and stick it out Karen I'm sure Austin won't mind." Bo answered.

"Okay I will." Out went her tongue.

"Austin when you get back in the truck you will need to teach your wife a little more about sticking her tongue out." Bo was glad to tell Austin what his wife had done.

"Bo did she do it again?" Austin asked.

"Yes she did." Bo was smiling at Karen. "See young lady I told on you. Now your husband will be showing you again what you can do with that tongue of yours. Austin I'm beginning to think she likes your lessons."

"Bo I do not." Karen answered.

"I think you are right Bo. I think my young wife is getting to enjoy a lot of the things we do." Karen stuck her tongue out at Austin this time. "Woman I think I'm going to love growing old with you."

"I hope so because that is exactly what you are going to be doing with me and all of our children and our grandchildren." Karen answered.

"Now she already has me as a grandpa. I guess Bo you are one too." Austin answered.

"Yes I must be, because our two wives have marriage plans for all of our children already." All of this made the two men very happy.

"So we will be keeping them all in the two families." Austin said. "Yep I think that's their plan." Bo didn't mind that at all and neither did Austin.

"Are you two going to get us something to drink or are you just going to stand there talking about your grandchildren?" Karen had her hands on her hips looking at both men.

"Karen we will go right now." Bo quickly answered.

"Thank you Bo. I'm very sure you two don't want a big pregnant woman falling down onto the ground right here in front of you." Karen still had her hands on her hips

"No we sure don't. So don't do it." Bo answered.

"Well Bo I won't if you and Austin would go on in there and get our drinks." Karen answered.

"Well we are going now. Don't you see our back sides?" Bo asked. "Yes we do and we like looking at them. Don't we Margo?" Karen answered.

"Yes Karen we do." The girls smiled at each other. It took another thirty minutes before they were back on the road. Bo and Margo were in the front seat and Austin and Karen in the back seat with him rubbing her stomach.

"Bo, this time two months from now you may be delivering our boy." Austin said from the back seat.

"Yep Austin you are right I may. I need to remember to get a new memory stick for my camera to use that day when I'm dragging that boy out of you Karen. I would not want to miss any of it and I'm sure Austin will want as many pictures of his son's birth as he can get from every angle." Bo knew Karen would not like what he had said at all.

"Hold it I have already told you two over sexed boys no pictures and I mean it. Margo, slap your husband." Karen was not giving in to letting Austin making pictures and she sure was not going to let Bo make any; not from where he would be sitting.

"I will Karen if he does that you can count on me." Margo answered.

"Margo honey, are you saying you don't want pictures of our baby coming into this world either?" Bo asked.

"That is exactly what I'm saying Bo." she answered.

"Austin what's wrong with our two wives?" Bo asked as he drove down the long road.

"They are cootchie shy Bo." Austin answered.

"No we are not. We just don't want our husband showing other people our cootchie. Can't you two men understand that at all?" Karen asked.

"Yes Karen we can, but we were not going to show everyone just us and Bo will have already seen your cootchie." Austin answered.

"Yes Austin he may. But you won't have seen it." she answered. "Karen I'm your husband." Austin said.

"Yes, but you are only one of our husbands. You aren't Margo's husband or her doctor." Karen was holding her ground.

"No Austin, you are not, so no pictures." Margo was staring at Bo. Austin started to laugh. "Bo, they really mean it don't they?"

"Yes Austin I think so." Bo still thought that maybe the girls would change their minds later.

"Yes we do mean it. Can't you two understand or do we need to do something drastic like not having sex with you. Will that make you understand, we mean it?" Karen asked.

"No you don't need to go that far. We understand perfectly." Austin answered. He knew his wife would do just as she said and he would be without sex for an even longer time than he was already going to have.

"Well I would hope so. Aren't you two grown men with big old educations?" Karen asked.

"How big of an old education are we talking about?" Bo asked. "Bo, don't ask me. I just know all three of you have more education than me." Karen answered.

"Honey none of us finished first in our class like you." Austin answered.

"But you could have if you would have studied your lessons as much as you studied the girls." Karen said.

"Austin we have been caught." Bo answered.

"I'm afraid so Bo. She knows us well." Austin smiled down at his wife as she lay in his lap

"I sure do know you well. Margo, do you see how bad our husbands are and I had to put up with all of this all by myself before you married Bo." Karen was smiling up at her husband.

"Karen I'm so glad I could come along and save you." Margo answered from the front seat.

"Me, too Margo I'm really glad to have another female here to help me live with theses two big boys."

"Karen do you think Austin and I are just two big boys?" Bo asked.

"Yes I do Big, Big, Big, Boys." she answered.

"Okay that's alright just as long as we are that big." Bo said with a smile.

"I didn't say, you were big at everything Bo." Karen answered

"Austin you are not doing your job. Your wife is doing way too much talking for someone who has been sticking her tongue out at me so much."

"You are right Bo I had forgotten all about that little job. I will get right to it." Austin answered.

Karen still had her head in Austin's lap. He just leaned down and started kissing her, but Karen did not resist him. Austin knew she was the right woman for him. She proved that over and over to him each day. He knew he was the only one for her. She had made that quite clear to him. They had been kissing for awhile when little Austin began to do his own little thing causing Karen to jump.

"Karen, are you alright?" Austin quickly asked.

"Yes, little Austin just gave me a big kick. I think he meant it for you." Karen answered.

"I'm sure he did." Austin would gladly take their son's kicks if he could.

Chapter Forty One

Later that day they got to Bo's parents house. It was a very large house with a long front porch with lots of rockers and a swing on each end of the porch. Their grass was still very green even though it was already October. Bo was very anxious for his family to meet his new wife.

"Mama we are here." Bo yelled.

His mother came running to see her son, but she stopped as soon as she saw them all. "Bo, tell me who these two beautiful women, are and whose baby is this one having?"

"Mine Mrs. Brooks. This is my wife Karen and she is seven months pregnant and we are so happy." Austin answered. Mrs. Brooks then gave Austin a hug. She was very happy for him and his wife.

"Austin this is shocking. I never expected you to get married, but I can see why you would want to marry her. She is beautiful and Bo who is this beautiful woman?"

"Mama this is Margo Brooks." At first Bo's mother just gave Margo a hug then she stopped and stepped back to look at her son. "Who did you say she was?"

"Margo is my wife. And you are going to be a grandmother." Bo answered.

"Bo I'm shocked once again, but I'm very happy. Welcome to our family Margo. Come on in. Bo how far along is she?" Mrs. Brooks was as happy as she could be. She stopped once again and gave Margo a big hug. "Honey I could not be happier." She told Margo as she hugged her.

"Oh Mama she's only two months along so we will be having a baby in May right in time for Mother's Day." Bo answered.

Bo that is so wonderful. Now let me give your Dad a call. He will be right home that is if there are no patients there. Austin I'm so glad you and your wife came." Mrs. Brooks had a big smile on her face.

"Thank you Mrs. Brooks, but Karen and I are going to ride on down the road and let Bo and Margo have this time with their family and I want to have a little time with my wife." Austin answered.

"Austin you are such a good and thoughtful man. Karen you got yourself a good one here." Mr. and Mrs. Brooks had known Austin and his family as long as the boys had known each other. They all were great friends.

"Yes M'am I know." Karen answered. "You are Southern?" Mrs. Brooks asked. "Yes M'am I am." Karen answered.

"I'm glad; Austin needed a good little Southern girl in his life. He was around all of those big tall beautiful women too much." Mrs. Brooks was not exactly a short woman herself.

"Yes M'am he was, but I changed all of that for him." Karen answered.

"I can see that, but I'm sure it has not hurt him one bit." Mrs. Brooks like Karen a lot. She wished Bo had met a southern girl, but Margo was his wife and she would love her.

"No it hasn't Mrs. Brooks, because Karen has already been a lot better for me than anyone else could ever be. She is as good of a wife as I will ever want." Austin answered.

"That's nice Austin. Not many men would say that; only you and my son Bo." Mrs. Brooks gave both men a big smile.

"Mama did you notice Austin's big black truck?" Bo asked.

"Yes I did and I also notice you both brought your motorcycles. Have you two men been riding them any on your way down here?" She asked.

"Yes we rode some yesterday and some today. Margo rode on the back of mine with me some of the way." Bo answered.

"Bo Brooks your wife is pregnant and she doesn't need to be riding on the back of your motorcycle." Mrs. Books did not want anything to happen to her new daughter in law or her first grandchild.

"Mama she is alright. After all I am her husband and her doctor." Bo may be a man and a doctor, but to his Mama he was still her little boy.

"Austin is Bo you wife's doctor too?" Mrs. Brooks asked. "Yes he is."

Mrs. Brooks quickly turned to the two girls. "Girls you do have a lot to handle with these two men."

"Mama our wives think we are just two big boys." Bo answered. "Well they are right. That's just what you and Austin, are, two big over grown boys. Now let me get you all some lemonade and call your Dad."

Bo's mother went into the house and called Bo's father and made them some very good homemade lemonade. They were all enjoying the fresh lemonade when Dr. Brooks arrived home.

"Bo son you look great. Austin it's always a pleasure to see you and you are also looking good very good. Now who are these two young ladies?" Dr. Brooks asked.

"Daddy, this is Karen she is Austin's wife."

"Austin you are married? Well I guess you are I see your wife is expecting and who is this?" Dr. Brooks asked.

Bo's mother had a big smile on her face. She could hardly keep from telling her husband who that pretty girl was herself, but she wanted Bo to tell his Daddy.

"Daddy this is Margo my wife and we are also expecting." Bo answered.

"What? How long have you two been married?" His Daddy asked.

"Two months." Bo answered.

"Two months and you haven't said one word to us. Son I'm shocked. Sara honey, did you know anything about this before today?" Dr. Brooks asked his wife.

"No, I'm just as surprised as you are, but happy as I can be." she answered.

"Son, I will say you a pick good one. She is a living doll and so is Austin's wife. Are you two girls as good of friends as these two boys are?" the doctor asked.

"Yes sir we are." Karen answered. Margo had not said much of anything yet.

"Margo let your old father in law have a little hug. It's not every day I get a daughter in law."

Margo got up from her chair and gave Bo's Daddy a nice friendly hug. "You sure are a pretty little thing. You boys both have beautiful wives. How did you both do that? Did you catch them both off guard?" he asked. Karen and Margo could tell right then where Bo got his personality from. His Daddy was just as big of a joker as Bo.

"We just got real lucky Dr. Brooks." Austin answered.

"Yes we did Daddy. Margo is so sweet that you would think she was from the South, even though she's not." Bo answered.

"Sara have you called the girls and told them that Bo has a wife yet?" Dr. Brooks asked his wife

"No I haven't I thought I would let Bo tell them himself tonight when they all come for supper. Austin you and Karen will stay for supper won't you?" Mrs. Brooks asked.

"No we want to drive a little further and stop at one of those B & B's tonight. We want Bo and Margo to have this time with his family. In fact we should be going. I don't want Karen to get too tired." Austin answered.

"Austin let's take the trailer off and you can leave it all here. I know you aren't going to be riding your motorcycle any and that way you won't have to be looking for a safe place for it all tonight."

"Alright Bo, that's a very good idea." Austin answered. He wasn't sure where he would have put the motorcycles at night.

"Bo you and Austin pull your truck to the back and put it all in the barn. Austin it is your truck isn't it?" Dr, Brooks asked.

"Yes sir it is, but your son has a blue one just like it." Austin answered.

"I'm not at all surprised. How do you like it?" Dr. Brooks drove a pickup truck himself.

"I love it Dr. Brooks." Austin happily answered.

"Well you sure look like a man who drives a truck and who loves his truck."

Austin smiled down at Karen. She was sitting right by his side on the swing and he was holding her hand. Bo's parents went into the house and left the four young people alone on the porch.

"Austin let's go and get it done and you and Karen can get on down the road. I know what you want to do." Bo said.

"So do you Bo." Karen answered.

"I know, but it will have to wait. Karen, don't let this big boy of yours do too much or you will be calling me to come and delivery your son before you or he is ready." Bo told her.

"Bo, don't tell me that. Now I will worry every time Austin gets near me." Karen already had a worried look on her face.

"No, I will tell your husband what he can and cannot do with you." Bo knew he had just said something Karen did not want to hear.

"Could you have told him without me knowing you two were going to discuss my sex life?" she answered.

"Yes I could have, but it would not have been as much fun." Karen could not help herself she had to stick her tongue out at Bo.

"Austin you saw her. She did it again." Bo called out to his friend. "Yes Bo I did, but I think she has started to like her lessons." Austin knew he liked them a lot too.

"She must like them a lot or she would stop sticking out her tongue at me so much." Bo said. Then he winked back at Karen.

"Bo, don't forget our suitcases." Margo said.

"I won't Margo honey, but have you forgotten to give me a kiss for all I'm about to do?" Bo was already on the steps ready to go with Austin to take the truck to the barn and unhitch the trailer.

"No I haven't forgotten. Come here and I will give you your kiss." Margo answered.

Austin and Bo drove down to the big barn. Austin backed his truck into the barn and he and Bo unhitched the trailer with the two motorcycles still on it and then Austin drove them back to the front of the house. There they unloaded Bo and Margo's things and carried them into the house.

"Bo, don't take your things to your old room unless you and Margo want to sleep on twin beds. Remember Margo isn't Austin so you may want to pick another room for you and your wife." His Mama told him.

"You are right Mama I will. Sorry Austin, but the twin beds are great with you, but not with my wife." Bo answered.

"That's alright Bo I understand you have replaced me with Margo." Austin had a sad look on his face.

"You two boys are crazy. Who would ever believe you have even one brain between the both of you let long two?" Mrs. Brook said.

"Nobody I guess Mama." Bo answered. He knew his Mama was kidding. She knew he and Austin both were very smart men when they needed to be.

Bo and Austin put all of the suitcases into one of the nice guest rooms and soon went back downstairs to join their wives.

"Dr. and Mrs. Brooks, Karen and I are leaving now, but we will see you all in three days." Austin was ready to hit the road.

"Alright Austin it was so good seeing you again and Karen it was nice meeting you. Karen, how old are you?" Karen didn't say anything she just looked up at Austin.

"She is nineteen." Karen and Margo hurried out of the house and went back to the porch and took a seat in the rockers. They decided to let the men explain it all to Bo's family.

"What, boy you are married to a teenager?" Mrs. Brooks said.

"Yes M'am I have been told that many times by your son." Austin answered.

"Bo how old is Margo?" His Mama asked.

Bo smiled over at Austin before he answered his Mama. "She is twenty two."

"Well you two boys got yourselves two babies." Mrs. Brooks answered. The men were not sure if that was good or not as far as Mrs. Brooks was concerned.

"Yes, but they are not our babies they are our wives. They are very much grown up women." Bo answered.

"Bo Brooks don't you be smart with me. I will put you back in your old room right by yourself. It doesn't matter about your wives ages as long as you love each other and apparently you do." his Mama said.

"Yes we do. We both love our wives and they love us." Austin answered.

"They would have to love you for them to put up with all the teasing and kidding you two big boys will put them through." Mrs. Brooks said.

They all soon walked back out to the porch. Margo and Karen were sitting in the rockers waiting.

"Karen honey, are you ready for us to leave?" Austin asked.

"I will be if I can use their bathroom before we go." she answered. "Yes honey you sure can use our bathroom. There is one just inside.

Bo, go and show her where the bathrooms are." Mrs. Brooks told her son. "Okay Mama I will. Margo you may just as well come too. I know you and Karen don't go to the potty without the other. I just don't know what you two are going to do for the next three days." Bo said.

"Bo I will take you with me and Karen will have Austin to go with her." Margo answered.

Margo and Karen both followed Bo into the house, but Karen stopped before they got too far and went back to get Austin.

"Austin, do you need to go while we are here?" she asked. "Yes I guess so." Austin answered.

"Well then come on and you can go with me. See Mrs. Brooks they do love us." Karen said.

"Yes I see that." Mrs. Brooks said as Karen and Austin went in the door.

"Austin you know where the bathrooms are. You take your wife and I will take mine." Bo said as soon as Austin was in the door.

CHAPTER FORTY TWO

After Austin had Karen seated in the truck and her seatbelt on, he went to speak to Bo. "Bo, were you serious when you told Karen about being careful having sex?"

"Yes, but I'm sure you have already realized that for yourself. Just remember no rough stuff." Bo answered.

"We don't do any rough stuff ever you should know that." Austin answered.

"I know that, but I'm talking about you finding a way other than you being on top of Karen. That's all I mean." Bo did not want his friend upset with him.

"I have already done that." Austin answered. "Then you are good." Bo said.

"Thanks Bo. We will see you in three days." "Okay Austin, have fun. I know you will."

"The same to you my friend," Austin said and then got into his truck.

"Karen, are you alright?" Austin asked as soon as they were in their truck.

"Yes Austin I'm just happy to be with you." she answered.

"And I'm happy to be with you and our son. Now let's go and get something to eat and then we will drive to Savannah and get a room in one of those nice B & B's to stay in while we are there."

"Austin, that sounds like fun. Have you ever done that before?" she asked.

Austin had years ago, but not in Savannah, Georgia. "Yes Karen I have but not here in Georgia."

"Well I guess that's alright. At least I know she was not seven month pregnant with your son."

"No she was not. Karen I know it hurts and bothers you to know I have been with other women, but you, need to remember I'm a lot older than you. I'm thirty five years old and I have been with other women."

"I know Austin and I do understand. I just don't want you to compare me to them." She was so worried that she would come up short and she didn't mean in height.

"Karen I chose to marry you not one of them." Austin answered. "Yes, I know and I'm very glad you did." Austin reached over and took her hand. Mrs. Blackburn you are the only woman that counts. You are the only one wearing my wedding ring."

"Austin, do you think about your wedding band." she asked.

"Yes I think about it all the time. It reminds me and the world that I have a woman that I love and who loves me and I belong to her and she belongs to me." he answered.

"But Austin I didn't buy your ring for you. You bought it." This still upsets Karen some.

"So what is mine is yours too. Karen we are one. I don't have one cent that you don't have half of it." he told her.

"Austin I don't have one cent." she answered. "What do you mean?" Austin asked.

"I mean I don't have anything. I couldn't even buy a coke if I was even allowed to have one." Karen answered.

"What?" Austin didn't understand what she was saying

"I don't have any money. I have already used up all of my last pay check and now I don't have one cent to my name." Karen had not been this broke since leaving home.

"Karen I haven't given you even one cent since we have been married and it has been seven months. How could I have been so stupid. Why didn't you, say something to me?" he asked.

"I didn't want to ask you for money." she answered. "But Karen I'm your husband." Austin felt so bad. "Yes and I'm your wife." she answered.

"You, are right, you should not have to ask me for money. I will start giving you money every month. How much do you need? he asked.

"One hundred dollars should do it." she answered. "One hundred dollars?" Austin asked.

"Why is that too much?" Karen asked.

"No Karen that is nothing. You need more than that, you are a woman."

"Austin I don't go anywhere and the only time I ever went by myself I landed in jail so I'm never going off by myself ever again." Karen was not yet over her jail experience.

"Karen, that won't ever happen again. We will get you a little car. Something you and little Austin can go places in. I will give you money and a credit card."

"No Austin I don't want all of that. I want you to go with me when I go places." She was not happy with his answer.

"Karen I will always go with you just like I do now. I could quit work and be with you now if you want?"

"Austin I would love that, But I think it is important that you have your business to pass down to our children just as your Dad passed it down to you."

"Karen I'm glad you feel that way, but I don't have to be at work every day. I have people who can do some of it and you know you can always go into the office with me. Even after little Austin is born. We will just get another bed and rocker for my office. What good is it to be the boss if you can't do what you want to do sometimes." Now he was ready to put a baby bed into his office. This was a far cry from anything Austin would have done just a year ago.

"Austin I'm so glad you wanted to marry me." She was now happy again.

"So am I Karen. I just would have hated to know I was missing out on our life together."

Austin and Karen found a nice little restaurant and had a very good lunch. Austin wanted to let Karen rest outside of the truck so this time stay awhile longer in the restaurant and just talked. It was a lot less nerve racking then the first time they met and talked at the little coffee shop. Karen loved him now and she was not afraid of him like she was at the coffee shop.

"Karen do you need me to walk you to the restroom before we go?"

"Yes and you can use the men's while I'm using the ladies'."

"Okay let's go before there's a line." The restaurant had filled up quite a bit since they had arrived.

It wasn't long before they were back on the road. Austin checked his GPS to make sure they were going in the right direction.

"Austin, are we staying in Savannah the whole time?" Karen asked.

"We can if you want to, but we don't have to if you want to go someplace else." he answered.

"It's alright we can stay here. I just don't want to run into anyone I know." She was worried about her family finding out where she was. She did not want any of them in her new life.

"Karen, if that happens, just act as if you don't know them. That will put them off." Austin answered.

"Alright I will do that if you will help me."

"Karen honey you know I will always help you." Austin answered. It took two more hours to get to Savannah, but they enjoyed every second of the trip. They were together and that was all they needed. "Now to find a nice B&B" Austin was driving down the street looking as they went for a nice place to stay.

"Austin let's try and get one in town so we can walk to where we want to go."

"Alright we sure will try to do that." Before long, they drove right up on a very nice old house that just so happened to be a B&B.

"Stop Austin there is one. It's so beautiful. I hope they have a room we can rent." Karen was getting all excited. She had always wanted go to Savannah and stay in a Bed and Breakfast, but there was never enough money for things like that in her young life.

"Well we won't know until we try." Austin pulled his truck into the parking area.

"Karen, do you want to wait here until I find out if they have a room?" Austin asked before getting out for the truck.

"No I want to go with you in case they don't, but I will have seen some of the house then at least." she answered.

They both went into the Beautiful house. They were greeted by a nice elderly man. "Yes sir we have a beautiful room still available. Would you and your wife like to take it?"

"Yes sir we sure would." Austin was still holding onto Karen's hand.

"Where are you folks from?" The man asked. "We are from New York City." Austin answered.

"You sure are a far piece from home." He was getting the book out for them to sign. "How many days will you be here with us?" the old man asked.

"Three days we hope." Austin answered as he signed the book and paid for their room.

"Good now let me show you to your room." The man took them to a room way in the back of the house that had a private entrance that lead off to a small court yard with a gate that open out to the parking area.

"Austin it's beautiful and we have a canopy bed." He could tell that the room pleased her a lot.

"Yes we sure do. Karen you need to rest some before we go anywhere else." Austin was worried she may over do it and he did not want that to happen. This was somewhat of a honeymoon for them.

"Do you mean rest or mess?" Karen was sitting on the side of the bed.

"Both" Austin had to answer.

"I thought so, but I don't mind. If you didn't want to mess around then I would worry." she answered.

"Karen, then you, don't have anything to worry about." Austin was already taking off his clothes.

"Austin do I need to put on one of my gowns?" she asked.

"No not for me. You just take off your jeans, top and bra. You don't need anything on. I would say your granny drawers, but I know you aren't going to give them up until you have to."

"You are so right I want to hide as much of my big stomach as I can from you. So give me my gown."

"If you were going to put it on all of this time why did you ask me if I thought you needed it?" Austin asked.

"I just did Austin, but I have decided to take it all off." Karen said that as she jumped into bed and under the sheet. "Aren't you coming to bed Austin?"

"Karen, are you naked under that sheet?" Austin asked. He sure hoped so.

"Why don't you get in here and find out." she answered.

"I will and I hope you are." She just smiled at him. "I'm waiting Austin you need to get a move on it."

"I'm coming as fast as I can honey." Austin dropped his boxers and got into bed with Karen.

"You are naked!" Austin said out loud.

"Yes Austin I am, but you didn't have to tell everyone here." Karen answered.

"Who is here except you and me?"

"That's all we need. Oh, I forgot little Austin is here so don't you forget that." Austin and Karen made love; the best that they had ever made even if they did have to be very careful.

"Karen you were amazing. I love you so much. I did not know that a person could love another person as much as I love you." Austin was so surprised at how he felt about his woman.

"Austin I love you. You make my life so complete." They lay in each other's arms for another half an hour before they got up and showered.

"Karen, are you sure you want to try walking all over this town." "Yes Austin, if I get tired we can stop and rest." Karen knew she wanted to be able to stand and look at all the sites as long as she could and in a the truck they would have to keep moving with the traffic.

"I guess so, but I don't want you to push yourself. Do you remember what Bo said about us not doing anything that could cause little Austin to come early?" Austin reminded her.

"I won't Austin. I want him to stay right inside of me until it is time for him to be born." They walked out of the B&B and started walking toward town.

"Karen would you like to take one of these horse driven carriage tours?" Austin knew that they would be riding and Karen would not be walking everywhere.

"Okay that could be fun. I've never been inside of any big pretty houses like these before."

Austin and Karen went on the first tour they came across. They were gone three hours. That put them right into their supper time.

"Austin I'm starving and I feel a little weak."

"Karen, sit down right here on this bench and I will go and find you something to drink and a little snack to eat." Austin hurried to find Karen something to eat. He was worried about her and their unborn son. He was back in less than ten minutes.

"Dear is that tall man your husband?"

"Yes M'am he is." Karen answered.

An elderly lady was sitting on the bench on the other side of Karen. "He is a handsome one and he loves you I can tell."

"Yes M'am he sure does." Karen answered.

"Are you here to visit with your family?" The lady asked.

"No M'am we are here on vacation. We live in New York City." Karen answered.

"Oh that's a big place. I have always wanted to go there, but I have never been. My name is Ellen Pittman. I've just retired from teaching school for over forty years."

"Oh how nice. I'm Karen Blackburn and this tall handsome man is my husband Austin."

"Young man you are a movie star or something like that I know." Miss Pittman said.

"No M'am I'm not a movie star or anything like that." Austin was just sitting and enjoying listening to the two women talking.

"But you are someone who is important because I recognize you from some place and it has something to do with entertainment I'm very sure." Miss Pittman was a smart and well read woman.

"Yes M'am I own an entertainment promotion agency in New York." Austin answered.

"Yes I remember now. You are a very wealthy man. It said you were one of the richest men in the United States."

Karen's eyes began to get real big. This was the first time it had even started to sink into her head that her husband Austin was a very rich man.

"Yes M'am, but my wife here doesn't know that yet." Austin smiled at Miss Pittman and then down at Karen.

"Oh have I said something I should not have said?" Miss Pittman had a worried look on her face.

"No M'am not at all. It's just my little wife here doesn't believe I can afford to buy her things." Austin answered.

"Oh my goodness you can afford to buy anything and everything you want. I wish I had a husband and we could afford to do things. Honey your husband is very well off." She was patting Karen on the hand now like a grandmother would pat her granddaughter's hand.

"Well, Miss Pitman it's just that I was raised poor and I have not gotten used to having everything, but all I want is Austin. He is all I want besides our son." Karen answered.

"I see you would love him even without his wealth. That is a very good thing. You can't just love someone for what they can give you that will one day make you miserable." Miss Pittman answered.

"Yes M'am you are right, but my wife married me without knowing anything about my wealth." Austin answered.

"Then young man you're a lucky man and I can sure see you have a big baby coming soon." Miss Pittman was looking at Karen's stomach. "Yes M'am and it's a boy and we are naming him Austin after his Daddy. He is due in two months." Karen was now rubbing her stomach.

"How nice, is this your first child?" Miss Pittman asked. "Yes M'am it's our first everything." Karen answered.

"Oh that is nice." She could see how happy the young couple was about having their baby.

"Miss Pittman, are you here with your family?" Austin asked.

"Oh no, I don't have any family anymore. I'm what they used to call an old maid. Now we are career women, but it all means the same. We are all alone in the end. People who took the time to love someone and have their families will most likely have someone later in life. I know all relationships don't always work out, but if you don't even try you won't ever know if they would have. That is my only regret. I didn't even try." Miss Pittman answered. She looked a little sad to Karen.

"So you are here alone?" Austin felt so sorry for this nice lady. He wished everyone could meet a person like her when they were away from home. It would make them feel as if they had met an old friend. "Yes I'm just here for the day. I live about thirty miles from here, but I enjoy coming and just sitting and watching all the people who come here to visit." This was one of the ways Miss Pittman spent her time after she retired. It keeps her from being totally alone.

"Miss Pittman my wife and I are going to have supper in that nice restaurant over there. Would you like to join us as my guest?" Austin asked.

"Oh that is so sweet of you, but you don't know me from a hill of beans." she answered.

"No, but we would still love for you to join us for dinner. Then maybe we could get to know you much better." Austin was amazed by this older woman. She was so well mannered and well spoken.

"Please Miss Pittman we would love to have you join us." Karen liked this elderly lady a lot. She reminded her of some of the teachers she had in school who helped her so much.

"Alright if you both are sure and you don't mind an old lady tagging along. I don't get asked out to eat very often."

"That is a shame, because you are such a lovely person." Austin answered.

"Thank you young man it is so nice of you to say that to an old lady. We sometimes need to hear that we aren't useless people as so many young people think these days. Even at my age I still have so much I can contribute to society and so do other seniors if just given the chance." Miss Pittman said as she smiled over at Karen.

The three of them had a nice meal. Austin had managed to slip off from the two women and had called his office back in New York and had Miss Pittman checked out completely. He always did that whenever he was approached by anyone he didn't know. Miss Pittman checked out to be just what she said she was.

"Miss Pittman I want to give you my card and I want you to call me in three weeks at my office back In New York if you don't mind?" Austin already had an idea he wanted to talk over with Karen.

"No Mr. Blackburn I won't mind at all. It has been a real pleasure meeting you and your lovely wife. Now I need to find the bus station it's getting late and the bus leaves at eight thirty and I don't want to miss it." She was looking around to see exactly where she was.

"Miss Pittman you came on the bus here today?" Karen asked.

"Yes dear I find it much easier than driving my car places these days. With so many of us tourist it makes it very hard to find a parking space and with gasoline so high."

"Austin" Karen said as she looked up at him with sad eyes.

"Yes honey." He already knew what Karen wanted. "Miss Pittman, will you allow us to take you home tonight? We are staying in a B&B just down the street. I will go and get our truck and we will be happy to drive you home."

"Mr. Blackburn won't that be putting you to a lot of trouble?" she asked.

"No M'am that will not be putting us to any trouble at all. I have enjoyed talking to you so much and so has my husband." Karen had not had anyone to talk with like Miss Pittman since she had left school in over three years.

"Alright if you don't mind I will be very happy to accept." Miss Pittman was getting a little tired herself and she would still need to walk home from the bus station if she rode the bus back to her home town.

"Karen you and Miss Pittman sit here and I will be back with our truck shortly." Austin gave Karen a kiss and walked off.

"Miss Pittman I'm very glad we got to meet you. Please do call Austin in three weeks. He is a wonderful man and I'm very sure he will make your call worth the trouble." Karen wanted to keep this nice lady in her life. It was like having a grandmother again and all of those nice teachers she had in school.

"Karen dear, I have been to a lot of places and I have met many people, but you and your husband have been the nicest two people I have ever met. Your husband makes everyone feel as important as he is. I dare say I never expected to ever meet him when I read all of those articles about him and saw his picture in all of those newspapers and magazines so many times. I was totally shocked when I recognized him."

"Well, Miss Pittman he is the best husband in the world. I love him so much and I know he will be the best father ever."

"Yes Karen dear, and he loves you as much and that is what makes it all work. You try and remember how you feel about him now and every time he upsets you or does something you don't care for, remember he is the same man he is today."

"Miss Pittman, I see Austin coming, so let's get ready to get into the truck." Karen knew it would take her awhile to get out to the truck and she didn't want to slow down her new friend.

"Oh my, is that big truck yours?" Miss Pitman could not imagine driving anything that large.

"Yes M'am that's it." Karen answered.

Austin pulled his truck into a nearby parking lot. He knew he would need to help Karen and Miss Pittman into the truck.

"Honey, are you feeling well?" Austin asked.

"Yes Austin I'm just fine." He kissed her and then he turned and helped Miss Pittman into the front seat. She gave Austin direction to the nearby town where she lives and then to her house. Austin didn't have any trouble at all finding the small town. Then he drove them to Miss Pittman's front door. It was a nice little Victorian house.

"Miss Pittman you have a nice home and it's Victorian. I love it. Our brownstone is Victorian too." Austin was so happy to hear Karen say our. It made him feel as if she was trusting in him and his love for her more and more.

They only stayed a short while with Miss Pittman. They all were tired and Austin and Karen still had the ride back to Savannah ahead of them.

"Karen, Miss Pittman is a very nice person and you two got along so well together." Austin wanted to hear what Karen thought of her.

"Yes Austin we did. It was like talking to a grandmother or one of my teachers." Karen was up front with Austin now. "Austin I'm very tired tonight and I don't think I can take one more step."

"You don't have to take another step, I will carry you in when we get to our B&B sweetheart." Karen leaned her head back and in a matter of seconds she was asleep.

"Karen, honey, we are here." Austin said. "Honey wake up."

"Oh Austin I fell asleep." Karen looked as if she didn't know where she was.

"Yes you did. Now let me get you out and up these steps." Austin carried her all the way into their room before he put her down.

"Karen let me get your gown on you. You can shower tomorrow morning." Austin got Karen's gown out and helped her to get her clothes off and the gown on. "Now go to the potty and brush your teeth and then get into the bed young lady." Austin got into the shower while Karen brushed her teeth. They both slept hard all night. They were both worn out.

CHAPTER FORTY THREE

"Austin wake up Little Austin is hungry." Karen was saying. Austin rolled over. "Who's hungry?" he asked.

"Little Austin, he has been kicking me all morning." Karen answered. Karen lay back down, but this time she got real close to Austin's back just as Little Austin gave another big strong kick. "Karen was that Little Austin kicking me or you?"

"Yes of course it was him. If I had kicked you, you would be getting up off the floor right now." she answered.

"Karen he kicks just like you." Austin answered.

"He's hungry Austin and so am I. Do you want me to give you a little kick too?" She was ready to go eat.

"No you don't need to kick me. I don't want to get up off the floor. So let's get up from here and go and get you two hungry babies something to eat." Austin was as happy as any man had ever been.

"Okay, but I need to take a quick shower first." Karen said as she climbed out of bed.

"No, we will take a quick shower Mrs. Blackburn." Austin answered. He was ready to join her in the shower.

"Austin there is no such thing as quick when you and I do anything together." Karen answered.

"Then junior will just be hungry a little longer because I'm taking a shower with his mother." Austin had already taken off his boxers and was getting into the shower.

One hour later they were dressed and walking out of the B&B. "See Karen we can do something quick."

"Yes we can, but only because you are hungry too." Karen answered.

"Yes you are right, so where should we go?" Austin asked. "We can go to Hardee's." Karen answered.

"Alright we will go to Hardee's, but don't you want something more than they have?" Austin asked. He wanted his wife to have a good breakfast.

"No, they have a lot to pick from and I will just get some of it all if I'm still hungry after I eat my first order." Karen answered.

"I bet you will." Austin said as he helped her into the truck.

While in line a young mother was there waiting her turn with her young daughter who was about five years old. "Mama I want my own food." The little girl kept saying.

"Terri, Mama doesn't have enough money for that today. You and I will share." The mother and little girl were right behind Austin and Karen. There was no one else in line. Austin ordered for Karen and himself then he told the cashier to take the lady's and her daughter's order that he was paying. The young woman was so surprised she just stood there. But she did finally order breakfast for her little girl and for herself. Austin gave the little girl a twenty dollar bill. The women thanked Austin several times for the breakfast and for the money.

"Austin that was so nice of you. I remember my mama not having money for me because she bought beer and that other stuff." Karen didn't want to say dope.

"Karen it was only a few dollars and it made their day better. What good is it to have a lot of money and not help someone who really needs your help?"

As soon as they were back in their truck Austin was asking Karen what she wanted to do the rest of the day.

"I don't know Austin this is the first vacation I have ever been on in my life. So you will need to tell me what we should be doing."

"What, Karen you have never been on a vacation before?" Austin had never known anyone who didn't go on vacation at least one week every year somewhere. Most the people he knew personally took at least a month off for vacations.

"No Austin I haven't. Only rich people take vacations poor people stay home." she answered.

"Karen when our little Austin is born I'm going to take you on a real vacation to France and England. I want to take you to some nice places."

"You mean like to Tennessee?" Karen answered.

"Yes if that is where you want to go." Austin would take her to Tennessee.

"Austin I thought this was a nice trip. Aren't you enjoying it?" she asked.

"Yes I am Karen." he answered.

"But not like you did when it was only you and Bo riding your motorcycles all around. Austin I could have stayed home. I told you to come by yourself. Now you are unhappy because you aren't able to do the things you wanted to do all because you feel as if you have to be with me. Austin, go back to Bo's parents' house and get your motorcycles and go where you want to go. I can stay at the B&B for as long as you want to be gone." Karen did not want him to feel he had lost everything by marrying her.

"Karen I did not marry you to leave you anywhere. I am happy. Just being with you makes me happy and letting the world know you are my wife and that you are having my son makes me very proud."

"Austin I just don't want you to be giving up everything just because I married you and took so much away from you. You have had to share everything you have with me and I'm not good enough for you."

"Karen, stop it right now. I have not given up anything. I chose to share my life with you and that means my possessions and my time. Karen Blackburn I love you more every day so you can't stay anywhere I'm not. Woman do you understand me?"

"Yes Austin I understand." Karen started to cry. "Karen what's wrong now?" Austin asked. "Nothing," she answered.

"Oh yes there is. Now tell me what it is?" Austin pulled his truck off the road and stopped. "Now Karen tell me what is the matter because until you tell me we are not moving." Karen looked over at Austin, but she did not say anything. "Tell me Karen. It really hurts me to see you crying." Austin got out of the truck and came around to Karen's side of the truck and opened the door. "Move over Karen." Austin said as he got into the front seat. "Now get into my lap. She did just as he said. "Tell me Karen what's wrong?"

"Austin, you deserve so much better than me. You should have married some tall beautiful rich woman. Not all of this." Karen was pointing to herself.

"Karen I saw you and I wanted all of this. I stopped wanting anyone else a long time ago. You and only you are the one I want forever. You and I will have many children together because we want each other that much. No tall rich beautiful woman could ever be more beautiful than you. I have learned that God made me for a five foot one and a half inch woman just like he made you for just me. Now I don't want you to say ever again that you aren't good enough for me. Karen Blackburn you are the best thing in my life." Austin began to kiss her. "Now we will go and do something. I will just chalk all of this up to hormones."

"Austin I love you. I guess I just see everyone as being tall and thin and me and little Austin as being the only big wide and short people in the world."

"Nope, my wife is pregnant, not big and wide, she is just pregnant that's all." Austin answered.

"Oh Austin you make me feel so good."

"I'm supposed to Honey that's one of my jobs. Now are we ready to get on down the road?"

"Yes just as long as you are getting on down that road with me." she answered.

Austin drove around until they found a nice place to stop. "Austin that's a nice park and it has a lot of statues in it. Do you want to walk around in it for awhile? Little Austin wants me to take him for a little walk."

"Yes we can do that if you promise not to overdo it."

"I promise Austin because I don't want to have little Austin to soon. We don't even have any diapers yet and he will need them right away." "Karen I will have time after he is born to get them before you and little Austin come home from the hospital." Austin had no idea at all about what a baby would need other than a bed and the things he and Karen had already gotten for their son.

"No Austin we will come home the day after he is born and you will be at the hospital the whole time with me in my room helping me with our son." Karen answered.

"Are you kidding me? You will have little Austin one day and come home the next day?" Austin had never heard of such a thing.

"No Austin I'm not kidding. I thought you knew that was the way it is done. I will just pop him out and then go home. That's the way it is done these days."

"Well I will get you a nurse for when you get home." Austin did not know if he would be able to do all the things a father needed to do.

"No Austin I won't need a nurse I have you." Karen had all the faith in the world that Austin would be able to handle it all.

"Yes you do." Austin answered.

"Yes I do what? Yes I do have you or yes I do need a nurse?" Karen asked.

"Both" he answered.

"Austin I do not need a nurse. Women have babies all the time. I won't be the first one. Your mother even had you." Karen said.

"Yes and she was in the hospital for four days after I was born." Austin thought that would be enough to convince Karen she needed a nurse.

"Well that was in the old days. Things are done just a little different today." Karen told him.

"Well if things have changed so much maybe the babies come out a different place today." Austin answered.

"That has not changed Austin and neither has how they get there." Karen answered.

"And Karen, aren't you glad?" Austin had a big smile on his face. "Yes Austin we both are." she answered.

"Karen let me hold to your hand." "Austin you always hold my hand."

"Yes but I like to remind you to let me do it." he answered.

"Oh you are such a good old husband." Karen said as she smiled up at him.

"Yes I am and you are such a good little pregnant wife." Austin smiled back at her.

Austin and Karen began to walk all around the park. Stopping at every statue and reading who they were and what they did.

"Austin," Karen said in a very low voice.

"Yes Karen," Austin was busy looking at another statue.

Karen was getting tired of it all. She had given up reading and looking at the statues and had started watching the people. "Austin" she said again.

"Yes Karen what is it?" Austin asked.

"I see a girl I went to school with and I think she has recognized me. She keeps looking over here at us." This was making Karen very nervous.

"Alright let her look. We will simply act as if your name is not Karen. I will call you Linda. Now remember, you are Linda Blackburn." Austin was already to do anything that would help his wife.

"Alright Austin if she comes over here I will be Linda Blackburn. Austin you need to remember my new name too." Karen was so afraid that he would slip up and call her Karen.

"I will Linda." he answered. Then he gave her a big smile.

"Austin, don't turn around, but she is coming this way. Just stand still and act as if you are reading the plaques." Karen could feel her hands beginning to sweat.

"You mean the same way you have been doing for the last thirty minutes." he answered.

"Oh Austin you could tell I wasn't reading them anymore?" This made Karen feel so bad.

"Yes, I could. I do know my wife a little by now." he answered. "Excuse me, but aren't you Karen Belmont?" The girl had come up on them while they were still talking.

"No, I'm Linda Blackburn and this is my husband we are here on vacation is your friend from here?" Karen asked.

"No we are from a small town about one hundred fifty miles from here." the girl answered. She was staring at Karen as if she wanted to say prove it.

"Well I'm so sorry, but my name is Linda and I'm not from around here at all." Karen hoped the girl would not notice her southern accent.

"Well you sure do look like her and she was such a pretty girl too like you. She was several years younger than the rest of us in our class. She was a real smart student and she graduated three years earlier than she should have. I wish you would have been her. It would be nice to see her again." Karen remembered this girl from school well and she was a nice person, but Karen just did not want anyone to be able to say anything back in her home town about her that may get back to her family.

"Well you sure have the wrong person for sure. All I know how to do is to have babies and this will be our fourth. I hope you find your friend though." Karen felt bad because she was lying to the girl.

"Thank you. I'm so sorry I disturbed you." the girl said.

"I didn't mind it at all." Karen answered. Then the young woman walked away.

"So Mrs. Blackburn we have three children already at home." Austin liked his wife's little lie.

"Yes we do Mr. Blackburn Daddy." Karen answered.

Austin started laughing. "You know Karen one of these days that will all be true. We will have three children, but they won't be back at home they will be right with us."

"Yes in three years Mr. Blackburn." Karen answered.

"Karen, are you sure you want to go through this every year for eight years?" Right now he wasn't sure if he would be willing to let her go through it even one more time.

"Yes I am Austin. Are you changing your mind about wanting all eight of our babies?" Karen asked.

Austin smiled at Karen as he looked down at her stomach. "Honey if you still want all eight of our babies, I will be happy to do my part." "I'm so glad you will still be willing to do your part." s he answered.

CHAPTER FORTY FOUR

"Karen, are you ready to do something else?" Austin had walked all around the park and he knew Karen had to be getting tired.

"Yes I have looked at all the dead people I want to for one day. Austin, do you want to do something you have never done before?" she asked.

"Karen have you been holding out on me?" Austin asked. "Holding out what?" Karen asked. She had no idea what her husband was talking about.

"I guess not." Austin answered.

"You guess not what? Mr. Blackburn you need to tell me what you are talking about." Karen was not happy with the way this conversation had gone.

"I was wondering if you were talking about doing something in bed that I have never done before." Austin was just joking with her, but she didn't know that right then.

"What would that be Austin?" she asked.

"I don't know that's why I was asking you Karen." He was still playing with her.

"You were asking me. You thought I knew something to do in sex that you have never done before." Karen could not believe what she had hearing.

"Yes" he answered.

"Are you crazy, I don't know anything about sex that you haven't done with me. Austin, are you asking me if I have had sex with some other man than you?" Karen was sitting in the front seat of the truck.

"No I was not. I don't even know how all of this got started. All I was doing was playing along with you." Austin was as upset now as Karen.

"Austin, don't start up this truck because I don't want to hurt my baby when I'm getting out of here." Karen had already unfastened her seatbelt and had started to open the truck's door, but Austin reached over and grabbed her arm.

"Karen what are you doing?" he asked. "I'm leaving you." she answered.

"And just where to do think you will go?" he asked.

"Anywhere I can go to get away from you Austin. Austin I have never had sex before I married you and I have only had it with you. I was talking about going to the Wal Mart, but all you can think about is sex. So if you think I'm doing it with someone else who do you think it is?" Karen's face was blood red.

"Karen I know you aren't having sex with another man and I know you have never. Honey I was just joking with you. Please settle down. Your face is way too red. Honey I love you and I never believed for one second you have had sex with anyone, but me. I'm very sorry if I upset you. Please calm down all of this is not good for you or little Austin." Austin was beside himself.

"Austin it hurt me when I thought you believed I knew something about sex that you had not taught me." Karen was in tears.

"Honey I know you are only mine and I'm only yours. Can we get over this?" he asked. "I was just playing with you. I knew you had something else in mind other than sex. I was just playing with you. That was all I was doing. I did not mean anything by what I said." Austin was almost as upset as Karen.

"Yes we can get over it. I'm over it already. Is my face still red?" Austin nodded his head yes. "Austin how do I get my face unred?" Karen asked. Now she was getting a little scared.

"You have got to relax honey and let's put your seatbelt back on. I'm calling Bo." Austin answered.

He wasted no time in getting Bo on the phone. "Hello Austin what's wrong with Karen. I know there's something wrong with her or you would not be calling me." Bo was afraid that Karen was going to delivery and he would need to be there with her.

"Yes Bo, its Karen. Her face is blood red." Austin's voice told Bo just how scared he was.

"Take her to the nearest fire station and have her blood pressure checked. I will stay on the phone until you get there. Now give Karen the phone." Bo knew he needed to calm Karen down some.

"Karen Bo wants to talk to you." Austin said as he handed her his phone.

"Bo" Karen said as Austin drove and at the same time looking for a fire station.

"Karen why is your face so red? Did you and Austin get upset with each other?" he asked.

"Yes, but not anymore. We have made up." Karen was glad to answer.

"Does that mean you had sex?" Bo asked.

"No we are in the truck and in town. So how could we have had sex?" she asked.

"So you haven't had sex yet." Bo asked. "No I'm just relaxing." she answered.

"No you are not relaxing. Has Austin found a fire station yet?" Bo asked.

"Yes he is pulling into one now." she answered.

"Karen let Austin help you out and give him back the phone, but don't hang up do you understand me?" Bo was really worried about Karen and he knew Austin was going out of his mind by now.

"Austin, Bo said to give you back your phone, but for you not to hang up and for you to help me out." Karen was still red in her face.

"Karen I always help you out. Bo, are you there?" Austin asked. "Yes Austin, I'm here, now take her on into the station, but don't hang up. Is her face still as red?" Bo did not want to sound as upset as he was he was afraid it would cause more harm than good. He didn't want Austin to get anymore upset than he already was. He needed to stay as calm as possible so he could help Karen.

"No not quite, but it is still very red." Austin answered.

As they walked into the fire station a fireman stop them. "Sir, could I help you?" He could already tell there was something wrong with Karen.

"Yes my wife needs to have her blood pressure checked. I have her doctor on the phone right now." Austin was feeling a little better knowing there was someone there that could help his wife.

"Okay little lady come with me, but you need to relax some." Karen was getting real scared and she didn't feel right, but she was not going to say anything. "Now you just sit down here and I will take your pressure." Karen sat down in the chair. Austin was right there at her side. "You say her doctor is on the phone." The fireman asked.

"Yes he is right here." Austin answered.

"Let me speak with him if you don't mind." Austin handed the fireman his phone. "Hello sir I'm EMT Ed Roberson your patient's blood pressure is a little high, but not dangerously high right now, but I think she should be under a doctor's care."

"Thank you now let me speak with her husband again." The man handed Austin's phone back to him and then he started taking Karen's pressure once again.

"Bo, its Austin what do I need to do?" he asked.

"Take her back to your room and put her to bed with her legs elevated. You rub her legs and stomach. You do everything you can to get her to relax or that boy will be born too early." Bo wanted his friend to know how important what he was telling him was.

"Bo I will get her to relax some way." Austin got Karen back into his big truck and drove them back to the B&B.

"Karen, Bo said you had to relax do you hear me? I mean just what I say." Karen could hear the concern in her husband's voice for her and their baby son.

Yes Austin I hear you and I will do the best I can at relaxing, that has never been one of my good points." she answered.

"Karen I want you to stop worrying about the women I could have had. You are the one I chose to have. All those other women are out of my life. You are my wife and no one else. There will never be any other Mrs. Blackburn in this generation. Tall, short, fat, or thin it's you and only you. We made that decision seven months ago when we got married. Do you understand that Karen?" All Austin wanted to do was relieve her mind from worrying about all the women he had ever been with and could have had for his wife.

"Yes Austin I understand, but it don't make me stop wondering how I did what the others could not do." she answered.

"Karen God wanted you and I to be together so stop fighting it and just be happy. Do you think you can just accept what God wants?" He knew if everything else failed she would believe in what the Lord had planned for them.

"Austin I'm sorry. I will accept what God wants." she answered.

"Karen I'm really glad because our little son is counting on you." Austin knew knowing their son was counting on her would help some.

"Oh God, Austin, I'm sorry. I don't want anything to happen to little Austin or to me. I want us to have each other. I don't know if I could go on if I let anything happen to Little Austin. I would never be able to forgive myself."

"I know honey so put on your gown and get into that bed. We need to elevate your legs Bo said and you need to relax." Austin was working as hard as he could to get her into her gown and into the bed. Then he helped her to lay back into the bed. He put two big pillows under her legs then he began to gently rub her body. After a while she began to relax. Austin could feel her tense body relaxing. It wasn't long before she was asleep. Austin decided to give Bo a call and let him know how she was doing.

"Bo she is asleep." Austin was happy to say.

"Let her sleep. I'm already on my way. I should be there within the next thirty or forty minutes. Where are you staying?"

CHAPTER FORTY FIVE

Austin told Bo the name of the street and the B&B they were at. When Bo got there Karen was still asleep.

"Austin we may need to cut our trip short. When she wakes up I will need to check her and you will need to help because you know she is not going to just give in." Bo had a worried look on his face.

"Bo I think this time she may." Austin answered. "I will need my bag." Bo told Austin.

"It's in here in the closet I didn't want to leave it in the truck. You never know what may happen if you leave anything in your vehicles anymore." Austin answered.

"Good now we will just wait for her to wake up. Has anything upset her?" Bo asked. He and Austin were sitting at the little table in their room.

"I just don't know. We got up and went to eat breakfast. She got upset when we were coming back into town. Lately she gets upset so easily."

"Austin she is pregnant and all she sees is tall beautiful woman looking at her husband. She doesn't see you just looking at her. You need to assure her she is the only one and that's why she is the one pregnant and not one of them." Bo was trying to help his friend.

"I have tried Bo, over and over again. Then we went to the park. She said little Austin wanted her to take him for a walk. So we took him for a nice long walk." Austin was so confused.

"Yes he probably did want to go for a walk." Bo answered.

"We then went walking in the park and that's where she saw the girl from her home town. She didn't want to see anyone that could go back and tell her family anything about her new life." Austin wanted to tell Bo as much about their day as he could remember. He hoped it would help Bo to decide what had bought all of this on today.

"Did she talk with this person?" Bo asked.

"Yes the woman came right over to us and asked Karen if she was Karen Belmont."

"What did Karen say?"

"She said no I'm Linda Blackburn and that we were expecting our fourth baby."

"She told the woman you had three other children?" "She sure did" Austin said with a big smile on his face.

"Austin, you just as well accept it you are going to be the daddy to a house full of kids." Bo hoped that someday he would have the same thing himself.

"Oh Bo I already know that." Austin answered.

"Then what happened?" Bo could not see how any of this would bring on what Karen was going through right now. In fact it was all sort of amusing in a funny way.

"Then we started to leave the park to go back to the B&B. We had just gotten into the truck when all hell broke loose. She asked me if I wanted to do something with her that I had never done before. Of course I thought about sex and she thought I was saying she had been with someone and he had done something with her that we had not done. She was getting out of the truck and away from me. She said I didn't believe she had not been with anyone, but me, but Bo that is not true. I know she has never been with anyone but me. I was just joking with her."

"Austin I don't think right now you and I need to be teasing her. She gets to upset about you being what you are and how all the other women see you. All she sees is she is short and fat, which she is not. She is the most beautiful woman Austin I have ever seen and I love Margo, but I'm just being honest. Karen is nothing but beautiful."

"Bo I know that. I told you the second I laid eyes on her I wanted to marry her." Austin was so glad he had placed the ad and that Karen had answered it.

"Austin I hope you never think I would do anything to jeopardizes our friendship." Bo never wanted to lose his best friend's friendship.

"Bo I know you and I'm not worried. You have Margo and soon you will be in my shoes trying to deal with her." Austin knew his friend was a good and honest man.

"Yes you are so right, but it will be worth it all." Both men were happier than they had ever been before in their life.

"Austin, are you here" Karen asked? She could not see him from the bed.

"Yes Karen honey I'm here and so is Bo." Karen was moving around in the big bed.

"Karen, how are you feeling?" Bo asked.

"Bo, I'm feeling fine. Why are you here? You're supposed to be with your family."

"I came to see about my most beautiful patient." Bo got up from his chair and was going over to the bed.

"You didn't come all this way just for that I know." Karen knew he was worried about her and Little Austin.

"Yes I did. Now Karen I need to give you a good check up and I need you to let me do it."

"Okay Bo I will." Austin looked at Bo. He was glad Karen had given in so quickly, but he thought after her face being so red she would.

"Can I go to the potty first?" she asked.

"Yes you can and Austin will help you." Bo and Austin both knew Karen had at last realized she needed to do what Bo tells her to do. "Alright I'm ready." Bo got his bag. "Karen I'm just going to check your blood pressure first. And then we will go from there." "You mean you will check little Austin?"

"Yes that's what I mean." Karen didn't say any more she just sat down on the edge of the bed. Austin was right beside her. Bo started to do his job.

"Karen it is still a little high, but not bad. Lie back down and let me check little Austin. Austin helped her up a little farther on the bed, but not too far." Austin helped Karen up in the bed just like Bo said for him to do. Bo felt all around Karen's stomach. "Well Karen he seems to be just fine." Both Karen and Austin said thank you Lord. "Karen I'm going to stay here with you and Austin tonight to be sure you aren't going into labor. Karen I'm telling you right now you need to calm down. Austin is married to you and only you. He never felt the way he feels about you with any other woman. So believe us both when we tell you Austin loves only you and that little boy you are carrying. Karen you cannot continue to get so upset. I have already told Austin he and I would have to stop teasing you until little Austin is born."

"No I don't want you two to stop that it would not be you if you did that and I would not feel loved by you if you didn't tease me."

Austin was still sitting on the side of the bed. Bo was sitting next to him. Karen was lying in bed with tears running down her cheeks. Austin took out his handkerchief and wiped the tears away.

"Honey, please don't cry. I love you so much and all I want is for you and Little Austin to be alright."

Bo got up off of the bed and went around to the other side and took off his shoes and laid down beside Karen.

"Austin you should get in bed with us."

"Thank you Bo, I think I will." Austin took off his jeans and soon Bo did the same. It wasn't long before the three of them were asleep. Karen slept there between the two men. It was like before Bo had married Margo when they were all three together so much. During the night Karen had rolled over on her side and had put her arms around Bo's neck.

"Karen I'm not Austin he is on the other side. Karen just turned over to the other side and put her arms around Austin. Austin was sleeping away. By morning Austin was hugging Karen and so was Bo.

"Austin, wake up. I think I'm in bed with two of you."

Bo opened his eyes. "Hello Karen." He still had his arm around her.

"Bo I love you, but I don't think this would please Margo very much." Karen said.

Austin woke and found Bo's hand on his wife's stomach. "Is she alright?" he asked.

"Yes she is fine. Karen did you sleep well?"

"Yes I did Bo. How about you, did you sleep well?" she asked. "I slept real well." Bo answered with a big smile.

"I know you did because you were hugging me all night and so was Austin." Karen said.

"See honey, we both love you, but I love you the most. Bo just loves you second." Austin said. Neither man said anything about Bo being so near to Karen.

"Well which one of you two men is going to get up and let me go to the bathroom?"

"I will honey. Bo can just rest a while longer while you and I use the bathroom first." Austin was as ready as Karen to use the bathroom.

"That's fine with me. I will just give Margo a call while I wait." Bo had forgotten to call Margo last night and he knew he was in trouble.

"Hello."

"Margo, it's Bo" Bo said as he waited to hear what she was going to say.

"Bo I was so worried, but I knew I could have called you, but I was so busy with your sisters and before long it was real late. So tell me how is Karen?"

"She is okay, but not good. So I think I'm going to sent them back home and you and I will rent a car for the rest of the time."

"Bo do we have to rent a car, can't we just use your motorcycle?" "Do you want to do that Margo?" Bo was happy that Margo enjoyed riding his motorcycle with him.

"Yes Bo it was so much fun and I'm not, but two months along and I feel great. So can't we try? We won't be able to do it again for awhile." Margo waited for Bo's Answer.

"Margo, if you really want to we will." He was smiling.

"Oh yes Bo I do." Bo was so glad he had himself a Karen because deep down inside he thought at one time he was falling in love with Karen and that just could not happen she was his best friend's wife. Now he had Margo and she was his Karen. Margo was not a substitute for Karen, but Margo was to him what Karen was to Austin. She had become his everything.

"Margo I miss you and I love you."

"Bo I love you and I'm trying real hard not to miss you so very much, but I failed. I miss you like crazy. We just spent our first night apart since we got married."

"Oh honey that makes me very happy."

"Bo, where did you stay last night?" Margo asked. "I stayed right here with Austin and Karen."

"Bo you stayed in the room with them?" Margo asked.

"Yes and in their bed with them, but don't worry Karen slept between us so Austin didn't get near your husband." Bo answered.

"Bo I'm not sure if that makes me feel any better. If it was anyone other than Karen and Austin I would be very upset right now." Margo answered.

"Yes Margo, but it was Karen and Austin and you have nothing to worry about. If anything it only made me want you more. I woke up this morning with my hand on Karen's stomach. It made me so happy to know we will be just like them in a few months. Austin is so in love with his wife just as I am with my wife."

"And Bo that is me," Margo answered.

"Yes Margo Brooks that is you. Woman I can't wait to see you again." Bo had that look in his eyes that Margo had learned to love in the few short months they had been married.

"Bo I will be right here waiting. Bo, don't hurry back if Karen needs you. I will understand."

"Honey I won't leave here until I'm sure she is stable and then I will ride along with them back to you. Austin will need to get the trailer and his motorcycle before they can start home. I will let you go. They are coming out of the bathroom now. I love you and I will give you a call when we start back."

"Okay Bo I love you and I will see you soon." Margo felt so bad for Karen she has had such a bad time. "Bo was that Margo?"

"Yes honey it was and she said it was alright for me to sleep with you anytime I wanted to." Bo was smiling at her.

"Bo I know you want me to give you a big kick like I give Austin when we are in bed and he says or does something I don't like." Karen was back in bed and Bo was still right there under the covers with her. "Austin, come and get back in bed with me and your wife you know you want to." Bo was having such a good time. He was having even a better time since his friend had married Karen and he and Austin had some real good times back then.

"Bo I was just about to ask you if I could be in bed with my wife by myself for awhile." Austin wanted to hold his wife in his arms without his friend in bed with them.

"Alright if that's the way you want it. I will get up and potty and get my shower and brush my teeth Austin which toothbrush is Karen's?" Bo asked.

"Bo Brooks you are not using my toothbrush. You may sleep with me, but you cannot use my tooth brush. Tell him Austin." Karen was getting just a little upset with her friend Bo.

"Karen, don't get so upset he has his own toothbrush and his own underwear." Austin answered. He felt he needed to save his friend from his little wife.

"Yes I remember I was the one with no underwear." Karen answered.

"Yes Karen I remember your sweet round butt." Bo teased. "Austin he looked. I told you he would see my butt."

"Karen I didn't see your naked butt; however I can imagine how it looks." Bo answered.

"Yes, real big" Karen answered.

"Austin tell your wife her butt is not real big it is just right." Bo told his best friend.

"Well, Bo I think you have already done that for me." Austin answered.

"Well Austin I guess I was just saving you the time and trouble." Bo answered.

"Karen, Bo did not see your butt. I'm the only one who has ever seen your butt since you became a woman and I will get Bo for him describing it as well." Austin answered.

"Alright, Austin, just as long as you get him for it real good. What awful thing are you going to do to him?" Karen was watching Bo in the bathroom mirror.

"Austin she is looking at me." Bo said as he watched Karen.

"I know Bo and she wants me to hurt you." Austin answered.

"No I don't really I was only teasing you Bo. Austin don't hurt Bo Margo may want to do that herself when she is as far along as I am." Karen said.

"Yes she will and I may want to help her." Austin answered. "Austin why would you want to hurt your very best friend?" Bo asked.

"Maybe, after all Bo you did sleep with my wife last night." Austin answered.

"But the clue word there is slept and I really did sleep with her and you." Bo answered, but all he could do was laugh.

"Bo I was only kidding you. I know Bo that was all you did if you don't count you and Karen hugging each other during the night because she thought you were me."

"Yes and I sent her right over to you. I know I felt her and little Austin. I would say Bo we are one big happy family. You and I got real lucky when we got our two wives." us."

"Yes Austin that is true. We have two women who love and trust us

Later when Bo came back to the bed room he saw a red spot on the bed. He went and got his doctor's bag without saying one word. "Karen I need to check you all over and I do mean all over. Austin is going to help me."

"Karen, don't get upset."

"I won't Austin I love you and I trust you and Bo"

Karen laid in bed while Bo checked her. "Austin I'm going to tell you to take your wife home and keep her in bed for the next two months. You must take time off from your work and stay with her. Karen needs bed rest. No more messing around until after little Austin is born. Do you two understand me?"

"Yes we do" Austin was pulling the covers up over Karen.

"See here, she is spotting and that is not good." It was clear that Bo was worried about Karen and her son."

Austin was shocked. He had no idea things like this could happen from just being pregnant. He took Karen in his arms and held her.

"I was going to stay and Margo and I were going to ride my motorcycle around and then go back home, but with Karen spotting I think we need to get home. Austin your son may come a little too soon if we can't keep Karen from getting upset and if she doesn't stay off her feet. I know you don't want that to happen."

Bo could see how upset this news had made both Karen and Austin. "Bo let's get packed up and get on the road. We will follow you back to your parents and then we will go home. I don't want to take even one chance with my wife or son."

Austin carried his wife to the truck and placed her in the back seat. She was still in her gown. "Austin I'm so sorry I didn't know that funny feeling I had all day yesterday would cause all of this. It made me very nervous and scared."

"Karen you were not feeling right all day yesterday? Is that why you were acting so weird?" Austin was still standing with the truck door wide open.

"Yes, but Austin I didn't know there was anything wrong. I just thought it would soon go away or I was just crazy."

"Honey you aren't crazy. In a couple of hours we will be at Bo's parents and then we will load up the trailer and be on our way home."

Bo put two pillows under her legs. In less than an hour from the time he had checked Karen they were on the road.

"Karen you are not taking another step. I will take you everywhere you will need to go. I will take you to the potty even if we have to rent a motel room every time you need to go until we get home."

They had been on the road for over an hour and a half. Austin was driving right behind Bo as he rode his motorcycle.

"Austin there is something wrong I don't feel very well." Austin began to blow his horn at Bo. Bo pulled off the road. Austin was right behind him. Bo jumped off his motorcycle the second it stopped and ran back to the truck. Austin had already gotten out and was getting into the back seat of the truck with Karen.

"What's wrong Austin?"

"Karen is not feeling right, something is happening." Austin was as scared as his wife.

Bo hurried into the back seat. "Karen what's going on?" Bo asked. "I don't know Bo I just began to feel very odd like I was starting my period." Karen answered. "Let me see" Bo said.

"What?" Karen answered. She was still trying to put up a fight. "Karen let Bo see if you are bleeding." Austin's face was almost as white as Karen's.

"Austin you check me not Bo" Karen said as she looked with pleading eyes up at her husband.

"Okay Austin, check and see if your wife is bleeding."

Austin started to pull Karen underwear down however he did not need too. He could see the blood already. "Yes Bo she is" Austin sadly answered.

"Alright Karen I'm going to raise your legs even higher and then I'm going to call my Daddy and tell him we are on our way to his hospital."

"Bo, what about your motorcycle?" Austin asked.

"I will drive it and you and I will both drive as fast as we can to that hospital. Austin put you emergence blinkers on. Karen you just try to relax. We should get there in about twenty five minutes. If it gets worst Karen you tell Austin and he will blow his horn at me and we will stop. Now let's get going I don't want anything to happen to our girl or our boy."

"Thanks Bo" was all Austin could say.

Austin and Bo drove as fast as traffic would allow. Somewhere about half way a police car came by going the other way, but as soon as the police spotted them he turned the police car around. He got a head of Bo and turned on his lights while picking up speed he led them into town. Bo's father was waiting for them at the back door of the hospital. His daddy had sent the police car out to find them and to bring them there.

CHAPTER FORTY SIX

Karen was in the hospital for three days. On the fourth day they started their trip home. Bo and Margo stayed and would ride Bo's motorcycle home the next week. Karen rode all the way home lying on the back seat of their truck.

"Karen honey how do you feel?" Austin asked.

"Austin stop worrying I feel wonderful. Little Austin is moving all around and having a lot of fun. He said to tell his Daddy to stop worrying so much."

"Oh so you two talk to each other now."

"Yes we do and we do a lot of talking about you. He loves you as much as I do, but in a different way."

"That's real good to know Honey." Austin said as he thanked God for them both.

Austin had called his parents while Karen was in the hospital and told them all about Karen and little Austin. His father told him to stay home with Karen as long as he needed that he Bridget would come back to the city and stay. He would go back to work until Karen had little Austin and longer if they needed him to. They did not want to lose Karen or their Grandson.

"Karen I'm staying home with you until after little Austin is born. My Dad is taking my place at the office until I go back. My parents, are already back at our house."

"Oh Austin, that is so nice of them." Karen never expected to have such nice in-laws.

"They are happy to do it for us Karen. They love you and little Austin and right now you need me more than the business does."

"Austin I will always need you more than your business will ever need you." Karen was still lying on the back seat.

"Karen that is nice to know. Now you rest and if you need something let me know in time so we can get off the interstate."

"I will Austin, Wow" Karen said. "What's the matter honey?"

"Your son has just given me the hardest kick ever. He must be mad at me again."

"Honey I'm sorry he hurts you, but I'm so glad he is still in there and is kicking."

"Oh Austin so am I. I just wished you got to enjoy your vacation more." Karen's voice sounded sad to Austin.

"Karen honey we can go on a vacation any time we want to, but taking care of you and our son has to be done now and that is what I'm going to do."

They both were quiet for a few miles. Austin just drove and listened out for Karen. Karen rested and listened to the country music on the CD player.

"Austin I hope this doesn't mean we won't have our other seven babies."

"No Karen it won't. It just means we will know to do less while you are pregnant or should I say while we are pregnant."

"Yes while we are pregnant. I like that way better."

"I thought you would, so do I. You didn't get pregnant by yourself. It took the both of us to do it and it's our baby so we are both pregnant."

"Austin I love you so much."

"I know you do Karen and I feel the very same way about you." They didn't say anything else for a long while. Austin could tell that Karen had fallen off to sleep by her breathing. He drove another hundred miles then he pulled off of the interstate just as Karen woke up.

"Austin where are we?"

"Honey we are about three hundred miles from Bo's parents house."

"That far already; I must have slept for a long time."

"Yes you did, but we have also been making good time. I'm going to stop here and gas up and we will get out and you can go potty, after I gas up and pull closer to the building."

"Alright Austin I will get my shoes and sweater on."

"Yes it's a little cooler here." Austin pulled his truck up to the first available pump and began to fill it up.

"Mr. you sure have a nice truck." "Thank you." Austin answered. "How does it do on the road?"

"It does great." Austin answered again.

The man on the other side of the truck was talking to Austin. "I see you have a nice big Harley too."

"Yes I do and it's great too." Austin talked as he put gas into his truck.

The man was driving a small compact car that was a few years old. "How much does a truck like that cost?"

"Oh around seventy thousand dollars" Austin answered.

"Your payments must be out of this world." The man quickly said.

"Nope, I paid cash for it and the motorcycle."

"Man you are so young. What kind of job do you have?" "I'm an entertainment promoter," Austin answered.

"I wish, I was something like that man. Well good luck to you and your wife."

"Thank you sir," Austin answered as he finished filling up his truck and then he filled up his motor cycle. "Karen I'm going to move us up to the building now. Do you have your shoes on?"

It wasn't long before they were back on the road again. "Karen lay back down right now. I can see you sitting up." "Okay. Austin I'm laying back down."

"Don't forget to put those pillows under your legs."

"I won't." Austin turned the radio on. Karen sang along with the radio while she laid and rubbed her stomach. Austin just smiled, he was so thankful to still have her and little Austin.

At one o'clock that afternoon Austin pulled off the interstate again.

"Karen we need to eat some lunch. What do you want?" "You are asking me that?" Karen answered.

"Yes I am, so tell me something quick." "Burgers," she quickly answered.

"Okay, we will get burgers." Austin pulled in at a local hamburger joint. He got out and went inside to get their food. Karen stayed in the truck. It didn't take long. Austin came back with two burgers, two fries, two drinks and two pieces of cake. He opened the front door of the truck and put the food on his seat. Then he opened the back door and told Karen to let him carry her to the front seat, so that she could sit with him and eat. Karen was so happy to be up front with Austin.

She put her arms around his neck and began kissing him. Austin pulled away. "Karen you can't be getting me worked up like this. We can't be doing anything until after little Austin is born."

"Austin does that mean that we can't kiss anymore?" "No we can kiss, but we can't have sex."

"Okay, we will not do that."

Karen began to eat her lunch and Austin began to eat his, but Austin had something else on his mind now. He decided he would call Bo and ask him, what they could still do, and keep Karen and little Austin safe.

"Karen how is your burger?"

"It's good Austin, do you like yours?"

"Yes I do, but not as much as I like your, cooking. However Karen that doesn't mean when we get home that you will be doing any cooking. You are not doing anything, but resting for the next two months. I mean what I say. I will be home with you to be sure that you are doing just that. I am a big man and you are a little woman, so I can make you do as I say."

"Austin Blackburn, do you really think if I didn't want to do what you said that I would do it?"

Austin grabbed Karen's hand. "Karen this is one time you will do as I say, that is my son in your stomach and I want him to be alive and healthy when he is born. Do you understand me?"

"Yes Austin I understand, so I will do everything that you and Bo tell me so do. But you don't have to hurt me to get me to do it." Austin had not realized how tight he was holding her hand.

"Oh honey I'm so sorry I just wanted to hold your hand and I guess I got to intense about little Austin."

"I guess so my hand has a cramp in it now." Austin began to rub Karen's hand. "Honey does it still hurt?"

"No, it is alright now, but I like it a lot better when you kiss me to make things better."

Austin leaned way over to Karen's side of the truck and began to kiss her. He kissed and kissed. "Honey I've done it to myself now. I need to give Bo a call before tonight."

"Austin, are we stopping tonight?"

"Yes, you do not need to ride more than ten hours Bo said and we will stop for the night at four o'clock."

"But that's not ten hours" Karen said from the front seat.

"I know it's only eight hours, but that's long enough. After all we will have one more night alone in a motel."

"Austin we can't do anything so why would we care if we were alone or not?"

"Karen, don't give up so fast. I will be glad to just kiss you and hold you in my arms if that's, all that Bo says we can do."

Karen looked at Austin. "Bo already told you that we could not do anything and now that is all you want to do."

"Yes I will always want to do it with you even when I'm eighty. So get used to it woman."

Karen smiled. "Austin I'm already used to it and I will still be wanting, you when I'm eighty."

"I know you will, I can already tell, that's just another way I have of knowing we are so right for each other." Austin kissed Karen again. "Now young lady let me get this trash out of the truck and I will be back to put you into the back seat. You stay right there." Karen smiled at Austin. He took their leftover food and all the other trash they had managed to collect to the big waste can outside of the small restaurant.

"Now let me get you up into my arms. I have been missing you all day."

"Austin I miss you so much." Austin kissed his wife. "Karen you are a big temptation to me."

"Austin I don't mean to be. I'm trying real hard not to tempt you at all."

"Honey you don't need to do anything. I just look at you and I want you just like that first day and all the days since."

"Austin you are so sweet. I want my tall handsome husband just as much. I had to sit there in that diner with my hands in my lap the whole time because they were shaking so much. I had never met anyone like you before. You were so handsome and smart and you were so much in control. The whole time I thought you didn't like me and that you were mad at me for wasting your time."

"No Karen I was not mad at you. I was very mad about you. If your hands had been on top of that table I would have been holding them the whole time. I wanted to touch you just to see that you were real."

"Oh I'm real alright and we both have exactly what we went to get that day." she answered.

Austin rubbed her stomach with his free hand. "Yes we did. Now let me put you into the backseat before I get into anymore trouble. Karen, do you need to go to the potty before we leave?"

"Yes I do" Karen answered.

"Alright let me get your shoes and we will go inside."

In less than fifteen minutes they were back in the truck and going down the road.

"Honey, are you okay?"

"Yes Austin I feel great and so does little Austin. He is kicking and playing right now."

"Good I'm so glad our son is playing. Tomorrow night we will be back in our own bed and that brings up something else. You will be carried up and down the stairs. You are not taking one step until after our son is born. Do you understand that Mrs. Blackburn?"

"Yes sir, Austin. Mr. Blackburn do you realize you will be carrying me up and down those stairs every time I want to go to some place and to the potty all day long?"

"Yes that's what I'm going to be doing for the next two months." "Well I just hope all that carrying of me doesn't hurt your old back."

Karen had a big smile on her face the whole time she was saying all of that to Austin. Austin was watching her in his rear view mirror. Little Austin gave Karen a big kick just as she finished talking. "Oh."

"Did Little Austin kick you?" Austin asked as he gave her a big smile in the mirror.

"Yes your son sure did." Karen was still rubbing her stomach. "Maybe, because you were making fun, of his old Daddy's back" Austin said.

"Maybe so, but his Daddy knows I don't think he is old. He is way too much of a stud to be old."

"Now that's a lot better" Austin said. "See a little kissing up will do a lot more for you than saying my son's Daddy is old."

Right at four o'clock Austin pulled off the interstate. "Karen, are you awake?"

"Austin I have been awake all afternoon. I was just not talking. I didn't want to get you all upset about you being almost as much older than me as little Austin Jr. will be younger than me. I'm almost right in the middle of you two men."

"So you have spent the whole afternoon lying back there thinking that up just to hurt your old husband feelings?"

"No I did not. Austin I love you. I love you."

"Karen I know you do. I'm just kidding you sweetheart. I'm fully aware of how young you are and how old I am."

"No you aren't old, because we aren't old or young. Together we are perfect for each other. We are only twenty seven each if you add our ages together and divide it by two. So see, we are perfect for only each other."

"Yes Karen, we are perfect for each other and if we were any other age we would still be, perfect for each other. I feel you know that more than even I do. After all it's you who fits me so well."

"Austin Blackburn you have sex on your mind again." "Yes I do. Now let's find a place to stay tonight."

"Yes and that has a big, big, big bed so you are not bothered by me in it."

"Karen Blackburn I love to be bothered by you in bed." "But Austin we can't do anything, but tease each other."

"You're right so I guess we could pretend we are dating and sex is still out of the question."

"Mr. Blackburn if we are just dating I must be a real fat woman and you like your women fat. Must I remind you I don't sleep with men I'm not married to?" Karen quickly said.

"Yes I know, but for the next two months we will pretend we are just in the back seat of a Chevy and we can do some things, but nothing all the way."

"Austin I have never been in the backseat of a chevy." Karen said. "Well Mrs. Blackburn we will get us a chevy and you will be able to try it."

"No we will not need to get a chevy. We can just pretend we are in one if that will make it easier for us because I know it's going to be very hard for both of us."

Austin just wanted to kiss his wife. She was so wonderful, but she was still in the backseat and he was way up front.

"Karen there is a nice motel right in front of us. I will go in and get us a room; you just stay here."

"Okay Austin I will wait right here."

Austin asked for a room on the ground floor. He carried Karen into the room and then their suitcases. Then he checked to be sure his motorcycle was secured. Then he went in and closed the door. He then called Bo.

"Hello Austin how are things going?"

"We have stopped for the night and Karen is feeling real good. Now I have a question."

"Austin I already know what your question is. You and Karen cannot have intercourse now work around it."

"Alright that's what I wanted to know."

"Good luck Austin, but I don't believe you need any luck. You will enjoy your wife these next two months almost as much as you have these last seven months. Give Karen a kiss for me. I mean a real wet one like I would do."

"Yes I'm sure you would. How is Margo? Remember her, your wife."

"Yes he remembers me sometimes when he doesn't have Karen to sleep with him."

"Hello Margo"

"Hey Austin tell Karen I love her and I will see her when we get back home."

"I will Margo and we love you both." "Austin was that Margo and Bo?"

"Yes sweetheart it was. She said to tell you she loves you and would see you when she gets back home and Bo said for me to give you a big wet kiss like he would give you."

"Austin he would never do that with me."

"I know honey all Bo is doing is letting me know how lucky I am to have you all to myself."

"Austin I love you. I hate to think how awful my life would still be if I had not answered your ad."

"Karen I'm so glad you did. I saw you and I had to have you. That was all there was to it. You were so beautiful and when you spoke you were just as beautiful inside as you were on the outside. I was so in love."

"So was I. Austin, aren't we glad we got married so little Austin can be born in two months."

"Yes sweetheart I am and our other seven babies can be born. Now I want to get you to bed. Bo said we could mess around, but not to go all the way. So Karen, are you up to doing a little messing around. Now if you're not just say so and we won't do anything."

Karen just started taking off her clothes. Austin just stood there watching her.

"Austin, are you just going to stand there and watch me get naked?"

"Yes Karen I am. Then I'm going to do all I can with you. You are too beautiful for words. Being pregnant has only made you even more beautiful. I love you Mrs. Blackburn."

"Austin I'm already naked. Are you ever going to take your clothes off or am I going to be naked all by myself?"

"Never, I'm taking them all off now. Get under that sheet so I can uncover you and look at that whole beautiful body."

Karen watched as Austin undressed. "Get those boxers off right now Austin while I'm watching. I want to see all of you. I love your body and I want to see it now."

"Woman look all you want, it's all yours."

Karen looked her husband all over before he got into bed. They didn't even turn out the light. They did all they could without going all the way. That would have been the only thing that would have made it better.

"Karen, are you alright?"

"Yes Austin I feel wonderful and big." "You look wonderful and pregnant."

Later they showered together and Karen went back to bed and Austin went out and got their supper. Tomorrow night they would be sleeping in their own bed again. However tonight before they would go to sleep they would do some more messing around. Austin was happy and so was Karen and little Austin was also happy.

The next morning they started home again. Once they were back on the road Austin started worrying about his wife once again.

"Karen, are you comfortable?"

"Yes Austin I'm as comfortable as I can be. I can't see over my stomach, but what is there to see under my stomach?"

"I could tell you what I see under your stomach if you wanted me to?" he said from the front seat. red.

"No Austin, don't tell me that." Karen face was already turning

"I won't because I don't want you to hide it from me."

"Austin Blackburn I know what you have been looking at. So you might as well watch our son being born now. There is nothing left of me that you haven't seen now."

"Well at last my wife realizes I have seen every inch of her." "Austin, are you smiling?" She knew he was.

"Yes I sure am Karen and real big in fact."

CHAPTER FORTY SEVEN

Austin and Karen had a good trip home. They laughed and talked all the way. They felt even closer than before. Austin knew he had made the right decision by marrying Karen.

"Austin I enjoyed our trip home."

"So did I sweetheart, but I'm glad to be parking our truck in front of our front door tonight." Austin was happy to be back home and he was sure so was Karen.

Austin's Dad came out of the front door as soon as he had stopped the truck. "Son, we have been watching for you. Do you want me to carry Karen in for you?" Maxwell asked.

"No Dad I can do it. She is all mine, and I'm so glad to still have a wife and son, but Dad if you will, you can drive the truck and trailer to the back and I will meet you back there and then we can get it all unloaded."

"Yes I will be glad to. Karen, are you alright? Bridget and I have been so worried about you."

"Yes sir I'm just fine, but poor Austin is all worn out from having to talk to me all the way home."

Austin looked over at his Dad. "No I'm not. I loved every second we spent together talking. Dad I love this woman."

"Son, I can tell and I think she feels the very same way about you. Karen I think you have grown a lot since we were here last."

"Yes sir that's all I've been doing. I just grow. You don't even have to water me to get me to grow."

"Well you look great and my smiling faced son looks great too. It seems as if marriage agrees with the both of you."

"Yes sir because we are married to each other."

"Karen I agree with you one hundred percent. You and my son belong together."

"Oh Mr. Blackburn that makes me feel so good."

"If you two would stop talking I will get her into the house and out of my arms."

Karen looked up at Austin, "what do you mean out of your arms?"

Austin just kissed her and whispered "The quicker we get everything done the quicker we can do something better."

"Okay Mr. Blackburn your son wants us to put a move on it. I will see you later inside and then I can tell you how good your son is at everything." Karen was smiling up at Austin.

Austin was carrying Karen into the house. "You will have me in trouble with my parents. They don't know their son knows so much about the bedroom."

"Austin they should just look at me if they don't know you know anything about the bedroom."

"I'm just hoping they don't realize what has caused you to be pregnant."

"Austin Blackburn, are you ashamed of what you did with me in our bedroom?"

"No, of course not honey, I just do not want to discuss, it with my parents, that's all."

"Okay I will do all the talking and you can play dumb like you have no idea at all what caused this." Karen pointed to her big stomach.

"Karen you are pulling my leg aren't you?"

"Yes Austin. I would faint if either one of your parents ever asked me one thing about our sex life."

"Good let's keep it that way. Mom we are home." Austin called out as he and Karen came through the front door.

Bridget came out of the kitchen. "Austin, Karen I'm so glad to see you. Karen how do you feel" Bridget asked as she hugged them both.

"Wonderful" Karen answered.

"Austin she is lying I know because I was pregnant once. Give your Mom a kiss."

Austin kissed his mother on the cheek while holding Karen in his arms.

"Austin put me down on the sofa in the den. Your Dad is waiting for you to help him unload the truck."

"Yes Austin I will take care of my daughter and besides I still need to get my kiss and hug from her and I also want to see how much my grandson has grown." Bridget was very happy to see her son and daughter-in-law.

"Mrs. Blackburn, our son is very big. Bo said he would weigh anywhere from eight to ten pounds when he is born."

"That's quite big. My, my, my, and you are such a little thing. Austin, it's all, your fault." Bridget said."

"My fault, how is it my fault?" he asked.

"You are big and your son is big Karen on the other hand is small. You figure it out." Bridget said as she looked over at her big son.

"So what am I supposed to do about all of that?" Austin asked. "Nothing Austin, I like you big. I will just have a big baby that's all.

Austin get outside your Daddy is waiting."

"Okay I'm going" down the basement steps he went.

His Dad already had the garage door opened. "Son, let's get the trailer off and unloaded first. You get your bike off and then I will unhitch the trailer."

"Alright Dad" Austin went to the back of the truck and started unloading his motorcycle.

"Son, did you get to ride it any?" Maxwell asked as he watched his son unload his favorite motorcycle.

"Yes Dad I did. Bo and I rode the day we left here. I enjoy riding my motorcycle, but I love Karen even more. I would give up anything for her."

Maxwell was very proud of his son. "Son, that's a great attitude to have. I have all of your things out of the truck you didn't really have much in it."

"No we didn't just our clothes and pillows." "Yes I found all of them in the back seat."

"Dad we are really thankful to be home and Karen is still pregnant."

"I know son it's written all over your and Karen's faces." They soon had it all in the garage and locked up.

"I see you and Mom came in your new white truck. How do you like it" Austin asked?

"Son, we both love it. I never knew your Mom was a hauler until we got this truck. Now we are hauling something all the time. I really don't know how we lived this long without a truck."

"I see you both have on jeans." "Yes that's our other new thing."

Austin laughed "I guess Karen has had an effect on all of us."

"Yes son she has and we love her."

After the men got back upstairs Bridget was ready for them all to eat. "Austin are you and Karen ready to eat supper?"

Austin looked over at Karen. Then Karen answered "Yes we are." "Karen, do you need to go to the potty first?"

"Yes I do Austin" Karen started to get up off of the sofa.

"Stop Karen I will take you. You are not to take one step for the next two months do you hear me. I don't want you going into labor before it's time."

"Yes Austin, so let's go I need to go now."

After supper they were all sitting in the den. Austin was telling his parents about their trip. Karen and Austin were on the sofa. Karen was not lying down she was sitting up with her back leaning on Austin.

"Austin, I want to say something." "What is it Mom" Austin asked?

"You cannot have sexual intercourse with Karen until our Grandson is born." Bridget said.

Karen just passed out. Bridget jumped up as fast as she could. "What happen to Karen, what's wrong with her?"

"I don't know! One second she is sitting here the next she has passed out." Austin answered.

Bridget and Maxwell both were right there. "Karen, wake up. Maxwell, get me a cold wet towel." As soon has the cloth touched her skin she came to.

"Karen, are you alright?"

"Yes Austin I'm fine. I told you what I would do if they ever said anything."

"What is she talking about?"

Austin had Karen now lying flat on the sofa. He was still at her head, his Mom was wiping her face and Maxwell was standing nearby. "Mom I will tell you later." Austin was not going to run a chance Karen would pass out again.

"Son, do you think we need to call Bo?"

"No Mom not this time because she seems to be alright now and I do know what caused her to pass out."

Bridget looked over at her husband, but she did not say anything. "Karen I think it is time to get upstairs, it has been a long day."

"Yes Austin, get her upstairs. I don't want her passing out again and I don't want my grandson coming too soon." It was very clear that Bridget was very concerned about her Daughter in law, but she knew her son would take very good care of his wife.

"Son, you and Karen sleep in tomorrow morning. Your mother and I will go to church and give you two sometime alone."

"Thank you Dad we can sure use it believe me." Austin scooped Karen up in his arms and carried her up to the third floor as if she was a small child. Austin was a very strong man. Austin got their things ready for their shower. It wasn't long before they were in bed and asleep. They were both worn out.

Sunday it turned cool. Austin and Karen spent most of the day in their bedroom. Austin read the newspaper and Karen wrote in her journal. She had been keeping it since she and Austin were married. She wanted each of her babies to know about her during the time she was carrying each of them.

"Karen what are you doing?"

"Austin I'm writing in my journal." Karen was sitting up in bed next to Austin.

"I can see you are writing, but what are you writing?"

Karen laid her pen down and turned to Austin. "Austin I have been writing about us and little Austin. I want him to know everything about how he came to be. I want him to know what we did for the nine months we waited for him to be born."

Austin put down the newspaper. "Karen you aren't writing everything are you?"

"Like what" she asked? "Like us in bed."

"Yes Austin I did. I just got through writing about us in bed. Do you want me to read what I wrote about you?"

"Yes, because I'm not sure I want our children to know what I do with their mother in our bedroom."

"Okay let me read it to you." Today is Sunday your Grandmother Bridget and your Grandfather Maxwell, went to church, leaving your Daddy and me at home alone in our bedroom. We woke up late and had breakfast and then we read the newspaper. Actually your Daddy did the reading I just listened and wrote to you. We will be in our bedroom a lot for the next two months until you are born. Daddy will be at home to help your Mama. He is a real good husband and Daddy. You will love him a lot. I sure do. See I wrote about us in bed."

"Karen that was sweet. I'm glad you are doing that for our son. Did you tell him how we met?"

"Yes Austin I did because it is important that he knows how close we came to not having him."

"Yes honey it is, but we didn't come close to not having him, we did what God lead us to do." Austin pulled Karen into his arms and kissed her. "Honey our children and I are very blessed to have you as my wife and their mother."

CHAPTER FORTY EIGHT

The next week went by fast. Thursday night Bo and Margo got home. Karen was glad to have her friend Margo back home. Bo was glad to be home and near Karen. He didn't want her to need him and him be off in Georgia somewhere.

Friday morning Bo went over to see Karen. He still had one more week before he had to be back to work.

"Come on in Bo we are having breakfast would you like to have some with us?"

"Sure why not. Margo is still asleep. She doesn't even know I'm gone. Where is Karen?"

"She is upstairs having her breakfast in bed with my son." Bo and Bridget were just walking into the kitchen. "Take a seat and I will get you a plate. Maxwell is going into the office for a while. But he is not staying all day like Austin does."

"Mr. Blackburn has got the right idea if you can do it that way." Bo said.

"Yes it is Bo. Bo I wish you would talk to Austin about spending some of his money. He needs to hire a cook and a housekeeper. Karen can't do it anymore. Did you know she has been doing all of the cleaning of this big house plus the washing and ironing and of course she has been doing all the cooking as well. She even goes to work with Austin when he wants her there at the office with him. She would just work a little harder to get all her house work done so she could be with him all day. I have never seen a woman so in love with her husband and a man so in love with his wife."

"No neither have I" Bo was eating his breakfast now.

"Good morning Bo." Maxwell said when he got into the kitchen and saw Bo at the table.

"Good morning Mr. Blackburn." Bo was busy eating his breakfast.

"Are you here to check on our girl?" Maxwell was as concern about Karen and their unborn Grandson as anyone.

"Yes sir I sure am." Bo answered in between bites of food. "Well you take good care of her we love her a lot."

"Yes sir so do I."

Bridget heard him and she wondered if Bo was really in love with his wife Margo or did he marry her because Karen was already married to Austin and he knew he would never have her. Karen loved Austin with all of her heart. She never gave anyone one second of doubt about her feelings for Austin. Austin was Karen's one and only love and Bo was Bridget's son's best friend. Bridget would not say anything about this to them. Those three friends would live with it and work it out. She was sure that Margo would never know Bo's true feelings even though she was sure Austin knew. Bridget knew her son had nothing to worry about. He trusted his friend Bo and his wife. After all she was very sure that Karen was innocent of the whole thing she had no idea Bo had such feelings for her.

When Karen and Austin had finished their breakfast Austin took their tray back down to the kitchen.

"Hello Bo, so you made it home. How is Margo this morning?" Austin was setting the trays on the island.

"She is still asleep. It was a long hard day for her." Bo answered. "Yes I remember a few times when it was too long and hard for even us." Austin answered.

"Yep, but we are tough and we could do it" Bo said.

"Yes Bo, we are tough, but I'm beginning to think that women, are a lot tougher than men. When I see all that Karen is going through to have our son my heart goes out to her and all she does is smile and tells me how much she loves me and our son."

Bridget was so glad her son was telling Bo all of this although she knew Bo would never break his vow to Margo. He and Austin were the two most honest men you would ever want to know.

"Did you come to eat or check on my wife?" Austin asked.

"I came to eat and to check on you and your wife. You said you both were pregnant didn't you?" Bo answered.

"Yes we are. We are both in this together all the way. Karen is not in this by herself. I love her more and more every day if that is possible." "It must be son because I have been doing it for years. I've loved your mother more every day for almost forty years. So it can happen.

day and know it's all there for only you." Maxwell said.

"Maxwell that was so sweet" Bridget said.

Maxwell got up from the table he was already dressed for work. He kissed Bridget and patted Bo and Austin on top their heads like he always did when they were still young boys.

"Dad I could still go in each day for a couple of hours." Austin didn't want his Father feel that he needed to do more than he wanted to do.

"No Son you have a job right here to do for the next two or three months. So I will do the easy job while you son do the hard one. Now I'm leaving I don't want to be late every day. My son may fire me." Maxwell said as he smiled over at Bo.

"No I won't" Austin answered.

"I know, but it's good to come and go when you want to. Karen, can't so son don't get upset if she sometimes gets upset."

"I won't Dad I know this is hard on her."

"Bridget I will see you at lunch time." Maxwell said as he was ready to leave.

"Yes Maxwell I will be there." They kissed and Maxwell left. "Austin let's go and check my patient. She has to be lonesome up there by herself." Bo had finished his breakfast and was now ready to do his job.

"Yes she does, but she lets me have time down here during the day to make phone calls that Dad can't handle. Bo she is so good.

"I know Austin so let's go and see how good she is." Bo told Austin as they left out of the kitchen.

Both men went up to the third floor. Karen was lying on the bed with her earphones on her ears. She didn't hear them come into the room. She had her gown up and another set of earphone on her stomach so little Austin could hear the music with her. All you could see was her big stomach and her beautiful legs and her breast. She had her eyes closed and was listening to the music, Country music of course, George Strait.

"Bo I don't believe my wife is expecting company. Let me pull her gown down."

"Why I'm only going to pull it back up."

"Okay I will leave it there. Karen, Karen" Austin said as he touched her arm making her jump and open her eyes.

"Austin I didn't hear you come up the stairs."

"And you didn't hear me either" Bo was standing right behind Austin.

"Bo, are you here too?" Karen asked.

"Yes Karen I'm here." Karen was taking the earphone off her stomach and was trying to pull her gown down at the same time.

"That was a waste of time. Now I have to pull it all back up. Karen I need to check you and little Austin." Bo said as he sat his doctor's bag down on the floor beside the bed.

"Austin did he see me?" Karen face was a light shade of red.

"Yes he did, but Karen it wasn't the first time remember." Austin reminded her.

"Austin, are you just going to let Bo look at me?" Karen was trying to get under the sheet.

"Karen I came to check you and to see how my little nephew is doing." Bo said.

"Alright, but Austin you stay in here with me just in case I need you to pop Bo."

"Now, Karen why would you want Austin to pop me?" Bo was looking into his doctor's bag to get out his stethoscope so he could listen to her heartbeat as well as Little Austin's heartbeat and his blood presser cup.

"I don't know yet, but I am very sure I will want Austin to do it before you get finished with me." She did not look happy about having to be examined.

"So it's sort of an in case of thing?" Bo smiled and said. "Yes that's just what it is." Karen answered.

"Austin you get on the other side of your wife so you won't be able to pop me so easily."

"Austin you get right into this bed with me. I'm very sure Bo will be in bed with us before it's over." Austin looked over at Bo. He just smiled.

"Okay honey I will get right here on my side. Bo can check you from_."

"My side," Bo answered. "Now Karen I'm going to take your blood pressure and then I'm going to check the rest of you." Bo began to work with Karen. Austin laid on the bed next to her.

"Karen your blood pressure is real good today. Now let's check little Austin who seems to be becoming big Austin while old big Austin watches. Bo pulled the sheet and Karen gave up.

"Karen I'm going to apply a little pressure to your stomach. I need to find your son."

"Okay Bo, but remember my husband is lying right here and he is ready to pop you if I say for him to do it."

"Then let's hope you won't need to say so."

Karen looked over at Austin. "Are you ready to pop your best friend?"

"Yes I am if my little wife tells me to pop him I will just have to do it. Sorry Bo."

Bo and Karen were looking at each other. Bo winked. "Karen, lay back and be still and try to be quiet. I know it's hard for you to do that, but just try."

"Yes Bo I will try" Karen answered.

"See you just could not do it. You had to say something back." Karen stuck her tongue out at Bo. "Austin I thought you had taken care of your wife's little bad habit."

"Bo I have tried, but she keeps doing it again and again. What should I do about it?" Austin knew his friend would say something that would get under Karen's skin.

"I would teach her all I could if I were you." Bo answered.

"But Bo you are not Austin and he don't want to teach me anything." Karen was watching Austin.

"Honey I do want to teach you. In fact I would like to teach you everything." Austin said.

"What do I not know? What could there be left that you haven't already tried with me?" Karen asked.

Bo was smiling from ear to ear. He loved to hear Karen spilling the beans about her and Austin's love life.

"A whole lot of things honey" Austin answered.

Bo Brooks stop smiling you are just leading Austin on."

"No Karen I don't need anyone to lead me on except you and you can lead me anywhere." Austin answered.

"Austin we can't be doing this Bo said so."

"Hey you two, have you forgotten that I'm here" Bo asked?

Austin had moved closer to Karen and he was holding her in his arms. "Yes Bo we had and we are very sorry" Karen answered.

"No you aren't Karen you just want me to get through with you so you and your husband can finish what you two have already started."

Karen looked up at Bo "We can't finish anything and you know that." she said.

"Yes I do, but there is still a lot you two can still do." Bo could see Karen's face turning red again.

Karen put her fingers in her ears. "Don't, you say one word I don't want to hear it. La, la, la, la, la, la," Karen kept saying over and over again.

Karen, take your fingers out of your ears Bo is not going to say anything. Don't you know, I know what Bo knows?" Austin said as he took hold of her hands.

"No I don't; how would I know. I haven't been with Bo so how would I know if you two know the same thing." she answered.

"You won't if that is the only way you will have of believing me." Austin said.

"That is right. I want you two men to know I am only one person not two. Well maybe I am right now, but I only have one husband and that is you Austin and you are the only one I want to teach me anything. So Bo Brooks stop smiling so big and go home and teach your wife Margo. I'm sure she doesn't know any more than I do."

"Yes you are right and Austin and I love it that way."

"So Bo, tell me how am I doing and how is my little precious baby?"

"Oh now you know that boy is no little anything he is a big boy like his daddy. He is great and as for you, you are still a pain."

"Austin pop Bo. He said I was a pain."

"Oh honey he didn't mean it. You are only my pain, if you are anyone's pain." Austin said.

"See Bo I'm no one's pain, but Austin's."

"Well you are doing great. I may let you go down stairs one hour a day if you don't walk down those stairs yourself."

"She won't Bo because I will carry her anywhere she needs to go" Austin said.

"Alright little smart mouth if your husband is willing to take you down to the den and bring you back up here in one hour I will let you go and sit in your rocking chair for one hour only. Then its back to bed, do you hear me?"

"Bo you really mean it! Bo I can go downstairs and sit in my rocker?"

"Yes Karen you can." he answered.

Karen grabbed Bo and kissed him. That caught Austin and Bo off guard. "Wow Austin your wife does kiss great."

"Yes I know that's why I married her so I would be the only one getting all of those kisses." Austin answered.

"Well big boy you didn't get that one." Bo told his friend.

"Yes, but he will be getting all the rest won't you Austin?" Karen said

"Yes I will get all of the rest" Austin answered. They all three looked at each other and started laughing.

"Now I'm going home and do something with my own wife. I'm sure she is awake by now and she will be wanting me real bad I know. Austin, remember what I said. She cannot walk."

"I will remember that Bo and I will not let her do anything that will hurt her or little Austin." Austin was as happy as Karen about her getting to go down to the den even if it was for only one hour.

"I will see you two later." Then Bo left.

"Karen, are you ready for a shower?" Austin asked.

"Yes Austin I am. I can't wait to get down stairs to our den and seat in my rocking chair."

Austin was so glad to hear Karen speak of their things as ours, but she never said ours when it came to Austin's money. It was always his and his alone. He hoped one day she would understand he had worked all of those years for them not, just for him.

They didn't stay in the shower very long. Austin didn't want Karen to be on her feet for more than a couple of minutes at a time.

"Now we need to get you dressed. Do you want a gown or a dress to put on?"

"Which do you think would be best Austin?"

"I would think a gown would be more comfortable for you." "Alright then I will take a gown. What are you going to put on

Austin?" He was still walking around in his boxers.

"My jeans of course" Austin answered. "My wife told me that she likes me in my little tight Jeans."

449

"Yes I sure do" Karen said as she took a good look at her husband. "And your long sleeve white shirt."

Austin got Karen's gown out and then he helped her to get dress. "Mrs. Blackburn, are you ready to go downstairs to our den?"

"Yes Mr. Blackburn I sure am. Austin I'm getting too fat for you to carry up and down these stairs."

"Oh so you think one hundred and twenty pounds is too much for me to haul around in my arms?"

"Yes I do especially up and down stairs. So why don't you just let me sleep in one of those rooms you don't have any things in." Karen wanted to make thing easier for her husband.

Austin didn't answer her until they were almost half way down the stairs. "No."

"Why Austin" Karen asked?

"Because Karen, if you slept down stairs I will sleep downstairs too." he answered.

"Austin what is in those rooms?"

"Nothing right now haven't you been into them?" he asked.

"No I've only been in the rooms you showed me when I first came here." she answered.

"Karen, after all these months and you didn't just open the door and at least look in?" Austin could not imagine anyone not opening a door and looking into the room when it was in their own home.

"No it wasn't my place to look into your rooms." Karen said. Austin stopped. They were still on their way down the stairs. "Karen I thought you had gotten over this thing about mine and not ours. Those three rooms are completely empty. Bo and I just never finished them in case I decided to make them into another bedroom suite after I got older and didn't want to travel up and down the stairs anymore. There's a big bathroom with a tub and a separate shower and two big walk-in closets in there. The only thing it doesn't have is a bedroom suit and the floors haven't been finished yet. So do you want us to move down to that room until after our son is born?"

"Austin I can't ask you to move out of your beautiful bedroom because of me."

"Karen Blackburn it's our bedroom in fact they are all our bedrooms all eight of them. I will call and get the floors done next week and we will get another bedroom set. You and I will be sleeping in our new bedroom by next weekend."

"Oh Austin you would do all of that for me?" She could almost cry she loved him so.

"Yes Karen and a lot more."

Austin carried her into the den and put her into her rocking chair. "Oh Karen, you are up." Bridget said as soon as she saw her son put his wife down into her rocking chair.

"Yes Mrs. Blackburn, Bo said I could come down here for one hour each day. That will give Austin some time to be free of me."

"I don't think my son wants to ever be free of you Karen." Bridget gave Karen a kiss and a hug just as little Austin gave her a big kick. "Oh I can tell my grandson is very active."

"Yes he is just like his Daddy." Bridget loved her son and his Father very much.

"Karen may I get you something to drink?"

"No Ma'm I find if I drink anything Austin has to take me to the potty a lot." Karen said.

"That's alright he likes to have you in his arms, I can tell, so I'm getting you some juice."

Karen was rocking in her chair when Austin came into the den. "Karen I called and a crew will be here Monday morning to finish the floors in our new bedroom."

"Austin, will that cost you a lot of money?" Karen asked. "No" was all Austin said.

"Austin would you like a glass of juice?"

"No Mom I'm fine. Mom next Monday morning I'm having the floors in those three empty rooms finished. Karen and I will be moving into them until after little Austin is born."

"That will be nice for you Karen. Then you will be near all of us during the day." Bridget was giving Karen a napkin for her juice. "Austin if you are going to be down here with Karen I will run up stairs and get ready to grab a cab and go meet your Dad for lunch."

"Austin, why don't you drive your Mom to meet your Dad. That way you will have a little extra time away from me." Karen hated for her husband to be so home bound.

"No way, I'm not leaving you here for even five minutes by yourself. Mom is a big girl and knows how to get into a cab and go anywhere she wants to go."

"I know that, but I thought you would enjoy just getting out of the house for a little while."

"Then Mrs. Blackburn, you thought wrong. I'm here to be with you so I'm staying right here."

"Mrs. Blackburn would you like Austin to drive you to meet your husband?"

"No Karen you cannot be left alone. What if something went wrong while you were here alone?"

"I would call Margo or Bo." she answered.

"The answer is still no" Austin just went over and got into his big recliner. "Karen, keep on rocking because your hour is almost up." Austin said.

"Austin, are you just trying to be mean to me?"

"No, I'm just not leaving you here by yourself. Now don't get mad just enjoy the rest of your time downstairs."

"Austin I'm not mad, I just think you need some time away from me so you don't get so tired of me in the next two months." Karen was rubbing her stomach and making a face as if she was in pain.

"Karen is there something wrong?"

"No I just think little Austin is in one of those knots again and it hurts a lot." Karen had tears running down her cheeks.

"Karen let me put you on the sofa and I will rub your stomach like we did before." Austin had Karen up and in his arms. "Karen honey, this is the reason I won't leave you alone. We never know when little Austin is going to do this very thing." Austin carried her over to the sofa and put her down then he began to rub her stomach. Little Austin was not cooperating at all. Karen was in more pain. She was only seven and a half months along. Austin called Bo right away.

"Bo can you come back over here Karen is in a lot of pain." Austin sounder scared.

"Yes Austin I will be right over."

Karen was all tense, she could not relax. Little Austin was scaring her and she did not know what was happening. Bo and Margo both came over.

"Where is she" Bo asked as he walked in the door.

"She is in the den on the sofa." Austin followed Bo and Margo into the den. Bo could hear Karen talking, to little Austin. "Little fellow you need to stop getting mad at me. Mama loves you so much and so does your Daddy."

"Karen lay back. I know it's not all that comfortable, but do it for just a little while." Karen didn't ask any questions she just did what Bo told her to do.

"There is nothing wrong he is just moving and there is not a lot of space for him to move around in. It seems his Mother is a small woman and his Daddy is a big man. That makes Little Austin a big boy. Karen you will just have to endure this until he is born. However I will always come when you call because we never know what it may be the next time."

"So Bo I'm not hurting my sweet baby?" Karen asked.

"No Karen you are not in fact he is fine. You're the only one in pain. He is playing and having all kinds of fun."

"Oh thank goodness I can deal with the pain as long as he is alright." Austin was holding to Karen now.

"Bo I'm sorry, but we don't know anything else to do, but to call you every time."

"It's alright Austin I had much rather you call and it be nothing than for Karen to lay here in pain and it be something. After all he is my little nephew. I love him too."

CHAPTER FORTY NINE

The next week the men came and did the floors in Austin and Karen's new downstairs bedroom suite. Austin went and bought them a new bedroom set while Bridget stayed with Karen. Austin had Karen to stay upstairs in bed until he returned. By the following weekend just as Austin had said they were sleeping in their new bedroom.

"Austin it is beautiful, but I love our old bedroom the most because it was just yours."

"I would have thought you would love this one the most because it is just ours."

"I do love this room, but I love the other one for a lot of reasons. We spent our first night together there and I got pregnant in that room and I just love everything about it and everything about this room too I just love any room I will be sharing with you." Karen said.

The next week was Halloween. Austin bought lots of candy to give out. He put Karen's big rocker in the entrance way so she could be with him while he gave out their candy to all the little children that came by trick or treating.

The next week they started Christmas shopping on line. Karen had never before had enough money to buy any one other than her mama and Grandmother a Christmas gift.

"Austin what do we get for little Austin for Christmas?" Karen asked as she looked at all the things displayed on her their lap top.

"Karen I don't now I have never been around a baby before." Austin said.

"Well you will be getting use to it very soon. Our son will be here in one month." Austin was on his lap top and Karen was sitting next to him in their bed.

"Austin I think we should plan to have a good Thanksgiving dinner."

"That would be nice, but who will cook it?" he asked. "Me" Karen answered.

"No you will not. We will have it catered. After all there will only be the four of us. Bo and Margo are going to fly to Georgia for Thanksgiving."

Karen was rubbing her stomach. "Austin?" "Yes Karen."

"I didn't think I could get any larger last month, but look I went from large to huge and next month I will go from huge to gigantic."

"But Karen little Austin will be ready to come by then."

"Oh I hope so. I haven't seen my feet in so long. Sometimes I don't even know if I have on matching shoes."

"Honey if you didn't I would tell you. I'm only happy you are able to get out of bed a little by yourself."

Karen stopped rubbing her stomach and looked over at Austin. "You have gotten tired of me already haven't you?" Her voice told Austin she was very serious about what she had said.

He stopped doing his work and closed up his laptop immediately. "Karen, no, I have not gotten tired of you. How could I? I love you so much I may not even want to go back to the office after little Austin is born. Only because you will be here and I will be there."

Austin knew this was one of those times Bo said he would need to be sure Karen knew he loved her and only her. Austin slid down into the bed. Then he pulled Karen down until she was next to him. Then he started kissing her. Karen had her arms around his neck and she was kissing him when Bridget knocked on their bedroom door. "Come in Mom."

"Austin there is a man at the door who said he was a friend of Karen's. I didn't let him in I just told him to wait."

Austin got out of bed and went to the front door. It was Rev. St. Johns. "Mister you need to leave my house and never come back here again. I thought you understood that the last time you were here." The reverend had not said a word. "Now leave before I call the police."

"Sir I did not come to see you I came to see Miss Belmont." He said at last.

"Well you just missed Miss Belmont by eight months. My wife does not wish to see or speak to you." Austin was ready to kick the good reverend way into next week.

"Sir you and Miss Belmont are living in sin." Austin just gave the good reverend a punch in the face. "Now leave I'm calling the police and my attorney will notify your church members about your conduct."

The good reverend hurried away while still rubbing his jaw. He did not want Austin to call anyone and most of all the members of this church.

"Austin who was at the door" Karen asked?

"No one Karen just a salesman trying to sell us something we don't want or need," he answered.

"Oh" Karen just kept on looking at her magazine. Austin knew Karen did not need to know that it was the good reverend at their door again. Austin was glad he was at home with her this time when the good reverend showed up.

Later while Karen took her nap Austin called his attorney and explained the situation with the Rev. St. Johns. "Austin most likely he will never say one word about you hitting him to anyone, most of all, his wife or the good members of his church. But we can send a letter out to all of his church members stating his intention towards your wife."

"Pete, why don't you get a letter written up and the names and addresses of all of his church members then we send the good Rev. St. Johns a copy of the letter along with a list of all of his church members and their addresses and in this letter. We will let him know if he ever tries to contact my wife or comes to our home ever again or even come near her; all of his members will be receiving a copy of the letter he has just received."

"I will get right on it Austin." Pete could tell how much his friend had changed in the last few months. Austin was a different man.

"Okay Pete that should take care of the good reverend." Austin said.

"Yes Austin I would hope so." Pete answered.

CHAPTER FIFTY

L ater that day Austin decided to give Miss Pittman another call and confirm her visit. "Hello" a soft voice on the other end said.

"Miss Pittman it's Austin Blackburn how are you doing today?" "Mr. Blackburn I'm doing quite well. I'm really excited about my trip to New York City. I still can't believe I'm really going. It still seems like a beautiful dream."

"Miss Pittman did you find someone to make the trip with you?" Austin sure hoped she did. He knew ladies Miss Pittman's age did not like traveling alone.

"Yes Mr. Blackburn I sure did a lady out of my Sunday school class. She is retired like me and has never been to many places. She was so excited about being asked."

"Well would you like to ask one more friend to come with you two?" Austin wanted this sweet woman to enjoy her visit in New York and if her having a couple of her friends with her would make it more enjoyable he was willing to pay the extra cost.

"Do you mean that Mr. Blackburn?" Miss Pittman was so happy. "Yes by all means ask another friend to join you." Austin could hear

Miss Pittman's joy in her voice

"Oh Mr. Blackburn you are such a good person. I would love to have my other dear friend to join us. She is also retired and alone. Thank you for being so generous to three old ladies whom you do not know or owe anything at all to."

"You are most welcome and I will have your three tickets waiting for you at the airport. I have also arranged for a car to pick you up Saturday morning to take you and your friends to the airport so you will all need to be ready very early. Then there will be another car and driver that will meet you in New York. This car and driver will be for your use while you and your friends are in the city. I don't want you to worry or be afraid of anything while you are here in our city. We will see you all Saturday."

"Thank you again Mr. Blackburn." Miss Pittman said just before she hung up her phone.

Austin had not told Karen about Miss Pittman coming for a visit. He was afraid she would get too excited. He also had enlisted his parents in helping him with his surprise.

CHAPTER FIFTY ONE

K aren only had one month to go and like she had said she was huge. However Bo said she was big, but no larger than he had expected her to be. After all she was small and any extra weight only made her look a lot larger. That made Austin and Karen feel better even if it was not the truth.

Karen was still going to have a very big boy. There was no way of getting around it. Austin's son had taken after him.

The rest of the week drug by for Karen. She was miserable. Austin did all he could to make her comfortable. She could not find a way to sleep at night so she was awake a lot during the night.

On Thursday Austin took her to Bo's office for her weekly check up. "Karen, get up on the scales I need to weigh you."

"No I'm too big, and I will break your scales," she answered.

"No you will not they go up to five hundred pounds" Bo said back to her.

"Bo I may weigh five hundred and one pound" Karen answered.

"No you do not. Bo, tell her she does not weigh five hundred and one pounds."

"Karen honey like Austin said you do not weigh five hundred and one pounds. Now get your butt up there and let me weigh you."

Karen stepped up on the scales one twenty seven. "See you can gain a little bit more before you break my scales."

"Will she gain any more before little Austin is born?" Austin asked. "Yes she will right along with little Austin. However he will be gaining most of the weight." Bo said.

"No" Karen said. She did not want to hear that from Bo. "Yes Karen he sure will" Bo answered.

"Austin you have to give birth to our son. I can't, I have decided he's just too big." Karen was very serious.

Bo could not help himself, he had to laugh. "Karen Austin can't do that, you are the only one who is equipped to do the job. So you will have it to do. All Austin and I will be able to do is help you."

"And look," Karen said.

"Yes and look, but I have seen it all and it's not that much." Bo said.

"Austin pop Bo" Karen said. "What for Karen?" Austin asked.

"For saying my cootchie was not that much," she answered.

"Now Bo I must say Karen is right there. So I will need to pop you for that one." Austin was standing behind Karen so she could not see him smiling over at his friend Bo.

"Austin, how did you get this woman to marry you so quickly?" Bo asked.

"He asked and I wanted him. If he had not asked me I was going to ask him" Karen answered.

"Karen, are you very sure you would have done that?" Bo teased. "Yes I'm very sure. I saw how handsome he was and I knew I had nothing to lose by asking. All he could do was say no and then I would have cried real loud."

"That alone should have convinced Austin to marry you. I'm very sure he would have done anything to stop you from crying. I sure would have." Bo said.

"But Bo you aren't Austin and he did ask me and I love him and he wants me even if I do cry."

"Yes I do Karen, but I don't like it when you cry," Austin said. "Karen lay down now and let me check your son. Austin do you have this much trouble getting her to lay down in bed?" Bo asked.

"No he does not. I'm always glad to lay down in bed for Austin. That's why I'm pregnant can't you tell?"

"Yes Karen I can tell, but I was talking to my good old friend Austin."

"No, Bo she lays down for me without any trouble." Austin was smiling at Bo again.

"See he said the very same thing."

"Karen you and our boy are doing so well I'm going to let you and Austin go back to living a normal life."

"Bo does that mean Austin won't be at home with me anymore?" Karen asked.

"No honey I will still be at home with you." Austin quickly answered.

"Yes he will it just means you can do things" Bo answered. "Like what?" Karen asked.

"Karen do you want me to tell you or do you want to put your fingers in your ears and start singing la, la, la, la, la." Bo asked.

"Austin is he going to tell me something personal?"

"Yes he is honey" Austin answered. Karen's face was already turning red.

"There she goes Austin turning red and I haven't even started to say any of those things to her yet."

"Bo, are you sure everything will be alright" Austin asked?

"Yes just as long as you don't go too far. Karen I'm sure will let you know when that happens."

Karen had her fingers in her ears now and like Bo said she was singing la, la, la, la.

"Austin, have a wonderful night."

"We will if my wife can take her fingers out of her ears long enough for us to have that night." Austin was sure he could get Karen to do everything he wanted once they were in bed.

"Now I know what I have to look forward to" Bo said.

Later that evening everyone was sitting in the den watching television, but television was not what Austin wanted to be doing. "Karen, are you ready for bed yet?" Austin asked.

"What do you mean yet? Austin it's only eight thirty." Bridget turned to her son and said.

"Mama I know exactly what time it is." Austin answered.

"So why are you so anxious to get to the bed? Oh I bet Bo told you Karen could have sex again." Bridget got a big smile on her face Karen's face turned a bright shade of red and Austin's face turned just as red.

"Bridget, I think you have managed to embarrass your grown up son." Maxwell had been watching his son as well as Karen.

"Oh Maxwell how did I do that?" she asked.

"I don't think he wanted us to know what he had on his mind to do with his wife tonight." Maxwell said.

"Oh is that all. It's not like we don't know he has done that with Karen. She is pregnant and she is his wife."

"Yes she is my wife, but I still think what we do in our bedroom is personal." Austin said.

"Austin Blackburn don't you speak to your mother that way even if she tells you what we should do in our bedroom. I for one hope she won't need to tell us what we should do or not do in our bedroom. But Austin she loves you and she only wants you to be happy."

"Yes and all I want right now is to be happy and that means being in bed with you."

Maxwell and Bridget were watching both Karen and Austin. All at once Austin scooped Karen up out of her rocker into his arms. "Since everyone knows what I'm about to do, I see no reason to wait. Woman we are going to our bedroom right now."

Maxwell smiled over at Bridget "Why should they have all the fun?"

"Let's go Maxwell" Bridget answered.

As soon as they had closed their bedroom door Austin said. "Karen, get out of those clothes."

"I am Austin it just takes me a little longer to undress than it used to." Karen answered while trying hard to get her clothes off.

"Let me help you turn around and I will unzip your dress." Austin was already behind her helping with her zipper.

"Austin, I need to get my gown."

"No you don't. Let me undo your bra." Austin had already taken off his shoes, socks, shirt and pants. He was just in his boxers now. "Karen, take off your shoes."

"Austin they are already off," she answered. "Well get in bed," he told her.

"Alright I'm getting there" Karen answered as she struggled to get her gown over her head.

"Karen you do not need that gown on just get into the bed." "Austin, don't be wasting all that sweet talk on me just get to it." Karen told him.

"What" Austin asked?

"Austin slow down we have all night and we can do it more than once."

"I know and that's just what I plan to do." Karen was already in bed. Austin got in next to her. He started kissing her. "Karen I have waited two whole months for this night."

"I know Austin. I have been waiting all that time right along with you. So now we don't need to wait any longer. Come here." Austin was right there. He was so gentle with his wife. He and Karen were so in love. They made love twice before going to sleep.

"Karen I love you so much and I know I will be getting you pregnant all the time so I'm very glad you want a lot of babies."

"Me too Austin, because I want you all the time too," Karen said. A big family was what she had always wanted.

CHAPTER FIFTY TWO

The next morning when Austin saw his Dad they both had smiles on their face. "Did you two have a nice evening" Maxwell asked?

"Yes we did Dad how about you," Austin asked?

"Son, your mother and I had just as nice of an evening as you and Karen did." Maxwell answered. That told Austin all he needed to know and more.

"Karen, are you going to stay up or are you going to lie back down for a while?" Austin asked when Karen came into to the kitchen.

"Maybe after awhile I will need to lie down, but right now I want to stay up for awhile." Karen answered.

"Son, don't try to wear it out." Austin looked over at his Dad with a puzzled look on his face. "Don't you look at me with that look on your face as if you don't have any idea at all what I am saying to you?"

"Oh Maxwell, don't make our big grown up son's face turn red let me do it." Bridget said.

"Will you two stop teasing me?" Austin said in his own defense. "Know they won't. They love you and they know what you want to do with me all the time." Karen said.

"I know they do Karen, but I just don't want them to know I know they know." Austin said.

Maxwell and Bridget could not hold it back any longer, they both burst out laughing.

"So you are playing like you have never done that with me?" Karen asked.

"Something like that you could say." Austin smiled and said.

"Well it's too late to play now. They can see for themselves that you have been doing that with me. Even little Austin knows it now." Karen said.

Maxwell and Bridget again busted out laughing and then Austin even started to laugh. It was all very funny to the three of them.

"What's so funny?" Karen asked.

"Me, they are laughing at me." Austin answered for his parents. "Now let's eat breakfast. Mom, you don't need to do this every day. I could go and get us something every day and save your all this trouble."

"Austin if Karen was able she would be doing it every day and along with whatever else that comes about." Bridget was only doing what she knew her daughter-in-law would be doing if she was able.

"Mrs. Blackburn I can start doing it all again. Bo said we could go back to normal. Well if you overlook my big stomach I'm normal at least. I'm as normal as I will be for the next month. So I can start back to doing my work today." Karen did not want her Mother-in-law waiting on her.

"No you are not little lady, you are going to play with my son and have our grandson." Bridget was not going to let Karen do anything.

"No Mrs. Blackburn I'm a grown woman and I have things I need to do and I need to do them."

"What do you need to do Karen?" Austin asked.

She looked at him with a blank look on her face. "I don't have any idea at all what I'm supposed to do as your wife Austin."

"Karen all you need to do is to be my wife and have our son and love me." Austin answered.

"Oh Austin I do love you can't you tell?" Karen asked.

"Yes I can tell and that's why I've hired a cook and a housekeeper." Austin thought this was as good of a time to tell Karen as any.

"Austin you don't need to spend your money on people to do my work. You are already off from work and we don't even have a pay check coming in each week any more. I don't know how long we will be able to keep on living like this with you not working." Karen was very serious.

Austin, Maxwell and Bridget looked at each other and said at the same time. "Karen we all three need to talk with you about something that is very important. Son, go and get our bank statements. I thought she had started to understand all of this?" Maxwell said. Austin went into his office and returned with both his and his parents' bank statements.

"Karen I'm your Father-In-Law and Austin's Dad, but I feel like your father as well. My wife Bridget and I along with our son your husband Austin own the entire business that your husband and I go to each day. Although Austin has not gone into work for the last month he still gets a pay check. If Austin decided to stay home with you and all eight of your children he would still get a pay check. Your husband owns this house, his car, his truck and all things you see in this place. He does not owe anyone any money and the same goes for me and Bridget. Now, here is where the hard part starts." Maxwell opened his bank statement. "Karen do you see this number?"

"Yes sir" Karen answered.

"Is it a lot?" Maxwell asked his daughter in law.

"Yes sir it is." Karen answered. She had never seen such large numbers on a bank statement before. Not even the church where she had worked for many years had numbers this large on their bank statement.

"Karen do you know how long a person can live on that much money?" Maxwell was trying to show her how well off they all were.

"No sir" Karen answered in a soft voice.

"We all could live very comfortable for over a hundred years with just what we have now, not what we will still be making in the future. Karen this is only Bridget and my statement your husband has three to four times this amount. Karen, that makes you a rich little girl do you understand what I have said to you so far?" Maxwell wasn't sure she was getting any of it by the look on her face.

"Sir I think so" Karen answered.

"Karen do you remember when we were in Savannah and we met Miss Pittman." Austin was trying to show her that other people knew of his wealth.

"Yes Austin I remember her" Karen answered.

"Then, do you remember what she said about recognizing me?" Austin thought he had at last found a way of helping her to understand.

"I think I remember Austin, but I was not feeling right. I was feeling real odd at that time. Do you remember?"

"Yes honey I do remember. Well anyway she said she recognized me from a magazine, because I was in that magazine."

"Yes I remember and Austin I was going to ask you why you were in a magazine?" Karen still had not really understood what her husband and her in-laws were telling her.

"Karen I was in the magazine because of my money." Austin said.

"Your money" Karen asked? She had never known anyone with so much money that they would be featured in a magazine.

"Yes Karen my money then, but now your money too. Karen we have over nine hundred million dollars not including the business we own with my parents. Honey, we don't need a pay check."

"Karen if you two don't have enough money of your own to have all those grandchildren for us you and our son can have our money too, but I'm very sure you and Austin have plenty of money. Austin and Bo have made several very good investments over the years and they have accumulated quite a large sum of money on their own. I dare say that Bo is worth in the neighbor of one hundred million dollars himself." Maxwell said and Bridget agreed.

Karen was turning as white as a sheet. "Karen, say something" Austin said.

"What do you want me to say?" She asked her husband. "Austin you, must be thinking I saw that magazine and that is why I wanted to marry you not because I love you at all." Karen felt sick.

"Honey I don't think any such thing. I know you had never seen that magazine or any of the others. I know you did not know who I was and you still don't know who I am. All you know is I'm your husband and I love you and I know you love me and soon we will be having our son."

"So you are telling that we can afford a housekeeper and cook." Karen said.

"Yes, yes, yes she gets it" Austin said with his hands up in the air. "But can we afford them all the time or just until little Austin is born?" Karen asked. She did not understand at all.

"Karen Blackburn we can afford them forever and we will. All you need to do is breast feed our son and me."

"What?" Karen asked.

"I mean take care of me. Now don't you go and faint on me." Austin said.

"I'm not going to faint I just hope your parents know their son is not going to be breast fed by me."

Maxwell and Bridget started laughing. "Son, you have a beautiful young wife and she doesn't like it when you embarrass her in front of people especially your parents. In your bedroom it may be alright, but I'm just saying maybe even there."

"Karen you look very pretty this morning." Bridget said trying to get Karen's mind on something else.

"Thank you Mrs. Blackburn I thought I needed to wear those clothes that Austin bought me before I'm not pregnant anymore."

"Well honey I don't think they will be going to waste. I think you will be pregnant in no time. My son is a real pistol."

"What does that mean?" Karen asked.

"Honey, I will let your husband explain that to you later in your bedroom." Bridget said.

"Oh well I most likely will have forgotten all about it by then." Bridget kicked Maxwell under the table.

"Bridget, why don't you go with me this morning and we can go and do some Christmas shopping later. I will be happy to wait for you to dress."

"Alright Maxwell I will love to go with you this morning. I'm very sure Austin won't mind being here by himself with his wife. He could chase her around the house naked."

"Oh no M'am Austin will never do that with me." Karen quickly answered.

"Karen has he ever tried" Bridget asked? "No" Karen answered fast.

"Well he should." Now Austin's face was red and Karen's face was not.

"Mom, go and get your clothes on before Dad decides to go without you."

Bridget got up from the table and was leaving when Karen asked the question. "Austin, have you ever wanted to chase me around the house naked?"

"Yes and I still do" he answered.

"Well take your clothes off and start running I will sit here and watch you." Karen was serious.

Maxwell just sat there for awhile and waited to see what was going to happen. "Son, what are you waiting for? Your little wife said for you to take off your clothes and she would watch."

"Karen I didn't want to run around naked by myself. I want you to be naked with me."

"So Austin you want to chase after Humpty Dumpy do you?" Karen answered.

"No I just want to chase after my beautiful pregnant wife. So will you take off your clothes and let me chase after you?"

"Yes I will as soon as hell freezes over." Karen then smiled up at Austin and at Maxwell then she started cleaning off the breakfast dishes from table.

"Then I take it that's a no" Austin said?

"Yes Austin that is a no. Can't you see there is a real good reason I would not even try that right now. Austin, look at me." "I'm trying to," he answered.

"No you are not, because if you were looking at me you would see how large and ugly I have become and without my clothes on I'm ever uglier."

Austin got up from the table and went to Karen and held her in his arms. "Karen you are not ugly you are so beautiful. I don't see one thing about you that turns me off. You being pregnant only turn me on even more."

"Austin you are so sweet. Isn't he Mr. Blackburn? Now let your Daddy, tell you how large I am. Mr. Blackburn, tell your son I'm big. Tell him that my toes look like those tiny sausages." Karen waited for Maxwell to say something.

"Karen you are big, but you are one beautiful woman and the only reason you are this big is because you are pregnant with my grandson by my son."

"Mr. Blackburn, my face is round, my stomach is big. And I haven't seen my feet all morning. I don't even know if I have on matching shoes or not. Tell him that my toes look like those tiny sausages that come in a little can, but three times larger."

"Well I will tell you. Your shoes match. You are pregnant and you only have one more month to go and then you will be your old self once again. You will be all curvy and sexy and my son will have you pregnant again in no time. As for your toes I'm sure they don't look anything like those tiny sausages that come in those little cans." Maxwell said.

As soon as Bridget soon came down from their second floor bedroom she and Maxwell left for the office.

CHAPTER FIFTY THREE

"Austin now that we are alone what do you want to do?" Karen asked.

"Guess?" Austin said. "Make cookies?" Karen asked.

"No, I haven't ever done that before." And that sure was not what he had in mind for them to do while they were alone. Karen got out her cookbook and they made cookies all morning. They made hundreds of all kind of cookies.

"Now what do we do with them?" Austin asked.

"We, put them into zip bags and into the freezer to have all during the holiday." Karen said.

"I hope Bo still likes cookies the way he did when we were boys." Austin had never seen so many cookies before in his life.

"Austin you are still a boy." Karen said with a big smile. "Yes I guess I am when I'm with my wife."

"Austin you look so cute in your apron. It makes me want to hug you." Karen said as she put a hand full of flower all over his face.

"Is that all it makes you want to do with me except what you just did?" Austin asked.

"No, but it's all I can say right now, because I hear your parents coming in the front door."

"Just my luck my parents return just as I was getting somewhere with my wife." Austin was putting the last of the cookies into the storage bags when his Dad came into the den.

"Son, I see you have your clothes back on. Did Karen, enjoy the show?" Maxwell asked.

Karen started to laugh. "No, Mr. Blackburn we made cookies instead." Austin took a bag of cookies and handed them to his Dad.

"I smell something baking." Bridget said as she came into the kitchen.

"Yes you do. Austin and I made cookies the whole time you were gone." Karen answered.

"Austin you cooked?" Bridget had never known of her son cooking anything.

"Yes Mom I cooked. Now we need to eat them all." There were cookies everywhere.

Maxwell was already eating one of the cookies. "Son, they are very good. Karen, you and your husband made some real tasty cookies."

"Thank you Mr. Blackburn would you like some milk with them?" Karen was just walking back into the kitchen.

"Karen I think I will make a pot of hot coffee to have with them." "Okay I can do that for you" Karen said.

"No Mrs. Blackburn you are going to rest. You have already done all of this and now you are going to rest. We are all bigger than you so mind us." Austin led her into the den and to the sofa where he made her lie down. "I will get you some milk for your cookies."

"Austin I only need one cookie that will be enough for me and little Austin."

"See Dad she thinks one cookie is enough and here we are having a lot of cookies."

"Her loss, our gain is all I can say son." Maxwell said as he took out another cookie from the bag.

"You are right Maxwell. It will be our gain. Our daughter-in-law is right. We should all be doing it her way." Bridget said.

"Mom, if we did it Karen's way we would have these cookies all year. We need to eat them and get rid of them."

"Oh son, they taste really good have you tried them yet?" Bridget had a couple of cookies and she was eating away.

"What are we going to do about supper Austin?"

"I don't know. Karen what would you like us to do?" Austin asked.

"Stop eating so many cookies would be a very good start. None of you will be wanting any supper if you keep eating all those cookies."

"Alright we will just eat a few more of them and then we will stop. Do you want to go out to eat tonight?" They all went out and had a wonderful meal. Karen felt the best she had in weeks.

"Austin it feels so good to go somewhere other than only to Bo's office." Austin and Karen were holding hands as they walked out into the restaurant's parking lot.

"Austin Blackburn, I haven't seen you in years. What have you been up to?" A man said as he came walking up to them

"Well, it's good to see you. I have been working as always." Austin answered.

Sam looked right at Karen. "It doesn't look like it has been all work to me." The man said.

"No Sam it hasn't. This is my wife Karen and we are expecting our first child in less than a month." Austin looked so proud.

"Karen this is Sam Winters, he went to school with Bo and me years ago." Austin was very happy to see his old friend again.

"Austin, tell me how is Bo doing? I'm very sure you two are still the best of friends, but that was twenty years ago. Things do have a way of changing we know."

"Yes they do. However Bo and I are still best friends. That has not changed and I hope it never will. Bo is a doctor now, in fact, he and his wife live next door to Karen and I. They are also expecting. Bo will be delivering both babies."

"That's nice, I'm glad you and Bo are still such good friends. It's hard to keep a friend as long as you and Bo have been friends. I hope you are always friends. Austin is that you Mom and Dad?" Sam was looking out in the parking lot as Maxwell and Bridget came walking hand and hand up to the restaurant.

"Yes Sam that's them." Austin said as he watched his parents walking towards them.

"They have not changed one bit. Hello Mr. and Mrs. Blackburn, I'm Sam Winters. I was in boarding school with your son here." Sam was shaking Maxwell's hand.

"Yes Sam I remember you. Didn't your father become Governor of your state?" Maxwell said.

"Yes sir he sure did three times. Now he wants me to follow in his footsteps." Sam was very proud of his entire family.

"Not at all bad footsteps to follow in as I remember," Maxwell said.

"No sir they surely are not. Austin, give me a call and let's get together sometime soon. I have to go now I'm meeting my date here. Wish me good luck." They exchanged cards and then they went their own way.

"Austin, why do rich men have so much trouble finding wives?" Karen asked.

"Because too many women only want a rich man for his money and they don't care about the man at all." Austin had met a few of those kind of women in is life and lucky for him he did not fall for any of them. He and Bo did not want that kind of women to be their wives

"Oh well I hope your friend's woman isn't like that and they fall in love like us and get married and she ends up with a big old stomach like I have." Karen was so happy and she wished everyone could be as happy as she and Austin were.

Austin gave Karen a little squeeze. "Honey it is almost over. In less than a month our little son will be lying in his little bed."

"And I can get pregnant all over again" Karen said.

"Yes, but Karen you don't have to right away unless you really want to."

"Austin Blackburn you already know I want all eight of our babies and I want them now."

"I guess you will be pregnant again then" Austin said.

"Austin, Sam looked good. In fact he looks a lot better now than when he was younger." Bridget said.

"Yes Mom he does he doesn't have braces on his teeth now." Austin said.

"Yes that's right he did have braces back then." Bridget was happy to see the young man looking so handsome.

"Honey boys do grow up. See our son did and now he has found the way to be a Daddy."

"Maxwell he is just like you." Bridget said.

"Yes he is and I'm very proud of my son and his wife and you, of course, Bridget." Maxwell was a good man.

"Maxwell we do have a perfect life."

"Yes Bridget, we sure do, only because we wanted our life together. Now our son is having the same kind of life. He found a woman who only wanted him."

CHAPTER FIFTY FOUR

The next day Miss Pittman and her two friends arrived in New York. Their driver was at the airport to meet them just as Austin had said he would be. He took them to their hotel and told them he would be back at seven thirty that night to pick them up. The three ladies were waiting in the hotel lobby when the driver arrived back at hotel to take them to Austin and Karen's house.

Maxwell, Bridget and Austin were ready to go out to dinner, but Karen was only told to put on her nicest dress which she did. She knew something was up, but she did not know what?

Austin was whistling and when he wasn't doing that he was all smiles. Karen did just what she was told. She looked so pretty Austin could not keep his eyes off of her.

"Austin what is the matter with you? Why are you, looking at me so much."

"Karen I was just thinking in a few weeks you won't be pregnant anymore and I've only know you one day that you haven't been pregnant. I just don't know how it will be without you being pregnant." Austin was staring at Karen as if there was something wrong.

"Austin, are you trying to tell me you only want me as long as I'm pregnant and after little Austin is born you won't need me anymore." Karen started to shake and tears started running down her cheeks.

"No Karen, no I love you and I never want a day without you. I was just thinking how we have spent our whole married life so far. We have spent it together planning our future and I have loved every second of it only because you are my wife. Please Karen don't cry." Austin was holding her as close as he could.

"Austin I love you so much and the thought of you not wanting me in your life kills me."

"Karen I will always want you in my life, besides you have a job to do and you are the only one who can do it."

"What job" Karen asked? She was looking up at Austin's handsome face.

"The job of having all of our babies and loving me at the same time I will be loving you." Austin answered.

"Yes that's right I get to do all of that. I wonder how many will be short?" Karen said.

"Only their mother" Austin answered.

By the time Miss Pittman and her two friends got to the brown stone Karen was alright. She knew her husband loved her and all he wanted in life was her and their eight children.

The door bell rang just as the clock struck eight. "Karen, would you mind answering the door? I have my hands full right now."

"Not at all Mrs. Blackburn," Karen answered as she hurried to the front door. Austin and his parents waited in the other room. Karen opened the door and there stood Miss Pittman.

"Miss Pittman, how did you get here?" Karen said real loud. She could not believe her eyes.

"Your nice husband paid for me and my two friends to come to New York for two weeks." Miss Pittman said with a big smile.

"Come in I'm so glad to see you. I just can't believe you are really here." Karen and Miss Pittman were hugging when Austin and his parents got to the door where their guests and Karen were still standing.

"Hello Ladies" Austin Said.

"He is a tall handsome one Ellen."

"Yes he is and he is all mine" Karen answered. "Do I need to watch you ladies when you are around my husband?"

"Only if we were forty years younger," one of Miss Pittman friends said.

"Yes Ladies I'm all hers." Austin had his arms around Karen. "Yes we can sure see that for ourselves" the other lady said. "Karen you look radiant." Miss Pittman said.

"Yes she is Miss Pittman. My wife is the most beautiful creature on earth." Austin said.

"Miss Pittman you will have to excuse my husband he only sees what he want to see."

"Oh I'm going to get lucky tonight." Austin said with a big grin on his face.

"What did you say" Karen asked?

"You said I only see what I want to see and I want to see it all." Austin answered.

"Oh and he is a hot one too," The first friend said.

"Yes M'am I am and so is my little wife. Now are you three ladies ready for a night out on the town?" Austin could tell that Miss Pittman and her two Sunday school friends were going to have a fun time in his town while they were there.

"Yes we are Mr. Blackburn, we are so ready." Miss Pittman said. "Now ladies these people here are my parents, Maxwell and Bridget Blackburn. I'm not sure if they like me best or Karen, but it doesn't matter because they love our baby the most."

"Yes we do. I'm Maxwell, glad to meet you ladies. Our son has told us so much about you Miss Pittman." Maxwell shock all three of the ladies hands.

"Oh please call me Ellen. I have been Miss Pittman for over sixty two years. Now I only want to be called Ellen. I want to look young and dress young and be young."

"We all three do" one of the other two ladies said.

"Austin we can do that can't we? There are places here that make people look altogether different from the way they usually look aren't there Austin?" Karen wanted her new friends to be able do the things they wanted to do while they were in New York.

"Yes Karen, there are and I'm very sure my Mom knows where the best of them are."

"Yes Austin, there are and I will be very happy to handle that for these three lovely ladies." This was something Bridget would enjoy doing.

"Son, we need to be going. Your mother and I will go with the ladies and you and Karen can follow in your car or truck." Maxwell go his and Bridget's coats from the hall closet.

"I think tonight we are taking our car. I haven't used it for a while and I need to drive it some." Austin and Karen went down to the basement garage and the others went out of the front door to the waiting limousine.

"Karen, are you comfortable enough in our car? We can always drive our truck."

"Austin I'm fine. Don't I look comfortable?" "No not really" he answered.

Karen was doing the best she could. "Well this is the best you get until little Austin is born. Then he and I won't ever get to ride with you in your pretty little red car again. All the women who will see you in it will think you are single and they will all be flirting with my husband."

"No they won't because I will get a tag that will read TAKEN." Austin knew that would make his little wife very happy.

"Austin, would you do that for me?"

"Yes after all I am very much taken and so are you." Austin picked up Karen's hand and kissed it. "I love you Karen."

"I love you Austin" Karen answered back.

They arrived at the restaurant just behind the limousine.

"Hello Mr. Blackburn nice to see you again. Come this way, we have your table waiting.

They had their dinner and Austin's parents and the three ladies hurried down town to see their play. Austin took Karen home.

"Honey this was too much on you I should have known it would be."

"No Austin it was so nice. I'm so glad you brought Miss Pittman and her two friends to New York. They are so sweet."

"Karen I was thinking about offering Miss Pittman a job teaching our children. What do you think about that?"

"You mean home school them?" "Yes" Austin answered.

"I love it, but little Austin won't be ready for school this soon. Austin you sure do not know anything about babies I can tell."

"No, but he will need someone to read to him and show him things."

"Austin you don't think I can teach our children to read or is it that you don't think I read well enough to read to your children?" The very thought of Austin not thinking she could read well enough to read to her own children hurt her so much.

"Karen I don't know anything you don't do well. All I know, is I want to have all those babies and still have my wife. With Miss Pittman here to help you I will be able to have some of you too."

"Alright Austin I do love Miss Pittman and I think our little sweetie will learn a lot from her. Yes Austin I like that idea."

"Alright then I will speak with her before she goes back home. We could make part of the basement into a real nice apartment for her."

"Oh Austin, that is so sweet. No wonder I love you so much." That night Karen slept right next to Austin. He could feel her stomach every time little Austin moved.

"Karen, how do you ever rest or sleep with little Austin kicking so much?" They were still in bed.

"Why?" Karen asked?

"I could feel your stomach on my back last night and I felt our son kicking and carrying on all night."

"Oh I'm sorry, was I too close to you?"

"No I want you close. I just don't know how you get any rest at all."

"I just do. If he didn't move that would worry me so I feel better if he moves."

"Are you ready to go to the bathroom?" Austin knew he would need to help her out of bed.

"Yes our son is sitting on my bladder right now." Karen answered. "Alright let me help you up. Do you want to shower with me this morning?" He hoped she would.

"Austin, do you want me to?" Karen was out of the bed and on her way to the potty.

"Woman I will always want you to shower with me." All he could do was watch her as she walked away.

"Even if I take up more of the shower than you" Karen asked? "Yes even then" Austin answered.

"All right I will shower with you and I will look at you." Karen said just before going in to the little potty room.

"I know you will that's why I want you to shower with me. I'm going to look at you too." Austin answered.

The next two weeks flew by. Miss Pittman took the job Austin offered her. She would be back in a few months to start living in her new home. While she was still living in Georgia Austin would have her, a new apartment built in their basement and it would be all ready for her to move into when she gets back.

CHAPTER FIFTY FIVE

"Karen, Karen, Karen what am I going to do with you?" Bo was standing next to his scales waiting for Karen to get up on them to be weighed.

"Bo a lot I think maybe too much" Karen answered.

"Austin your wife won't get up on the scales again. I thought after last week she would just get up here and let me weigh her, but no she just won't do it."

"Bo I don't see what good it does for me to weigh every week. You already know I'm big, and fat and heavy so you want to see me get mad at you too?" Karen was not a happy camper.

"No, but I still need you to get up here and let me weigh you." Bo gave her one of his best looks. He hoped that would help to sway her. "Austin you get up on the scales and let Bo weigh you this week for me. I'm very sure we weigh the very same thing." Karen was also miserable.

"Karen honey, if I could I would do it all for you." Austin answered.

"Austin all you have to do is step up on the scales and Bo will do the rest." Karen told her husband.

"Alright Bo, weigh me." Austin stepped up on the scales and waited.

"Two hundred and five pounds, now Karen it's your turn unless you want me to put your husband's weight in your chart as your weight." Bo said and he waited for her answer.

"Alright" Karen reluctantly got up on the scales.

"One hundred and thirty one pounds, see Austin is still the big one." Bo said as he smiled over at Austin

"Not much bigger" Karen replied.

"Alright Miss Blimp let's go into this room and you take off everything." Bo said as he entered her weight into her record.

"What?" Karen did not want to do that for sure. "Karen you heard me" Bo answered.

"Karen honey, do what Bo tells you to do." Austin knew his friend was only having Karen to do what she needed to do.

"Austin how do I know if this is right?" Karen said while all the time she was giving Bo a funny look that only she could make.

Bo smiled at Karen "You don't, but you will still do it." And of course she did.

"Austin, feel here. This is your son's head. He is getting ready to be born. Austin she has only eight days to go. That means your wife could have little Austin any time now. Karen are you alright?" Bo asked.

"I will be as soon as you two men get through sticking your hands all up me." Karen answered.

"Karen I'm your doctor and Austin is your husband and—" "And I'm naked" Karen quickly answered.

"Yes you are and we all know that" Bo answered. "Austin you need to pop Bo now."

"Honey I can't right now I'm still checking out our son. Can it wait until I finish doing this?" Austin answered.

"So that's your big hand that's up there now? Karen said. "Yes honey that's me" Austin answered.

"Are you ready to stop playing doctor and get your hand out of me?" Karen was not happy with all that was going on right then. She was feeling more like a biological project than anything else right then.

Karen got off the table and got dressed. She was glad that the examination was all over. She only hoped Austin didn't want to play doctor after they got back home. Now that he knew how to do it.

"Mama our son is already to be born. He has already dropped I could feel his head." Austin was very happy Bridget could tell. "How did you do that" Bridget asked?

"Bo let him play doctor again." Karen answered.

"Karen we did not have our hands in you. We were only mashing down on the very bottom of your stomach." Austin told her.

"Oh I bet. Then why did I feel little Austin trying to get away from yours and Bo's big old hands? I just may call the whole thing off." Karen said.

"Honey I don't think you can do that or even would want to do that would you?" Austin asked.

"No I don't, but I don't like being the one you and Bo are always doing all of that to." Karen answered.

"Would you rather we be doing it with some other woman?" Austin asked?

"No I would not. So I guess I will just let you two play doctor all you want and hope you will grow out of wanting to do it one day. I guess by the time we have all eight of our babies you will be getting your doctoring license." Karen was sitting in her rocking chair in the den.

"Tomorrow is Thanksgiving so I think I will go and set the dining table. Karen is that alright with you?" Bridget asked.

Karen looked over at her mother-in-law and the over at Austin. "Austin is that alright?"

"Yes Karen, I thought you had already decided we would eat all of our holiday meals in our dining room." Austin answered.

"I did, but I didn't know if it was going to be alright for us to do at your house." Karen answered.

"Karen Blackburn this is our home as much as it is mine." Austin was shocked.

"Yes Karen this is your and Austin's home not just Austin's anymore" Bridget said.

"I know, but it is still very hard for me to accept all of this. I still feel like I am on a visit and any day I could be sent back home."

"Honey you are home and if you ever go anywhere I will go right along with you." Austin answered.

"And so will we" Maxwell said as he walked into the den where they had all gathered.

"So are we eating in the dining room or not Karen?" Maxwell asked.

"Mr. Blackburn, I guess we are" Karen answered. "Now Karen, tell me all about your doctor visit."

"Mr. Blackburn, your son stuck his big old hand up me and felt my son's little head today."

Maxwell looked over at his son. "Did you really do that Austin?" "Yes Dad I did, but I did not feel his head." Austin answered. He knew Karen was still a little if not mad she was at least upset. "Was he alright" Maxwell asked?

"Yes he was Mr. Blackburn until Bo and your big handed son started messing with him. Now he wants to be born so he won't have those two men bothering him while he is enjoying being in his Mama's stomach." Karen answered.

"Dad, Bo said our son" Austin stopped and looked over at Karen. "As I was saying our son could be born anytime now. Karen has only eight days to go."

"Karen honey, I know you were glad to hear that today." Maxwell said.

"Yes Sir, I was. In fact I feel like it may even be sooner. I sure don't want to have to go through another doctor appointment where your big handed son and his little big handed friend, wants to play doctor." "Karen I know Austin is just anxious to be a part of it all." Maxwell gave his son a funny look. As if to say I can't believe you really did that son?

Karen was still sitting there looking at Austin. "Karen, don't give me that look. I wanted to feel where our son was. How else could I have done that, if I had not used my hand?"

"Austin Blackburn, am I going to go through that with everyone, of our babies?" She asked.

"Yes I think so. Karen I want to know what you are going through." Austin said. He wanted to share in with it as much as he could.

"Austin when we get to our bedroom I'm going to check you out." Karen said as she looked at him.

"How do you think you are going to do that to me Karen?" Austin asked.

"I don't know yet, but I will find a way you can be sure." Karen answered.

"In that case I may not go to bed with you tonight." Austin told her.

Karen stopped rocking. She didn't say one word she just got up out of her rocker and went to their bed room and locked the door.

"Son, I think you just made a big mistake and mostly likely one that you are already regretting." Maxwell said

"Yes I am. So I'm going into that bedroom and make up with my wife." Austin went to try to open their bedroom door, but it was locked. From the other side of the room Karen could hear Austin trying to open the door. Then he began to knock on the door, but Karen did not answer. "Karen, open this door right now. You hear me? Karen you know I didn't mean it. I don't want to sleep anywhere without you."

Still Karen did not open the door. She was busy packing her suitcase for the hospital. Her water had broken, and she knew she would be having their son soon. She took time and called Bo.

"Hello" Bo said. He was sitting in the den watching the evening news on the television.

"Bo, its Karen, my water has broken." She was in a lot of pain already and she knew she needed help.

"Alright Karen go lie down. I will be right over." Bo hung up the phone and went to find Margo. She was in the kitchen. "Margo that was Karen on the phone her water has just broken. I'm on my way over to check her and then we will be going to the hospital I'm sure."

"Alright Bo I will wait right here, but call me and let me know how things are going for Karen." Margo looked a little tired to Bo.

"I will, but Margo honey I want you rest some. You are four months along yourself." Bo said as he got ready to leave.

"Yes I am and I'm so glad." Margo was so happy about being Bo's wife and about having their baby.

"Now give me a kiss so I can go." Bo took Margo in his arms and kissed her.

When Bo rang the door bell Austin was still standing outside their bedroom door waiting for Karen to let him in, but she was not opening that door until Bo was there.

"Get the door Austin." Karen hollered from the other side of the door.

Austin stopped knocking on their bedroom door and went to the front door. "Hello Bo"

"Austin where is Karen?" Bo asked.

"She is in our bedroom, but she is mad at me and she won't let me into our room, why?" Austin asked?

"Oh, you don't know? I guess you have really made her mad this time." Bo asked.

"No, Bo I guess I don't." Austin answered.

"Austin, your wife's water has broken and she is in bed. I told her to get into the bed now I need to get in there to her."

"We can't get in she has the door locked" Austin answered. He was beside himself now. All he could think was his wife being in labor and her not opening the door.

"Well then you will need to open it. Your wife is already in labor man." Bo was ready to kick down the down.

"Are you sure Bo?" Austin asked.

"Well that's what they told us in medical school and I'm here to find out for sure so open that door Austin." Right then Karen opened the bedroom door. She was in labor big time.

"Karen!" Austin said as he picked her up and carried her back to their bed. "Bo, help her. She is in so much pain."

"I know Austin now let me check her." Bo had to do his job now and he needed Karen's help.

"Bo how did you know her water had broken?" Austin asked. "Karen called me and told me it had broken." Bo said.

"How did she know that her water had broken?" Austin asked.

"I was all wet. Austin didn't you see my clothes and my chair when I left the den to come in here?" Karen was trying very hard not to let Austin see how scared she was.

"No I just thought you were mad because I said I was not going to sleep with you and that you didn't want to be in the same room with me."

"I am mad at you Austin, but if you don't want to sleep with me anymore you don't have to that's all I can say. You can go right back up to that third floor and I will stay right here with my baby." Karen said between her pains.

Bo looked over at his friend. "Austin, don't do this. This is not the time for anything like that. Don't tell me, that you and Karen are having trouble, I don't want to hear this from you two now."

"We aren't having any trouble Bo." Austin answered.

"No we aren't have any trouble anymore, it's all settled he doesn't sleep in the same room with me anymore." Karen answered.

"Karen Blackburn I do so. I love you and I won't sleep anywhere you aren't sleeping. I have already told you that awhile ago."

"It's time for you two to make up. Your son is on his way." Bo said as he closed his bag.

"Austin, I love you." Karen began to say. Karen was in her husband's arms.

"Oh Karen I love you too honey." Austin could not stop loving her if his life depended on it.

"Austin, son, what in the world is going on in here?" Bridget said when he came into the room.

"Mrs. Blackburn, I'm in labor and it's hurting really bad." Karen said.

"Karen, honey can I do anything for you?" Bridget asked his daughter-in-law.

"No I don't think so. Do you still want a grandson?" she asked. "Yes Karen I do and now more than ever." Bridget answered. Just knowing that Karen was so close to having her Grandson made it all the more real to Bridget, she was going to be a Grandmother soon.

"Alright I will try to get him here as fast as I can." Karen smiled and said.

"Good girl" Bridget said.

"Bo, are we going to the hospital now?" Austin was getting nervous.

"Yes Austin we are Karen is all ready." Bo answered. He could tell by the look on his friend's face that he was as anxious for this to be all over as his little wife was.

"Mom, will you ask Dad to bring my truck around to the front of the house. Karen needs to get to the hospital, her water has already broken."

"I know Austin, Karen told me and I will tell your Dad to go and get your truck. You take it easy." Bridget could see how nervous her son was she hoped he would still be able to drive.

Maxwell came in to the bedroom while Austin and his Mom were still talking. "Dad Karen's water broke."

"Yes son I know. I cleaned it up off the floor in the den and out of her rocker. Now I will go and get your truck and bring it around to the front for you." Maxwell got Austin's keys and hurried down to the basement. In less than five minutes he had his son's truck at the front door.

"Austin son, your truck is at the front and here are your keys. Your mother and I will drive our truck to the hospital."

"Thank you Dad." Austin took the keys from his Dad.

"Karen honey we love you. Bridget and I will be at that hospital with you." Maxwell had learned to love this young girl so much. He now regretted the words he had said to his son about him marrying her when they first met Karen.

"Thank you Mr. Blackburn. Austin, get my suitcase." Karen called out.

"I will Karen you stop worrying about everything. I will get it all done." Austin had never had so much going on in his life before that he was not in control of completely until now.

"Give me that suitcase. We will bring it to the hospital. You just take Karen to that hospital." Maxwell told his son.

Karen was having a lot of hard pains now. She could not even walk anymore all she could do was hurt and that did not want to stop.

"Bo, help her" Austin begged.

"Austin there is nothing I can do right now. We just need to get her to the hospital." Bo knew he would be going through the same thing when it came Margo's time to delivery.

"Bo I hate seeing Karen of all people in such pain. I love her so much."

"Austin it hurts so much" Karen had now laid back down on the bed.

"Honey I love you so much. I can't stand to see you in so much pain. What can I do for you?" Austin was already doing all he knew to do, but if she asked him to do anything he was ready to do it.

"Austin, help me. I can't do this it hurts too much." Karen had tears running down her face and her whole body was shaking.

"Karen, listen to me." Bo didn't want her to hurt anymore than was necessary.

"Yes Bo I will try." Karen was so scared. She had never been in so much pain before in her life.

"Honey, you can do this." Bo was rubbing her back and his voice was so calm.

"No, Bo I cannot it hurts too much. My whole body is hurting." Karen was almost in a little ball.

"Austin let's get her out of the house and into your truck and I will ride in the back with her and you drive. Now let's pick her up together." Bo had never before felt this anxious about any of his other patients, but Karen was a lot more than only a patient to him.

Austin gently picked Karen up in his arms and then he kissed the top of her head. "Honey I love you so much." Was all he, could say. There were tears in his eyes now.

"I sure hope so Austin if we plan for me to do this seven more times. Knowing that you love me will help." Karen answered.

Bo got into the back seat with Karen and Austin got up front by himself. "Is she buckled in?" He asked before leaving his parking spot.

"Yes Austin we both are." Bo answered. "Bo this really hurts." Karen was crying.

"Yes Karen I know honey." Bo felt so sorry for his friend.

"Oh no, you don't you just think you do." Karen was in so much pain she was bending way over. Then out of the blue, "Austin we can't have our baby yet." Karen said.

"What?" Austin answered. He almost hit the brakes.

"We haven't been to the Wal-mart yet to get our diapers. We don't have any diapers at all at home." Karen said from the back seat.

Bo was holding Karen's hand now." Karen don't worry we will get your son some diapers because with or without diapers he is coming. There is no holding him back, by tomorrow you will be holding him in your arms."

"Bo I can't do it this hurts too much." Karen kept saying.

"You can Karen and you will. I will see to it that you and your son get through all of this." Bo would die himself if anything happen to Karen or Little Austin.

"Honey, please try to relax a little it will help." Austin said knowing there was no way for her to do that because he couldn't do it either and he wasn't even in labor. He was driving as fast and as careful as he could.

"Karen your contractions are three minutes apart." Bo told her. "No Bo they don't quit." Karen said between cry.

"What do you mean, they don't stop?" Bo knew if they were one long hurt they had no time to spare.

"What do you think I mean?" she asked. "Karen, are you in pain right now?" Bo asked. "Yes, Bo can't you tell" she asked?

"No I'm sorry Karen, but no I cannot tell."

"Well believe me I'm in pain and it is just hurting all the time now and it don't want to stop." Karen had tears still running down her face.

"Karen, listen to me. Are you feeling much pressure?" Bo was trying to check her out as they rode to the hospital.

"Pressure where Bo?" Karen asked.

"Pressure at the place where your baby will be coming out where else woman?" Bo was still amazed at how innocent Karen was about some things even after almost a year of marriage.

"Yes a lot of pressure like little Austin really wants out right now." Karen answered.

"Austin I need to check her to see if your son is on his way out. You just keep driving. Karen I don't need you to fight me on this. I really do need to check you." Bo was not going let her talk him out of doing his job.

"Who's fighting Bo, I'm in so much pain I could scream." Karen said in a weak voice.

Bo checked her and like she said her son was wanting out. "Austin your son is on his way out so we need to get going."

"Bo, how can it be she has only been in labor an hour?" "No I've been in labor five hours" Karen answered. "What" Both men asked?

"Yes it all started when we were leaving your office this afternoon."

"Karen why didn't you tell us" Bo asked?

"I didn't know it was labor at first" Karen answered. "I thought it was from you two playing doctor OH, OH, OH," Karen was squeezing Bo's hand.

"Bo is she alright?" Austin was very nervous. He had no idea having a baby hurt so much. "Karen I never dreamed it would hurt you this much."

"Really Austin, did you think our son would just fall out. I have got to push a little you out of my bottom and it ain't no picnic I can tell you two right now OH, OH, OH." Karen had a hold of Bo's hand again and she was not letting go.

CHAPTER FIFTY SIX

"**I** can see the hospital now. Karen, just keep holding on honey." Austin said from the front seat.

"Oh she is. However my hand may not work ever again." Bo said.

"Bo, aren't you and Margo suppose to be on an airplane on your way to Georgia?" That had slipped Karen's mind when she call him for help.

"Yes Karen we are." Bo answered. He had forgotten all about the trip to Georgia. "But I have a baby, a very special baby to delivery tonight."

Austin pulled right up to the emergency room door. Bo got out and got Karen a wheel chair.

"Karen, honey" Austin had gotten out and had gotten into the back seat with his wife. "Karen, honey I'm so sorry I didn't mean one word I said. I will always want to sleep with you."

"Well tonight you may not get to sleep with me or anyone." At that time Bo open the door to the back seat. "Karen let's go." Austin got out and lifted her out of the truck and into the wheelchair.

"Austin, go and park and then you will need to check her in at the front desk. I will take her right on up to the 8ᵗʰ floor. We will see you up there." Bo said.

"Austin I love you" Karen managed to say.

"Honey I love you so much." Austin said and then he gave his wife a quick kiss and then he watched as Bo pushed her away.

Austin found a parking spot and hurried into the hospital he needed to get Karen checked in before he would be able to go up to the 8ᵗʰ floor. As soon as he had it done he hurried to the 8ᵗʰ floor to find Karen. His parents were already in the waiting area.

"Austin" Maxwell called out as he saw his son hurrying by. Austin stopped and turned around. "Bo said for us to wait here for you and then all of us to go to room 8017. Karen and Bo are already there."

"Son, she will be alright. I know I have been there." Bridget said hoping to comfort her son some.

"I know Mom, but it hurts so much to see someone you love in so much pain." Austin was thinking right now that one child may be all he and Karen would ever need.

"Son, if you and Karen plan to have eight children this is how they will all come into this world." It was as if his Mother had read his mind.

Austin didn't answer. His thoughts now were all with Karen. All he wanted to do was to get to her so she would know he loved her and she was not alone. When they got to her room Karen was already in a hospital gown and Bo was right there with her.

"Austin her contractions are very hard and your son is very large and Karen is very small as we both know. We may need to do a C section on her. I'm going to try to get him to be born vaginally, but we may not have a choice." Bo did not want to wait too long before deciding what he needed to do.

"Yes we do" Karen said. "He is coming now." "No Karen he is not" Bo said.

"Yes Bo he is look." She said.

Bo and Austin both looked. They could see the top of little Austin's head. "You are right Karen he is. Now let me do my job."

"Austin did Bo say your son was coming?" "Yes, Mom I saw the top of his head."

"Oh son that is so wonderful." Bridget was all smiles.

Bridget stepped outside to let Maxwell know their grandson was on his way. "Maxwell come on back in, he is on his little way." Bridget had a big smile on her face.

He had not gone into the room yet. He was waiting to see if it was alright with Karen for him to be there. After all this was a very private thing.

"Maxwell, come on in before you miss the birth of our first grandson."

They both went back into Karen's hospital room, but from where they were standing they could not see anything because of Bo and three nurses that were standing at the foot of Karen's bed. Austin was at Karen's side.

"Honey, do you want to hold my hand?"

"Yes Austin and your neck" Austin smiled. Karen was not going to just take all of the pain and smile she was going to give him a little pain of her own. Austin did not mind that at all.

"Austin, do you want to see your son being born?" Bo asked' "Yes of course I do Bo."

"Well come down here. It's not happening up there."

"Mom, you and Dad come over here and stand beside Karen." "Sure son, we will be glad to do that" Maxwell on one side and Bridget on the other.

"Karen when I say push, I want you to do some hard of pushing. Mr. and Mrs. Blackburn you two can help her. Your grandson is a very big boy." Bo wanted them all to have apart in the born of this special little baby.

Maxwell took one of Karen's hands and Bridget took the other. "Karen push" Karen pushed as hard as she could. The nurses were holding her legs. Karen was getting real tired. "Push Karen, now breathe honey."

"Bo I'm so tired. Oh, oh, it's coming again" Karen was soaked in sweat.

"Karen push, push as hard as you can. Here he comes. Now Karen can you give me just one more big strong push?"

"I will try Bo" she pushed as hard as she could.

"Karen, please push" Austin said. Karen gave one more big push. "Austin see you son" Bo was holding their little boy in his hands.

"Karen, are you alright?"

"Yes Bo" was all the energy she had left in her to say anything with.

"Austin do you want to cut the cord?" Bo asked.

"Yes I do" Austin was so happy that he had a son and a wife he loved.

Karen was lying back in the bed and Bridget had a damp cloth wiping Karen's face. "Honey you did good."

"Thank you Mrs. Blackburn is our baby alright?" Karen asked. "Yes he is" Bridget said proudly. At that very moment little Austin let out a big cry. You could hear him all over the place.

"Oh so he took after his Mama some too." Bo said as a nurse handed Austin his son. "Austin I need to get busy again the after birth will be coming out soon so you may want to move. It can be very messy sometimes."

Austin had his son wrapped in a little blanket. "Go give that boy back to his Mama. She needs to see him too."

Austin walked to the head of the bed where Karen laid looking so worn out. "Karen, look at our son. He is a very big one. I love you both so much thank you honey for giving us our son."

"Dr. Brooks," A nurse called out from the other side of the room. "The Blackburn boy weighs nine pounds and twelve ounces and he is twenty two inches and a half inch long."

"Karen did you hear that? Your son is almost as tall as you." Bo said. Karen was too tired to answer. All of her fight was gone.

Austin had laid their son up on Karen. "Karen honey, how are you feeling now?" Austin asked.

"Austin I'm so tired, but I'm so glad it's over." She answered as she looked at their beautiful little boy.

"Honey the drugs didn't help you any?" Austin asked.

Bo raised his head from his work. "Austin Karen didn't have time to get any drugs. She had to do it all by herself." Bo was so proud of this little girl.

"What, my wife didn't get anything to help her with all of that awful pain?" This made Austin feel sick all over.

"No Austin it was too late. She was too far along." Tears came into Austin's eyes. All he could remember was all the pain his little wife was in for the last hour.

"Son, she did real well and she is now doing great." Bridget said. She wanted to help her son She did not want him to feel guilty about Karen.

"Mom I can't let Karen do this ever again." Austin was very serious. He was ready to call off having all the other babies he and Karen had planned to have.

"Yes, yes you can" Karen was kissing their son. "I want seven more babies and little Austin, wants lots of brothers and sisters and anyway you have already said we would have them."

"But that was before I saw how a baby is born." Austin was serious.

The nurse came over and took little Austin. "Mrs. Blackburn I will bring him back in a few minutes."

"Alright, but don't forget to bring him back to me." Karen said. "I won't" the nurse answered.

"Bo is Karen alright" Austin asked?

"Her pressure is good, her heart rate is good and all my work for tonight will be done as soon as I finish up down here." Bo answered.

"What are you doing down there still" Austin asked?

"Why don't you come down here and look for yourself." Bo told his friend as he continued to work.

Austin went to the foot of Karen's bed. Bridget went over to Karen's bed and held her hand and kissed her on her cheek she was so proud of her daughter-in-law. Then they both talked about little Austin.

Austin was watching what Bo was doing. He didn't say anything and neither did Bo. Bo was putting a lot of stitches inside and outside of Karen. Bo looked over at Austin. "Are you alright" he asked in a very low voice so Karen would not hear.

"I don't know if I am or not. What happened?" Austin asked.

"Your son did all of this coming out of your wife." Bo was still working.

"Is she alright?" Austin asked.

"Yes she will be, healing will just take some time. Now Austin when I say no sex I mean no sex. Do you see why?"

"Yes Bo I see why." Austin could not take it any longer. He could not stand seeing all the work Bo, had to do on Karen to get her back together. "Mom I will be back in a second." Austin went out to the men's room where he washed his face and had a good cry.

"Son, it's alright. Karen is doing great." Maxwell had followed his son into the men's room.

"Dad you didn't see what this did to Karen's body." Austin's eyes were all red.

"No, but I can imagine. Now you get back in there and take care of your wife. She needs you son."

"I know Dad and I need her too. She means more to me than I ever thought a woman would ever mean to me." Austin and his Dad went back to Karen's room. She was holding little Austin in her arms and kissing him.

"Austin isn't he beautiful?" she said as she kissed her son little head.

"Yes Karen he is" Austin answered.

"Bo did good, didn't he Austin?" Karen didn't feel real well, but she sure felt a lot better than she did a few minutes ago.

"Yes honey Bo, did very good." Austin was so thankful for what his friend had done.

"Are you two talking about me?" Bo asked. "Yes we are." Karen had a smile on her face.

Bo was so glad to see that smile. He had done a lot of work on her. More than he had ever had to do on any other patient before. "Karen, how are you feeling?"

"I am feeling wonderful now," she answered.

"Honey I'm sorry you didn't get any drugs to help with your pain, but you will be better soon. Tomorrow morning you will go home. Austin will stay in here with you tonight and I will be back here early tomorrow morning to check you out. Now let Austin have your son and then you let me do another little check on you."

Austin took little Austin and he was holding him so tight. "Son, you are going to break him if you keep holding him so tight."

"Mom I'm afraid to let go of him."

"Let me have him." Bridget said as she took her grandson from Austin arms. "Maxwell, look how perfect our grandson is." She held little Austin so Maxwell could get a good look.

"Yes sweetheart he is definitely perfect and large."

"Yes Maxwell too large for Karen to have had him, but she did it. Our son needs to get her something very special something out of this world for giving him and us such a wonderful gift."

"Yes I agree and so do we."

Bo was checking her over good. After all he cared a lot for Karen. "Honey, you will be sore and hurting some for a few days, but it will gradually start going away. I don't want you to lift anything not even little Austin. Let someone else do that for you. You can hold him in your arms, but I don't want you lifting him and walking around with him in your arms. Austin do you hear me and do you understand all your wife has just gone through?"

"Yes Bo I do."

It was after midnight and they all were worn out and most of all Karen. "Austin I have a private nurse that will be in here with you and Karen tonight or should I say with the three of you."

"Who is the third person that will be staying in our room with us tonight Bo?" Austin asked.

"Austin your son will be in here in that little bed over there." Bo pointed to the little bed sitting on the other side of the room. "The nurse will take care of your son and Karen you won't need to do anything until you get home tomorrow." Bo told his friend.

"How do we get him home tomorrow Bo?" Austin asked.

"In your big truck and in a car seat of course, how else do you think you would do it?" Bo answered.

"Karen, do we have a car seat?" Austin asked. He had not thought about getting a car seat.

"No, I told you we could not have him yet, that we needed to go to the Wal-mart." Karen said from her bed.

"Mom you and Dad need to go to the Wal-mart right now. We need a car seat and diapers." Austin was now in a panic.

"You don't have a car seat?" Bridget asked.

"No Mom we don't or diapers." Austin answered.

"Alright Maxwell let's go and find a Wal-mart." Out the door they went but not before Bridget, gave little Austin back to his Daddy and Austin put his son into the little bed.

"Bo why didn't you tell me we needed all of those things?" Austin asked.

"Austin I thought you knew you would need those things. Most people know that their baby will not come with all the things they will need." The two men were walking out of the room.

"How would I know about all of those things? I have never even held a baby in my arms before tonight." Austin felt like a fifteen year old boy who had gotten his girlfriend pregnant and knew nothing. Maybe the fifteen year old boy would even know more than him. "Bo I have a lot to learn about being a Dad. There is a lot I'm responsible for now besides myself and it all happened in just nine short months. I have a family now that counts on me and only me. Bo I'm not sure I'm ready for all of this." Austin face was looking a little pale.

Austin and Bo were standing just outside of the door to Karen's room in the hall talking. "Austin my friend you sound just like someone who has just woken up and realized you did something you are not so sure you want now. I do hope that is not true." Bo looked a little pale himself now.

"Bo nothing could be farther from the truth. I love Karen even more for what she just did and my son. Bo I didn't know parents really felt this way, but I know now they do. No way, am I sorry about marrying Karen and having our son. I could not be happier. I'm just scared that I won't be as good of a Daddy as I had." Austin and Bo hugged. Austin had tears in his eyes.

"Bo, what about your family in Georgia" Austin asked?

"We will just be late. There was no way I was going to let someone else delivery my nephew."

"Thank you Bo, but is Karen alright with all that you had to repair?" Austin had a worried look on his face.

"Austin right now no, but it will all heal in time. I'm just not going to let this happen with the next seven. The next time, when she feels like she is in labor we are bringing, her to the hospital because each baby will come quicker each time. Austin she did exceedingly well. She did not panic one time. She did exactly as I told her to do and she got the job done. Now are you ready for the second one?" Bo was smiling at Austin who was shaking his head.

"Bo not yet, but next year I'm sure we will be here again."

"Now that your parents have gone I will need a ride home." Bo said.

"Here take my keys and drive my truck back home and then you can come back in it tomorrow morning and then we four, will go home together like we came." Austin said.

"Yes we can, but I will be sitting in the front seat with you and Karen and your son will be in the back seat." Bo took Austin's key and left.

"Honey I guess we are here for the night, but I don't have anything with me."

"Yes you do Austin look in my bag."

Austin went to the other side of the room where his Dad had left Karen's bag on a low consol table. Karen had packed all of the things Austin would need for their stay at the hospital. She had even packed Austin's camera. "Does this mean I can make some pictures?" Austin was now holding his camera in his hand ready to make a few pictures. "Yes now that he is here and I'm all covered up." Karen smiled at her husband.

"Karen, when did you do all of this?" Austin could see he had everything he would need for tonight and in the morning.

"I did it when I left out of the den and went to my bedroom." "Karen, it's our bedroom. I didn't mean it when I said I would sleep without you and you know it."

"Yes Austin I know it, but you hurt me when you said it."

"I'm so sorry Karen I won't ever say that to you again because it is just not true. I will always want to sleep with you." Austin went over to Karen's bed. "Honey you mean everything to me I'm not worth anything without you." Austin held Karen in his arms and was giving her a little kiss on her cheek when there came a knock on the door. It was Austin's parents back from the Wal-Mart

"Hello are we disturbing anything" Bridget asked?

"No mam' Austin, was just giving me a kiss on my cheek" Karen answered. Karen felt there was something different now between them and it was scaring her even after all he had just said to her.

"Son, we have us all some supper since we all missed eating and I'm very sure Karen could use something after all she has done for all of us tonight." Maxwell was as excited as all the others over the birth of his Grandson.

"Thank you Dad. My wife really is something." All Austin wanted to do was smile.

"Yes she is." Bridget said as she opened a nice take out dinner for Karen to eat.

"Dad is that the car seat?" Austin had never even look close up a car sear before.

"Yes it is son and it's a dandy" Maxwell answered.

"Did they happen to show you how to work it?" Austin asked. "No, but we did get instructions with it. I feel the four of us will be able to figure it out." Maxwell didn't see a little car seat as being too much trouble.

"Austin, are you staying with Karen tonight" Bridget asked?

"Yes I am and little Austin will be staying in here with us too." he answered.

"Are you going to be taking care of Karen and your baby son?" Bridget asked. She wasn't sure if she could leave her daughter-in-law and new Grandson in only her son's care for a whole night.

"No Mom, Bo got a nurse to come and be with us tonight. She will be the one taking care, of them."

"Good that scared me for a couple of minutes" Bridget said. "What, don't you think I could take care of my wife and my son?"

If Austin wasn't as scared as he was of Little Austin he would tell the nurse that they did not need her service. Then he would take care of his wife and his child.

"No I don't" Bridget answered.

"You are right Mom. It scares me to death." Austin had both of his hands on his face. "He is so small and she is so torn up. How, did I do this to her?"

"Austin Karen will heal and she will do it again and again until you two get all eight of your babies here. Son you will learn how to take care of them just like Karen. They're your babies too. Not just hers."

"I know Mom, but he is so small" Austin said.

"Son right now I don't believe Karen would agree with you."

"No I don't guess she would. He is so wonderful and she is so wonderful. Mom how did I get so blessed?"

"Son, you are a good man. Now go and get your food and get up there with your wife. She needs you to be with her now. She needs you to tell her what she has just gone though was worth it, that you, are so proud of her and of your son; which I know you are, but Austin you have left Karen alone so much tonight when you got upset or when things got to be more than you could handle you just left the room. Karen didn't get to do that. She had to bite the bullet and grin and bear it. Now you get over there and let your wife know how much you love her."

Austin's Mom had never before talked to him this way. After all he was a grown man, but he knew she was telling him the truth. He had let Karen down and he did need to reassure her of his love for her.

Austin went right to Karen's bed with his carry out box. "Honey, do you mind if I share your tray with you or do you feel too bad for me to sit on your bed with you?"

"Oh Austin I want you here. I have been waiting for you to come to me. I was about to think you had picked me to be your surrogate." Karen started to cry. Austin got up in the bed with her and held her in his arms.

"Honey, I could never love anyone more than I love you this very minute. You were never my surrogate I have already told you that many times. I wanted you to be my wife the second I laid eyes on you. Karen Blackburn I will always be in love with you and want you to be my wife. You gave me a beautiful son tonight and I could not be prouder."

Karen put her arms around Austin's neck "Austin I love you so much." She was crying. He was so happy to have it all over.

"Karen, stop crying and let's eat. It's almost two o'clock in the morning." Austin said.

"What, we have kept little Austin up this late" Karen was shocked.

"Yes we sure have, but I really think he is asleep over there in his little bed. My Mom has been keeping an eye on him. She is going to be a real good grandmother."

"Yes I know. It's his Daddy I'm worried about" Karen said. "Why would you be worried about me?" Austin asked.

"Because Austin I know little Austin and I came into your life real quick, but we do love you and I hope you love us the same way." Karen didn't want her husband to be disappointed with either her or Little Austin.

"Oh Karen I do, can't you tell?"

"No, not all the time tonight Austin I could I tell. Some of the time tonight I, didn't even see you here in my room. I needed you so bad and you were not here. Where were you?" Karen needed an answer.

"Karen I was outside crying." Austin did not think this was a good time to hide anything from his wife.

"Crying" Karen said.

"Yes I was crying because I saw how hard all of this was on you and you did it all without one time complaining." Austin didn't know if he had been in Karen place if he would have been able to have done what she did and she did it all without anything for pain.

"I had to do it Austin there was no one else here that could do it, except me. After all little Austin was in me." Karen said from her bed while still looking worn out.

"Yes he was, but he is not anymore and now my little wife can rest. Karen you look so beautiful."

"Austin you still want me don't you?" Karen needed some reassurance that she was not there only to give birth to Little Austin.

"Yes I do. Who else, but my beautiful wife could have eight babies with me?"

"Only me" Karen answered. Austin kissed Karen once again.

"Son, we are going home. We will see all of you tomorrow morning at home." Maxwell said. He and Bridget were ready to get some sleep. It had been a very long day for them all.

"Mr. and Mrs. Blackburn, thank you for coming." Karen wanted her in-laws to know she was glad that they were there at the birth of their Grandson.

"Oh Karen honey, we would not have missed it, no more than we will miss the next seven." Bridget answered.

"Oh that is so sweet. I hope I don't bore you with so many of them." Karen laughed and said.

"Never honey, you rest. Our son will be right here to take care of you. He loves you so very much and so do we." Bridget kissed Karen and Austin and so did Maxwell. As they were leaving the young nurse that Bo had arranged to care for Karen and Little Austin came into the room. She spoke to Maxwell and Bridget as they went out the door. Austin and Karen were so busy they didn't even notice her.

"Austin, where is little Austin?" Karen could not see his little bed from her bed no matter how hard she looked.

"Honey he is in his little bed. Do you want me to move his little bed closer to yours?" Austin had not realized that Karen was unable to see their son's bed from her hospital bed.

"Yes I do" Karen answered. Austin moved their son's bed right next to his mother's bed.

"Now Austin, where are you going to sleep?" she asked.

"I don't really know" Austin said as he looked around the room for another bed.

"Mr. Blackburn this chair makes into a bed. I will be happy to make it up for you." When the nurse said that it made Karen and Austin both jump. This was the first time they knew there was anyone else in the room with them except for their son.

"Thank you I'm not used to hospital things." Austin said as soon as he could regain his composure.

"Most people aren't" the young nurse answered. The nurse started making up Austin's bed. "Mr. Blackburn would you like me to move your bed near your wife's bed?"

"Yes I do. I want to be as near to her as I can get." Austin answered.

"Then why don't you just sleep in her bed with her? I'm sure your wife won't mind." The young nurse knew if this handsome man was her husband she would want him in bed with her.

Karen didn't wait to be asked. "Austin I don't mind at all." They both slept in Karen's bed with their son in his bed next to his Daddy. The nurse checked on them every hour during the night. They didn't get much rest at all. The next morning Bo was there to get them.

"Karen, how are you this morning?"

"Bo I'm fine, but poor Austin is worn out, he had a hard night." Karen answered.

"Oh poor baby" Bo said while looking at his friend.

"Bo, don't tease him. He has been up all night taking care of me and little Austin."

"Where was the nurse I got for you?" Bo asked.

"Outside, but she was in here every hour to check on us." Karen answered.

"Karen, are you breast feeding your son?" Bo hoped she had decided to do it.

"Yes I am and we have already done it twice." Karen answered. "How is it going" Bo asked?

"Alright I guess. I don't know. How do I know if he is getting enough?" she asked.

"Karen you could get a breast pump and then you could make little Austin's bottles, then anyone could help you feed him even his big old Daddy. Otherwise I could check and see if you have enough milk in your breast." Bo knew she would not like that at all.

"No, you will not. You have messed with enough of me. You know me better than Austin does."

"No he still knows you the most. He got to do all the good stuff with you. All I got to do was to clean it all up after he had all the fun."

"So Bo you think we need a breast pump now?" Austin asked.

"Yes I would get one and a lot of bottles. You two, were not really prepared for all of this were you?" Bo had never known any two people more unprepared for anything in his life as his two friends. Lucky for them they had him.

"No we are not. This is our first try at parenthood does it show?" Austin asked.

"Yes Austin it does all over. In fact I don't believe I have met two more unprepared people in my life." He had to just say it. He could not hold it back.

"Bo I didn't plan on being in bed for such a long time. Besides I didn't know a lot about being a mother." Karen said.

"Don't worry Karen you two will have time to learn it all. I dare to say Margo and I won't do any better. After all I couldn't even tell that my own wife was pregnant and me a doctor. Now Karen, are you ready to go home? Bo already knew the answer.

"Yes I am" Karen quickly answered.

"Well then lie down and let me check you. How is the bleeding?" Bo was back to being her doctor again.

"Awful" Karen answered.

"Awful meaning too much or I hate doing it?" "Both" she answered.

"Alright let me check." Bo began to check Karen out. "Karen, it is a little heavy, but I'm still going to let you go home, but you are not to lift anything at all. Austin do you hear me?"

"Yes I will do all of the lifting." Austin answered. "No sex" Bo said as he looked at his friend.

"Bo you don't need to worry about that" Austin answered.

"Good" Bo said knowing that they would fight him all the way on this as soon as Karen started to feel better.

"Now Karen do you have pads?" Bo asked. "No" Karen and Austin both answered.

"I should have known you would not have them." Bo said. He was not surprised at all.

"Bo I will call Mom. She and Dad will go and get Karen some. Now tell me where do we get a breast pump?" Austin remembered that Karen had told him something about a breast pump a couple of month back, but of course he had forgotten all about it.

"Austin you can get them at most drug stores. Karen I want to see you and Little Austin at my office in six weeks. You will need to call my office after the holiday and make an appointment."

Austin called his Mom. She and his Dad went and got everything Karen and Little Austin needed for now. The girl came with the wheelchair and Austin went to get his truck and to meet them at the front door of the hospital. He was waiting at the door when Bo, Karen and Little Austin got there.

"I see you found it." Bo said to his friend.

"Yes it was right there in your parking spot." Austin answered. "Karen I'm going to put little Austin in his seat."

"Alright Bo, that's another thing we will need to learn." Karen knew she and Austin had a lot to learn, but with Bo's help and her in-laws she was sure they would do it.

"Well you won't be going anywhere with him until you and Austin come for your six week checkup. That will be your first trip for you and little Austin other than this trip home. I believe in the old fashion way. It's still the best way." Bo told them.

Bo got little Austin into his car seat and buckled in. He was very sure this was another something his two friends would need to learn to do. In no time they were home. Bo went home to his house as soon as he and Austin had Karen out of the truck. He and Margo left for Georgia by noon.

CHAPTER FIFTY SEVEN

Austin was carrying little Austin in one hand and Karen's bag in the other. He was a happy man anyone could tell by the big grin on his face.

"Austin I'm so glad to be home." Karen said as soon as they got into the front door of their house.

"Karen I know you are. Now let's get you into bed." He led the way to their down stair bedroom.

"Austin our baby bed is upstairs." Karen said as soon as they were in the bedroom.

"Karen you don't need to go upstairs. Bridget and I got you a little bassinet for little Austin. It's upstairs in our room. I will go and get it right now." Maxwell went right up to the second floor and got their gift.

Austin placed little Austin in the middle of their bed to undo him from his car seat. He was still, sound asleep. Maxwell brought the bassinet down to the down stairs bedroom.

"Austin look how beautiful. I have never seen a bassinet this beautiful." Karen said. In fact she had not seen many bassinets at all in her life. Most of the women she knew from her small town could not have afforded them.

"Thank you Mom and Dad it is very nice." Austin had tears in his eyes.

"Son, he is worth every tear." Maxwell said. "Yes Dad he is and so is Karen."

"Austin your son looks just like you did the day we brought you home from the hospital."

"Was he, big too" Karen asked?

"What do you think Karen? Look at him now" Bridget said. They all started to laugh.

"Karen, how do you feel?" Bridget, remembered how she tried to act as if she felt great the day she came home from the hospital after having Austin. She knew she had four days in the hospital to recover in before she went home, but Karen had not even had twenty four hours. It had only been twelve hours and here she was home with her son.

Karen was sitting on the side of the bed. "I feel a little tired and a whole lot happier."

"Well you get into bed and we will take your son and watch after him while you and Austin get a little sleep. I'm sure neither one of you got any last night."

"Mrs. Blackburn I need to pump before I can do anything else or you won't have anything to feed your grandson."

They got it all ready and Austin helped Karen to get it done. "That should do it. Now you get into that bed and rest. This time yesterday you were still pregnant and you had no idea that little Austin would be in that bed this morning."

"You are right I sure didn't Austin."

Karen and Austin got their shower and then they went to bed. Maxwell and Bridget had moved the little bed to the den. They were so proud of their grandson.

Bridget called all of her family and Maxwell did the same. Several didn't even know Austin was married, but they all were very happy with the news.

"Karen, are you still asleep?" Austin asked. "No I'm awake." Karen answered.

Austin then moved over closer to Karen. "Honey did I tell you how much I love you and our son?"

"Yes I think I heard you say that before," she smiled and said. "Well I can't tell you that enough. You did something I could not believe last night." Austin was still beside himself. "Well believe it" Karen said.

"Honey I didn't know you had not been given anything for pain. How did you ever do all of that without getting something for pain?"

"Austin I just wanted him out it hurt so bad." Karen did not want to think about all she had gone through last night.

Austin pulled Karen even closer to him. "Karen we do not have to have any more babies if you don't want to go through that ever again."

"Are you crazy? How, else will we have our family if I don't do it? You are not putting anymore ads in the newspaper do you understand me?"

"Yes and I was not going to do that. I already have the woman I want to have all of my babies."

Yes and here I am and I will have all eight of our babies."

Karen and Austin soon got up. It was Thanksgiving Day, and the caterer had already delivered their Thanksgiving dinner. By one they were all in the big dining room ready to eat. Little Austin was still asleep in his little bassinet.

"Mom, Dad and my most wonderful wife, I have so much to be thankful for and they all are in this room, plus my job and home and of course my good friend Bo. Karen I love you. Thank you for our son."

"You are so welcome Austin" Karen answered as she patted him on his hand.

They were all still sitting at the table no one had started to eat anything yet. "Yes, Karen thank you and you too Austin, although your part in it all was only fun and games. We would like to say thank you to you both for giving us our first grandchild. He is so wonderful. He has already added so much to our life."

"Mr. and Mrs. Blackburn I would like to say thank you two for Austin. Without him I could have never done it." Karen had a big smile on her face. Her life was so much better than she had ever dreamed it would be.

They all, had a wonderful Thanksgiving being together and taking care of little Austin. Austin gave his son several bottles and changed his diapers several times. He didn't even ask for help he figured it all out for himself.

"Austin we have a lot to learn about raising our son and there are so many things we need to get yet." Karen could only see dollars marks.

"Like what" Austin asked?

"Baby oil, shampoo, towels, washcloths, the list goes on and on. Austin babies are expensive. I don't know how people can afford to have them."

"They just do Karen. Love is what makes them afford their children."

"Austin not all people who have babies together love each other. Some don't even love the baby. I know I was one of those babies." she answered.

Austin had forgotten what an awful life Karen had before she married him. He only hoped one day she would get over it. She never had to go back to her old way of life. He loves her so much and he would always take good care of her and their children.

"Karen you look so thin." Austin had almost forgotten how sexy his wife had looked.

"Yes, at last now I can see my feet again, but little Austin was worth every day of it." Karen was dressed in a pair of pants and a pretty sweater." Austin I need to get some new bras, so I can feed our son."

"Where do we go to find them?" Austin was sitting in the rocker with his son in his arms.

"At that mother to be shop where we got my clothes, they have them there. I saw them the last time we were there." Karen also remembered seeing a lot of other things there as well. Like one of his old girlfriends.

"Alright tomorrow morning you and I will go and get you some new bras and Mom and Dad can watch little Austin."

"Don't you think we need to at least ask them if they want to watch our son?" Karen said.

The second Maxwell and Bridget came into the den Austin asked them about watching Little Austin for them to go shopping for Karen some feeding bras. Of course they said yes right away. They would be more than happy to do it.

"Mrs. Blackburn are you sure you and Mr. Blackburn want to be left here babysitting all morning.

"Yes Karen we are sure, believe me. It seems as if that will be the only way we will ever get to touch our Grandson as long as Austin is around the house. Our son won't let go of him of his son so take the big boy off for the whole day and let us have a day with our grandson."

"Mrs. Blackburn, that's all, my fault. I told him it was his turn to carry little Austin for nine months, but after last night I may throw in another year."

"Yes Karen I would think so." Bridget was over at the rocker getting her grandson out of his Daddy's arms. "Karen you should do a little more shopping for yourself other than just feeding bras."

"I will later, but right now I really don't care how I look. Right now all I need is bras. Besides, tomorrow will be very busy at all the stores with people Christmas shopping."

"Yes it will be black Friday." Bridget said.

"Mrs. Blackburn, have you ever done your Christmas shopping on black Friday?"

"No Karen I haven't. We usually are at home in the country and I try to always have most of my shopping done before Thanksgiving like this year. Why, would you like to do that one of these years?" she asked.

"Yes, I have never done any Christmas shopping before and everyone was always telling me how much fun they have doing it on the Friday after Thanksgiving. So I would like to do it one time." Karen was sitting in Austin's big chair. "But not this year, I don't believe, I'm ready for all of that right now."

"Neither do I" Austin said as he got out of the rocker so his Mom could rock little Austin. "Karen, do you want to sit in my lap?"

"Yes if you are sure you want me to," she answered.

"Why would I not want you to sit in my lap?" Austin asked. "Because I'm sore, I hurt and I'm just one big mess. That's just a few of the reasons why." Karen answered. "Yes and I did it all to you didn't I?"

"Yes, but not by yourself." Karen said back to him.

"No, but I didn't have to go through labor either." Karen got up out of Austin's chair with his help and then he sat down and then she sat back down on his lap." Are you comfortable Karen?"

"As comfortable as I can get right now." "Karen honey, you are so light."

"I guess I am. The rest of me is in your Mama's arms." Austin put his arms around Karen and pulled her close to him. "And I have the rest of you in my arms where you belong." Austin started kissing Karen right then. He didn't care who saw them.

"Look little Austin your Daddy is trying to get all of your Mama's sugar. He's a big boy and one day you will be big just like him and you will get yourself a sweet girl like your Mama to marry you and then you will have a house full of babies just like your Mama and Daddy are going to do." Bridget was talking to her grandson.

"We don't have them all yet."

"No Austin you don't, but I can already see you will. I bet you don't give Karen six months before you have her pregnant again."

"Now Mom I don't think I will. I'm not in that big of a hurry to do that all over again. I need to get over this time first." Austin said as he gave Karen a little hug.

"What have you done that you need to get over?" Bridget asked. "Not me, Karen" Austin said.

Karen turned a little in Austin's lap so t h a t she could look up at him." Austin I do hope I have gotten over having our son before six months."

"So do I honey and I hope the next time Bo will be able to give you something for pain." Austin was still very much upset over Karen doing it all without any drugs. "Karen I don't know how you did it last night?"

"Austin I had to do it. What else could I do? Get up and run out. No I don't think so. I wasn't in the running mood at that time. Didn't you notice Austin, how they had me lying in that bed. I could not have left if I had wanted to."

"I know Karen it was awful, but we got our son here."

"Yes we did, meaning I got him here, you watched." Karen said. "Yes I did. It was the most fascinating thing I have ever seen in my entire life."

"Well you have seven more times to be just as fascinated."

"And I will be just as fascinated the eighth time as I was the very first time." Austin gave Karen another little hug.

"Austin I sure hope so."

"Karen I know I will. Mom did we get any dessert with that meal?"

"Yes we did. Why do you want some?" Bridget asked.

"Yes isn't that part of the Thanksgiving meal?" Austin said while still holding Karen in his lap.

"I guess if you want some you can get up and get yourself and Karen some. Maxwell, are you awake?"

"Yes, I'm awake." Maxwell answered from the sofa.

"Would you like some cake and pie?" Bridget asked her husband. "Yes I could eat some."

"Alright Austin I will have some too." Bridget said. "So you want me to get you all some cake and pie?"

"Yes son it sure sounds that way. I will just lay here until you get it. I may want a cup of hot coffee with it too. How about you, Bridget honey, do you want a cup of hot coffee with your pie and cake?" Maxwell didn't even look Austin's way.

"That sounds great; I think I will have a cup too." Bridget said. "Karen sweetheart do you want anything?" Austin asked while still sitting in his chair.

"No Austin I'm still full from dinner," she answered.

"Well let me up and I will feed my old parents before they both starve to death."

"Yes son see to it that you do. Oh I think I want a few of those sugar cookies you have in the freezer too." Maxwell said.

"You mean the ones Karen and I made all by our little selves?" "Yes those are the ones I want."

"Alright Dad, Mom do you want anything else?"

"No, yes I have changed my mind I will have some of those sugar cookies too."

"Karen, are you sure you don't want something?" I will be glad to get it for you."

"No Austin I'm fine, but I will go to the kitchen with you if you want me to."

"Yes I do. Now let me help my little mother up." Austin said. Karen looked up at Austin "What did you say?" she asked. "Little Mother" Austin repeated.

"Austin I'm a mother." Karen started to cry.

"Oh, sweetheart, don't cry. You will wake up our son and he will cry just as loud as he can."

"Austin I love being a Mother and I almost didn't answer your ad."

"Yes, but you did and look what it got you." Austin was looking over at their son in his Mother's arms.

"Yes a very sore bottom." Karen said. "Karen is that all it got you?" Austin asked.

"No it got me you and you got me little Austin."

"Karen Blackburn, I love you so much." Austin had Karen in his arms kissing her again.

"Son, are you going to get our snacks or not?" Maxwell asked. "Yes, we are on our way."

"Austin I will put a pot of coffee on. Do you want a cup?" Karen said as soon as they were in the kitchen.

"Yes since you are making it and not me," he answered.

"Austin, get that big tray and we will put everything on it. It will make it easier to carry." Austin got the big tray and began to load all the food and dishes on it. He then took it into the den.

"My, my, it all looks, so good." Bridget said. Austin put the tray with all the goodies on the big coffee table.

"Karen did you make the coffee?" Maxwell asked after taking his first sip.

"Yes sir" Karen answered.

"It's good I knew Austin had not made it."

"No sir, but he did cut the cake and pie." Karen answered.

"I guess that's why the pieces are so large." Both of Austin's parents were sitting on the sofa. Bridget had put little Austin in his little bed to sleep. Karen was sitting in her rocker again.

"Honey you don't want just a little?" Austin asked. "I may take a bit of yours." Karen answered.

"Alright get back over here in my lap woman and we will share all of this stuff." Karen eased up out of the rocker and walked very slowly over to Austin's chair. He put his dish down on the little table next to his chair and helped Karen into his lap. "You smell good."

"It's the perfume you gave me." Austin started kissing Karen's neck.

"Austin you are being mean to me. You know I can't fight back or even move."

"Yes I know. So you have to sit here and let me kiss you all over your neck."

"No I don't I can get up out of your lap and go back over to the rocker," she said as she smiled up at him.

"Would you do that?" Austin asked.

"Yes I will if you keep this up." Karen said and then she started to get up out of his lap, but he would not help her up nor would he let go of her.

"Alright I will give you a break," he answered.

"Give me a break. You are the one who needs a break or is it time out you need?" Karen answered then she turned to her Mother-in-law for help. "Mrs. Blackburn, tell your son to stop tormenting me."

"Austin you have teased Karen long enough. She doesn't feel like being tormented by you. Her body is too sore." Bridget said as she gave her son the same look she used to give him when he was a boy and had done something wrong.

"Oh God Karen I forgot all about that. I'm so sorry honey." Austin pulled Karen close in his arms. "I love you so much and you are so small and your, breasts are so large."

"Austin, don't talk like that in front of your parents they will think

I'm easy."

"No way Karen, we will never think that. After we finish eating let's make a few pictures."

"Mom we have made pictures all day long."

"I know Austin, but little Austin will never be one day old ever again. Austin I want a picture with you, your dad and little Austin. Three generation of Blackburns. Karen I want one of you and Austin and then the three of you and I want one of just Karen and little Austin." Bridget wanted her Grandson's first Thanksgiving well documented.

"Mrs. Blackburn, I look awful so just make pictures of Austin and little Austin they look good together, but I don't need to be in any pictures." Karen was worried that she looked so bad that no one would want to see any of the pictures that she would be in and most of all her.

"Yes you do need to be in them. You are his mother and my beautiful wife." Austin did not know what Karen was saying about looking bad she looked beautiful to him. Maybe a little pale, but she had just given birth to their son the night before.

"Austin I don't feel beautiful at all."

"Karen is there something wrong that you are not telling me?" Austin asked.

"No Austin I just think I look too awful to be in any pictures." "Karen honey you are just tired. You need to be in bed right now."

Bridget got right up and helped Karen out of her son's lap. "Come with me we are going to get your gown on you and you are going to rest. It' still hasn't been twenty four hours ago yet that you gave birth to our grandson. You have done way too much today. Maxwell and I will take care of little Austin tonight so you can sleep all night. What in the world have we been thinking? Karen should still be in bed not up making coffee for us and being tormented by you Austin."

By now Bridget had walked Karen all the way to her and Austin's bedroom. "Mrs. Blackburn, I can take care of little Austin." Karen said.

She did not want her Mother-in-law to feel that she was pushing her son's care off on her

"No Karen, let me do it tonight. I still know how to do that and you already have several bottles made and I know you will be pumping again soon."

"Yes, I need to be doing it right now. My breast, are leaking right through my bra I can feel my milk running down me."

"Alright let me get Austin in here to help you."

"Mrs. Blackburn I can do it by myself. Austin doesn't need to help me."

"No, but he needs to be with you. Your husband needs to help you with everything. He needs to learn what it is to be a parent just like his Daddy did. That's what made him the father he is."

"Alright if you say so" Karen decided her Mother-in-law knew best.

"I do Karen you will see it will make my son, your husband a better husband, daddy and man."

Karen got her gown on with Bridget's help and got ready to pump. "Karen I will go and get Austin and your pump and bottles. You just relax. Austin will be right in." Bridget hurried out the door and back into the den where Maxwell and Austin were still sitting. "Austin, Karen is ready to pump." Austin just sat there he did not move an inch.

"Austin did you hear your mother?" Maxwell asked. He knew Bridget was not just telling their son what his wife was up to she was telling him to get up and get into that bedroom and help her. That it was his son too.

"Yes sir I did. Mom said Karen was going to pump now." Austin answered as he still sat in his big chair.

"Yes and so are you. You need to get in there and be with your wife. Son, she, just gave birth less than twenty four hours ago to your son and that's not all Karen has done she has been taken care of your son, you and us today. She doesn't feel well Austin. In fact you will never feel as bad as your wife feels today."

"What?" Austin asked.

"Have you already forgotten about what you saw Bo having to do to Karen last night after she gave birth to your son?" Maxwell was ready to take a big paddle to his gown son.

"No" Austin answered, but he still sat in his big chair without moving.

"Then you need to get into that bedroom and help that little girl." Maxwell was even more ready to use his paddle on his grown son if for no other reason than because he was still sitting in his chair.

"Alright I will do anything for Karen after all I do really love her." Austin said.

"Son, we know you do we can see it for ourselves. Now get a move on it."

Austin was just getting up out of his chair when his mother came back through the den carrying Karen's breast pump. "Are you still here?" Bridget asked her son.

"Yes I'm still here, but I'm on my way. Do you want me to take all of that to Karen?"

"Yes you may. Now Austin you help her, she is all worn out." Bridget did not want to go back into her son and daughter-in-law's bedroom and find her son stretched out all over the bed while his wife sat pumping her milk. She felt that her son needed to help his wife more.

"Alright Mom I'm going."

Karen was leaning back on the headboard of their bed when Austin walked in. He could see her milk running down her. "Karen, wake up honey."

"Oh Austin did I fall asleep?

"Karen here is your pump and six bottles." Austin said as he put it all down on their nightstand.

"Austin I don't think I will have that much milk." Six bottles seemed an awful lot to her right then.

"Well just do all you can, and I will help you. Let me get you some warn water then you can wash off your breast."

"Alright Austin I'm just so tired." Karen did not have any energy left.

"I guess so little Mother you just had our son. Now let me take care of you."

"Austin did your Mother tell you that she and your Dad are going to take care of little Austin tonight so we can rest?"

"That's nice we can have a night alone."

"Austin we have had all of our nights alone except for last night." Karen said as she sat up in bed.

Austin started laughing "was that just last night?" It was hard to believe what all had happened last night now.

"Yes Austin, I'm afraid so, but it was a real long night for me." Karen said.

"Yes it was Karen. Now all I want to do is to hold you close to me without having to worry about hurting you or our son. I want us to have some time for just us and of course our son."

"Well let's get our son's food out of me and we can do some holding then." Karen wasn't sure she had even enough energy to even be held by her husband.

That night she slept in Austin's arms like she did when they were first married only nine months ago.

The following Monday when Maxwell went back to work he announced to all of their employees that he was a grandfather and that Austin was a Daddy. This excited the whole office. The following week they gave Karen and Austin a big party with tons of baby gifts. They got more things than they would ever use. Of course Karen found a very good place to give some of their baby things. She knew there were lots of families who did not have enough money to buy everything they needed for a new baby and they could use their extra things.

CHAPTER FIFTY EIGHT

The next few weeks flew by for Karen, but not for Austin. He was missing his wife. Christmas week marked four and half weeks there was still one and a half weeks to go.

"Bo can't you just check Karen and see if she is healed." Austin wanted his wife.

"No Austin, this is her time to heal and there is no rushing it she is either healed or not no matter how horny you are." Bo was enjoying seeing his friend in this way.

"Some friend you are." Austin said as he worked.

"Yes I know." Bo had one of his big smiles on his face. He was remembering all the times his friend had sex and he didn't. Pay back was hell.

Bo and Austin were down in the basement cleaning up their motorcycles. "Austin, do you think we will ever get another trip on our bikes?"

"I don't know Bo, but I think we made two good decisions when we decided to marry our wives. I would not trade my life now for my old life even if I could. We both love our wives and they love us. I have a son and that is worth me giving up all the trips I could still be making on these bikes if I had not met and married Karen."

"Austin I can't wait to hold my little girl in my arms." Bo said with a smile that covered his whole face.

"Don't you mean my son's wife?" Austin said with the same kind of smile on his face.

"Yep, I guess so. Our little wives have it all planned out for our two families." Bo said as he continued to polish every little part of his bike. "Austin what did you get Karen for Christmas?"

"Nothing yet" Austin answered.

"Nothing, man Christmas is in two days what are you waiting for? You wanted to wait to see if she was worth something?" Bo was really ready to get upset with his old friend.

"No I already know she is worth everything."

"Then what are you going to give her?" Bo asked once again.

"Five million dollars" Austin answered while still polishing on his bike.

"What?" Bo asked as if he had not understood what his friend had said.

"I'm giving Karen Five . . ." Austin didn't get to finish what he wanted to say.

"I heard that, but why five million dollars?" Bo asked. "Now you are going to have Margo wanting the very same thing."

"So give it to her. Bo, you know you have it and ten times that much." Austin said without looking up at his friend.

"I know, but she doesn't know that yet." Bo answered.

"Now who's keeping secrets from their wife?" Austin teased Bo. "Alright I will do it. Then she can go and get anything she wants and I won't have to shop for her a gift." Bo decided that may be the best way to always do Christmas.

"Now, that we have all of our Christmas shopping done what would you like to do?" Austin asked Bo.

"Austin I want to go upstairs and check on Karen, Merry Christmas." Bo answered.

"Bo, do you mean that?" Austin could not believe his good luck. "Yes, Austin, but it can only happen if Karen is willing to let me check her." Bo said.

Austin and Bo stopped polishing their motorcycles immediately and hurried up the basement stairs. Karen was feeding little Austin when they got upstairs. "Karen, how are you doing?" Bo asked as soon as they were in the den.

"Bo I'm doing great, why?" Karen knew the two men had to be up to something.

"Well Karen I want to get all of my Christmas shopping done today and you are part of my gift to Austin." Bo answered.

"Oh I see. So what part do I play in your shopping?" Bo was sitting in Austin's chair and Austin was in her chair.

"Well Karen I'm glad you asked." Bo smiled over at Austin.

"I'm sure you are and how did Austin get you to do this?" she asked as she looked from Bo over to Austin.

"Well Karen your husband just looked so pitiful." Bo said as he looked over at his friend who was doing his very best to look as pitiful as Bo had said he looked.

"And I'm the only one who can change all of that for him with your help." Karen answered.

"Yes Karen it seems that way" Bo said.

Austin was still sitting in the other chair and he was not saying anything. Karen was still breast feeding little Austin.

"Austin what do you want?" Karen asked.

Austin looked at Bo and then he looked over at Karen. "You, I want you."

"So you want me to give into your over sexual needs? Karen answered again.

"Yes" Austin answered back. "No" she quickly said.

"Is that your answer?" Austin asked. He could not believe she had said no.

Karen looked over at her husband and he did look pitiful and she missed him too. "No, it's not. What do I need to do?" she asked.

"All you need to do is to come with Austin and me to my office and let me examine you." Bo answered. Things were now going very well for him and Austin.

"What am I suppose to do with our son while his Daddy and you play doctor again?" Karen asked. "Or have you two thought about that?"

"I will get Margo to come over and watch him while we go to my office." Bo hurried home to get Margo to stay with little Austin.

"Austin, are you going to tell your parents tonight where we went today?" Karen asked.

No it's not any of their business. Karen you do know you don't have to do this if you don't want to." Austin hoped he had not said the words that would make her change her mind.

"Austin Blackburn, don't you know I know that. I love you and I've missed you too. I'm ready to get this all over with and I feel great so why should we keep waiting."

Karen got finished feeding little Austin and then his daddy took him and put him into his little bed.

"Austin, are we ever going to move back upstairs to our room?"

Karen asked. He loved their downstairs master bedroom, but there was something more special about their upstairs master bedroom. "Do you want to honey?" Austin asked?

"Yes, that's where I want to get pregnant with all of our babies." Karen answered.

Austin finished pulling the blanket up on his son and then he turn to his wife. "Karen I hope you don't get pregnant the first time again. I want you to have a little time to rest in between our babies."

Then it's up to you Austin to see I don't get pregnant. I've never been pregnant before I met you, so it must be you who caused me to get pregnant."

Austin could not help, but laugh. "Yes I am the one who did it and I'm the one who will be doing it again and again." Karen was sitting in Austin's lap now.

"Austin I need to go and get a shower will you watch little Austin for me?"

"Karen did you need to ask?"

"No, but I didn't want you to have it to do if there was something else you needed to do," she answered.

"Karen I have only two things in my life to do. One is to take good care of you and the other is to take good care of our son. Now go and get your shower woman."

Karen got up off Austin's lap and hurried to the bathroom. Bo and Margo were there when Karen came out of the bedroom.

"Wow Karen, you look beautiful." Margo said when she saw her friend all dressed.

"Margo you just think that because you are the one getting big now." Karen remembered having that same feeling herself.

"No I can see how beautiful you are Karen. Bo, tell her how beautiful she is."

"Yes Karen you are beautiful enough to tempt any husband." Austin had a big smile on his face from just thinking what was ahead for him tonight. "Karen you could be the ugliest women ever hit with the ugly stick and your husband would still be tempted." Bo answered.

"Oh is he that horny?" Karen asked as she smiled up at Austin. "Yes I am. So are you ready to go?" Austin asked as he took Karen's coat out of the hall closet.

"Not so fast. When are you planning this big time for you big boy?"

"As soon as we get back home from Bo's office and the sooner we get there the sooner we will get back." Austin was ready to leave so he could get back.

"Sorry not a chance." Karen answered as she put her coat on. "What? Why not Karen?" Austin saw no need in waiting once Bo said she was well.

"Austin, by the time we get back home it will either be time for me to feed little Austin again or to pump."

"Well then in that case tonight." Austin answered.

"Austin tonight means after ten o'clock not five thirty just because it is already dark." Karen said. She knew her husband would use any reason to get her into their bed.

Bo and Margo could hear everything Austin and Karen were saying to each other and they were having themselves a good laugh over it all.

"Don't you be laughing at me Bo Brooks you will soon be in my shoes." Austin said.

"That is right Bo, and I don't care if you are a doctor you will need to wait just like Austin." Karen had stopped disagreeing with Austin and now she was defending him.

"Margo, don't be listening to Austin and Karen. They just don't want me to be having all of the fun." Bo was almost laughing himself. "I'm sure Bo, but I will need to heal just like Karen and we women stick together." Margo was sitting in Karen's rocker." Bo said as he watched her stomach as she rocked. "Margo, are you sure our baby won't get sea sick while you are rocking?" Bo was beginning to feel a little sick himself from watching her stomach as she rocked.

Margo looked over at Karen and then over at Bo. "You're the doctor you tell me how many unborn babies have you had to see because their mothers rocked in a rocker while they were pregnant?" Bo didn't have an answer. "Just as I thought" Margo said as she kept rocking.

"Bo, are you ready to go?" Austin was ready to go.

"Yes Austin, even my wife wants to be mean to me today."

"No Bo I do not. I love you. You and Austin know that Karen and I love you two. However you two have a one track mind and you know it. Karen and I have to do all we can to keep you two big boys happy while at the same time trying very hard to be ladies."

Bo looked over at Austin and then they both said. "You don't have to be ladies for us we like it better when you two aren't ladies."

"No you don't, you just like what you get when we aren't being so much of a lady." Karen answered.

"I think our wives know us Bo."

"Are we going or not?" This time it was Karen asking the question.

"Yes Karen we are going. Right this minute we are going." Karen was over at the bassinet giving little Austin a good bye kiss. Before she had finished Austin was doing the same thing. Then Austin turned, "Karen thank you."

"Austin it was my pleasure that got him for you." "Mine too honey." Then they kissed.

"Alright you two let's go so I can get back here to my wife." Bo was ready to kiss Margo now.

"See you when you get back. Karen, don't worry about your son. I will be very careful with my daughter's husband." "I know you will Margo."

"Good luck Karen" Margo said.

"I will need it with these two big over grown boys and just think Margo they are the fathers of our babies" "Yes and aren't we glad."

"Yes I sure am. I do love this big one right here." Karen was reaching for Austin's hand. He took it and raised it to his lips and kissed it.

Now are you ready to go honey?" Austin took Karen by her hand and led her down the stairs to the basement.

Karen got into the backseat of their truck and Austin and Bo in the front. "Austin, don't forget we have little ears in the back and we don't want them to hear anything she and Margo can use against us later."

"Oh you think we need something you two may say to have something to use against you. We have the bedroom and without us it's not the same room." Karen was just sitting and looking at the back of Austin head. "Austin you need a haircut."

"I know honey I will get one tomorrow." Austin answered.

"Bo you could use one too. You don't want your father-in-law to think you are a hippy, do you?"

"No Karen I sure don't want him to think that, at all. I just want him to think I'm sex hungry for his daughter." Bo answered.

"Austin did you hear him? Bo wants his new father-in-law to whip his butt when he gets here."

Both men busted out laughing. "Karen honey I'm just as sex crazy about you as Bo is about Margo. Is there someone who would like to whip my butt?"

"I know Austin and that's why we are going to Bo's office right now. So he can check my cootchie for you and Bo, wipe that smile off your face right now and as for the last part of your question Austin will the good reverend do?" Karen could not pass up this opportunity.

"Never" Austin answered. "I hope we never see or hear from that man again."

"Me too Austin" Karen said.

"Now back to what you said Karen you can't even see my face from where you are sitting." Bo answered.

"No I can't, but I'm a mother now and I can see everything just like you have seen everything on me." Karen said. "Austin your friend now knows as much about me as you do."

"No he doesn't. He only knows you have all of the right parts, that's all he knows, but he doesn't know how good they all work." Austin was driving in the heavy traffic.

"Now he does Austin you have just told him." Karen wasn't happy about Bo knowing so much about their sex life.

"Karen don't you worry about that I had already guessed that a long time ago. I could tell by the way my friend goes around smiling all the time. You two belong together just like me and Margo. There is never going to be any divorce in our two families."

"Bo that was so sweet, but I still know you will be looking." Karen said in her usual sweet voice.

"Yes sweetheart he will and so will I." Austin said.

"Does that mean I will get to check you two out afterwards?" "I don't think so." Austin said.

"Alright Karen, are you ready to do this?" Bo asked

"Yes I guess. Austin you don't have to look so happy especially when I don't feel so happy." Karen said as she pulled the sheet up and over her head.

"But Karen sweetheart you will feel like smiling later tonight." Austin told her.

"Karen can you breathe alright with you head under that sheet?" Bo asked.

"Yes I can breathe, but I can't see you and that's the whole idea." Karen answered.

"Now you can" Bo said as he, raised up the sheet from the bottom of the table.

"Get out from under my sheet Bo. Austin?" "Yes Karen."

"You get out from under my sheet too."

"Now let's get down to business" Bo said. "Karen, are you having trouble with anything?"

"You mean other than you two boys? No." She quickly answered. "Are you still sore?" Bo asked?

"No" Karen answered again.

"Well everything looks great to me." Bo said as he smiled over at Austin.

"Austin do you hear Bo. We can put that on a cake. Karen's cootchie looks great."

"No Honey I don't think so." Austin answered.

"Austin you will be getting your Christmas present tonight. Karen you are all well." Bo smiled and told them both.

"Does this mean I'm all through with you Bo?" Karen asked.

"No I hope not. You do live next door to me and I did ride all this way over here with you and Austin." Bo answered.

"I mean I don't have to come back and do this ever again."

"No, but if you are going to get pregnant again I will see you and I do mean see you."

"Austin pop Bo" Karen said. "Honey he is right."

"I know, but I think he needs to be popped anyway."

"Karen I'm just going to let you be the one to pop me because it will have been worth it." Bo told her.

"Now may I get dressed?" Karen asked.

"Yes and hurry it's almost five" Austin said teasing Karen. She just gave him a little dirty look. "Woman I saw that look and we both know you don't mean it."

Bo had already gone to his office to finish up Karen's chart. He knew they wanted to hurry home and he did not want to be the one who slowed them down.

"Austin, come here and help me. My milk is starting to run down me. Give me some of those tissues." Austin did just as Karen asked.

"Karen you look so beautiful." Austin said as he hand her the tissues

"I'm sure I do with milk running down me."

"Even with that you are still beautiful. In fact you look more like a woman now instead of a girl."

"Austin I love you and if this makes you happy it makes me happy." She answered.

Austin pulled Karen into his arms and before long they were kissing. "Austin stop we need to get home."

"Alright, but it will be a fast ride." Austin said.

Karen finished dressing with Austin's help and then they went into Bo's office where he was waiting for them.

"Karen you have made a remarkable recovery now I will tell you that you can get pregnant while breast feeling no matter what some may believe. If you two aren't ready to go right back through this again in nine months then you need to use something."

"I could always say no." Karen said as she watched as both men's faces turned red.

"No, Karen, no you can't."

"Austin yes I can if I want to." She was smiling up at Austin. "But you won't will you?" he asked.

"No" she answered.

"Karen I think you have said enough nos' to last me a life time not only for today."

"Now are you two ready to go back home to your son? I want to go and get my wife before her daddy gets here and wants to whip my butt." Bo then looked over at Karen.

CHAPTER FIFTY NINE

"Margo we are home. How was little Austin?" Karen began to ask as soon as her feet hit inside their house. "Karen he is so sweet. I can't wait to have his little wife in my arms." Margo was as happy as Karen about being a mother.

"I know that Margo." Karen said as she turned to her son. "Little Austin Mama is here and so is your big old Daddy and even your uncle Bo is here. Did Aunt Margo get all of your sugar?"

"Aunt Margo got as much sugar as she could get." Margo said as she looked around for Bo.

"Margo are you ready to go home? I need to get in a little more husband work before your Daddy gets here and whips my butt for getting his little girl pregnant."

"Well let's go Bo because we can't get any more pregnant than we are already. Karen I gather you are back in commission."

"Yes Margo I am and if Austin's parents were not due here any second he would have me already in our bedroom jumping my bones."

"I guess Karen we are just lucky we have such good bone jumpers."

"They think we are." Karen answered.

"Come on Margo time is racing and your Dad will be here in no time." Bo had hold of Margo's hand and he was already to leave.

"Bo he won't even be here until tomorrow." Margo said.

"I know Margo, but he may not want me to sleep with his daughter." Bo didn't know how Margo's Father was going to react to their marriage.

"Bo, look at me. Don't you think it's a little late for him to be worrying about that? I'm five months pregnant and anyway my Dad will love you."

Thirty minutes later Maxwell and Bridget were at Austin and Karen's house with all of their Christmas gifts. Karen had not gotten anything for anyone except for the few things she and Austin had ordered on line.

"Austin I didn't get you anything for Christmas." Karen felt as if she had messed up their first Christmas together because she had not been able to go out shopping for Christmas' presents.

"Yes you did. He is lying in that little bed over there and tonight I will get his mother again." Karen was sitting in Austin's lap and he had both of his arms around her.

"Son, how are things going?" Maxwell asked.

Austin wasn't sure what to say. He just sat there and waited for his Dad to say more.

"I mean how was it being here this week by yourselves with a new born baby?" Maxwell remembered how it had been many years ago for him and Bridget.

"Oh, we did alright. I have learned to sleep with one eye open." Austin answered.

Maxwell laughed. "Yes that's the way parents do it and it don't get any easier no matter how old our children get. I know because I still worry about you all the time, but I must say after you married Karen I have stopped worrying so much. Son she has been very good for you and look what we all got from her."

"Dad I feel God sent Karen to me. How else would I have picked her to be the only one, I wanted to meet from all the letters I received from my ad."

"Son God has his hand in everything it is always us who messes things up." Maxwell answered.

Karen and Bridget were in the kitchen making supper. "Mrs. Blackburn I made a big pot of vegetable soup and I have corn bread muffins in the oven."

"Karen that sounds delicious. I haven't had homemade soup in years. I used to make it a lot." Bridget went over to the stove where the soup was still simmering and got a big smell of it. "Oh Karen this smells wonderful I can't wait to eat."

"Then I need to hurry and get our table set." Karen said as she hurried around the kitchen.

"Karen let me do that. How are you feeling?" Bridget asked.

"I feel great, I have lost all of my baby weight and I'm back into my jeans. Now I'm going to tell you something, but I'm not sure Austin would want you to know."

"Well Karen maybe then you should not tell me."

"No, it's not a secret or anything like that, it's just I went to Bo's office today and had my check up."

"I thought Bo's office was closed all this week."

"It is, but Bo and your horny son took me there this afternoon and they both played doctor again. So I had my check up today and I passed. Your son doesn't have to do without anymore."

"That's great, I mean the part about you being healed and well, but the part about my horny son I'm just not sure of. I hope he realizes you can get pregnant again right now." Bridget knew that Karen did not need to get pregnant right again away.

"Yes he knows, Bo told him. He has been told we need to use something if we don't want another new baby in nine months." Karen was getting the muffins out of the oven.

"Well then are you two going to use some protection?"

"I hope so. I told Austin it was his job to be sure I didn't get pregnant before we wanted me to be."

Bridget knew she would never trust that job with a man, but she knew Karen was very young and her son was old enough to know what he needed to do.

"Karen I will get the butter out and then we will be ready to eat." Bridget had been rushing around the kitchen as much as Karen.

"Alright Mrs. Blackburn then I will go and check on little Austin and get our husbands in here." Karen hurried into the den. "Oh little Austin mommy is right here." Little Austin had started to fuss a little. Karen picked him up and held him close to her. "I love you so much my big, big, beautiful boy. You look so much like your big handsome Daddy."

"Karen I will move little Austin's bassinet into the kitchen that way we will be able to keep an eye on him while we eat."

"Alright Austin, I will be right in as soon as I change his little diaper."

"Alright honey, don't be long." Austin decided to pick up the bassinet and carried it instead of rolling it into the kitchen.

"Austin Blackburn, is my grandson in that bed?" Bridget was ready to have a fit.

"No Mom his Mama has him in our bed room changing his diaper."

"Well I was just about to give you a piece of my mind if my grandson had been in that bed and you carrying it like you were."

"Mom I have a lot better sense than to do something like that, after all, he is my son and I do love him. Anyway Karen would kill me." Austin said with a little smile on his face.

"If I didn't do it first, now put the bed down and get to the table, but wash your hands first." Bridget said.

Karen came back into the kitchen carrying little Austin. "Sorry, but I will need to feed our son first. You all just go ahead and eat while it is still hot." Karen then turned around and went back into the den and sat down in her rocker and began to breast feed her son.

Austin followed her back into the den. "Karen I will wait until you are ready to eat. Can I do something for you?"

"No Austin I guess not unless you have a boob under that shirt somewhere."

"Nope I don't have one like you do, but I can keep you company." "I would love that." Austin gave Karen a little kiss. "Honey you look so beautiful no one would guess you had just given birth to our son four weeks ago." He said as he sat down in his chair.

"All this sweet talk I wonder if it's not for some little reason?" Little Austin was going to town on his Mama's breast. "Our son seems to like his Mama's breast a lot."

"Yes he does. He takes after his Daddy." Karen said as she smiled up at Austin.

"That's my son, but his time to have them will end, but my time won't. Karen the house looks real nice. I love the way you decorated our trees."

"Thank you Austin and thank you for helping me." "It was all my pleasure Mrs. Blackburn."

Austin's parents decided to wait for Karen too. They put the soup back on the stove and the muffins back in the warm oven.

"Austin I think our son has stopped eating and has fallen back to sleep. Do you want to take him into the kitchen and put him in his bed while I go and clean up?"

"Sure honey, I can do that." Austin got himself a kiss from Karen and then he gave their son a little kiss before taking him.

As soon as Austin got back into the kitchen he could tell that his Mother was waiting to ask him something. "Alright what is it you want to know?"

"Austin let us watch little Austin tonight. We have missed him this week. That way you and Karen can have a night alone." Bridget quickly said.

He knew right then that his mother had been told about their trip to Bo's office. "Alright if you really want to babysit him it's fine with me." "Sure, we want to babysit him. We love this little boy very much and we were young ourselves once." Maxwell said.

"Dad, Karen is so good and she goes along with whatever I ask her to do."

"Son, that's why you should be very careful about what you want her to always do. Karen doesn't need to get pregnant tonight."

"No I don't. I need a little rest at least, but not a year or more." Karen said as she came into the kitchen.

"Karen we were just telling Austin we would like to keep our grandson in our room to night." Karen was getting the muffins out of the oven and Bridget was getting the soup. "Are you real sure?"

"Yes honey we are. We missed him so much this past week. I just don't know what we will do when we go home and leave you three here." Karen could hear the sadness in her Mother-in-law's voice.

"Oh Mrs. Blackburn I'm sure you will be coming back and we could go and visit you if you would like?"

"Karen, honey we would be happy to have you three visit us. You have never been to our old farm house, but of course it has all of the modern conveniences. We love it and it's only three hours away, just a nice little drive from here. Austin could bring his family to see us all the time." Bridget was looking right at her son. Austin knew she was doing that because he didn't go out to their farm very often.

"How long have you lived there?" Karen asked.

"Karen, we have lived there since Austin was a baby, but we had an apartment in the city here for during the week and we went to the country on the weekends."

"You had two homes?" Karen had never known anyone with two places to live before.

"Yes we did up until Maxwell retired. We sold our apartment then because we didn't need it anymore."

"Karen this soup is delicious."

"Thank you Mr. Blackburn. Austin, do you like it or do you want me to make you something else?" Karen asked.

"No honey, it's all delicious." Austin said as he sat at the table. "See Dad, I got myself a good cook along with everything else Karen can do." That night little Austin slept in the room with his grandparents on the second floor.

"Austin would you like to go back up to the third floor tonight?" Karen asked. They had not slept in their third floor master bedroom in over three months.

"Sure honey if that's where you want to sleep tonight we will. It's our bedroom and we have everything up there just like we have down here so let's go." Austin was ready to run Karen right up to the third floor.

"Austin don't you think we need to let you parents know we are changing bedrooms for tonight?" Karen asked.

He could tell that she was worried about being away from their son. "Yes we should. We will stop by their room on our way up to the third floor and tell them."

Austin was doing all he could to get his wife upstairs and to bed. After a quiet stop on the second floor they hurried up to the next floor to their bedroom. Once there they shared a nice shower and then they got into bed.

"Austin, do you remember what Bo said about me getting pregnant?" Karen wasn't so sure she wanted to get pregnant again so fast.

"Yes honey I do and that is why I came prepared." Austin had a silly smile on his face as he showed Karen how prepared he really was.

"When did you get all of those things?" She asked.

"Right after little Austin was born. I knew we both wanted him to be an only baby for a while at least and I need to be a responsible father and husband. So Karen I came to bed tonight prepared."

"I guess you did, are you planning to get out of bed ever again?" Karen asked as she let Austin take her into his arms.

"Yes, but only after my supply has run out," Austin said as he kissed his beautiful wife.

THE END
Las Chance